Beginning SAS Programming

Yufeng Guo

10 9 8 7 6 5 4 3 2

First edition: June 2015

ISBN 978-1514218990

Printed in the United States of America

Contents

Preface

Its syntax is downright ugly, yet its approach is pure genius. Its scope is gigantic, yet knowing only 5% of it is probably sufficient for your job. It is likely the most expensive software package you will ever use, yet it is one of the most productive data management and analysis tools ever invented for business users. It is hardly the language you fall in love at first sight, yet it grows on you over time and may become a major tool for your career. It is SAS.

Search `www.indeed.com` and you'll find that SAS programming skills are highly sought after in today's big data world. However, learning SAS isn't easy for complete beginners primarily for three reasons.

First, the archaic syntax of SAS may frustrate many modern programmers and business users who are used to programming languages like Java and Python. The SAS DATA step was modeled after PL/I (programming language one). The SAS macro facility was modeled after the macro preprocessor of PL/I. In fact, SAS was originally written mostly in PL/I and later ported to C. PL/I had its heyday in the 1960s and is on the verge of extinction. Some even say that it's been long dead.

Fortunately, the overall language design of SAS is coherent. If you can overcome the initial syntax shock of SAS, you'll open yourself up to its immense power.

Second, getting the SAS software was, up until recently, expensive for independent learners not associated with a college or an employer. Fortunately, the SAS Institute, the company that makes the SAS software, woke to the alarm that its future could be bleak if only the privileged few could learn SAS while the open source data analysis software R and Python are free to anyone. It decided to make the SAS software in the cloud free for everyone to learn SAS. Today, an independent learner who has an internet connection can login to the SAS server in the cloud and write his first SAS program in 5 minutes.

An ambitious learner can even download and install the free SAS University Edition in virtualbox (see `http://www.sas.com/en_us/software/university-edition/download-software.html`).

Finally, SAS is a huge language to learn and newcomers often drown in the giant ocean of SAS. SAS is a software package for a full data analysis cycle, from data creation, extraction, cleaning, and transformation to advanced data analytics and data presentation. Often an overambitious newcomer attempts to learn everything in SAS but soon gets discouraged after realizing that he'll need to spend his lifetime to gain full mastery of SAS.

Fortunately, there's a strategy to cope with the enormous scope of SAS. The strategy is called the 5% principle:

> *My life is short. I don't have time to learn everything in SAS. I just need to learn*
> *5% of it. 5% is good enough. For the remaining 95%, my answer is that I don't know*
> *and I don't care. I can always Google when I need it.*

You can think of SAS as the Microsoft Office counterpart for data management and analysis. You don't try to master the full Microsoft Office suite: Word, Excel, Access, Outlook, OneNote, and Publisher. No one can master all the products in Microsoft Office. Rarely can one master everything even in one Office product. You start by learning one or more Office products that are most relevant to you, such as Word and Excel. Even if you focus on Word, most likely you just need to know 5% of its features that you use regularly and rely on a search engine such as Google or Bing to find the features you use rarely. For example, most people don't need to know how to create a table of contents or do a mail merge in Word.

The same is true for SAS. SAS was invented to solve virtually every major problem imaginable in the full data analysis cycle. No one has the time or need to master everything in SAS.

Which 5% of SAS to learn? A good starting point for anyone to learn is how to get the data. The full data analysis cycle can be roughly divided into two phases: getting the data (data retrieval, cleaning, and transformation) and making sense of the data. In a typical real-world project, getting the data is 80% of the work; analyzing the data is 20%.

Getting the data consumes most of the time on an analytics project. Knowing how to retrieve and manipulate data is beneficial even if your job is mostly making sense of the data. Even if someone else fetches the data for you, you almost always need to clean and reformat the data before you can analyze it.

However, even getting the data is too much for most people to master. One has to narrow his focus even further.

PROC SQL, the DATA step, and the macro facility are the cornerstones of SAS programming. They are the 5% of SAS programming every aspiring SAS programmer needs to learn. If you can master the fundamentals of these three areas, the immense power of SAS as a data extraction and manipulation tool will be at your disposal. With Google on your side to help you find details of the SAS language that are too numerous to remember, you'll be able to write complex SAS programs and solve challenging real-world problems.

This book focuses on PROC SQL, the DATA step, and the macro facility.

Origin of the Book

This is the book I needed when I was first learning SAS. None of the books on the market seemed to be right for a true novice like me. Most SAS books focused on statistical analysis with a sprinkling of SAS programming. Their coverage of SAS as a data extraction and data manipulation tool was insufficient for a newcomer to be up and running with SAS programming.

Though there were a handful of books on SAS programming, some of them didn't tell me much more than what I could find by reading the SAS documentation, while others were reference books for someone who already knew SAS programming fundamentals. In addition, almost all the SAS programming books threw too much stuff at me too fast.

In the end, I muddled through SAS by trial and error without using any books. I learned it the hard way.

While there were a plethora of books on Java, Python, or almost any other programming language that would bring a complete beginner to the advanced level, there was none for SAS. I wrote this book to fill the void. I hope it will teach you SAS programming from the ground up and transform you from a complete novice to an advanced programmer.

What You Get from This Book

This book is a fast paced tutorial on SAS data programming. It assumes that you know nothing about SAS and builds your knowledge from the ground up to the advanced level. It starts from a simple Hello World program and gradually moves onto advanced topics such as the macro facility.

The focus of this book is the SAS programming language, not the statistical analysis features of SAS.

One distinguishing feature of this book is that it teaches SAS by solving real-world problems.

Prerequisites

An absolute requirement for you to learn SAS from this book is that you have access to the SAS software. If you run PC SAS on your computer or SAS on a Unix server, you are good to go. If you installed the free SAS University Edition in virtualbox, you are good to go. Finally, if you have a computer and an internet connection, you are good to go; you can access SAS in the cloud for free via a web browser.

It will be easier for you to learn SAS if you have some programming experience in whatever software tools or computer languages you happen to use. For example, if you know how to use the `sumif` or `vlookup` function in Excel or if you can create a simple table in Access, you are ready to follow this book. If you have programmed in Visual Basic, Python, Javascript, or any other programming languages, you are ready to go.

If SAS is your first programming language, you can still follow this book, but you'll have to work much harder.

Target Readers

The intended audience for this book is beginning and intermediate SAS programmers. If you belong to one of those two groups, you'll find that this book answers many of the questions you have about SAS as a data extraction and manipulation tool.

A true beginner can quickly learn how to program in SAS by reading Chapters 1 – 6. An intermediate SAS programmer can enhance his knowledge by reading the remainder of the book, which covers advanced topics including the macro facility, combining tables, and regular expressions.

If you are an expert SAS programmer, you might learn something here and there, but most of the content should be familiar to you.

Advice for a True Beginner

First and foremost, be patient with yourself. Unless you are a PL/I veteran, SAS syntax will be new to you. It will take some time for you to get comfortable with the syntax, the vocabulary, and how things are done in SAS.

Second, when you learn SAS, focus on learning enough to solve one problem a time. Don't try to learn many things all at once. If you try to understand everything before solving anything, you'll get so sidetracked and overwhelmed that you want to quit.

Third, though you may fall in love with the DATA step, learn relational database basics and SQL. SAS is often used to extract and analyze large tables from a third party relational database. Virtually every complex real-world project requires a programmer to write SQL.

Finally, write a lot of SAS code. Some say that you are not an experienced driver unless you have driven more than $100,000$ miles. Though no one can foretell how many SAS programs you need to write to reach the advanced level, you clearly have a long way to go if you have written only a handful of programs. Besides, even advanced programmers need to keep up with the major changes introduced by each new release of SAS.

Why Chapter 1 is PROC SQL, not the DATA Step

Most SAS books start from the DATA step. However, this book teaches PROC SQL first.

The SAS DATA step is nothing short of a miracle of ingenious software design. It avoids the need to write complex SQL and allows a user to create and manipulate a table with simple procedural syntax. Want to drop Column X from a table? Just write `drop=X`. Want to rename Column X to Y? Just write `rename=(X=Y)`. Want to add a `tax` column which is 3% of the `sales` column? Just write `tax=0.03*sales`. Want to create ten character columns `var1` to `var10` each with a column width of 8? Just write `length var1-var10 $8`. Tired of writing CASE statements in SQL? Just write IF-THEN-ELSE in a DATA step.

As the popular saying goes, with great power comes great responsibility. To use the power of the DATA step, one must take on the responsibility of learning relational database fundamentals. SAS is a database engine for manipulating tables, not a procedural language for manipulating variables.

For example, a novice SAS programmer tends to create more variables in a DATA step than is truly necessary. Creating a variable incurs little overhead in a procedural language; a variable is just a memory cell to store a value. An extraneous variable in a procedural language is not the best thing to do but the harm is minimal.

However, an extraneous variable in a SAS DATA step is far more costly because a variable introduced in a DATA step automatically becomes a column of the output table unless it is dropped in the end. If your input table has ten million rows, then the extraneous variable `x=1` will cause the output table to have a column x filled with ten million rows of the constant value 1. This increases your table size and slows down your program execution, not to mention how confused your users will be when they see a column filled with row after row of the same value.

Here's another example where the ease of the DATA step can lead an inexperienced programmer astray. Newcomers tend to make multiple trips to a large table when only one pass to the table is truly needed to perform all the operations. When this happens, operations on a table that should take only thirty minutes can take three hours.

The SAS DATA step is a shortcut to the traditional SQL (structured query language) approach. As multiplication is a shortcut to addition and one must learn addition before learning multiplication, one needs to learn how to create and manipulate a table the hard way before learning the easy way.

How to Best Use This Book

This book alone cannot make you an advanced SAS programmer. You have to do your part. The best thing you can do is to write a lot of code. You won't become an advanced coder if you speed read this book without trying my programs in SAS.

Though I posted all the program code on my website for you to download, you'll learn most by resisting the temptation to copy and paste the code to your SAS code editor. Instead, manually type each line of code. Create your own prime number generator in SAS. If you are an expert in another language such as Python, rewrite your favorite Python programs in SAS.

In addition, recreate at least some, if not all, of the programs in the *Further Reading* section at the end of each chapter.

Adjust the File Path for SAS in the Cloud

Most programs in this book work in both PC SAS and SAS in the cloud out of the box. However, if a program reads from or writes to an external file, you'll need to adjust the SAS code that references the external file.

Some SAS programs in this book read in an external text file such as `abc.txt`. Other programs export an existing SAS table to a CSV file such as `xyz.csv`. In my PC SAS code, I assume that both `abc.txt` and `xyz.csv` are stored in the `C:\LearnSAS` folder. My SAS code will reference these two files as:

- `C:\LearnSAS\abc.txt`

- `C:\LearnSAS\xyz.csv`

In my code for SAS in the cloud, however, I assume that both `abc.txt` and `xyz.csv` are stored in the `/home/userid/myProgram` folder, where `userid` should be replaced by your user ID for SAS in the cloud. My SAS code will reference these two files as:

- `/home/userid/myProgram/abc.txt`

- `/home/userid/myProgram/xyz.csv`

To follow this book, create the `C:\LearnSAS` folder if you use PC SAS.

If you use SAS in the cloud, create the `myProgram` subfolder under `My Folders`. The full path of `My Folders` is `/home/userid`, where `userid` is your ID for SAS in the cloud. To find the full path of

My Folders, right click My Folders and select "Properties." Then the "Folder Properties" window will open up. The "Location" property is /home/userid. My Folders is the home directory of SAS in the cloud. The full path of the myProgram subfolder is /home/userid/myProgram.

To avoid repetition, I may show you only the code for PC SAS. If a program doesn't reference any files or folders in the operating system, the PC SAS program will also work for SAS in the cloud. However, if a program references a file path in the operating system, you'll need to adjust the file path so the operating system can recognize the file path.

For example, if you need to read in C:\LearnSAS\sales.txt into SAS, first create sales.txt in the C:\LearnSAS folder. Then you can reference the text file in a PC SAS program via an infile statement:

```
infile 'C:\LearnSAS\sales.txt';
```

If you use SAS in the cloud, upload sales.txt from your computer to the myProgram folder in the remote SAS Unix server in the cloud. Next, adjust the file path so the infile statement becomes:

```
infile '/home/userid/myProgram/sales.txt';
```

Here's another example. This is how to export the work.employee table to the employee.csv file in the C:\LearnSAS folder using PC SAS:

```
proc export
    data=work.employee
    outfile='C:\LearnSAS\employee.csv'
    dbms=csv
    replace;
run;
```

This is how to export the work.employee table to the employee.csv file in the myProgram folder in SAS in the cloud:

```
proc export
    data=work.employee
    outfile='/home/userid/myProgram/employee.csv'
    dbms=csv
    replace;
run;
```

Unlike in Windows, in SAS Unix servers in the cloud, folder names and file names are case sensitive. In addition, while both forward slashes and backslashes can be used in a file path in Windows, only forward slashes can be used in a file path in SAS in the cloud (see Section 1.6.3).

About Me

I grew up in China and immigrated to the United States in 1996. I received a master's degree in accounting and business information systems from Indiana University. After graduation, I worked in the IT department of an insurance company for two years and then became an actuary. I have been programming in SAS since 2009.

Where to Download the SAS Program Code in This Book

All the SAS programs in this book can be downloaded from my website:

saszero2hero.com

Submit or View Errata

If you find typos or programming errors, please email me at yufeng.guo.actuary@gmail.com.

The errata will be posted at my website:

saszero2hero.com

Acknowledgements

I couldn't have written this book without the support of my family. My wife Tonya helped me cut out dead wood (including some cute Chinese proverbs) in the preface. My oldest son Abraham proofread each chapter and helped set up the support site http://saszero2hero.com/. My second oldest son Benjamin designed the book cover.

I would like to thank the SAS Institute for making the SAS software in the cloud and the SAS University Edition free for anyone to learn SAS.

Finally, I would like to thank many SAS users who published papers to share their programming techniques. I have benefited greatly by reading papers by other SAS programmers.

Chapter 1

Hello World and PROC SQL Basics

In this chapter, you'll learn how to create a table using PROC SQL. You'll begin with a trivial Hello World example and move on to more serious programs.

1.1   Where to Get the SAS Software

If you are reading this book, most likely you already have SAS installed on your computer perhaps through your employer or your school.

If you don't have SAS installed in your machine, you can access the SAS software in the cloud via a web browser for free. You don't need to install anything special in your machine. As long as you have an internet connection, you can access SAS in the cloud, write and submit the code, and see the result.

The SAS Institute offers SAS in the cloud for anyone to learn SAS. Go to the SAS OnDemand for Academics Control Center at `https://odamid.oda.sas.com/SASODAControlCenter/`. Create an account and you can access the SAS server in the cloud right away.

This book uses SAS OnDemand and SAS in the cloud interchangeably.

Here's one major advantage of SAS in the cloud over SAS on your computer. SAS in the cloud not only uses the latest version of Base SAS, it also includes many other useful packages such as SAS/ACCESS Interface to PC Files, SAS/STAT, and SAS/IML, to name a few. In contrast, the SAS software installed in your machine may be several versions behind the most current version; it may not have SAS/ACCESS Interface to PC Files or other packages.

Since this book focuses on SAS programming, the most relevant package included in SAS in the cloud is SAS/ACCESS Interface to PC Files. The most common use of this interface is reading Excel files into SAS or exporting SAS tables into Excel files.

SAS in the cloud is slightly slower than SAS installed in your machine. Besides, SAS in the cloud may be down temporarily for maintenance.

1.2 SAS Windowing Environment

SAS runs on various operating systems including Windows, Unix, Mac dual boot, and mainframe. On each operating system, SAS lets a user, through a windowing environment, write and submit code, check the program log and output, and open the data tables generated by the SAS program. By the way, the windowing environment should be not confused with the Windows operating system.

This book uses PC SAS (e.g. SAS in Windows) and SAS in the cloud (e.g. SAS in Unix servers) to teach you how to program in SAS.

The SAS Institute published SAS companion guides for various operating systems. Search the web and you should find the following online documentation or pdf files:

- *SAS Companion for Windows*

- *SAS Companion for Unix*

- *SAS Companion for z/OS*

These companion guides are mostly reference books for advanced users. However, some content in Chapter 1 of these guides is friendly to new SAS users.

If you use SAS in the cloud, please Google the *SAS Studio User's Guide*. SAS Studio is the windowing environment for SAS in the cloud.

1.3 PC SAS Main Windows

This section is for PC SAS. Skip this section if you use SAS in the cloud.

Launch your SAS software by selecting Start ⟩⟩ All Programs ⟩⟩ SAS ⟩⟩ SAS x , where x is your SAS version number. SAS will open 5 windows:

- `Editor - Untitled1`, the enhanced editor window. The enhanced editor window typically has a running man icon with a plus (+) sign. The plus sign means "enhanced" (enhanced editor). Your cursor should be blinking in this window after you launch SAS. This is where you type your SAS code.

- `Log - (Untitled)`, the log window. The log window generally sits on the top of the enhanced editor. After you launch SAS, the log window will just display copyright information. If you write any code in the enhanced editor and submit the code, SAS will provide feedback in the log window, telling you whether your code has executed successfully or has failed.

- `Output- (Untitled)` window. When you initially launch SAS, your `output` window will be blank. However, if you submit any SAS code and your SAS code generates any output, the `output` window will have some content.

- `Explorer` window, sitting in the left of the SAS window pane. In the explorer window, you should see a file cabinet icon called `Libraries`. Double click `Libraries` and you'll see several items (libraries) such as `Sashelp`, `Maps`, `Sasuser`, and `Work`. We are mostly interested in the `Work` library. By default, the `Explorer` window is selected.

- Results window, sitting to the far left of the SAS window pane. When you initially launch SAS, this window won't have any results yet. After you execute your SAS program, if your SAS program generates any outputs, the Results window will show clickable links to the outputs. By default, the Results window is not selected.

If by any chance you don't see any of these windows, you can always go to the View menu and select any of these five windows.

1.4 Configure PC SAS Windows

This section is for PC SAS. Skip this section if you use SAS in the cloud.

1.4.1 Show Line Numbers in the Enhanced Editor

While your cursor is still blinking in the enhanced editor window, do the following:

- select Tools >> Options >> Enhanced Editor
- check "Show line numbers"

1.4.2 Configure PC SAS 9.3+

SAS 9.3 or above, among other things, defaults the output to HTML instead of plain text. While this change might be welcomed by experienced SAS users, most new learners will find that the plain text output is less overwhelming. If you use SAS 9.3 or higher, you can switch the default output to plain text:

- select Tools >> Options >> Preferences >> Results
- check Create listing
- uncheck Create HTML
- uncheck Use ODS Graphics

For more details, see SAS documentation at http://support.sas.com/documentation/cdl/en/odsug/65308/HTML/default/viewer.htm#p0xidv7ssklgg2n1lzf7u6wuei7z.htm.

1.5 First Program - Hello World with SQL

SAS is for analyzing tables. A table is like an Excel spreadsheet, where columns represent data names and where rows represent data values. Here's an example of a sales table with 5 columns and 2 rows:

```
CustomerID   LastName   FirstName   OrderDate   OrderAmt
    1         Smith      John        3/12/2014    287.45
    2         Johnson    Mary        9/22/2014    135.74
```

SAS has another set of vocabulary to describe a table. A table is a data set. A column of a table is a variable. And a row of a table is an observation.

Our first program will create a table.

1.5.1 Create helloWorld.sas in SAS In the Cloud

If you use SAS in the cloud, please watch the official video tutorial at http://support.sas.com/training/tutorial/studio/index.html on how to write a basic SAS program in SAS Studio.

Let's create a Hello World program in SAS in the cloud. After you login to the SAS server in the cloud, in the left pane of SAS Studio, right click "My Folders." Choose New ⟩ Folder to create a new folder and name it myProgram. You can use the myProgram folder to store all your SAS programs.

Press F4 to open the SAS code editor window. Type the following program and save it as helloWorld.sas in the myProgram folder:

Program 1.5.1 *helloWorld.sas*

```
1   proc sql;
2   create table work.MyNum
3   (
4       N num
5   );
6   quit;
```

Make sure you spell sql correctly. The last letter is l as in **light**, not the number one. Next, submit the program by pressing F3 or clicking the running man icon. The log window will open up displaying something like this:

```
1           OPTIONS NONOTES NOSTIMER NOSOURCE NOSYNTAXCHECK;
57
58          proc sql;
59          create table work.MyNum
60          (
61           N num
62          );
NOTE: Table WORK.MYNUM created, with 0 rows and 1 columns.
63          quit;
NOTE: PROCEDURE SQL used (Total process time):
      real time          0.00 seconds
      user cpu time      0.00 seconds
      system cpu time    0.00 seconds
```

The main message in the log is NOTE: Table WORK.MYNUM created, with 0 rows and 1 columns. This warns you that the work.MyNum table is blank with no data in it (because we haven't put any data in it). Nothing to worry about.

To see the newly created work.MyNum table, in the left pane of SAS Studio, click the Libraries. This opens up a new window. Click the triangle icon to the left of My Libraries to open up all the sub-libraries under My Libraries. You should see WORK as one sub-library. Under WORK, you should see the MYNUM table. Double click to open the MYNUM table. Since the MYNUM table is blank, you just see the column header N without any data.

Congratulations! You've successfully created a blank work.MyNum table.

1.5.2   Create helloWorld.sas in PC SAS

In your SAS enhanced editor window, type the same helloWorld.sas program.

Program 1.5.2 *helloWorld.sas*

```
1   proc sql;
2   create table work.MyNum
3   (
4     N num
5   );
6   quit;
```

How to submit a program   To submit the code you just typed in the enhanced editor, issue the submit command in one of the following ways:

- Press the F8 key while your enhanced editor window is active

- Select Run ⟫ Submit

- Click the running man icon

- Enter submit in the command bar. The command bar is at the top left corner of the SAS window, below the File menu. The command bar has a check mark to its left.

Submit the helloWorld.sas by one of the four ways above.

What you should see   Your Log window should display copyright information followed by feedbacks to your submitted program:

```
NOTE: Copyright (c) yyyy-yyyy by SAS Institute Inc., Cary, NC, USA.
NOTE: SAS (r) Proprietary Software Version x
      Licensed to xyz, Site xxxxxxxx.
NOTE: This session is executing on the WIN_PRO  platform.



NOTE: SAS initialization used:
      real time           0.01 seconds
      cpu time            0.01 seconds

1    proc sql;
2    create table work.MyNum
3    (
4      N num
5    );
```

```
NOTE: Table WORK.MYNUM created, with 0 rows and 1 columns.
6    quit;
NOTE: PROCEDURE SQL used (Total process time):
      real time            0.01 seconds
      cpu time             0.00 seconds
```

The SAS log records everything you did in your SAS session or with your SAS program. Your original program statements are identified by line numbers. Mixed with SAS statements are messages generated by SAS. These messages typically begin with the words NOTE, INFO, WARNING, ERROR, or an error number, and they may refer to a SAS statement by its line number in the log.

When you submit Program 1.5.2 the first time, the line number in the log starts from 1.

However, if you submit Program 1.5.2 the second time, a new log will be added to the end of the previous log. In the new log, the starting line number will be the ending line number of the previous log plus 1.

This is the main message in the log:

```
NOTE: Table WORK.MYNUM created, with 0 rows and 1 columns.
```

The `work.MyNum` table is blank with no data in it.

Next, let's see the `work.MyNum` table. Select View ⟫ Explorer to open the explorer window. You should see the `Work` folder displayed in either side of the explorer window. Click to open the `Work` folder on either side of the window. You should see the `MyNum` table. Click to open `MyNum` table. A message box pops up saying:

```
NOTE: Data set has 0 observations.
```

This message warns you again that the `work.MyNum` table is blank.

Click OK to exit the pop up window. Then you should see a blank table with a column header `N`.

Congratulations! You've successfully built your first SAS program and produced a blank table.

1.6   Understand helloWorld.sas

Program 1.5.2 can be shortened to three lines:

```
1    proc sql;
2        create table work.MyNum (N num);
3    quit;
```

This is a complete, fully working SAS program. It generates a blank table `work.MyNum` with a numeric column `N`. This table sits in the `work` folder.

SAS uses a two-level name such as `work.MyNum` to unambiguously identify a table. The first level `work` identifies the folder that contains the table. The second level `MyNum` is the name of the table.

If you omit the first level name, SAS will use `WORK` as the default first-level name. The statement `create table MyNum (N num)` is the same as `create table work.MyNum (N num)`.

In Section 1.8 you'll learn how to create a different first level name than `work`.

Statements This program has three statements. Each statement ends with a semicolon.

The first statement invokes the SQL procedure. Many pre-built procedures are shipped with Base SAS to enable users to perform specific tasks. For example, you can use the SORT procedure to sort a table by one or more columns, in ascending or descending order (see Program 9.1.1).

`SQL` stands for structured query language, a special-purpose programming language designed for managing data held in a relational database management system (RDBMS). `Proc sql` is a pre-built procedure shipped with Base SAS. Its main functionality is `CRUD`, that is, to create, read, update, or delete a table.

The second statement `create table work.MyNum (N num)` creates a new table that has one numeric column `N`. The word `num` is short for `numeric`.

Finally, the `quit` statement terminates the SQL procedure.

1.6.1 How SAS Is Different from Other RDBMS

It's debatable whether SAS should be called a RDBMS. Though SAS has PROC SQL, the SAS database engine is different from most relational databases. Most RDBMS engines are designed for transaction processing and allow multiple users to have concurrent access to data. As such, most RDBMS engines have record locking to ensure data integrity when multiple users are attempting to read or update the same row simultaneously. In addition, most RDBMS engines have transaction rollback to return a database to its previous state.

However, the SAS database engine is designed for data analysis. In many companies, copies of transactional data were made solely for data analysis so data analysis won't interfere with real time transaction processing. And a copy of transactional table can be exclusively used by a single user while he is reading the data. After the user finishes reading the data, the data sits idle until the next user reads it and has the exclusive access to it. Then the second user releases the data after he finishes reading it. Hence the SAS database engine doesn't have to worry about maintaining data integrity due to concurrent access and can sequentially read large amounts of data quickly.

Here's another difference between SAS and other databases. While a table in a typical relational database is a collection of unordered rows, a SAS table is a collection of ordered rows in a SAS DATA step program (the DATA step is explained in Chapter 2). If you use a DATA step to manipulate a table, the order of the rows in the output table is the same as the order of the rows in the input table. To change the order of the rows of a table, you must purposely reorder the rows using PROC SORT.

However, similar to other database engines, SAS does not guarantee the order of the rows in the output of PROC SQL. If you use PROC SQL to query a SAS table, the output of the query is not guaranteed unless you specify a sort order using the ORDER BY clause.

The third major difference between SAS and other databases is how null is handled. This becomes an issue when you use SAS to retrieve a table from a third party database system such as DB2, Oracle, and Microsoft SQL server. For more information, see `http://support.sas.com/kb/23/225.html`. If you are new to SAS, skip this topic for now and come back to it later.

1.6.2 SAS Case Sensitivity

In PC SAS and SAS in the cloud, the log generated by `helloWorld.sas` calls the `WORK.MYNUM` table, but the table is spelled `work.MyNum` in the code. SAS is case insensitive. `WORK.MYNUM` is the same as `work.MyNum`. The N column is the same as the n column. Program 1.5.2 can be rewritten in uppercase or in the mixture of uppercase and lowercase:

```
1  PROC SQL;
2  CREATE TABLE WORK.MYNUM
3  (
4      N NUM
5  );
6  QUIT;
```

```
1  PROC SQL;
2  CREATE TABLE work.MyNum
3  (
4      N num
5  );
6  QUIT;
```

However, quoted strings or literal strings are always case sensitive in SAS. 'US', 'Us', 'uS', and 'us' are four different literal strings. If your table has a country column and the United States is entered as any of the above four quoted strings, then to do a case insensitive comparison, you can write:

```
if upcase(country)='US' then ... ;
```

The `upcase` function converts all letters in an argument to uppercase.

1.6.3 Case Sensitivity: SAS in the Cloud Versus PC SAS

Though SAS is case insensitive, your operation system can be case sensitive or case insensitive.

Windows is case insensitive in folder names and file names. For example, `C:\LearnSAS` is the same as `C:\learnsas`. If you already have the `C:\LearnSAS` folder and you want to create another folder named `C:\learnsas`, your Windows computer will warn you that a folder with the same name already exists and asks you whether you want to replace the existing folder.

Similarly, in Windows, you can't create `abc.txt` and `Abc.txt` in the same folder because they refer to the same file.

The following three statements are equivalent in PC SAS. Each statement creates the same file nickname `myfile` pointing to the same external file `abc.txt` in the `C:\LearnSAS` folder:

```
1  filename myFile 'C:\LearnSAS\abc.txt';
2  filename myfile 'C:\learnSAS\Abc.txt';
3  filename Myfile 'C:/learnsas/ABC.txt';
```

Because SAS is case insensitive, `myFile`, `myfile`, and `Myfile` are equivalent. Because Windows is case insensitive, the three full file paths are equivalent.

By the way, in Windows, a backslash and a forward slash are interchangeable as a file path separator.

Unlike Windows, the Unix operating system is case sensitive. Since SAS in the cloud is hosted in Unix servers, a file path and a file name are case sensitive in SAS in the cloud. For example, in the `/home/userid` folder in SAS in the cloud (where `userid` should be replaced by your user ID for SAS in the cloud), you can create two subfolders, one named `myProgram` and the other `myprogram`. Similarly, you can create two text files, `abc.txt` and `Abc.txt` in the same folder in SAS in the cloud.

In addition, Unix uses a forward slash as the path separator.

If you use SAS in the cloud, when you need to reference a folder name or file path, the folder name and the file path you specify are case sensitive. For example, in SAS in the cloud, the following three statements are equivalent:

```
1   filename myFile '/home/userid/sasuser.v94/abc.txt';
2   filename MyFile '/home/userid/sasuser.v94/abc.txt';
3   filename myfile '/home/userid/sasuser.v94/abc.txt';
```

The file nicknames, `myFile`, `MyFile`, and `myfile` are equivalent because SAS is case insensitive.

However, in SAS in the cloud, `/home/userid/sasuser.v94/abc.txt` cannot be specified, for example, as `/home/userid/sasuser.V94/abc.txt`.

Since a forward slash as a path separator works in PC SAS and SAS in the cloud, if you use a forward slash in your file path, your SAS program will work in PC SAS and SAS in the cloud.

1.7   Second Program - Populate a Table with SQL

The next program works in both PC SAS and SAS in the cloud.

Program 1.7.1 *one2tenWork.sas*

```
1    /* clear previous log and output */
2    dm log 'clear';
3    dm output 'clear';
4
5    /*********************************************************/
6    /* create and populate MyNum (only one numeric column N) */
7    /*********************************************************/
8    proc sql;
9
10   * Define table structure ;
11   create table work.MyNum
12   (
13       N num
14   )
15   ;
16
17   * Populate the blank table with 1 to 10 ;
18   insert into work.MyNum
19   values ( 1 )
20   values ( 2 )
21   values ( 3 )
22   values ( 4 )
23   values ( 5 )
24   values ( 6 )
25   values ( 7 )
26   values ( 8 )
27   values ( 9 )
28   values ( 10 )
29   ;
30
31   *Display work.MyNum in Output window unless noprint is on;
32   select * from work.MyNum;
33
34   ************************************************************ ;
35   * When done, always use quit to exit sql procedure         ;
36   * Otherwise proc sql keeps running, wasting computer resources ;
37   ************************************************************;
38   quit;
```

Output:

```
       N
    --------
       1
       2
       3
       4
       5
       6
       7
       8
       9
      10
```

Submit the program. A new `work.MyNum` table will be created with integers from 1 to 10. You'll get the following log:

`NOTE: 10 rows were inserted into WORK.MYNUM.`

Open the `work.MyNum` table. It has ten rows populated with 1 to 10 respectively.

What just happened

Comment   Line 1 is a comment. SAS has 2 comment styles:

```
/* one line or multi-line comment */
*  one line or multi-line comment  ;
```

The first style is widely used in many programming languages. The second style, however, appears to be specific to SAS.

Under the second style, a comment starts from the star sign *, can run many lines, and ends with a semicolon.

This program has two pretty boxes (Lines 5–7 and Lines 34–37). A pretty box is just disguised comments. The first pretty box is several one-line comments using the first comment style; the second is several one-line comments using the second comment style.

DM statements   The `dm` statements (Lines 2 and 3) are for PC SAS. If you use SAS in the cloud, you don't need them, though adding them won't cause any harm.

These two lines instruct the SAS display manager to clear the `log` window and the `output` window before executing the rest of the code.

Every time when you submit a SAS program via any of the four ways described in Section 1.5.2, a log is written to the log window indicating whether the SAS program has executed successfully. And the output, if any, is written to the output window.

Without the DM statements, the logs and the outputs generated by all the previously submitted PC SAS programs will stay in the `log` window and in the `output` window respectively. And the new log and the new output generated by your current program will be appended to the previous logs and to the previous outputs, making it hard for you to see your current log and current output.

The two DM statements erase any previously created logs and outputs. As a result, only the log and the output generated by the newly submitted SAS program will appear in the `log` window and the `output` window.

If you are using SAS 9.3+, you'll want to configure it according to Section 1.4.2. Otherwise, the `dm output 'clear'` statement won't work.

INSERT   This is the main code. The `insert` statement (Lines 18–29) adds new rows to a table. The `values` clause lists the values to be inserted into each new row. Each data type in the `values` clause must match the data type of the corresponding column.

SELECT   The `select * from work.MyNum` statement (Line 32) retrieves all the columns from the source table `work.MyNum`. The `from` clause indicates the source table. An asterisk * represents all the columns of the source table.

`work.MyNum` has only one column N. Hence `select * from work.MyNum` can be replaced by `select N from work.MyNum`.

By default, all the retrieved columns in the `select` statement will be displayed in the `output` window. However, you can prevent Line 32 from writing the query result to the `output` window by specifying the `noprint` option. Change Line 8 into

```
proc sql noprint;
```

Resubmit the program. You won't see the 10 rows of integers from the `work.MyNum` displayed in the `output` window.

Finally, the ending `quit` statement terminates the SQL procedure.

1.8 Third Program - Store a Table in a Permanent Folder

1.8.1 PC SAS

Now close the SAS software by clicking the top right [X]. Re-launch SAS from the Start menu. Select [View] [Explorer] to open the SAS explorer window. Open the Work folder on either side of the window. What's in the Work folder? Nothing. The MyNum table generated by Program 1.7.1 is gone.

The Work folder is a temporary storage of your tables. If you close SAS, SAS will automatically delete all the files stored in the Work folder.

The next program stores MyNum table in a permanent folder C:\LearnSAS. Create the folder C:\LearnSAS before running Program 1.8.1.

Program 1.8.1 *one2tenPermFolder.sas*

```
1   /**********************************************/
2   /* Store MyNum table permanntly in C:\LearnSAS  */
3   /* First, create C:\LearnSAS                    */
4   /* This program works in SAS 9.0 and above      */
5   /**********************************************/
6   dm log 'clear'; dm output 'clear';
7
8   proc sql;
9   create table 'C:\LearnSAS\MyNum'
10  (
11     N num
12  )
13  ;
14
15  insert into 'C:\LearnSAS\MyNum'
16  values ( 1 )
17  values ( 2 )
18  values ( 3 )
19  values ( 4 )
20  values ( 5 )
21  values ( 6 )
22  values ( 7 )
23  values ( 8 )
24  values ( 9 )
25  values ( 10 )
26  ;
27
28  select * from 'C:\LearnSAS\MyNum';
29  quit;
```

Output:

```
        N
   --------
        1
        2
        3
        4
        5
        6
        7
        8
        9
       10
```

Submit the program. If you are using SAS version 9, this program will run without errors. The output window will display integers 1 to 10.

Check your C:\LearnSAS folder. You should see the mynum.sas7bdat table. The .sas7bdat is the file extension of a SAS table. Click to open the mynum table and you should see ten rows filled with integers 1 to 10 respectively.

In this program, we identify the MyNum table by its full path and name, C:\LearnSAS\MyNum. As a result, SAS will create the MyNum table in the C:\LearnSAS folder. Now if you exit SAS and re-launch it from the START menu, the MyNum table remains in the C:\LearnSAS folder.

What if later you want to change the folder from C:\LearnSAS to another folder? You'll need to replace each occurrence of C:\LearnSAS in Program 1.8.1 with the new folder name. Sure you can do a find-and-replace in the enhanced editor by selecting Edit ⟩ Replace, but there is a better way.

Program 1.8.2 *one2tenLibname.sas*

```
1   dm log 'clear'; dm output 'clear';
2
3   /* create C:\LearnSAS first before you nickname it as mylib */
4   /* works in all SAS versions */
5   libname mylib 'C:\LearnSAS';
6                                                              Output:
7   proc sql;
8   create table mylib.MyNum
9   (                                                               N
10      N num                                               --------
11  )                                                              1
12  ;                                                              2
13                                                                 3
14  insert into mylib.MyNum                                        4
15  values ( 1 )                                                   5
16  values ( 2 )                                                   6
17  values ( 3 )                                                   7
18  values ( 4 )                                                   8
19  values ( 5 )                                                   9
20  values ( 6 )                                                  10
21  values ( 7 )
22  values ( 8 )
23  values ( 9 )
24  values ( 10 )
25  ;
26
27  select * from mylib.MyNum;
28  quit;
```

Program 1.8.2 works for all SAS versions. Next, highlight the `libname` statement:

```
libname mylib 'C:\LearnSAS';
```

Submit Program 1.8.2. You should see the following log (Vx is your SAS version number):

```
NOTE: Libref MYLIB was successfully assigned as follows:
      Engine:        Vx
      Physical Name: C:\LearnSAS
```

SAS creates a folder nickname `mylib` that points to the actual folder C:\LearnSAS. Once `mylib` is created, C:\LearnSAS\mytable can be referenced by a short name `mylib.mytable`.

Now unhighlight the `libname` statement and submit Program 1.8.2. Go to C:\LearnSAS. You should see the `MyNum` table.

If later you decide to use a different folder, just update the `libname` statement and point `mylib` to the new folder.

For simplicity, I nicknamed C:\LearnSAS as `mylib`. You can use a different nickname such as `folder` or `dir`. Make sure that the nickname is no more than 8 character long. In addition, the folder nickname can not be a SAS reserved word like `work`, `user`, or `sashelp`.

1.8.2   SAS in the Cloud

Similar to in PC SAS, in SAS in the cloud, the `work` folder is a temporary storage. If you exit SAS in the cloud by clicking "Sign Out" at top right of SAS Studio and re-login to SAS in the cloud, the `work` folder will be empty. All the tables previously stored in the `work` folder were deleted.

In SAS in the cloud, as in PC SAS, we can use the `libname` statement to create a permanent folder to store our SAS tables. We'll use the `myProgram` folder created earlier as the permanent location to store our tables. Create the following program in SAS in the cloud:

Program 1.8.3 *one2tenLibnameCloud.sas*

```
 1   libname mylib '/home/userid/myProgram';
 2   proc sql;
 3   create table mylib.MyNum
 4   (
 5      N num
 6   )
 7   ;
 8
 9   insert into mylib.MyNum
10   values ( 1 )
11   values ( 2 )
12   values ( 3 )
13   values ( 4 )
14   values ( 5 )
15   values ( 6 )
16   values ( 7 )
17   values ( 8 )
18   values ( 9 )
19   values ( 10 )
20   ;
21
22   select * from mylib.MyNum;
23   quit;
```

```
Output:

       N
 --------
       1
       2
       3
       4
       5
       6
       7
       8
       9
      10
```

In `'/home/userid/myProgram'`, replace `userid` with your user ID for SAS in the cloud.

You can save Program 1.8.3 in the `myProgram` folder. Press F3 to submit the program. Now under the `myProgram` folder, you should see the newly created `MyNum` table.

Here's another way to view the newly created `MyNum` table. Click to open the `Libraries`. You should see the `MYLIB` folder. Under the `MYLIB` folder, you should see the `MYNUM` table.

1.8.3   WORK Pointing to Which Physical Folder?

`Work` is also a nickname pointing to some temporary folder in your hard drive. To find out which folder `work` points to, after you submit Program 1.7.1 and the table `work.MyNum` is created, submit the next program:

Program 1.8.4 *one2tenWork2.sas*

```
/*show content of the table; prints library and physical path*/
proc contents data=work.MyNum;
run;
```

Your output should be similar to the following no matter you submit the program in PC SAS or SAS in the cloud:

```
                    The CONTENTS Procedure

Data Set Name: WORK.MYNUM        Observations:         10
Member Type:   DATA              Variables:            1
Engine:        Vx                Indexes:              0
Created:       date time         Observation Length:   8
Last Modified: date time         Deleted Observations: 0
Protection:                      Compressed:           NO
Data Set Type:                   Sorted:               NO
Label:


-----Engine/Host Dependent Information-----

Data Set Page Size:        4096
Number of Data Set Pages:  1
First Data Page:           1
Max Obs per Page:          501
Obs in First Data Page:    10
Number of Data Set Repairs: 0
File Name:                 path\_TDxxxx\mynum.sas7bdat


-----Alphabetic List of Variables and Attributes-----

#    Variable    Type    Len    Pos
1    N           Num     8      0
```

Under the Engine/Host Dependent Information section, the File Name tells you where the MyNum table is. If you use PC SAS, the File Name may contain _TDxxxx. TD stands for temporary directory and xxxx is a combination of random integers and characters generated by SAS. _TDxxxx is the temporary directory that contains the MyNum table. The work library points to the path_TDxxxx folder. Open the path_TDxxxx folder and you should see the MyNum table.

If you use SAS in the cloud, your File Name may look like this:

/saswork/.../.../mynum.sas7bdat.

Unfortunately, you won't be able to access the folder that contains the MyNum table:

/saswork/.../.../.

However, you can still access the MyNum table by opening the work library in SAS Studio.

Let's experiment with PC SAS. Go to the path folder, which is the parent folder of the _TDxxxx folder. Next, close the SAS software and you'll witness that the _TDxxxx temporary folder disappearing right in front of your eyes. Now re-launch SAS from the Start menu and you'll see that another temporary folder _TDyyyy appears in the path folder. Every time you launch SAS, SAS creates a temporary folder whose name begins with _TD. This temporary folder is deleted when you close SAS.

Open the _TDyyyy folder. The folder contains some utility files but it doesn't have the MyNum table yet. Now submit Program 1.8.4 and you'll see that more files are added to the _TDyyyy folder. One of the files added is the MyNum table.

The MyNum table you see in the work folder is not the physical table, but a pointer to the physical MyNum table stored in the _TDyyyy folder. That's why the MyNum table in the work folder doesn't have the file extension .sas7bdat.

By the way, if you delete the MyNum table from either the _TDyyyy folder or the work folder, the MyNum table will disappear from both the _TDyyyy folder and the work folder.

Go to the path_TDxxxx folder and delete the MyNum table. Then go to the work folder. Now the work folder is empty because we just deleted the physical MyNum table.

Now re-submit Program 1.8.4. A new temporary directory _TDxxx with different integers and characters will be generated.

1.8.4 Manually Delete PC SAS Temporary Folders

After your PC SAS programming job is done and you exit the SAS software, you'll want to manually delete all the temporary _TDxxxx folders that SAS failed to delete. If everything goes well, there shouldn't be any _TDxxxx folders in your hard drive after you close SAS. However, if your SAS program has errors, SAS may not be able to delete a temporary folder. Over time you'll have many temporary folders taking up space and slowing down your SAS program. You'll want to periodically delete all the temporary folders that SAS failed to delete.

1.9 Fourth Program - Calculate the Total with SQL

Often we need to find the total of some values such as integers from 1 to 10:

$$1 + 2 + ... + 10 = 55$$

Your first instinct probably is to implement the following loop in SAS:

```
int i, sum=0;
for(i=1; i<=10; i++)
{
  sum+=i;
}
```

You can certainly do that (see Program 9.1.5). However, for a large table, it's typically inefficient to scan each row. A better approach is to ask SAS to get the sum for you. After the work.MyNum table is created, submit the next program:

Program 1.9.1 *one2tenSum.sas*

Output:

```
proc sql;
create table MyTotal as
select sum(N) as total                          total
from MyNum;                                     --------
                                                   55
select * from MyTotal;
quit;
```

For a big table, Program 1.9.1 is can be more efficient because internally SAS may use a faster approach to finding the sum than performing a full table scan.

1.10   Fifth Program - Create the Worker Table with SQL

Program 1.10.1 *worker.sas*

```
1   dm log 'clear'; dm output 'clear';
2   proc sql;
3   create table worker
4   (
5       id num,
6       sex char(1),
7       firstName char(12),
8       lastName char,
9       salary num
10  );
11
12  insert into work.worker
13  values(1,'M','John','Smith',60000)
14  values(2,'F','Jane','Johnson',70000)
15  values(5,'F','Mary','Williams',80000)
16  values(20,'M','Robert','Walker',90000)
17  ;
18
19  select * from worker;
20  quit;
```

Output:

id	sex	firstName	lastName	salary
1	M	John	Smith	60000
2	F	Jane	Johnson	70000
5	F	Mary	Williams	80000
20	M	Robert	Walker	90000

This program specifies `sex` to be a 1-character column and `firstName` a 12-character column.

In the `create table` statement, if you don't specify the length of a numeric or character column, that column gets the default 8 bytes. As a result, ID and `salary` are both 8-byte numeric columns; `lastName` is an 8-character column.

You can verify that `sex` is a 1-byte character column. If you use SAS in the cloud, expand the `worker` table in the `work` library and you'll see all the columns in the `worker` table. Double click the `sex` column and the column properties window will show up. The column properties window should display the 6 properties of the `sex` column, `name`, `label`, `length`, `type`, `format`, and `informat`. Verify that the length of the `sex` column is 1.

If you have PC SAS, open the `work.worker` table. Highlight the `sex` column. Select $\boxed{\text{Data} \rangle}$ $\rangle \boxed{\text{Column Attributes}}$. The following window pops up:

```
-------------------------------------------------
Column Attributes
```

```
        General | Colors | Fonts

Name:     sex
Label:                    ----------------------
Length:   1              | Type (radio button)  |
Format:   $1.            |   Character (checked) |
Informat: $1.            |   Numeric             |
                         ----------------------
```

In the Type radio button, the `Character` is checked, indicating that `sex` is a character column. In addition, the attribute window indicates that the column `name` is sex; the `label` is blank; the `length` is 1 byte; and the `format` and the `informat` are both $1.

Each column in a SAS table has these six attributes (or properties): `name`, `label`, `length`, `type`, `format`, and `informat`. `Name` and `type` are mandatory in the `create table` statement; you must specify them in your `create table` statement. In contrast, if you don't specify the remaining four attributes, SAS will assign each one a default value.

`Label` is a string of text that helps explain what a column is. Its default value is blank. If your column has a cryptic name, consider creating a meaningful `label`.

An `informat` tells SAS how to read raw strings from an external file into SAS. For example, the `yymmdd10.` informat will interpret the raw string 01/01/1960 as January 1, 1960. Without any `informat` to guide SAS, SAS will read in the raw string 01/01/1960 as text and you won't be able to do math on dates such as finding the number of days between two dates. The `informat` is solely for a DATA step to read in raw data from an external file; it is not used in PROC SQL.

A `format` controls how column values are displayed in the SAS table, in the output window, and in a printed report. For example, the `mmddyy10.` format will display the integer 0 as 01/01/1960, while the `yymmdd10.` format will display the same date as 1960-01-01.

An `informat` and a `format` must end with a period to distinguish from variable names. In addition, the `format` and the `informat` of a character column must begin with a dollar sign.

Under the `$1.` format, `sex` will be displayed as a 1-column string. Since the CREATE TABLE statement defines `sex` as 1-character column, SAS automatically assigns the `$1.` format to `sex`.

Similarly, this is the attribute window for the `salary` column:

```
--------------------------------------------------
Column Attributes
        General | Colors | Fonts

Name:     salary
Label:                    ----------------------
Length:   8              | Type (radio button)  |
Format:   BEST12.        |   Character           |
Informat: 12.            |   Numeric   (checked) |
--------------------------------------------------
```

The BEST12. format tells SAS to display `salary` with maximum precision subject to the limitation that salary has the maximum width of 12 characters. This is the default format of a numeric column.

You can open the attribute window for all the other columns in the worker table.

Another way to check the column attributes is to use the pre-built CONTENTS procedure. After the work.worker is created, run the following program:

Program 1.10.2 *workerProcContents.sas*

```
proc contents data=worker;
run;
```

No matter you use SAS in the cloud or PC SAS, this is part of your output:

```
-----Alphabetic List of Variables and Attributes-----

    #    Variable    Type    Len    Pos
    ---------------------------------
    3    firstName   Char    12     17
    1    id          Num     8      0
    4    lastName    Char    8      29
    5    salary      Num     8      8
    2    sex         Char    1      16
```

The next program illustrates how to define optional attributes.

Program 1.10.3 *worker2.sas*

```
1    dm log 'clear'; dm output 'clear';
2    proc sql;
3    create table worker
4    (
5       id num format=8. informat=8. ,
6       sex char(1),
7       firstName char(12) format $12.,
8       lastName char,
9       salary num label="annual$" format=best12.
10   );
11
12   insert into work.worker
13   values(1,'M','John','Smith',60000)
14   values(2,'F','Jane','Johnson',70000)
15   values(5,'F','Mary','Williams',80000)
16   values(20,'M','Robert','Walker',90000)
17   ;
18
19   select * from worker;
20   quit;
21
22   proc contents data=worker;
23   run;
```

Submit the program. This is part of the output:

```
      id  sex  firstName    lastName      annual$
      ------------------------------------------------
       1   M    John         Smith          60000
       2   F    Jane         Johnson        70000
       5   F    Mary         Williams       80000
      20   M    Robert       Walker         90000
```

The CONTENTS Procedure

-----Alphabetic List of Variables and Attributes-----

#	Variable	Type	Len	Pos	Format	Informat	Label
3	firstName	Char	12	17	$12.		
1	id	Num	8	0	8.	8.	
4	lastName	Char	8	29			
5	salary	Num	8	8	BEST12.		annual$
2	sex	Char	1	16			

Though `id` is assigned an informat `8.`, the informat is not used in PROC SQL.

Even though the `salary` column is now shown as `annual$` in the `worker` table and in the output window, `salary` is still the name of the column. If you need to reference the `salary` column, don't use `annual$`; the label `annual$` is just a decorative string.

In the next program, the lengths of two numeric columns, `id` and `salary`, are specified to be different than the default 8 bytes, but SAS resets their lengths to 8 bytes.

Program 1.10.4 *numLength.sas*

```
1   dm log 'clear'; dm output 'clear';
2   proc sql;
3   create table numLength
4   (
5      id num(3), /*will still default to 8 bytes*/
6      sex char(1),
7      firstName char(12),
8      lastName char,
9      salary num(12) /*will still default to 8 bytes*/
10  );
11
12  quit;
13
14  proc contents data=numLength;
15  run;
```

Submit the program. You'll see the following as a part of the output:

-----Alphabetic List of Variables and Attributes-----

#	Variable	Type	Len	Pos
3	firstName	Char	12	17

```
1    id          Num       8      0
4    lastName    Char      8     29
5    salary      Num       8      8
2    sex         Char      1     16
```

All the numeric columns in the **create table** statement get the default 8 bytes, even if you purposely assign to them a length that is less or greater than the default 8 bytes. So id and **salary** get the default length of 8 bytes.

However, you can assign to a character column a length different from the default 8 bytes, subject to the limitation that the maximum length of a character column is $32,767$ bytes.

Here's one thing that often trips SAS newcomers. Though an 8-byte character column stores up to 8 characters, the greatest integer that can be stored in an 8-byte numeric column under Windows is $2^{53} = 9,007,199,254,740,992$, not 99999999 as one might think.

Though character data is stored one character per byte in SAS, numeric data is stored as floating point numbers in real binary representation, which allows for 16− or 17−digit precision within 8 bytes. 8 bytes are equal to 64 bites. The maximum base 10 value of a 64 binary is 2^{64}. However, some bits are reserved for representing the negative sign, the decimal point, or the exponent. Consequently, the base 10 value of a floating point number of a 64 binary is less than 2^{64} in Windows and Unix. The decimal precision of a full 8-byte number is effectively 15 decimal digits.

Be careful when you want to set the length of a numeric column to less than 8 bytes. If the value of a variable becomes large or has many significant digits, you can lose precision in the results of arithmetic calculations if the length of a numeric variable is less than 8 bytes. Even for an integer column, you may want to set its length wide enough to allow room for future growth.

1.11   SAS Session - Three Experiments

If you use PC SAS, you don't need to do any configuration. If you use SAS in the cloud, for the first two experiments, however, you need to change the mode from the default batch mode to the interactive mode. You do so using one of the following two methods. While the CODE window is active, click the "Go Interactive" icon. Alternatively, click the "More application options" icon, which is located to the right of the "Sign Out" button. Select "Preferences." Check "Start new programs in interactive mode."

1.11.1   First Experiment

PC SAS and SAS in the cloud   Instead of submitting the three statements in Program 1.5.2 all together, let's submit one statement a time and see what happens. Once again, this is our helloWorld.sas program:

```
proc sql;
create table work.MyNum
(
   N num
);
quit;
```

Highlight the first statement:

```
proc sql;
```

Submit the program. SAS will execute only the highlighted code while ignoring the unhighlighted code. After the program is submitted, no table is generated. However, if you use PC SAS, the top left corner of the enhanced editor window should display the following title:

`PROC SQL running`

This message indicates that the SQL procedure is invoked and that SAS is ready to do a `CRUD` job.

If you use SAS in the cloud, you will not get the `PROC SQL running` title. You'll get this log:

```
NOTE: This session is in interactive mode.

        proc sql;
```

This indicates that PROC SQL was invoked.

Next, highlight the second statement:

```
create table work.MyNum
(
    N num
)
;
```

Submit the program. Once again, only the highlighted code is executed. You will get this log from PC SAS and SAS in the cloud:

`NOTE: Table WORK.MYNUM created, with 0 rows and 1 columns.`

A new `work.myNum` table is generated, overwriting the existing table with the same name.

Finally, highlight and submit the third statement:

```
quit;
```

This terminates the SQL procedure. In PC SAS, this causes the title `PROC SQL running` to disappear from the top left corner of your enhanced editor window. In addition, you'll get a log similar to this:

```
56   quit;
NOTE: PROCEDURE SQL used:
      real time           3.86 seconds
      cpu time            0.00 seconds
```

In SAS in the cloud, submitting the `quit` statement will generate a log similar to this:

```
16         quit;
NOTE: PROCEDURE SQL used (Total process time):
   real time           6.10 seconds
   user cpu time       0.01 seconds
   system cpu time     0.01 seconds
```

The effect of you sequentially submitting each statement in Program 1.5.2 is the same as submitting Program 1.5.2 all at once.

1.11.2   Second Experiment

PC SAS and SAS in the cloud   After PROC SQL is terminated, highlight and submit the second statement of `helloWorld.sas`:

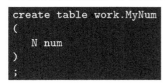

In both PC SAS and SAS in the cloud, you get this error log:

```
ERROR 180-322: Statement is not valid or it is used out of proper order.
```

You got an error in the log because you were trying to create a table without first invoking the SQL procedure. The `create table` functionality is contained in the SQL procedure. To create a table, you must first invoke the SQL procedure.

1.11.3   Third Experiment

PC SAS   First, create a new program:

Program 1.11.1 *worker3.sas*

```
1   dm log 'clear'; dm output 'clear';
2   libname mylib 'C:\LearnSAS';
3   proc sql;
4   create table mylib.worker
5   (
6       id num,
7       sex char(1),
8       firstName char(12),
9       lastName char,
10      salary num
11  );
12
13  insert into mylib.worker
14  values(1,'M','John','Smith',60000)
15  values(2,'F','Jane','Johnson',70000)
16  values(5,'F','Mary','Williams',80000)
17  values(20,'M','Robert','Walker',90000)
18  ;
19
20  select * from mylib.worker;
21  quit;
```

Output:

id	sex	firstName	lastName	salary
1	M	John	Smith	60000
2	F	Jane	Johnson	70000
5	F	Mary	Williams	80000
20	M	Robert	Walker	90000

We'll partition `worker.sas` into 5 subprograms:

Program 1.11.2 *worker3Sub1.sas*

```
1   dm log 'clear'; dm output 'clear';
2   libname mylib 'C:\LearnSAS';
```

Program 1.11.3 *worker3Sub2.sas*

```
1   proc sql;
2   create table mylib.worker
3   (
4       id num,
5       sex char(1),
6       firstName char(12),
7       lastName char,
8       salary num
9   );
```

Program 1.11.4 *worker3Sub3.sas*

```
1   insert into mylib.worker
2   values(1,'M','John','Smith',60000)
3   values(2,'F','Jane','Johnson',70000)
4   values(5,'F','Mary','Williams',80000)
5   values(20,'M','Robert','Walker',90000)
6   ;
```

Program 1.11.5 *worker3Sub4.sas*

```
1   select * from mylib.worker;
```

Program 1.11.6 *worker3Sub5.sas*

```
1   quit;
```

It doesn't matter where you store `worker3.sas` and the 5 subprograms. However, for easy tracking, we'll store these 6 programs in the `C:\LearnSAS` folder.

Next, make sure all the 5 subprograms are opened under the same running instance of SAS. For example, while Program 1.11.2 is open, from the same running instance of SAS, use File ⟩ Open to open Program 1.11.3. Now these two subprograms are opened under the same running instance of SAS.

Next, submit Program 1.11.2, 1.11.3, 1.11.4, 1.11.5, and 1.11.6 in that order. This will create the same output table `mylib.worker` as does Program 1.11.1.

The effect of executing these 5 seemingly independent SAS programs under the same running instance of SAS is the same as submitting their combined program 1.11.1.

Multiple SAS programs under the same running instance of the SAS software is said to share the same SAS session.

The effect of executing several SAS programs under the same running instance of SAS is the same as executing a bigger SAS program that combines each executed program, with the earlier executed program appearing earlier in the combined program.

SAS in the cloud   First reset the mode to the batch mode. Next, create the following program:

Program 1.11.7 *worker3cloud.sas*

```
1   libname mylib '/home/userid/myProgram';
2   proc sql;
3   create table mylib.worker
4   (
5      id num,
6      sex char(1),
7      firstName char(12),
8      lastName char,
9      salary num
10  );
11
12  insert into mylib.worker
13  values(1,'M','John','Smith',60000)
14  values(2,'F','Jane','Johnson',70000)
15  values(5,'F','Mary','Williams',80000)
16  values(20,'M','Robert','Walker',90000)
17  ;
18
19  select * from mylib.worker;
20  quit;
```

mylib.worker table:

id	sex	firstName	lastName	salary
1	M	John	Smith	60000
2	F	Jane	Johnson	70000
5	F	Mary	Williams	80000
20	M	Robert	Walker	90000

We'll partition worker3cloud.sas into 4 subprograms:

Program 1.11.8 *worker3cloudSub1.sas*

```
1   libname mylib '/home/userid/myProgram';
```

Program 1.11.9 *worker3cloudSub2.sas*

```
1   proc sql;
2   create table mylib.worker
3   (
4      id num,
5      sex char(1),
6      firstName char(12),
7      lastName char,
8      salary num
9   );
10  quit;
```

Program 1.11.10 *worker3cloudSub3.sas*

```
1   proc sql;
2   insert into mylib.worker
3   values(1,'M','John','Smith',60000)
4   values(2,'F','Jane','Johnson',70000)
5   values(5,'F','Mary','Williams',80000)
6   values(20,'M','Robert','Walker',90000)
7   ;
8   quit;
```

Program 1.11.11 *worker3cloudSub4.sas*

```
1   proc sql;
2   select * from mylib.worker;
3   quit;
```

Submit Program 1.11.8, 1.11.9, 1.11.10, and 1.11.11 in that order in the batch mode. This creates the same output `worker` table as does Program 1.11.7.

If you invoke PROC SQL in the batch mode in SAS in the cloud, to avoid server overload, SAS in the cloud automatically terminates PROC SQL after the program is executed regardless of whether you have an ending `quit` statement. As a result, you'll need to invoke PROC SQL in each program to perform CRUD.

If you use SAS in the cloud, you'll want to use the default batch mode most of the time. If you use the interactive mode, different SAS programs are independent from one another as if they were created under different running instances of the SAS software.

1.12   Sixth Program - Create the Employee Table

The next program creates the `work.employee` table and exports it to a CSV file in `C:\LearnSAS`.

Program 1.12.1 *employee.sas*

```
1    dm log 'clear'; dm output 'clear';
2    proc sql;
3    create table work.employee
4    (
5       SSN num,
6       Gender char(1),
7       Dept char(11),
8       JobClass char(3),
9       HireDate num,
10      Salary num
11   )
12   ;
13
14   insert into work.employee
15   values(123456789,'M','Engineering','EA1','31Dec1959'd,60000)
16   values(234567890,'F','Engineering','EA2','1Jan1960'd,70000)
17   values(345678901,'M','Engineering','EA3','2Jan1960'd,80000)
18   ;
19   quit;
20
21   proc export
22   data=work.employee
23   outfile='C:\LearnSAS\employee.csv'
24   dbms=csv
25   replace
26   ;
27   run;
```

This is part of the log:

```
NOTE: 3 rows were inserted into WORK.EMPLOYEE.

3 records created in C:\LearnSAS\employee.csv from WORK.EMPLOYEE
NOTE: C:\LearnSAS\employee.csv was successfully created.
```

This is the newly created `C:\LearnSAS\employee.csv` file:

SSN	Gender	Dept	JobClass	HireDate	Salary
123456789	M	Engineering	EA1	-1	60000
234567890	F	Engineering	EA2	0	70000
345678901	M	Engineering	EA3	1	80000

If you use SAS in the cloud, change the `outfile` line to:

`outfile='/home/userid/myProgram/employee.csv'`

Submit the program. It will create the same `employee.csv` file in the `/home/userid/myProgram` folder. This is the log:

```
3 records created in /home/userid/myProgram/employee.csv from WORK.EMPLOYEE.

NOTE: "/home/userid/myProgram/employee.csv" file was successfully created.
```

This is the syntax of `proc export`:

- `data` specifies the source table.

- `outfile` specifies the full path of the CSV file to be created.

- `dbms=csv` specifies that the output file type is csv.

- `replace` forces the newly generated csv file to overwrite any existing csv file with the same name.

Unlike PROC SQL, PROC EXPORT ends with the `run` statement.

You can open the CSV file with Excel and save it as an Excel file. If you use SAS in the cloud, download the CSV file to your hard drive before saving it as an Excel file.

1.12.1   SAS Dates

In Program 1.12.1, the `HireDate` column was declared to be `numeric`. In SAS, a date is an integer that represents the number of days between January 1, 1960 and a specified date. For example,

- December 30, 1959 is -2 (Day negative 2)

- December 31, 1959 is -1 (Day negative 1)

- January 1, 1960 is 0 (Day 0)

- January 2, 1960 is 1 (Day 1)

- January 3, 1960 is 2 (Day 2)

January 1, 1960 is expressed as the integer 0 or more conveniently '1Jan1960'd in SAS. If you don't know the integer corresponding to the date mm/dd/yyyy, you can express it as 'ddmmmyyyy'd.

Make no mistake. '1Jan1960'd is not a string, but the number 0. The expression '1Jan1960'd=0 evaluates to true. This makes date math simple. For example, '1Jan1960'd+1=2, meaning that one day after Jan 1, 1960 is January 2, 1960.

The followings are some of the equivalent ways of representing January 1, 1960:

- 0

- '01jan1960'D

- '01JAN1960'd

- '01jAn1960'd

You can use the mdy() function to find the integer value of a random date. For example,

- mdy(12,31,1959)=-1

- mdy(1,1,1960)=0

- mdy(1,2,1960)=1

Conversely, to find the month, the day, and the year of a given SAS date, use the month(), day(), and year() functions. For example,

- month(-1)=12

- day(-1)=31

- year(-1)=1959

1.12.2 Explore Informats and Formats

Program 1.12.2 *dateInformatFormat.sas*

```
1  dm log 'clear'; dm output 'clear';
2  proc sql;
3  create table work.HireDateTable
4  (
5     HireDate num
6  )
7  ;
8
```

```
 9    /*  method 1 - use date integer*/
10    insert into work.HireDateTable
11    values('31Dec1959'd)
12    values('1Jan1960'd)
13    values('2Jan1960'd)
14    ;
15
16    /*  method 2 - use mdy function*/
17    insert into work.HireDateTable
18    set HireDate=mdy(12,31,1959)
19    set HireDate=mdy( 1, 1,1960)
20    set HireDate=mdy( 1, 2,1960)
21    ;
22
23    /*  method 3 --use informat date9.*/
24    insert into work.HireDateTable
25    set HireDate=input('31dec1959',date9.)
26    set HireDate=input('1jan1960', date9.)
27    set HireDate=input('2jan1960', date9.)
28    ;
29
30    /*  method 4 --use informat date11.*/
31    insert into work.HireDateTable
32    set HireDate=input('31 dec 1959',date11.)
33    set HireDate=input('1 jan 1960', date11.)
34    set HireDate=input('2 jan 1960', date11.)
35    ;
36
37    /*  method 5 --use informat mmddyy10.*/
38    insert into work.HireDateTable
39    set HireDate=input('12/31/1959', mmddyy10.)
40    set HireDate=input('1/1/1960',    mmddyy10.)
41    set HireDate=input('1/2/1960',    mmddyy10.)
42    ;
43    quit;
44
45    options linewidth=min nonumber nodate;
46    /*  method 1 - display date as integer*/
47    proc print data= work.HireDateTable;
48        title 'method 1;default best12. format; all the rows;';
49    run;
50
51    /*  method 2 - display date as integer*/
52    proc print data= work.HireDateTable(obs=3);
53        title 'method 2;best12. format; first 3 rows';
54        format HireDate best12.;  /* default format*/
55    run;
56
57    /*  method 3 - display date as mm/dd/yyyy */
58    proc print data= work.HireDateTable(obs=3);
59        title 'method 3; 4.2 format; first 3 rows';
60            format HireDate 4.2;
61    run;
62
63    /*  method 4 - display date as mm/dd/yyyy */
64    proc print data= work.HireDateTable(obs=3);
65        title 'method 4;mmddyy10. format; first 3 rows';
66        format HireDate mmddyy10.;
```

```
67  run;
68
69  /*  method 5 - display date as dd/mm/yyyy */
70  proc print data= work.HireDateTable(obs=3);
71      title 'method 5;ddmmyy10. format; first 3 rows';
72      format HireDate ddmmyy10.;
73  run;
74
75  /*  method 6 - display date as dd MMM yyyy */
76  proc print data= work.HireDateTable(obs=3);
77      title 'method 6;yymmdd10. format; first 3 rows';
78      format HireDate yymmdd10.;
79  run;
80
81  /*  method 7 - display date as ddMMMyyyy */
82  proc print data= work.HireDateTable(obs=3);
83      title 'method 7;date9. format; first 3 rows';
84      format HireDate date9.;
85  run;
86
87  /*method 8 - display date as weekday, full month-name dd, yyyy*/
88  proc print data= work.HireDateTable(obs=3);
89      title 'method 8;WEEKDATE. format; first 3 rows';
90      format HireDate WEEKDATE.;
91  run;
92
93  /*  method 9 - display date as 3-letter month-name dd, yyyy */
94  proc print data= work.HireDateTable(obs=3);
95      title 'method 9;worddate12. format; first 3 rows';
96      format HireDate worddate12.;
97  run;
98
99  /*  method 10 - display date as yyyyQquarter-name */
100 proc print data= work.HireDateTable(obs=3);
101     title 'method 10;yyq6. format; first 3 rows';
102     format HireDate yyq6.;
103 run;
```

This is the output:

```
method 1;default best12. format; all the rows;

              Hire
       Obs    Date

         1     -1
         2      0
         3      1
         4     -1
         5      0
         6      1
         7     -1
         8      0
         9      1
        10     -1
        11      0
        12      1
```

```
                    13      -1
                    14       0
                    15       1
       method 2;best12. format; first 3 rows


           Obs          HireDate

            1              -1
            2               0
            3               1
       method 3; 4.2 format; first 3 rows


                      Hire
           Obs        Date

            1      -1.0
            2       0.00
            3       1.00
       method 4;mmddyy10. format; first 3 rows


           Obs          HireDate

            1      12/31/1959
            2      01/01/1960
            3      01/02/1960
       method 5;ddmmyy10. format; first 3 rows


           Obs          HireDate

            1      31/12/1959
            2      01/01/1960
            3      02/01/1960
       method 6;yymmdd10. format; first 3 rows


           Obs          HireDate

            1      1959-12-31
            2      1960-01-01
            3      1960-01-02
       method 7;date9. format; first 3 rows


           Obs          HireDate

            1      31DEC1959
            2      01JAN1960
            3      02JAN1960
       method 8;WEEKDATE. format; first 3 rows


        Obs              HireDate

         1     Thursday, December 31, 1959
         2         Friday, January 1, 1960
         3       Saturday, January 2, 1960
       method 9;worddate12. format; first 3 rows


           Obs          HireDate

            1      Dec 31, 1959
```

```
        2       Jan 1, 1960
        3       Jan 2, 1960
method 10;yyq6. format; first 3 rows

                    Hire
        Obs         Date

          1         1959Q4
          2         1960Q1
          3         1960Q1
```

The 5 `insert` statements (Lines 10, 17, 24, 31, and 38)) each write the same three dates, 12/31/1959, 1/1/1960, and 1/2/1960, to the output table `HireDateTable`.

The INPUT function converts a character expression using a specified informat. The informat determines whether the resulting value is character or numeric.

The `date9.` informat converts a raw string '`ddmmmyyyy`' to a SAS date. For example, `date9.` reads the raw string '`31dec1959`' as the date of December 31, 1959 or the integer negative 1.

The `input('31dec1959',date9.)` function returns the integer date for December 31, 1959. Notice that the width of '`ddmmmyyyy`' is 9, hence the number 9 in the `date9.` informat.

The `date11.` informat interprets '`dd mmm yyyy`' as a date. Notice that the total width of '`dd mmm yyyy`' is 11. Similarly, the informat `mmddyy10.` interprets string '`mm/dd/yyyy`' as a date.

Finally, the ten PROC PRINT steps in Program 1.12.2 display the integer `HireDate` as various string representations.

In PROC PRINT, the `linesize=min` option tells SAS to use for each variable the minimum column width that accommodates all the variable values. The `nonumber` option tells SAS not to print the page number. Finally, the `nodate` option tells SAS not to display date in the output.

1.12.3 Set Column Format Attributes

You specify the `format` option in the `create table` statement to set a column's format attribute.

Program 1.12.3 *ssnTable.sas*

```
1   dm log 'clear'; dm output 'clear';
2   proc sql;
3   create table ssnTable1
4   (
5      ssn num format ssn11.
6   )
7   ;
8   insert into ssnTable1
9   values(123456789)
10  values(234567890)
11  values(345678901)
12  ;
13  quit;
14
15  proc print data=ssnTable1;
16   title 'ssnTable1 using ssn11. format';
17  run;
18
19  proc sql;
20  create table ssnTable2
21  (
22     ssn num
23  )
24  ;
25  insert into ssnTable2
26  values(123456789)
27  values(234567890)
28  values(345678901)
29  ;
30
31  quit;
32
33  proc print data=ssnTable2;
34    title 'ssnTable2 using ssn11. format';
35    format ssn ssn11.;
36  run;
37
38  proc print data=ssnTable1;
39    title 'ssnTable1 using best12. format';
40    format ssn best12.;
41  run;
```

Output:

ssnTable1 using ssn11. format

Obs	ssn
1	123-45-6789
2	234-56-7890
3	345-67-8901

ssnTable2 using ssn11. format

Obs	ssn
1	123-45-6789
2	234-56-7890
3	345-67-8901

ssnTable1 using best12. format

Obs	ssn
1	123456789
2	234567890
3	345678901

The ssn11. format displays a social security number such as 123456789 in the form of 123-45-6789.

1.12.4   Difference between Informats and Formats

To summarize. You use an informat to tell SAS how your raw data looks like so SAS can extract the correct value from your raw input data and store the correct value in a table. You use a format to tell SAS how to display the data stored in a SAS table to you.

Formats are for displaying purpose only. They don't alter or truncate the data stored in a SAS table. Informats, on the other hand, determine how to extract the correct value from the raw input data. With a wrong informat, SAS will retrieve the wrong value from the input data.

An informat and a format may have the same expression. For example, mmddyy10. can be used either as an `informat` or a `format`. As an `informat`, it instructs SAS to read the string `mm/dd/yyyy` as a date. As a `format`, it tells SAS to display a date in the string form `mm/dd/yyyy`.

1.13 Further Reading

The free official SAS tutorial pdf, *Step-by-Step Programming with Base SAS Software*, by SAS Institute Inc, 2001. Cary, NC: SA Institute Inc. Google it to download the pdf. Chapter 1, *What Is the SAS System?*

The free official SQL user guide pdf, *SAS 9.3 SQL Procedure User's Guide*, Chapter 4, *Creating and Updating Tables and Views*.

Step-by-Step Programming with Base SAS Software, Chapter 14, *Working with Dates in the SAS System*.

Introduction to SAS Informats and Formats

`http://support.sas.com/publishing/pubcat/chaps/59498.pdf`.

Choose your own adventure with SAS OnDemand for Professionals

`http://blogs.sas.com/content/sasdummy/2012/01/18/sasondemand-forpros/`

Free SAS!

`http://statisticalhorizons.com/free-sas`

On the difference between the batch mode and the interactive mode, refer to *Step-by-Step Programming with Base SAS Software*, Chapter 38, *Introducing the SAS Environment*, Page 645, *Selecting a SAS Processing Mode*.

Chapter 2

DATA Step Basics

There's almost always more than one way to do everything in SAS. Instead of using PROC SQL, you can use a DATA step to create or modify a table.

2.1 Hello World DATA Step Program

The next program creates a `work.MyNum` table with one blank row. A period represents a missing numeric value.

Program 2.1.1 *helloWorldDataStep.sas*

MyNum table:

```
1   data MyNum;
2   length N 3;
3   output MyNum;
4   return;
5   run;
```

	N
1	.

A DATA step begins with the `data` statement and ends with the `run` statement.

Line 1 declares that the `MyNum` table is to be created. `Data` in SAS means a table or a data set.

Line 2 declares the column `N` and specifies its length to be 3 bytes. Since the data type of `N` is not specified, SAS automatically sets `N` to be a numeric column.

Unlike the CREATE TABLE statement in PROC SQL, a DATA step can set the length of a numeric column to be less than the default 8 bytes, subject to the limitation that the minimum length of a numeric variable is 2 bytes in mainframe environments and 3 bytes in non-mainframe environments (Windows and Unix).

Line 3 writes the value of `N` as one row to the `MyNum` table. The `output` statement is similar to the `insert into` statement in PROC SQL. Since no value is explicitly assigned to `N` before the `output` statement, the `output` statement will write a missing numeric value to the `MyNum` table.

Line 4. The `return` statement does two things: (1) It causes the execution to stop at the current point in the DATA step, and (2) it returns control to the beginning of the DATA step so the DATA step can start its next iteration.

35

Every DATA step program is an implicit loop so the `output` statement can be executed multiple times to create multiple rows in the destination table specified in the `data` statement (more on this in Section 4.12). However, the DATA step loop in Program 2.1.1 has only one iteration and the `return` statement isn't necessary.

Next, open the `work.MyNum` table and verify that `N` is indeed a numeric column (see Section 1.10).

In Program 2.1.1, you can omit the `output` statement and the `return` statement altogether because SAS by default will automatically execute an implicit `output` statement and an implicit `return` statement at the end of the DATA step. Program 2.1.1 can be shortened to:

Program 2.1.2 *helloWorldDataStepShort.sas*

```
1  data MyNum;
2  length N 3;
3  run;
```

Though Program 2.1.1 and Program 2.1.2 are equivalent, newcomers to SAS are encouraged to use the coding style in Program 2.1.1 to spell out the DATA step. After they have a good grasp of SAS DATA step fundamentals, they can switch to a terse coding style as in Program 2.1.2.

The next program creates a blank table `MyNum` with no rows.

Program 2.1.3 *helloWorldDataStepBlankTable.sas*

```
1  data MyNum;
2  length N 3;
3  stop;
4  output MyNum;
5  return;
6  run;
```

MyNum table:

N

The newly created `work.MyNum` table has the column header `N` but doesn't have any rows:

The `stop` statement instructs SAS to immediately stop processing the current DATA step and to resume processing statements after the end of the current DATA step.

In Program 2.1.3, after the `stop` statement is executed, neither the `output` statement nor the `return` statement will be executed and the entire DATA step will come to an end. If there are any statements after Line 6, these statements will be executed next after the `stop` statement is executed.

In a SAS DATA step, a variable is numeric by default unless specified otherwise. The next program creates `MyChar` table that has a character column `N` with length 3.

Program 2.1.4 *helloWorldDataStepChar.sas*

MyChar table:

N
1

```
1  data MyChar;
2  length N $ 3;
3  output MyChar;
4  return;
5  run;
```

The newly created `work.MyChar` table has one row populated with a missing character value.

In the `length` statement, the dollar sign indicates that `N` is a character column.

In SAS, while a missing numeric value is represented by a period, a missing character value is represented by a blank.

Next, open the `work.MyNum` table and verify that `N` is a character column (see Section 1.10).

Similar to Program 2.1.3, the next program creates a blank `work.MyChar` table without any rows.

Program 2.1.5
helloWorldDataStepCharBlankTable.sas

MyChar table:

```
1   data MyChar;
2   length N $ 3;
3   stop;
4   output MyChar;
5   return;
6   run;
```

N

The newly created `work.MyChar` table has only the column header `N` but doesn't have any rows.

While PROC SQL ends with the `quit` statement, a DATA step ends with the `run` statement. This is largely an inconsistency in the SAS language implementation. More on this in Section 2.7.

By the way, this is the shortest DATA program you can ever write:

Program 2.1.6 *shortestDataStepProgram.sas*

```
1   data;
2   run;
```

Submit Program 2.1.6 the first time and you'll get this log:

```
NOTE: The data set WORK.DATA1 has 1 observations and 0 variables.
```

You have created the `work.data1` table but it doesn't have any columns. Though the `work.data1` table isn't useful, Program 2.1.6 is a valid DATA step program.

If you don't specify the destination table in the `data` statement, SAS automatically uses `dataN` as the destination table. The integer N starts from 1 and increments by 1.

Submit Program 2.1.6 the second time and you'll get this log:

```
NOTE: The data set WORK.DATA2 has 1 observations and 0 variables.
```

2.2 Populate a Table with Integers from 1 to 10

Here's the DATA step counterpart to Program 1.7.1:

Program 2.2.1 *one2tenDataStep.sas*

```
1   dm log 'clear'; dm output 'clear';
2   data MyNum;
3   N=1;  output MyNum;
4   N=2;  output MyNum;
5   N=3;  output MyNum;
6   N=4;  output MyNum;
7   N=5;  output MyNum;
8   N=6;  output MyNum;
9   N=7;  output MyNum;
10  N=8;  output MyNum;
11  N=9;  output MyNum;
12  N=10; output MyNum;
13
14  return;
15  run;
16
17  proc print data=MyNum;
18  run;
```

Output:

Obs	N
1	1
2	2
3	3
4	4
5	5
6	6
7	7
8	8
9	9
10	10

In the output, `Obs` stands for observation, which means a row in a table.

Every variable in a DATA step will automatically become a column of the output table specified in the `data` statement. Since numeric values are assigned to N, SAS automatically sets N to be a numeric column. Since no length is specified for N, SAS sets its length to the default 8 bytes.

Finally, the pre-built PRINT procedure writes the content of the `MyNum` table to the output window.

PROC PRINT is similar to the following SQL statements:

```
proc sql;
select * from MyNum;
quit;
```

Compare the output generated by PROC SQL and that generated by PROC PRINT:

```
select * from MyNum     PROC PRINT data=MyNum

         N                  Obs    N
--------
         1                   1     1
         2                   2     2
         3                   3     3
         4                   4     4
         5                   5     5
         6                   6     6
         7                   7     7
         8                   8     8
         9                   9     9
        10                  10    10
```

For debugging your code, the two methods are roughly the same. Both display the data values of a table in the output window. However, PROC PRINT offers finer controls over the final output and can produce headers, total lines, and grand total lines. You can use PROC PRINT to produce pretty documents to distribute to end users. In addition, using ODS (output delivery system), PROC PRINT can export a table to a CSV file, a PDF file, an HTML file, or a Microsoft Word document. To learn more about PROC PRINT and ODS, refer to Section 2.8.

2.3 More DATA Step Programs

The next DATA step creates the `work.MNO` table with three columns, M, N, and O.

Program 2.3.1 *MNO.sas*

```
1   dm log 'clear';   dm output 'clear';
2   data MNO;
3   M=1; N=10; O='abc'; output MNO;
4   M=2; N=20; O='def'; output MNO;
5   M=3; N=30; O='ghi'; output MNO;
6
7   return;
8   run;
9
10  proc print data=MNO;
11  run;
```

Output:

Obs	M	N	O
1	1	10	abc
2	2	20	def
3	3	30	ghi

Program 2.3.1 is equivalent to the following PROC SQL program:

Program 2.3.2 *MNOequivalent.sas*

```
1   dm log 'clear';   dm output 'clear';
2   proc sql;
3   create table MNO
4   (
5      M num,
6      N num,
7      O char(3)
8   );
9
10  insert into MNO
11  values(1,10,'abc')
12  values(2,20,'def')
13  values(3,30,'ghi')
14  ;
15
16  select * from MNO;
17  quit;
```

Output:

M	N	O
1	10	abc
2	20	def
3	30	ghi

2.4 Do-Loop and If-Then-Else in a DATA Step

So far a DATA step appears to be just another way to populate a table; nothing spectacular. But wait! Unlike PROC SQL, a DATA step allows a DO-LOOP. Program 2.2.1 can be rewritten as:

Program 2.4.1

Output:

one2tenDataStepLoop.sas

```
1   dm log 'clear'; dm output 'clear';
2   data MyNum;
3   do N=1 to 10;
4     output MyNum;
5   end;
6
7   return;
8   run;
9
10  proc print data=MyNum;
11  run;
```

Obs	N
1	1
2	2
3	3
4	4
5	5
6	6
7	7
8	8
9	9
10	10

The DATA step in Program 2.4.1 iterates only once. However, inside the DATA step, the DO-LOOP iterates ten times.

While a CREATE TABLE statement can create only one table, one DATA step can create multiple tables. The next program creates three identical tables MyNum1, MyNum2, and MyNum3. In each iteration of the DO-LOOP, the same value of N is inserted to three tables, MyNum1, MyNum2, and MyNum3.

Output:

MyNum1

Obs	N
1	1
2	2
3	3
4	4
5	5
6	6
7	7
8	8
9	9
10	10

MyNum2

Obs	N
1	1
2	2
3	3
4	4
5	5
6	6
7	7
8	8
9	9
10	10

MyNum3

Obs	N
1	1
2	2
3	3
4	4
5	5
6	6
7	7
8	8
9	9
10	10

Program 2.4.2

one2tenDataStepLoop3Tables.sas

```
1   dm log 'clear'; dm output 'clear';
2   data MyNum1 MyNum2 MyNum3;
3   do N=1 to 10;
4     output MyNum1 MyNum2 MyNum3;
5   end;
6
7   return;
8   run;
9
10  proc print data=MyNum1;
11   title 'MyNum1';
12  run;
13
14  proc print data=MyNum2;
15   title 'MyNum2';
16  run;
17
18  proc print data=MyNum3;
19   title 'MyNum3';
20  run;
```

In PROC SQL, you cannot use the IF-THEN-ELSE statement; you need to use the CASE expression instead. In contrast, a DATA step allows the IF-THEN-ELSE statement.

Output:

Program 2.4.3

one2tenDataStepLoopEvenOdd.sas

```
1   dm log 'clear'; dm output 'clear';
2   data Both Odd Even;
3   do N=1 to 10;
4     output Both;
5     if mod(N,2)=1 then output Odd;
6     else output Even;
7   end;
8
9   return;
10  run;
11
12  proc print data=Both;
13    title 'Both';
14    title2 'Contains integer 1 to 10';
15  run;
16
17  proc print data=Odd;
18    title 'Odd';
19    title2 'Contains integer 1, 3, 5, 7, and 9';
20  run;
21
22  proc print data=Even;
23    title 'Even';
24    title2 'Contains integer 2, 4, 6, 8, and 10';
25  run;
```

```
                  Both
        Contains integer 1 to 10

            Obs        N

             1         1
             2         2
             3         3
             4         4
             5         5
             6         6
             7         7
             8         8
             9         9
            10        10
                  Odd
    Contains integer 1, 3, 5, 7, and 9

            Obs        N

             1         1
             2         3
             3         5
             4         7
             5         9
                  Even
   Contains integer 2, 4, 6, 8, and 10

            Obs        N

             1         2
             2         4
             3         6
             4         8
             5        10
```

The unconditional `output Both` statement inserts every `N` into the `Both` table. The `mod(N,2)` function returns the remainder of N divided by 2. If the remainder is 1, then `N` is inserted into the `Odd` table; if the remainder is not 1 (e.g. 0), then `N` is inserted into the `Even` table.

The `title` statement adds a line of text to the top of the report. You can use up to ten `title` statements, `title1` (same as `title`), `title2`, ..., and `title10`, to include 1 to 10 lines of text at the top of the report. You must enclose the text of each `title` in single or double quotes.

Once you specify a `title` for a line, it is used for all subsequent output under the same running instance of the SAS software until you cancel the title or define a new title.

Let's experiment. After submitting Program 2.4.3, open a new enhanced editor window and create Program 2.4.4:

Output:

Program 2.4.4 *ByHundred.sas*

```
1   dm log 'clear'; dm output 'clear';
2   data ByHundred;
3   do i=100 to 1000 by 100;
4    output ByHundred;
5   end;
6
7   return;
8   run;
9
10  proc print data=ByHundred;
11  run;
```

```
                Even
  Contains integer 2, 4, 6, 8, and 10

        Obs        i

         1        100
         2        200
         3        300
         4        400
         5        500
         6        600
         7        700
         8        800
         9        900
        10       1000
```

To cancel a title, you use an empty **title** statement without an argument. The next PROC PRINT uses an empty **title** statement to reset the report title to blank.

```
proc print data=one2tenByHundred;
  title;
run;
```

The next program creates three big tables. The **Both** table has one million integers: $1, 2, ...,$ $1,000,000$. The **Odd** table contains $500,000$ odd integers: $1, 3, ..., 999,999$. And the **Even** table contains $500,000$ even integers: $2, 4, ..., 1,000,000$.

Output:

Program 2.4.5 *one2oneMillionDataStepLoop.sas*

```
1   dm log 'clear'; dm output 'clear';
2   data Both Even Odd;
3   do N=1 to 1e6;
4     output Both;
5     if mod(N,2)=0 then output Even; else output Odd;
6   end;
7
8   return;
9   run;
10
11  proc print data=Both(firstobs=999996 obs=1000000);
12   title 'last 5 rows from Both table';
13  run;
14
15  proc print data=Odd(firstobs=499996 obs=500000);
16   title 'last 5 rows from Odd table';
17  run;
18
19  proc print data=Even(firstobs=499996 obs=500000);
20   title 'last 5 rows from Even table';
21  run;
```

```
last 5 rows from Both table

      Obs          N

    999996      999996
    999997      999997
    999998      999998
    999999      999999
   1000000     1000000
last 5 rows from Odd table

      Obs          N

    499996      999991
    499997      999993
    499998      999995
    499999      999997
    500000      999999
last 5 rows from Even table

      Obs          N

    499996      999992
    499997      999994
    499998      999996
    499999      999998
    500000     1000000
```

The `data xyz(firstobs=m obs=n)` expression where $m \le n$ retrieves $n - m + 1$ rows from Table xyz, starting from Row m and ending with Row n. If `firstobs=m` is omitted, m defaults to 1.

Make sure $m \le n$ or you'll get an error log:

```
ERROR: FIRSTOBS option > OBS option - no data to read from file xyz.
```

Similar to Program 1.9.1, the next program finds the sum of the integers from 1 to 10:

Program 2.4.6 *one2tenSumDataStep.sas*

Output:

```
1   dm log 'clear';  dm output 'clear';
2   data MyNumTotal;
3   total=0;
4   do N=1 to 10;
5     total=total + N;
6     output MyNumTotal;
7   end;
8
9   return;
10  run;
11
12  proc print data=MyNumTotal;
13  run;
```

Obs	total	N
1	1	1
2	3	2
3	6	3
4	10	4
5	15	5
6	21	6
7	28	7
8	36	8
9	45	9
10	55	10

Can you explain the output of Program 2.4.7?

Program 2.4.7 *MNOTable.sas*

Output:

```
1   dm log 'clear';  dm output 'clear';
2   data MNO;
3   M=1; N=10; O='abc';
4   M=2; N=20; O='def';
5   M=3; N=30; O='ghi';
6   output MNO;
7   return;
8   run;
9
10  proc print data=MNO;
11    title 'MNO table';
12  run;
```

MNO table

Obs	M	N	O
1	3	30	ghi

The resulting table MNO has only one row, not three rows as one might expect. The DATA step has only one iteration and the `output` statement is executed only once. Only the final values of M, N, and O before the `output` statement are inserted into MNO.

Program 2.4.7 is equivalent to the following PROC SQL program:

Program 2.4.8
MNOTableSQLequivalent.sas

```
1   dm log 'clear';  dm output 'clear';
2   proc sql;
3   create table MNO
4   (
5      M num,
6      N num,
7      O char(3)
8   );
9   insert into MNO
10  values(3,30,'ghi');
11  quit;
12
13  proc sql;
14    title 'MNO table';
15    select * from MNO;
16  quit;
```

Output:

```
        MNO table


      M         N  O
-----------------------
      3        30  ghi
```

Can you explain the output of Program 2.4.9?

Program 2.4.9 *MNOTable2.sas*

```
1   dm log 'clear';  dm output 'clear';
2   data MNO2;
3   N=10; P=M+N;           output MNO2;
4   M=1; O='def'; P=M+N; output MNO2;
5   M=3; P=M+N;           output MNO2;
6
7   return;
8   run;
9
10  proc print data=MNO2;
11    title 'MNO2 table';
12  run;
```

Output:

```
        MNO2 table

Obs    N     P    M    O

 1    10     .    .
 2    10    11    1    def
 3    10    13    3    def
```

SAS scans all the variables in the DATA step to determine the column names of the output table. All the variable names automatically become the column names of the output table. The columns in the output table are in the same order in which the variables first appear in the DATA step.

The four variables in the DATA step first appear in this order: N, P, M, and O. SAS creates four columns, N, P, M, and O, in the order of each variable's first appearance in the DATA step.

In a DATA step, to determine the data type and the length of a column in the output table, SAS uses the rule of the first encounter. When SAS first encounters a variable in the DATA step, that variable's data type and length become the data type and the length for that variable in the output table.

Before the first output statement executes, only the variable N is initialized. The other three variables are not initialized and SAS sets them to missing. The output statement inserts N=10, P=missing, M=missing, O=missing into the first row of the MNO2 table.

Before the second output statement executes, SAS gathers the final data values up to that output statement and finds that N=10, M=1, O='def', and P=M+N=11. SAS inserts N=10, P=11, M=1, O='def' into the second row of the table.

Before the third output statement executes, SAS gathers the final data values up to that output statement and finds that N=10, M=3, O='def', and P=M+N=13. SAS inserts N=10,P=13, M=1, O='def' into the third row of the table.

The DATA step in Program 2.4.9 iterates only once.

2.5   DATA Step Boundary - PC SAS

Newcomers to PC SAS often have this experience. They create a DATA step program and submit it, but nothing happens. No table is created; no output is generated; and no log is produced to tell what has gone wrong. Here's an example.

Program 2.5.1 *dataStepNothingHappened.sas*

```
1   dm log 'clear'; dm output 'clear';
2   data A;
3   do i=1 to 10;
4     output;
5   end;
```

Submit the program. Open the work folder and you won't see the table A. Check the log and you won't see any WARNING or NOTE messages. The only clue you get is that the following message title will appear at the top left corner of the enhanced editor window:

```
DATA STEP running
```

What just happened? ANSWER: You forgot to end the DATA step.

To fix the error, first cancel the submitted SAS job:

- From the Application Toolbar, click the exclamation mark enclosed in a circle. Now the Tasking Manager window opens up.

- Select Cancel Submitted Statements from the Tasking Manager window.

- Next, a Break -> Submit window opens up.

- Select Y to cancel submitted statements. Click OK.

Now your submitted SAS job is cancelled. The DATA STEP running title will disappear from the top left corner of the enhanced editor window. Next, add the statement proc print data=A; after the end of Program 2.5.1:

Program 2.5.2 *dataStepExecutedButProcPrintNot.sas*

```
1    dm log 'clear'; dm output 'clear';
2    data A;
3    do i=1 to 10;
4      output;
5    end;
6
7    proc print data=A;
```

Submit this new program. You should get this log:

```
NOTE: The data set WORK.A has 10 observations and 1 variables.
NOTE: DATA statement used:
      real time             0.00 seconds
      cpu time              0.00 seconds
```

Open the `work.A` table and you should see that `work.A` is correctly populated with the integers from 1 to 10. However, there's nothing in the output window; PROC PRINT was not executed. The top left corner of the enhanced editor window has this message title:

```
PROC PRINT running
```

What just happened   When you submit a program, be it a DATA step or a PROC step, your program code goes into an area of memory called the input stack. Once your code is in the input stack, SAS will do the following:

- read the code in the input stack from left to right and from top to bottom

- send the code to the compiler

- stop sending code to the compiler when a step boundary such as a RUN statement, a new DATA step, or a PROC step is encountered

- execute the compiled code if there are no compilation errors

- repeat this process for any subsequent steps

In order for a DATA step or PROC step to be executed, SAS must find a step boundary such as a RUN statement or another DATA step or PROC step. The step boundary triggers SAS to execute the preceding step.

Program 2.5.1 doesn't have a step boundary to mark the ending of the DATA step. After you submit the program, SAS sends all your code to the compiler so your code gets compiled. Then SAS waits for you to type more code for it to send to the compiler. Without a step boundary, the compile phase never ends and your program never gets executed.

In Program 2.5.2, the PROC PRINT step after the DATA step serves as the implicit step boundary of the DATA step. However, there's no explicit or implicit step boundary to signal the ending of the PROC PRINT step. After Program 2.5.2 is submitted, the DATA step is executed, but the

PROC PRINT step will not be executed. SAS will wait forever for you to type more code in the PROC PRINT step for it to send to the compiler.

To execute the PROC PRINT step, at the end of Program 2.5.2, type the run statement. Highlight and submit the run statement:

`run;`

The run statement is the explicit boundary for the PROC PRINT step. It tells SAS that the compilation stage of the PROC PRINT step is over and the execution phase should begin. As a result, the PROC PRINT step is executed. You'll get a log similar to this:

```
        proc print data=A;
        run;

NOTE: There were 10 observations read from the dataset WORK.A.
NOTE: PROCEDURE PRINT used:
        real time            xx
        cpu time             0.00 seconds
```

where xx is the time in seconds it took SAS to complete the PROC PRINT job.

In addition, you'll get this desired output:

```
Obs      i

  1      1
  2      2
  3      3
  4      4
  5      5
  6      6
  7      7
  8      8
  9      9
 10     10
```

Though you don't need to use a run statement to explicitly mark the step boundary of a DATA step or a PROC PRINT step, it's considered the best practice to do so.

The next program use the run statement to explicitly mark the boundary of the DATA step and the PROC PRINT step:

Program 2.5.3 *useRunToMarkStepBoundary.sas*

```
1    dm log 'clear'; dm output 'clear';
2    data A;
3    do i=1 to 10;
4      output;
5    end;
6    run;
7
8    proc print data=A;
9    run;
```

2.6 DATA Step Boundary - SAS in the cloud

If you submit Program 2.5.1 in SAS in the cloud, you'll get the following error in the log:

```
ERROR 180-322: Statement is not valid or it is used out of proper order.

WARNING: The data set WORK.A may be incomplete.  When this step was
 stopped there were 0 observations and 1 variables.
```

If you re-submit Program 2.5.1 in SAS in the cloud, you'll get the following error in the log:

```
ERROR 180-322: Statement is not valid or it is used out of proper order.

WARNING: The data set WORK.A may be incomplete.  When this step was
 stopped there were 0 observations and 1 variables.
WARNING: Data set WORK.A was not replaced because this step was stopped.
```

Program 2.5.1 is missing a boundary for the DATA step. SAS in the cloud will throw an error in the log, whereas PC SAS will display a message title DATA STEP running.

If your PROC PRINT is missing a step boundary, PC SAS will display a message title PROC PRINT running. In contrast, SAS in the cloud will execute the PROC PRINT without throwing an error or issuing a warning in the log.

Program 2.6.1 *procNoBoundaryCloud.sas*

```
1   data A;
2   do i=1 to 10;
3     output;
4   end;
5   run;
6
7   proc print data=A;
```

Submit the program in SAS in the cloud. The content of the work.A table will be displayed in the RESULTS window, even though the PROC PRINT doesn't have a step boundary.

Even though SAS in the cloud executed your PROC PRINT job regardless of whether it has a step boundary, it's considered the best practice to explicitly mark the step boundary of PROC PRINT.

2.7 Quit Versus Run

You probably noticed that PROC SQL uses an ending quit statement but DATA steps or other procedures end with a run statement. What's the difference between quit and run?

In Section 1.11, you experimented with the quit statement. You found that in PC SAS once you invoke the SQL procedure, the SQL procedure is always running and that you can submit another CRUD statement without reinvoking the SQL procedure. To exit the SQL procedure, you submit the quit statement.

In PROC SQL, the step boundary is not important. Once PROC SQL is invoked, every `CRUD` statement you submit is executed immediately.

The SAS Institute adopted two different code-execution philosophies. For DATA steps and most non-SQL procedures, the SAS default behavior is not to execute the code until it sees a step boundary such as a `run` statement. For PROC SQL, however, the SAS default behavior is to execute the code immediately.

Why two different philosophies? My guess is that SAS evolved over time. In early versions of SAS, there wasn't PROC SQL and the SAS Institute felt that the "don't run unless the boundary is found" defensive philosophy was good for end users. Later when the SQL procedure was added, the SAS Institute switched its position and adopted the "always run PROC SQL unless told to stop" philosophy.

The SAS Institute perhaps should have adopted coherent syntax to free everyone from worrying about the difference between `quit` and `run`, but we live in an imperfect world.

2.8 Further Reading

Step-by-Step Programming with Base SAS Software, Chapter 2, *Introduction to DATA Step Processing*.

For the `output` statement, refer to

http://v8doc.sas.com/sashtml/lgref/z0194540.htm

PROC PRINT - the Granddaddy of all Procedures, Enhanced and Still Going Strong!

http://www.lexjansen.com/nesug/nesug11/ds/ds09.pdf

ODS Step by Step

http://www.lexjansen.com/nesug/nesug03/ps/ps020.pdf

PROC PRINT and ODS: Teaching an Old PROC New Tricks

https://support.sas.com/resources/papers/proceedings11/270-2011.pdf

Using 22 Easy Tricks with ODS to Generate Colorful Reports

http://www.mwsug.org/proceedings/2007/tutorials/MWSUG-2007-T10.pdf

Chapter 3

Build Up the Savings Account Balance

This chapter is a warm up exercise for the DATA step.

3.1 Calculate the Savings Account Balance

An annual deposit of $1 is made at the end of each year for the next 10 years into a savings account, the first deposit being made one year from today. The savings account earns a 10% compound interest rate per year. What's the balance of the savings account 10 years from today?

- $1 deposit made at the end of Year 1 will grow into 1.1^9 at the end of Year 10.

- $1 deposit made at the end of Year 2 will grow into 1.1^8 at the end of Year 10.

- . . .

- $1 deposit made at the end of Year 9 will grow into 1.1^1 at the end of Year 10.

- $1 deposit made at the end of Year 10 will still be 1 at the end of Year 10.

The savings account balance at the end of Year 10 is:

$$1.1^9 + 1.1^8 + 1.1^7 + ... + 1.1 + 1 = 15.9374246$$

3.1.1   Method 1

Program 3.1.1 *savingsAccount.sas*

```
1   dm log 'clear'; dm output 'clear';
2   data savings;
3   int=0.1;
4
5   balanceEOY10=   /*EOY=end of yr*/
6     (1+int)**9+(1+int)**8+(1+int)**7
7   +(1+int)**6+(1+int)**5+(1+int)**4
8   +(1+int)**3+(1+int)**2+(1+int)**1
9   + 1
10  ;
11  run;
12
13  proc print data=savings;
14    format balance best12.;
15  run;
```

Output:

Obs	int	balance EOY10
1	0.1	15.9374

3.1.2   Method 2

Program 3.1.2 *savingsAccount2.sas*

```
1   dm log 'clear'; dm output 'clear';
2   data savings;
3   balanceEOY10=0; int=0.1;
4
5   do year=1 to 10;
6     balanceEOY10=balanceEOY10 + (1+int)**(10-year);
7     output;
8   end;
9
10  run;
11
12  proc print data=savings noobs;
13    format balance best12.;
14  run;
```

Output:

balance EOY10	int	year
2.3579	0.1	1
4.5015	0.1	2
6.4503	0.1	3
8.2218	0.1	4
9.8323	0.1	5
11.2964	0.1	6
12.6274	0.1	7
13.8374	0.1	8
14.9374	0.1	9
15.9374	0.1	10

3.1.3   Method 3

Let $bal(n)$ represent the balance at the end of Year n. The initial balance is $bal(0) = 0$.

If a deposit amount k is made at the end of Year n:

$$bal(n) = bal(n-1) \times (1 + int) + k$$

If a deposit amount k is made at the beginning of Year n:

$$bal(n) = [bal(n-1) + k](1 + int)$$

Program 3.1.3 *savingsAccount3.sas*

```
1   dm log 'clear'; dm output 'clear';
2
```

```
3   data savingsEOY;
4   year=0; int=0.1; deposit=1; balance=0;
5
6   type=0;
7   /*type 0=deposits are made at the end of the year
8     type 1=deposits are made at the beginning of the year*/
9
10  do year=1 to 10;
11    if      type=0 then balance= balance*(1+int) +deposit ;
12    else if type=1 then balance=(balance + deposit)*(1+int);
13    output;
14  end;
15
16  run;
17
18  proc print data=savingsEOY;
19   title 'Type 0=deposits BOY; Type 1=deposits EOY';
20   format balance best12.;
21  run;
22
23  data savingsBOY;
24  year=0; int=0.1; deposit=1; balance=0;
25
26  type=1;
27  /*type 0=deposits are made at the end of the year
28    type 1=deposits are made at the beginning of the year*/
29
30  do year=1 to 10;
31    if      type=0 then balance= balance*(1+int) +deposit ;
32    else if type=1 then balance=(balance + deposit)*(1+int);
33    output;
34  end;
35
36  run;
37
38  proc print data=savingsBOY;
39   title 'Type 0=deposits BOY; Type 1=deposits EOY';
40   format balance best12.;
41  run;
```

This is the output:

Type 0=deposits BOY; Type 1=deposits EOY

Obs	year	int	deposit	balance	type
1	1	0.1	1	1	0
2	2	0.1	1	2.1	0
3	3	0.1	1	3.31	0
4	4	0.1	1	4.641	0
5	5	0.1	1	6.1051	0
6	6	0.1	1	7.71561	0
7	7	0.1	1	9.487171	0
8	8	0.1	1	11.4358881	0
9	9	0.1	1	13.57947691	0
10	10	0.1	1	15.937424601	0

Type 0=deposits BOY; Type 1=deposits EOY

Obs	year	int	deposit	balance	type
1	1	0.1	1	1.1	1
2	2	0.1	1	2.31	1
3	3	0.1	1	3.641	1
4	4	0.1	1	5.1051	1
5	5	0.1	1	6.71561	1
6	6	0.1	1	8.487171	1
7	7	0.1	1	10.4358881	1
8	8	0.1	1	12.57947691	1
9	9	0.1	1	14.937424601	1
10	10	0.1	1	17.531167061	1

3.2   Find the Number of Deposits to Meet the Target Balance

An annual deposit of \$1 is made at the end of each year for the next n years into a savings account, the first deposit being made one year from today. The savings account earns a 10% compound interest rate per year. What's the minimum n such that the balance of the savings account n years from today will be greater than \$30?

3.2.1   Method 1

Program 3.2.1 *savingsAccountSolve.sas*

```
1   dm log 'clear'; dm output 'clear';
2
3   data savingsEOY;
4   year=0; int=0.1; deposit=1; balance=0; target=30;
5
6   type=0;
7   /*type 0=deposits are made at the end of the year
8     type 1=deposits are made at the beginning of the year*/
9
10  do while (balance <= target);
11    if      type=0 then balance= balance*(1+int) +deposit ;
12    else if type=1 then balance=(balance + deposit)*(1+int);
13
14    year=year+1;
15    output;
16  end;
17
18  run;
19
20  proc print data=savingsEOY noobs;
21   title 'Type 0=deposits BOY; Type 1=deposits BOY';
22   format balance best12.;
23  run;
24
25  data savingsBOY;
26  year=0; int=0.1; deposit=1; balance=0; target=30;
27
28  type=1;
29  /*type 0=deposits are made at the end of the year
```

```
30     type 1=deposits are made at the beginning of the year*/
31
32  do while (balance <= target);
33    if      type=0 then balance= balance*(1+int) +deposit ;
34    else if type=1 then balance=(balance + deposit)*(1+int);
35
36    year=year+1;
37    output;
38  end;
39
40  run;
41
42  proc print data=savingsBOY noobs;
43    title 'Type 0=deposits BOY; Type 1=deposits EOY';
44    format balance best12.;
45  run;
```

Here's the output:

Type 0=deposits BOY; Type 1=deposits EOY

year	int	deposit	balance	target	type
1	0.1	1	1	30	0
2	0.1	1	2.1	30	0
3	0.1	1	3.31	30	0
4	0.1	1	4.641	30	0
5	0.1	1	6.1051	30	0
6	0.1	1	7.71561	30	0
7	0.1	1	9.487171	30	0
8	0.1	1	11.4358881	30	0
9	0.1	1	13.57947691	30	0
10	0.1	1	15.937424601	30	0
11	0.1	1	18.531167061	30	0
12	0.1	1	21.384283767	30	0
13	0.1	1	24.522712144	30	0
14	0.1	1	27.974983358	30	0
15	0.1	1	31.772481694	30	0

Type 0=deposits BOY; Type 1=deposits EOY

year	int	deposit	balance	target	type
1	0.1	1	1.1	30	1
2	0.1	1	2.31	30	1
3	0.1	1	3.641	30	1
4	0.1	1	5.1051	30	1
5	0.1	1	6.71561	30	1
6	0.1	1	8.487171	30	1
7	0.1	1	10.4358881	30	1
8	0.1	1	12.57947691	30	1
9	0.1	1	14.937424601	30	1
10	0.1	1	17.531167061	30	1
11	0.1	1	20.384283767	30	1
12	0.1	1	23.522712144	30	1
13	0.1	1	26.974983358	30	1
14	0.1	1	30.772481694	30	1

If deposits are made at the end of the year, it will take 15 deposits for the savings account balance to first exceed \$30. If deposits are made at the beginning of the year, it will take 14 deposits for the savings account balance to first exceed \$30.

3.2.2   Method 2

Program 3.2.2 *savingsAccountSolve2.sas*

```
1    dm log 'clear'; dm output 'clear';
2
3    data savingsEOY;
4    year=0; int=0.1; deposit=1; balance=0; target=30;
5
6    type=0;
7    /*type 0=deposits are made at the end of the year
8      type 1=deposits are made at the beginning of the year*/
9
10   do until (balance > target);
11     if      type=0 then balance= balance*(1+int) +deposit ;
12     else if type=1 then balance=(balance + deposit)*(1+int);
13
14     year=year+1;
15     output;
16   end;
17
18   run;
19
20   proc print data=savingsEOY noobs;
21    title 'Type 0=deposits BOY; Type 1=deposits BOY';
22    format balance best12.;
23   run;
24
25   data savingsBOY;
26   year=0; int=0.1; deposit=1; balance=0; target=30;
27
28   type=1;
29   /*type 0=deposits are made at the end of the year
30     type 1=deposits are made at the beginning of the year*/
31
32   do until (balance > target);
33     if      type=0 then balance= balance*(1+int) +deposit ;
34     else if type=1 then balance=(balance + deposit)*(1+int);
35
36     year=year+1;
37     output;
38   end;
39
40   run;
41
42   proc print data=savingsBOY noobs;
43    title 'Type 0=deposits BOY; Type 1=deposits BOY';
44    format balance best12.;
45   run;
```

Program 3.2.2 generates the same output as does Program 3.2.1.

3.3 Using the SAS Finance Function

The next program uses the finance function available in SAS 9.

Program 3.3.1 *finance.sas*

```
1   dm log 'clear'; dm output 'clear';
2
3   data savings;
4     rate = 0.1; nper = 10; pmt = -1; pv = 0; type = 0;
5     balance = finance('fv', rate, nper, pmt, pv, type);
6   run;
7
8   proc print;
9    title 'balance of 10 EOY deposits of $1 each';
10  run;
11
12  data savings2;
13    rate = 0.1; nper = 10; pmt = -1; pv = 0; type = 1;
14    balance = finance('fv', rate, nper, pmt, pv, type);
15  run;
16
17  proc print;
18   title 'balance of 10 BOY deposits of $1 each';
19  run;
20
21  data savings3;
22    rate = 0.1; pmt = -1; pv = 0; type = 0; fv=30;
23    n = finance('nper', rate,  pmt, pv, fv, type);
24    numDeposits=ceil(n);
25  run;
26
27  proc print;
28   title 'number of EOY deposits of $1 each to reach FV 30';
29  run;
30
31  data savings4;
32    rate = 0.1; pmt = -1; pv = 0; type = 1; fv=30;
33    n = finance('nper', rate,  pmt, pv, fv, type);
34    numDeposits=ceil(n);
35  run;
36
37  proc print;
38   title 'number of BOY deposits of $1 each to reach FV 30';
39  run;
```

Here's the output:

balance of 10 EOY deposits of $1 each

Obs	rate	nper	pmt	pv	type	balance
1	0.1	10	-1	0	0	15.9374

balance of 10 BOY deposits of $1 each

Obs	rate	nper	pmt	pv	type	balance
1	0.1	10	-1	0	1	17.5312

number of EOY deposits of $1 each to reach FV 30

Obs	rate	pmt	pv	type	fv	n	num Deposits
1	0.1	-1	0	0	30	14.5451	15

number of BOY deposits of $1 each to reach FV 30

Obs	rate	pmt	pv	type	fv	n	num Deposits
1	0.1	-1	0	1	30	13.8042	14

The finance function has the following 6 parameters:

- rate, the interest rate per period.

- nper, the number of periodic occurring equal payments per year.

- pmt, the periodic recurring equal payment amount.

- pv, the present value of one-time investment amount at time zero. Its default value is 0.

- fv, the future value of all the investments (the initial investment plus periodic payments).

- type. Type 0 means that deposits are made at the end of the period; type 1 means that deposits are made at the start of the period.

The finance function is similar to the time-of-money function found in many financial calculators. It accepts 5 of the 6 parameters above and returns the missing parameter.

A negative pmt means money leaving your hand, that is, you are depositing the amount into the savings account. If you make an annual end-of-year deposit of 1 per year for 10 years, the ending balance at the end of Year 10 will be a positive future value 15.9374. Positive 15.9374 means 15.9374 flowing into your hand.

On the other hand, pm=1 means that you borrow 1 per year. This will produce a negative balance 15.9374 at the end of Year 10 if each borrowing occurs at the end of the year. A negative 15.9374 means that you need to pay 15.9374 at the end of Year 10 to extinguish your debt.

Similarly, a positive pv means that you borrow money at time zero. A negative pv means that you deposit money at time zero.

Program 3.3.2 *finance2.sas*

```
1   dm log 'clear'; dm output 'clear';
2
3   data savings;
4      rate = 0.1; nper = 10; pmt = -1;
5      pv1 = -1;    pv2 = 0;    type = 0;
6
7      balance1 = finance('fv', rate, nper, pmt, pv1, type);
8      balance2 = finance('fv', rate, nper, pmt, pv2, type);
9      balance3=1.1**10;
10
11     x=balance1 - (balance2 + balance3);
12  run;
13
14  proc print data=savings;
15   title;
16  run;
```

This is the output:

```
Obs rate nper pmt pv1 pv2 type balance1 balance2 balance3 x

 1   0.1  10   -1  -1   0    0   18.5312  15.9374  2.59374 0
```

In this program, `balance1` is the account value at the end of Year 10 after you (1) make an initial deposit of 1 at time zero, and (2) deposit 1 per year at the end of the year for 10 years. The `pv1=-1` parameter means that you make a deposit of 1 at time zero.

`balance2` is the account value at the end of Year 10 after you deposit 1 per year at the end of the year for 10 years. The `pv2=0` parameters means no additional deposit at time zero.

`balance3` is the account value at the end of Year 10 after you deposit 1 at time zero.

Notice that `balance1` = `balance2` + `balance3`. Hence x=0.

3.4 Further Reading

Controlling Program Flow

http://www.okstate.edu/sas/v8/sashtml/sclr/z0662667.htm

Chapter 4

Give Everyone a 10% Raise

4.1 Power of the Input Statement

The next program is a DATA step counterpart to Program 4.1.1 and 1.10.2 combined:

Program 4.1.1 *worker.sas*

```
1   dm log 'clear'; dm output 'clear';
2   proc sql;
3   create table worker
4   (
5      id num,
6      sex char(1),
7      firstName char(12),
8      lastName char,
9      salary num
10  );
11
12  insert into work.worker
13  values(1,'M','John','Smith',60000)
14  values(2,'F','Jane','Johnson',70000)
15  values(5,'F','Mary','Williams',80000)
16  values(20,'M','Robert','Walker',90000)
17  ;
18
19  select * from worker;
20  quit;
```

Output:

id	sex	firstName	lastName	salary
1	M	John	Smith	60000
2	F	Jane	Johnson	70000
5	F	Mary	Williams	80000
20	M	Robert	Walker	90000

When `firstName` is assigned a value the first time, it is assigned a literal string beginning with `John` followed by 8 blanks to make `firstName` a 12 width string column. As explained in Program 2.4.9, in a DATA step, SAS uses the rule of the first encounter to determine the data type and the length of a column.

MNOTable2.sas

Similarly, `lastName` is an 8 width string column because its first assigned value is an 8 width literal string.

In the next program, the rule of the first encounter causes `firstName` to be a 4 width string column and `lastName` a 5 width string column. Any `firstName` longer than 4 columns and any `lastName` longer than 5 columns will be truncated.

Program 4.1.2 *workerDataStep.sas*

```
1   dm log 'clear'; dm output 'clear';
2
3   data worker;
4   id=1;  sex='M'; firstName='John        ';
5   lastName='Smith   '; salary=60000;
6   output worker;
7
8   id=2;  sex='F'; firstName='Jane';
9   lastName='Johnson'; salary=70000;
10  output worker;
11
12  id=5;  sex='F'; firstName='Mary';
13  lastName='Williams'; salary=80000;
14  output worker;
15
16  id=20; sex='M'; firstName='Robert';
17  lastName='Walker'; salary=90000;
18  output worker;
19
20  return;
21  run;
22
23  options linesize=min nonumber nodate;
24  proc print data=worker;
25  run;
26
27  proc contents data=worker;
28  run;
```

Partial output:

```
                            first    last
Obs     id    sex    Name     Name    salary

 1       1     M     John     Smith    60000
 2       2     F     Jane     Johns    70000
 3       5     F     Mary     Willi    80000
 4      20     M     Robe     Walke    90000
```

The CONTENTS Procedure

-----Alphabetic List of Variables and Attributes-----

```
#    Variable      Type    Len    Pos
------------------------------------------
3    firstName     Char     4      17
1    id            Num      8       0
4    lastName      Char     5      21
5    salary        Num      8       8
2    sex           Char     1      16
```

Question Is there a better way to read in raw data than the tedious `insert into` clauses as in Program 1.10.2 or the repetitive `output` statements as in Program 4.1.2?

Answer YES. When you use SAS to analyze workers' data, the raw data file such as `workers.csv` most likely already exists. You can use the `input` statement to directly read in the raw input file.

Program 4.1.3
readWorkerCSV.sas

```
1    /*first, create C:\LearnSAS\worker.csv
2    id,sex,firstName,lastName,salary
3    1,'M','John','Smith',60000
4    2,'F','Jane','Johnson',70000
5    5,'F','Mary','Williams',80000
6    20,'M','Robert','Walker',90000
7    */
8    dm log 'clear'; dm output 'clear';
9    data worker;
10   infile 'C:\LearnSAS\worker.csv'
11      firstobs=2 delimiter=',' dsd;
12   input
13     id
14     sex $
15     firstName $
16     lastName $
17     salary
18   ;
19   raise=salary * 0.1;
20
21   output worker;
22   return;
23   run;
24
25   option linesize=min nonumber nodate;
26   proc print data=worker;
27    format salary raise dollar7.;
28    title 'Confidential salary data';
29    title2 'For authorized use only';
30   run;
```

Output:

Confidential salary data
For authorized use only

Obs	id	sex	firstName	lastName	salary	raise
1	1	M	John	Smith	$60,000	$6,000
2	2	F	Jane	Johnson	$70,000	$7,000
3	5	F	Mary	Williams	$80,000	$8,000
4	20	M	Robert	Walker	$90,000	$9,000

This is how to create a similar program in SAS in the cloud. Create the worker.csv file on your computer and upload it to the /home/userid/myProgram folder in SAS in the cloud. You upload a file to SAS in the cloud by clicking the up arrow icon in the left pane of SAS Studio.

Next, change the infile statement to:

```
infile '/home/userid/myProgram/worker.csv' firstobs=2 delimiter=',' dsd;
```

Remember to replace userid with your ID for SAS in the cloud.

One major reason many companies use SAS given its high annual licensing cost is its universal data access capability. If you purchase the SAS Access software (which should not be confused with SAS/ACCESS Interface to PC Files), an add-on to Base SAS, you can read, write, and update data regardless of source or platform. With SAS Access installed, you can manipulate, analyze, and report data no matter whether it resides in the IBM mainframe, DB2, Oracle, Microsoft SQL server or another database. However, you'll need to purchase a separate SAS Access module for each platform your data resides in.

For the ease of learning SAS, however, in this book, the only external data source is a flat file on your computer's hard drive for PC SAS or a flat file you upload to SAS in the cloud. This way, you can learn SAS without installing the DB2, Oracle, SQL server, or another third party database. Nor do you need SAS Access installed in your machine. You are guaranteed to be able to run any sample program in the book and replicate the result without any additional software other than Base SAS.

4.2   Infile and dsd

In Program 4.1.3, the `infile` statement identifies the source file. The `firstobs=2` option tells SAS to start reading the source file from the second line.

The `delimiter=','` option specifies an alternate delimiter other than blanks. It tells SAS to interpret the comma not as a literal string, but as a delimiter.

The `dsd` (delimiter-sensitive data) does four things for you:

- It uses a comma as the default delimiter.

- It removes quotation marks from character values.

- It specifies that when data values are enclosed in quotation marks, delimiters within the value should be treated as character data. With `dsd`, SAS will interpret the comma in "JFK, Jr." not as a delimiter, but as part of the name.

- It treats two consecutive delimiters in the raw input data as a missing value. With `dsd`, a raw input line `1,2,,,4` will be read in as `1  2  .   4`, which is probably what you intended.

Program 4.1.3 uses only the first two features of `dsd`. Since `dsd` automatically uses a comma as the delimiter, the `delimiter=','` option is redundant. The `infile` statement can be written as:

```
infile 'C:\LearnSAS\worker.csv' firstobs=2 dsd;
```

4.3   Inner Workings of the DATA Step

Program 4.1.3 has only one `input` statement and one `output` statement, yet four raw input records are read from an external file and four rows of values are written to the destination `worker` table.

This is the working of the hidden loop in a DATA step. Every DATA step program has a built-in loop. The DATA step in Program 4.1.3 is executed not once, but many times. In each execution, the `input` statement reads in one row from the raw input file and the `output` statement writes one row to the destination table.

Let's see the loop. Add two PUT statements to Program 4.1.3:

Program 4.3.1 *readWorkerCSVshowLoop.sas*

```
1   /* C:\LearnSAS\worker.csv
2   id,sex,firstName,lastName,salary
3   1,'M','John','Smith',60000
4   2,'F','Jane','Johnson',70000
```

```
5    5,'F','Mary','Williams',80000
6    20,'M','Robert','Walker',90000
7    */
8    dm log 'clear'; dm output 'clear';
9    data worker;
10   infile 'C:\LearnSAS\worker.csv' firstobs=2 dsd;
11   put 'before: ' _all_;
12   input
13     id
14     sex $
15     firstName $
16     lastName $
17     salary
18   ;
19   raise=salary * 0.1;
20
21   output worker;
22   put 'after : ' _all_;
23   return;
24   run;
```

If you use SAS in the cloud, upload `worker.csv` to the following folder:

/home/userid/myProgram.

Change the `infile` statement to:

`infile '/home/userid/myProgram/sales.txt' firstobs=2 dsd;`

Submit the program in PC SAS or SAS in the cloud. This is the log:

```
before: id=. sex=  firstName=  lastName=  salary=. raise=. _ERROR_=0 _N_=1
after : id=1 sex=M firstName=John lastName=Smith salary=60000 raise=6000 _ERROR_=0 _N_=1
before: id=. sex=  firstName=  lastName=  salary=. raise=. _ERROR_=0 _N_=2
after : id=2 sex=F firstName=Jane lastName=Johnson salary=70000 raise=7000 _ERROR_=0 _N_=2
before: id=. sex=  firstName=  lastName=  salary=. raise=. _ERROR_=0 _N_=3
after : id=5 sex=F firstName=Mary lastName=Williams salary=80000 raise=8000 _ERROR_=0 _N_=3
before: id=. sex=  firstName=  lastName=  salary=. raise=. _ERROR_=0 _N_=4
after : id=20 sex=M firstName=Robert lastName=Walker salary=90000 raise=9000 _ERROR_=0 _N_=4
before: id=. sex=  firstName=  lastName=  salary=. raise=. _ERROR_=0 _N_=5
NOTE: 4 records were read from the infile 'C:\LearnSAS\worker.csv'.
```

The PUT statement writes the character string that you specify to the SAS log, to a procedure output file, or to an external file. If you omit the destination, then SAS writes the string to the log.

When the PUT statement writes the character string to the log, all leading and trailing blanks are deleted and each value is followed by a single blank, as illustrated in the next program:

Program 4.3.2 *put.sas*

```
1    data testPut;
2    x='  aa  ';
3    y='  bb  ';
4    z=1;
5    u=2;
6    put x y z u;
7    run;
```

Log:

```
aa bb 1 2
```

In Program 4.3.1, the `put _all_` statement writes to the log all the variables created in the DATA step. The `id`, `sex`, `firstName`, `lastName`, `salary`, and `raise` variables are created by you; `_error_` and `_n_` are automatic variables created by SAS but are not written to the output table. The `_error_` variable tracks whether an error has occurred in your DATA step. The `_n_` variable tracks the number of iterations your DATA step loop has gone through.

In the log, the `before` line marks the beginning of an iteration of the DATA step. The `after` line indicates that the user-created variables have been written to the output table and that the next iteration is about to start.

There are 4 pairs of `before` and `after` lines in the log. The DATA step has completed 4 iterations and written 4 rows to the output table.

At the end of the fourth iteration, the `return` statement hands over program control to the beginning of the DATA step and the fifth iteration starts. Next, the `input` statement executes. SAS attempts to read another record from the raw input file, but there's no more record to be read. The fifth iteration immediately stops and the DATA step terminates.

One peculiar thing about the DATA step is that it always starts one extra iteration after reading the last record from an external file or from an existing SAS table.

Conceptually, Program 4.1.3 does the following behind the scenes:

```
Open worker.csv
Skip first 2 rows

Scan variable names in the DATA step (total 6 variables)
Determine whether each variable is numeric or character
Determine each variable's length and other attributes

Create a blank Worker table with 6 columns:
  id, sex, firstName, lastName, salary, raise

Allocate memory area #1 for holding a raw input record
Allocate memory area #2 for building a final output record

Do until there's no more record to read from worker.csv
 1. Read in an input record into memory area #1
 2. In memory area #2, initialize the 6 variables to missing and
    build the 6 variables from scratch
 3. Write the 6 variables from memory area #2 into Worker table
Process the next raw input record from worker.csv

Close Worker.csv
```

Bear in mind that this is just the conceptual model of what's happened in Program 4.1.3. The physical implementation can be different. For example, instead of extracting one record a time from the raw input file and inserting one row into the destination table, SAS can bulk extract and bulk insert, reading in several records at once from the raw input file and inserting several rows at once into the output table.

However, no matter how much the physical implementation deviates from the conceptual model, the physical implementation must produce the same result as the conceptual model.

Memory area #1 is called the input buffer. The input buffer is a temporary holding place for a record of raw data as it is being read by SAS via the `input` statement.

Memory area #2 is called the PDV (program data vector). The PDV is the place where SAS builds the variables as one row to be inserted to the output table.

Let's use an analogy to bring home the concept of the input buffer and the PDV. The input buffer is like a refrigerator holding your raw ingredients. The PDV is like your kitchen table where you use the raw ingredients to prepare your final food.

4.4   Variables Created by the INPUT or Assignment Statement Are Initialized to Missing

In the five `before` lines of the log, `id`, `sex`, `firstName`, `lastName`, `salary`, and `raise` are initialized to missing. SAS uses a period to represent a missing numeric value and a blank to represent a missing character value. However, the automatic variables `_n_` and `_error_` are not initialized to missing.

At the beginning of each DATA step iteration, in the PDV, SAS initializes to missing all the variables created by the `input` statement and by the assignment statement. All the variables that were read from a raw input file during the previous iteration of the DATA step are erased from the PDV; all the variables created by the assignment statement during the previous iteration are erased from the PDV. The next DATA step iteration will extract and manipulate variables from a clean slate. After all, each employee record is independent. Why should SAS bother remembering any previous employee records before it processes the next employee record?

SAS initializing variables to missing at the beginning of each DATA step iteration is similar to you clearing the memory of a handheld calculator at the beginning of each independent calculation. The goal is to enhance data integrity. If the previous result is not needed for the next round of work, clear it out and start afresh to prevent it from being accidentally used in your next round of work.

4.5   The Conventional Way to Find the Cumulative Sum Doesn't Work

The following conventional programming technique to find the cumulative salary and the cumulative raise doesn't work. As the DATA step transitions from one iteration to the next, the ending values of `totalSalary` and `totalRaise` from the previous iteration are erased from the PDV.

Program 4.5.1
workerTotalNotWorking.sas

```
1   /* C:\LearnSAS\worker.csv
2   id,sex,firstName,lastName,salary
3   1,'M','John','Smith',60000
4   2,'F','Jane','Johnson',70000
5   5,'F','Mary','Williams',80000
6   20,'M','Robert','Walker',90000
7   */
8   dm log 'clear'; dm output 'clear';
9   data workerTotal;
10  infile 'C:\LearnSAS\worker.csv' firstobs=2 dsd;
11  put 'before ' _all_;
12
13  totalSalary=0; totalRaise=0;
14  input
15    id
16    sex $
17    firstName $
18    lastName $
19    salary
20  ;
21  raise=salary * 0.1;
22  totalSalary=totalSalary + salary;
23  totalRaise=totalRaise + raise;
24
25  output workerTotal;
26
27  put 'after  ' _all_;
28  return;
29  run;
30
31  options linesize=min nodate pageno=1;
32  proc print data=workerTotal;
33   format salary raise totalSalary totalRaise dollar7.;
34   title 'Workers total salary and total raise';
35  run;
```

Output:

```
                    Workers total salary and total raise                    1

              total    total              first
       Obs   Salary    Raise    id   sex   Name    lastName   salary   raise

        1    $60,000   $6,000    1    M    John    Smith      $60,000  $6,000
        2    $70,000   $7,000    2    F    Jane    Johnson    $70,000  $7,000
        3    $80,000   $8,000    5    F    Mary    Williams   $80,000  $8,000
        4    $90,000   $9,000   20    M    Robert  Walker     $90,000  $9,000
```

Here's part of the log:

```
before totalSalary=. totalRaise=. id=. sex=  firstName=
lastName=  salary=. raise=. _ERROR_=0 _N_=1
after  totalSalary=60000 totalRaise=6000 id=1 sex=M firstName=John
lastName=Smith salary=60000 raise=6000 _ERROR_=0 _N_=1

before totalSalary=. totalRaise=. id=. sex=  firstName=
lastName=  salary=. raise=. _ERROR_=0 _N_=2
after  totalSalary=70000 totalRaise=7000 id=2 sex=F firstName=Jane
lastName=Johnson salary=70000 raise=7000 _ERROR_=0 _N_=2

before totalSalary=. totalRaise=. id=. sex=  firstName=
lastName=  salary=. raise=. _ERROR_=0 _N_=3
after  totalSalary=80000 totalRaise=8000 id=5 sex=F firstName=Mary
lastName=Williams salary=80000 raise=8000 _ERROR_=0 _N_=3
```

```
before totalSalary=. totalRaise=. id=. sex=  firstName=
lastName=  salary=. raise=. _ERROR_=0 _N_=4
after  totalSalary=90000 totalRaise=9000 id=20 sex=M firstName=Robert
lastName=Walker salary=90000 raise=9000 _ERROR_=0 _N_=4

before totalSalary=. totalRaise=. id=. sex=  firstName=
lastName=  salary=. raise=. _ERROR_=0 _N_=5

NOTE: 4 records were read from the infile 'C:\LearnSAS\worker.csv'.
      The minimum record length was 26.
      The maximum record length was 30.
NOTE: The data set WORK.WORKERTOTAL has 4 observations and 8 variables.
```

At the beginning of the each iteration, in the PDV, `totalSalary` and `totalRaise` are first initialized to missing and then reset to zero. Later, `salary` is added to `totalSalary=0`, causing `totalSalary=salary`; and `raise` is added to `totalRaise=0`, causing `totalRaise=raise`.

4.6   The RETAIN Statement

The next program correctly calculates the cumulative salary and the cumulative raise using the `retain` statement.

Program 4.6.1
workerTotal.sas

```
1    /* C:\LearnSAS\worker.csv
2    id,sex,firstName,lastName,salary
3    1,'M','John','Smith',60000
4    2,'F','Jane','Johnson',70000
5    5,'F','Mary','Williams',80000
6    20,'M','Robert','Walker',90000
7    */
8    dm log 'clear'; dm output 'clear';
9    data workerTotal;
10   retain totalSalary totalRaise 0;
11   put 'before ' _all_;
12   infile 'C:\LearnSAS\worker.csv' firstobs=2 dsd;
13   input
14     id
15     sex $
16     firstName $
17     lastName $
18     salary
19   ;
20   raise=salary * 0.1;
21   totalSalary=totalSalary + salary;
22   totalRaise=totalRaise + raise;
23
24   output workerTotal;
25   put 'after  ' _all_;
26   return;
27   run;
28
29   options linesize=min nodate nonumber;
30   proc print data=workerTotal noobs;
31    format salary raise totalSalary totalRaise dollar8.;
32    title 'salary and raise - running total';
33   run;
```

Output:

salary and raise - running total

total Salary	total Raise	id	sex	first Name	lastName	salary	raise
$60,000	$6,000	1	M	John	Smith	$60,000	$6,000
$130,000	$13,000	2	F	Jane	Johnson	$70,000	$7,000
$210,000	$21,000	5	F	Mary	Williams	$80,000	$8,000
$300,000	$30,000	20	M	Robert	Walker	$90,000	$9,000

This is how the **retain** statement works. If a variable appears in the **retain** statement, then its value is retained in the PDV across iterations of the DATA step.

The **retain totalSalary totalRaise 0** statement does two things. First, it sets **totalSalary** and **totalRaise** to 0, instead of missing, at the beginning of the first iteration of the DATA step. Second, it preserves the value of **totalSalary** and the value of **totalRaise** in the PDV from one iteration of the DATA step to the next.

You can see the effect of the **retain** statement from the log:

```
before totalSalary=0 totalRaise=0 id=. sex=  firstName=
lastName=  salary=. raise=. _ERROR_=0 _N_=1
after  totalSalary=60000 totalRaise=6000 id=1 sex=M firstName=John
lastName=Smith salary=60000 raise=6000 _ERROR_=0 _N_=1

before totalSalary=60000 totalRaise=6000 id=. sex=  firstName=
lastName=  salary=. raise=. _ERROR_=0 _N_=2
after  totalSalary=130000 totalRaise=13000 id=2 sex=F firstName=Jane
lastName=Johnson salary=70000 raise=7000 _ERROR_=0 _N_=2
```

```
before totalSalary=130000 totalRaise=13000 id=. sex= firstName=
lastName=  salary=. raise=. _ERROR_=0 _N_=3
after  totalSalary=210000 totalRaise=21000 id=5 sex=F firstName=Mary
lastName=Williams salary=80000 raise=8000 _ERROR_=0 _N_=3

before totalSalary=210000 totalRaise=21000 id=. sex= firstName=
lastName=  salary=. raise=. _ERROR_=0 _N_=4
after  totalSalary=300000 totalRaise=30000 id=20 sex=M firstName=Robert
lastName=Walker salary=90000 raise=9000 _ERROR_=0 _N_=4

before totalSalary=300000 totalRaise=30000 id=. sex= firstName=
lastName=  salary=. raise=. _ERROR_=0 _N_=5

NOTE: 4 records were read from the infile 'C:\LearnSAS\worker.csv'.
      The minimum record length was 26.
      The maximum record length was 30.
NOTE: The data set WORK.WORKERTOTAL has 4 observations and 8 variables.
```

4.7 Another Example of RETAIN

Program 4.7.1 *readWorker2txt.sas*

```
1   /*First, create C:\LearnSAS\worker2.txt
2   ----+----1----+----2----+----3----+----4----+
3   id sex firstName lastName salary department
4   1  M    John    Smith      60000
5   2  F    Jane    Johnson    70000
6   5  F    Mary    Williams   80000  Finance
7   20 M    Robert  Walker     90000
8   30 M    Steve   Langston  100000  Sales
9   32 F    Jane    Adler     120000
10  */
11  dm log 'clear'; dm output 'clear';
12  data worker2;
13  retain dept;
14  infile 'C:\LearnSAS\worker2.txt' firstobs=3;
15
16  put 'before ' _all_;
17  input
18    id
19    sex $
20    firstName $
21    lastName $
22    salary
23    @
24  ;
25  if _n_ in (3,5) then input @32 dept $;
26  raise=salary * 0.1;
27
28  output worker2;
29
30  put 'after  ' _all_;
31  return;
32  run;
33
34  options linesize=min nodate nonumber;
35  proc print data=worker2 noobs;
36    title 'Data read in from a text file';
37  run;
```

Output:

Data read in from a text file

dept	id	sex	first Name	lastName	salary	raise
	1	M	John	Smith	60000	6000
	2	F	Jane	Johnson	70000	7000
Finance	5	F	Mary	Williams	80000	8000
Finance	20	M	Robert	Walker	90000	9000
Sales	30	M	Steve	Langston	100000	10000
Sales	32	F	Jane	Adler	120000	12000

This is part of the log:

```
before dept=  id=. sex=  firstName=  lastName=
salary=. raise=. _ERROR_=0 _N_=1
after  dept=  id=1 sex=M firstName=John lastName=Smith
salary=60000 raise=6000 _ERROR_=0 _N_=1

before dept=  id=. sex=  firstName=  lastName=
salary=. raise=. _ERROR_=0 _N_=2
after  dept=  id=2 sex=F firstName=Jane lastName=Johnson
salary=70000 raise=7000 _ERROR_=0 _N_=2

before dept=  id=. sex=  firstName=  lastName=
salary=. raise=. _ERROR_=0 _N_=3
```

```
after  dept=Finance id=5 sex=F firstName=Mary lastName=Williams
salary=80000 raise=8000 _ERROR_=0 _N_=3

before dept=Finance id=. sex=  firstName=  lastName=
salary=. raise=. _ERROR_=0 _N_=4
after  dept=Finance id=20 sex=M firstName=Robert lastName=Walker
salary=90000 raise=9000 _ERROR_=0 _N_=4

before dept=Finance id=. sex=  firstName=  lastName=
salary=. raise=. _ERROR_=0 _N_=5
after  dept=Sales id=30 sex=M firstName=Steve lastName=Langston
salary=100000 raise=10000 _ERROR_=0 _N_=5

before dept=Sales id=. sex=  firstName=  lastName=
salary=. raise=. _ERROR_=0 _N_=6
after  dept=Sales id=32 sex=F firstName=Jane lastName=Adler
salary=120000 raise=12000 _ERROR_=0 _N_=6

before dept=Sales id=. sex=  firstName=  lastName=
salary=. raise=. _ERROR_=0 _N_=7

NOTE: 6 records were read from the infile 'C:\LearnSAS\worker2.txt'.
      The minimum record length was 31.
      The maximum record length was 38.
NOTE: The data set WORK.WORKER2 has 6 observations and 7 variables.
```

How this program works is explained in the next section.

4.8 Hold the Pointer and Conditionally Input Raw Data

In Program 4.7.1, no delimiter option is specified in the `infile` statement. As a result, SAS uses blanks as the default delimiter unless `dsd` option is used in the `infile` statement.

The at-sign @ in the `input` statement tells SAS to hold the pointer at the current record in the input buffer so the next `input` statement if `_n_` in (3,5) then input @32 dept $; in the same DATA step iteration will read from the same record in the input buffer.

Without the at-sign to hold the pointer, if the condition `_n_` in (3,5) evaluates to true, then `input @32 dept $` will load the next record into the input buffer and extract `dept` from the record in the input buffer.

The statement if `_n_` in (3,5) then input @32 dept $ will extract the character variable `dept` only during the third or the fifth iteration of the DATA step. This is not a robust method to conditionally extract a field from a raw input file. It is impractical to specify which record from a large raw input file has the `department` field. Program 8.1.1 provides an example of how to conditionally read data from a raw input file using a robust approach.

The statement if `_n_` in (3,5) then ... is the same as:

```
if _n_=3 or _n_=5 then ...;
```

However, the `in` operator is more concise in case you need to search among a sequential list of integers. For example, instead of

```
if x=1 or x=2 or x=3 or x=4 or x=5 then ...;
```

you can write:

```
if x in (1:5) then ...;
```

Notice that dept is retained without an initial value. As a result, dept is still initialized to missing at the beginning of the first iteration of the DATA step. The missing dept remains in the PDV until it is updated to Finance at the end of the third iteration. Next, dept=Finance remains in the PDV until it is updated to dept=sales at the end of the fifth iteration. Finally, dept=sales remains in the PDV until the DATA step ends.

4.9 No Need to RETAIN When Cumulation Is within the Same DATA Step

Program 2.4.6 correctly calculates the running total of N without any retain statement. This is because total is calculated inside a DO-LOOP within the same DATA step iteration. Here's another example where retain is not needed.

Program 4.9.1 *sumInSameIteration.sas*

Output:

```
1   dm log 'clear'; dm output 'clear';
2   data sumWithinSameIterationOfDataStep;
3   do i=1 to 3;
4     total=0;
5     do j=1 to 3;
6       total=total +j;
7       output;
8     end;
9   end;
10
11  put 'i=' i ' j=' j;
12  run;
13
14  proc print;
15    title 'No retain needed to sum within';
16    title2 'the same iteration of the DATA step';
17  run;
```

```
No retain needed to sum within
the same iteration of the DATA step

Obs    i    total    j

 1     1      1      1
 2     1      3      2
 3     1      6      3
 4     2      1      1
 5     2      3      2
 6     2      6      3
 7     3      1      1
 8     3      3      2
 9     3      6      3
```

Here's a surprising detail. After the outer DO-LOOP finishes its execution, i and j are both 4, not 3 as one might expect. This is evident in the log generated by the PUT statement:

```
i=4   j=4
```

This is a peculiar thing about the SAS DO-LOOP. In a DO-LOOP, the increment occurs at the end of each iteration of the DO-LOOP. In the next program, the increment occurs after the doStuff statement is executed.

```
data myTable;
do i=1 to 3;
 doStuff;
 /*i increments by 1*/
end;

/*i is 4 during the remainder of the DATA step*/
doMoreStuff;
run;
```

At the end of the third iteration of the DO-LOOP, after doStuff is executed, i increments to 4, which is out of the range of the DO-LOOP. The loop terminates but i=4 persists in the rest of the DATA step.

In the next program, the second output statement writes i=4 to the output table:

Program 4.9.2 *doLoopQuirk.sas*

Output:

```
1   data doLoopQuirk;
2   do i=1 to 3;
3    output;
4   end;
5
6   output;
7   run;
8
9   proc print data=doLoopQuirk;
10   title 'doLoopQuirk table';
11  run;
```

doLoopQuirk table

Obs	i
1	1
2	2
3	3
4	4

You already know of another SAS quirk. When SAS reads in data from a raw input file via the input statement or reads in data from an existing SAS table via the set statement (the set statement is explained in Program 6.0.1), SAS starts an extra iteration before terminating the DATA step.

4.10   The SUM statement

SAS has a shortcut to finding a running total in a DATA step. Program 4.6.1 can be shortened to:

Program 4.10.1
workerTotal2.sas

```
1   /* C:\LearnSAS\worker.csv
2   id,sex,firstName,lastName,salary
3   1,'M','John','Smith',60000
4   2,'F','Jane','Johnson',70000
5   5,'F','Mary','Williams',80000
6   20,'M','Robert','Walker',90000
7   */
8   dm log 'clear'; dm output 'clear';
9   data workerTotal;
10  put 'before ' _all_;
11  infile 'C:\LearnSAS\worker.csv' firstobs=2 dsd;
12  input
13    id
14    sex $
15    firstName $
16    lastName $
17    salary
18  ;
19  raise=salary * 0.1;
20  totalSalary + salary;
21  totalRaise + raise;
22
23  output workerTotal;
24  put 'after  ' _all_;
25  return;
26  run;
27
28  options linesize=min nodate nonumber;
29  proc print data=workerTotal noobs;
30   format salary raise totalSalary totalRaise dollar8.;
31   title 'salary and raise - running total';
32  run;
```

Output:

salary and raise - running total

id	sex	first Name	lastName	salary	raise	total Salary	total Raise
1	M	John	Smith	$60,000	$6,000	$60,000	$6,000
2	F	Jane	Johnson	$70,000	$7,000	$130,000	$13,000
5	F	Mary	Williams	$80,000	$8,000	$210,000	$21,000
20	M	Robert	Walker	$90,000	$9,000	$300,000	$30,000

This is part of the log:

```
before id=. sex=  firstName= lastName=  salary=. raise=.
totalSalary=0 totalRaise=0 _ERROR_=0 _N_=1
after  id=1 sex=M firstName=John lastName=Smith salary=60000
raise=6000 totalSalary=60000 totalRaise=6000 _ERROR_=0 _N_=1

before id=. sex=  firstName= lastName=  salary=. raise=.
totalSalary=60000 totalRaise=6000 _ERROR_=0 _N_=2
after  id=2 sex=F firstName=Jane lastName=Johnson salary=70000
raise=7000 totalSalary=130000 totalRaise=13000 _ERROR_=0 _N_=2

before id=. sex=  firstName= lastName=  salary=. raise=.
totalSalary=130000 totalRaise=13000 _ERROR_=0 _N_=3
after  id=5 sex=F firstName=Mary lastName=Williams salary=80000
raise=8000 totalSalary=210000 totalRaise=21000 _ERROR_=0 _N_=3

before id=. sex=  firstName= lastName=  salary=. raise=.
totalSalary=210000 totalRaise=21000 _ERROR_=0 _N_=4
after  id=20 sex=M firstName=Robert lastName=Walker salary=90000
raise=9000 totalSalary=300000 totalRaise=30000 _ERROR_=0 _N_=4
```

```
before id=. sex=  firstName=  lastName=  salary=. raise=.
totalSalary=300000 totalRaise=30000 _ERROR_=0 _N_=5

NOTE: 4 records were read from the infile 'C:\LearnSAS\worker.csv'.
      The minimum record length was 26.
      The maximum record length was 30.
NOTE: The data set WORK.WORKERTOTAL has 4 observations and 8 variables.
```

These two statements are new:

```
totalSalary + salary;
totalRaise + raise;
```

The statement `variable+expression;` in a DATA step does the following:

- The `variable` is automatically set to 0 before SAS reads the first observation. The value of `variable` is retained from one iteration to the next, as if it had appeared in a `retain` statement. However, to initialize `variable` to a value other than 0, include it in a `retain` statement with an initial value.

- The `expression` is evaluated and the result is added to the accumulator `variable`.

- If `expression` is missing, it is set to 0 before it is added to the accumulator `variable`.

Program 4.10.1 does everything Program 4.6.1 does and more. If `salary` is missing in any observation, Program 4.6.1 will have a missing `totalSalary` and a missing `totalRaise` from that observation on, whereas Program 4.10.1 will use `salary=0` to calculate `totalSalary` and `totalRaise` for any observation that is missing `salary`.

The next two program compare and contrast two methods for finding a running total. Program 4.10.2 uses the explicit `retain` statement. Program 4.10.3 uses the SUM statement.

Program 4.10.2

workerTotal3A.sas

```
1   /*First, create C:\LearnSAS\workerUpdated.csv
2   id,sex,firstName,lastName,salary
3   1,'M','John','Smith',60000
4   2,'F','Jane','Johnson'
5   5,'F','Mary','Williams',80000
6   20,'M','Robert','Walker',90000
7   */
8   dm log 'clear'; dm output 'clear';
9   data workerTotal;
10  retain totalSalary totalRaise 0;
11  put 'before ' _all_;
12  infile 'C:\LearnSAS\workerUpdated.csv'
13      firstobs=2 dsd truncover;
14  input
15   id
16   sex $
17   firstName $
18   lastName $
19   salary
20  ;
21  raise=salary * 0.1;
22  totalSalary=totalSalary + salary;
23  totalRaise=totalRaise + raise;
24
25  output workerTotal;
26  put 'after  ' _all_;
27  return;
28  run;
29
30  options linesize=min nodate nonumber;
31  proc print data=workerTotal noobs;
32   format salary raise totalSalary totalRaise dollar8.;
33   title 'salary and raise - running total';
34  run;
```

Output:

```
salary and raise - running total

total      total        first
Salary     Raise id sex  Name  lastName  salary   raise

$60,000    $6,000  1  M  John   Smith    $60,000  $6,000
    .         .    2  F  Jane   Johnson     .         .
    .         .    5  F  Mary   Williams $80,000  $8,000
    .         .   20  M  Robert Walker   $90,000  $9,000
```

totalSalary and totalRaise are both missing in Observations 2 to 4 because salary and raise are missing in Observation 2.

Program 4.10.3

workerTotal3B.sas

```
1   /*First, create C:\LearnSAS\workerUpdated.csv
2   id,sex,firstName,lastName,salary
3   1,'M','John','Smith',60000
4   2,'F','Jane','Johnson'
5   5,'F','Mary','Williams',80000
6   20,'M','Robert','Walker',90000
7   */
8   dm log 'clear'; dm output 'clear';
9   data workerTotal;
10  put 'before ' _all_;
11  infile 'C:\LearnSAS\workerUpdated.csv'
12      firstobs=2 dsd truncover;
13  input
14    id
15    sex $
16    firstName $
17    lastName $
18    salary
19  ;
20  raise=salary * 0.1;
21  totalSalary + salary;
22  totalRaise + raise;
23
24  output workerTotal;
25  put 'after  ' _all_;
26  return;
27  run;
28
29  options linesize=min nodate nonumber;
30  proc print data=workerTotal noobs;
31   format salary raise totalSalary totalRaise dollar8.;
32   title 'salary and raise - running total';
33  run;
```

Output:

salary and raise - running total

id	sex	first Name	lastName	salary	raise	total Salary	total Raise
1	M	John	Smith	$60,000	$6,000	$60,000	$6,000
2	F	Jane	Johnson	.	.	$60,000	$6,000
5	F	Mary	Williams	$80,000	$8,000	$140,000	$14,000
20	M	Robert	Walker	$90,000	$9,000	$230,000	$23,000

The sum statement uses **salary=0** to calculate the two running totals for the second observation, which is most likely what you want.

4.11 Truncover

This is how the **truncover** option in the **infile** statement works in Program 4.10.2 and Program 4.10.3. **Truncover** causes the DATA step to assign the raw data value to the variable even if the value is shorter than expected by the **input** statement. When the DATA step encounters the end of an input record and there are variables without values, the variables are assigned missing values for that observation.

Besides **truncover**, there are three other major **infile** statement options to handle the situation where the structure of the data in the raw input file doesn't match its informat. They are **flowover**, **stopover**, and **missover**. For the difference among these four options, refer to *MISSOVER, TRUNCOVER, and PAD, OH MY!!* at http://www2.sas.com/proceedings/sugi26/p009-26.pdf.

4.12   Convention Over Configuration

SAS is one of the programming languages that use the convention over configuration principle. In SAS, especially in a DATA Step program, a programmer often doesn't need to spell out everything. He just needs to specify the unconventional. What's not specified by the programmer often gets the default value.

For example, SAS uses a two-level name to identify a table. If you omit the first-level name, SAS by default uses `work` as the first-level name.

Here's another example. In a DATA step, you can specify that a variable is character by appending a dollar sign after the variable name. However, if you introduce a variable in the DATA step without specifying its data type, the variable is numeric by default. Similarly, if you don't specify the length of a numeric or character variable, the length is 8 bytes by default.

Additionally, in a DATA step, you can omit the `return` statement at the end of the DATA step. Every DATA step program has an implied `return` as its last executable statement.

Similarly, every DATA step by default has an implicit `output` statement at the end of each iteration to insert one row into the output tables listed in the `data` statement. If you intend to insert one row to the output tables only at the end of each iteration of the DATA step, you can omit the `output` statement; SAS will automatically write the data values as one row to the output tables at the end of each iteration.

You can place any number of explicit `output` statements in a DATA step to override the implied `output` statement. An explicit `output` statement instructs SAS not to wait until the end of the iteration but to immediately write the data values as one row to the output tables.

Once you write an explicit `output` statement, however, there's no implicit `output` statement at the end of an iteration of the DATA step. You are fully responsible for writing data values to the output tables. Data values are written to the output tables only when an explicit `output` statement executes.

As a final example of the convention over configuration in SAS, you don't need the `run` statement to explicitly mark a step boundary if the step is followed by another step. For example, you can reduce Program 4.7.1 to:

Program 4.12.1 *readWorker2txtShort.sas*

```
1   dm log 'clear'; dm output 'clear';
2   data worker2;
3   retain dept;
4   infile 'C:\LearnSAS\worker2.txt' firstobs=3;
5   input
6     id
7     sex $
8     firstName $
9     lastName $
10    salary
11    @
12  ;
13  if _n_ in (3,5) then input @32 dept $;
```

```
14    raise=salary * 0.1;
15
16    /*output worker2;*/
17    /*return;*/
18    /*run;*/
19
20    options linesize=min nodate pageno=1;
21    proc print /*data=worker2*/;
22     title 'Data read in from a text file';
23    run;
```

In the PROC PRINT step, the `data=` option is omitted and PROC PRINT uses `worker2`, the last table created in the program, as the data source.

Similarly, Program 2.4.3 can be shortened to:

Program 4.12.2 *one2tenDataStepLoopEvenOddShort.sas*

```
1     dm log 'clear'; dm output 'clear';
2     data Both Odd Even;
3     do N=1 to 10;
4        output Both;
5        if mod(N,2)=1 then output Odd;
6        else output Even;
7     end;
8
9     /*return;*/
10    /*run;*/
11
12    proc print data=Both;
13     title 'Both';
14     title2 'Contains integer 1 to 10';
15    /*run;*/
16
17    proc print data=Odd;
18     title 'Odd';
19     title2 'Contains integer 1, 3, 5, 7, and 9';
20    /*run;*/
21
22    proc print /* data=Even */ ;
23     title 'Even';
24     title2 'Contains integer 2, 4, 6, 8, and 10';
25    run;
```

In the last PROC PRINT step, the `data=` option is not specified. Since `even` is the last table created, PROC PRINT uses `even` as the data source.

However, not everything can be reduced. For example, the three `output` statements in the first DATA step in Program 4.12.2 cannot be replaced by the implicit `output` statement.

Similarly, Program 2.2.1 is not the same as:

Program 4.12.3

one2tenDataStepTooShort.sas

```
1   dm log 'clear'; dm output 'clear';
2   data MyNum;
3   N=1;  /* output MyNum; */
4   N=2;  /* output MyNum; */
5   N=3;  /* output MyNum; */
6   N=4;  /* output MyNum; */
7   N=5;  /* output MyNum; */
8   N=6;  /* output MyNum; */
9   N=7;  /* output MyNum; */
10  N=8;  /* output MyNum; */
11  N=9;  /* output MyNum; */
12  N=10; /* output MyNum; */
13
14  /* return; */
15  /* run; */
16
17  proc print /*data=MyNum */;
18  run;
```

Output:

```
Obs      N

 1      10
```

Though coding by convention reduces the amount of code you have to write, its overuse can lead to cryptic code that is difficult to understand months later when you need to modify the code. Carefully balance the terseness of your code and its readability.

As a newcomer to SAS, you may want to spell things out so you know what you are doing. Once you are more experienced, you can reduce your code by using SAS defaults.

4.13   Datalines

SAS has a testing tool called `datalines`. It lets you put data directly in the SAS code.

Program 4.13.1

readWorkerDatalines.sas

```
1   dm log 'clear'; dm output 'clear';
2   data worker;
3   infile datalines firstobs=2 dsd;
4   input
5     id
6     sex $
7     firstName $
8     lastName $
9     salary
10  ;
11  datalines;
12  id,sex,firstName,lastName,salary
13  1,'M','John','Smith',60000
14  2,'F','Jane','Johnson',70000
15  5,'F','Mary','Williams',80000
16  20,'M','Robert','Walker',90000
17  ;
18  run;
19
20  proc print data=worker;
21    title 'Confidential salary data';
22    title2 'For authorized use only';
23  run;
```

Output:

Confidential salary data
For authorized use only

Obs	id	sex	first Name	lastName	salary
1	1	M	John	Smith	60000
2	2	F	Jane	Johnson	70000
3	5	F	Mary	Williams	80000
4	20	M	Robert	Walker	90000

You use the `datalines` statement with an `input` statement to read data directly entered in the program, rather than stored in an external file. The `datalines` statement needs to be the last statement in the DATA step.

4.14 Further Reading

Step-by-Step Programming with Base SAS Software, Chapter 2, *Introduction to DATA Step Processing*

Understanding DATA Step Processing

http://web.utk.edu/sas/OnlineTutor/1.2/en/60476/m22/m22_1.htm

Errors, Warnings, and Notes (Oh My)A Practical Guide to Debugging SAS Programs

http://support.sas.com/resources/papers/proceedings13/127-2013.pdf

Chapter 5

Data Step Walkthrough: Input Buffer, PDV, and Loop

This chapter builds upon the DATA step conceptual model in Section 4.3. It aims to cement your knowledge of the three core concepts of the DATA step: the input buffer, the PDV, and the DATA step iteration. We'll read a raw input file in a DATA step and walk through each iteration of the DATA step.

First, create a dummy sales text file C:\LearnSAS\sales.txt. If you use SAS in the cloud, upload sales.txt to the /home/userid/myProgram folder. This is the sales.txt:

```
CustID  OrderDate  Amount
----+----1----+----2----+----3
    104 01/01/2014  $2,245.08
 590194 10/23/2014 $26,820.07
1000000 05/11/2014      19.52
```

This text file contains five lines. Line 1 is the header. Line 2 is a ruler. Lines 3–5 are three orders.

We'll read the text file into a table called sales. The sales table has four columns, CustID, OrderDate, Amount, and Tax. Tax is 3% of the order amount.

The following is the pseudocode for reading the text file into a sqlite3 table Sales using Python.

Program 5.0.1 *readTextFileToDB.py*

```
Open connection to sqlite3 database
Create Sales table (4 columns): CustID, OrderDate, Amount, Tax
Open sales.txt
Skip first 2 rows

If hasn't reached the end of the file
    Extract CustID, OrderDate, Amount
    Calculate Tax as 3 percent of Amount
    Insert CustID, OrderDate, Amount, Tax into Sales table
End
```

```
Close sales.txt
Close connection to sqlite3 database
```

For simplicity, this Python program extracts one record a time from the input file and inserts one row at a time into the `sales` table.

The extraction routine to retrieve `CustID`, `OrderDate`, and `Amount` can be implemented like this:

```
1   Identify the start position and the ending position of each field
2   Extract CustID as integer.
3   Read the string mm/dd/yyyy as a date
4   Remove the dollar sign and the period and get Amount
```

Here are sample Python programs to import a CSV file into a table: `http://stackoverflow.com/questions/2887878/importing-a-csv-file-into-a-sqlite3-database-table-using-python`.

In the Python program, we need to parse the `Amount` field by removing the dollar sign and the period. Here's one way to convert the currency string \$26,820.07 into the number $26,820.07$ using the Python interactive shell:

```
>>> from re import sub
>>> from decimal import Decimal
>>> currency='$26,820.07'
>>> number=Decimal(sub(r'[^\d.]','',currency))
>>> number
Decimal('26820.07')
>>> number+100
Decimal('26920.07')
>>>
```

We add 100 to `number` to test whether `currency` was correctly converted to a numeric value.

Here's the equivalent PC SAS program:

Program 5.0.2 *readTextFile.sas*

```
data Sales;
infile 'C:\LearnSAS\sales.txt' firstobs=3;
input
@1  CustID $ 7.
@9  OrderDate mmddyy10.
@20 Amount comma10.2
;

Tax=Amount * 0.03;
run;
```

Admire the SAS code. How much simpler it is than the Python program. In Program 5.0.2, we create a character column `CustID` by extracting the substring of the raw input file from Positions 1 through 7. We then create a numeric column `OrderDate` by parsing the substring from Positions 9 through 18. The informat `mmddyy10.` convert the substring `mm/dd/yyyy` into a SAS date integer.

We could extract `OrderDate` using the expression `@9 OrderDate $10`. Then `OrderDate` will become a character column and no numeric calculations can be performed on `OrderDate`.

Next, we create a numeric `Amount` column by reading the substring from Positions 20 to 29 via the `comma10.2` informat. The informat `comma10.2` tells SAS that the raw amount string (1) has a total width of 10, (2) has one or more decimals, and (3) has extraneous characters such as dollar signs and periods that need to be removed.

`Comma10.2` requires the raw data to have one or more decimals. If the raw data is an integer without a decimal, SAS will divide the integer by $10^2 = 100$, producing a wrong amount. Fortunately, the order amounts in the raw input file all have decimals. To be safe, we can use the `comma10.` informat instead. This informat will read in an integer or non integer sales amount correctly as long as the width of the amount doesn't exceed 10.

Next, we create a numeric column `Tax` by an assignment statement. At the end of the DATA step, an implicit `output Sales` statement writes the data values as one row to the `Sales` table; an implicit `return` statement starts the next iteration of the DATA step. Finally, the `run` statement explicitly declares the DATA step boundary.

Make no mistake. Program 5.0.2 does everything Program 5.0.1 does. However, SAS does most of the heavy lifting for you in the background. You don't need to write any complex logic to parse the order date or the order amount; you just need to consult the SAS documentation and use a correct `informat` to parse a raw substring. Nor do you need to write SQL to populate the output table.

In data extraction, manipulation, and analysis, which is SAS's niche, a SAS program is typically shorter than an equivalent program written in a general purpose programming language.

However, there's a price to be paid for using SAS `informats` to parse a raw string. While a Python programmer who understands regular expressions and core Python functions can parse any strings, in SAS a separate `informat` has to be created for each commonly encountered string pattern. As a result, SAS has too many `informats` for anyone to remember and a SAS programmer almost always has to search the SAS documentation to find the correct `informat` to parse a raw input string.

To understand why SAS settles on using `informats` to parse most raw strings as opposed to using the more generic approach as in Python, one has to remember that SAS is created mainly for business users, not for IT professionals. A statistician, an employee in a marketing department, or a fraud detection specialist in an auditing department will most likely find that looking up an `informat` is easier than writing a regular expression.

Another major downside of SAS doing work in the background and making things so easy for you is that programming internals are not exposed to you. Let's dissect Program 5.0.2 using PUT statements to write variable values to the log:

Program 5.0.3 *readTextFile2.sas*

```
data work.Sales;
infile 'C:\LearnSAS\sales.txt' firstobs=3;
put 'Before: ' _all_;
```

```
input
@1  CustID $ 7.
@9  OrderDate mmddyy10.
@20 Amount comma10.2
;
Tax=Amount * 0.03;

put 'After:  ' _all_;
run;
```

Submit the program. This is the log:

```
Before: CustID=  OrderDate=. Amount=. Tax=. _ERROR_=0 _N_=1
After:  CustID=104 OrderDate=19724 Amount=2245.08 Tax=67.3524 _ERROR_=0 _N_=1

Before: CustID=  OrderDate=. Amount=. Tax=. _ERROR_=0 _N_=2
After:  CustID=590194 OrderDate=20019 Amount=26820.07 Tax=804.6021 _ERROR_=0 _N_=2

Before: CustID=  OrderDate=. Amount=. Tax=. _ERROR_=0 _N_=3
After:  CustID=1000000 OrderDate=19854 Amount=19.52 Tax=0.5856 _ERROR_=0 _N_=3

Before: CustID=  OrderDate=. Amount=. Tax=. _ERROR_=0 _N_=4

NOTE: 3 records were read from the infile 'C:\LearnSAS\sales.txt'.
      The minimum record length was 29.
      The maximum record length was 29.
NOTE: The data set WORK.SALES has 3 observations and 4 variables.
```

The variable _all_ represents all the variables created by you and by SAS in the DATA step. You created four variables, CustID, OrderDate, Amount, and Tax. SAS created two variables, _N_ and _ERROR_.

- _N_ is initially set to 1. Each time the DATA step loop passes the data statement, the variable _N_ increments by 1. The value of _N_ represents the number of times the DATA step has iterated.

- _ERROR_ is 0 by default but is set to 1 whenever an input data error, a conversion error, or a math error such as division by 0 or a floating point overflow error has occurred.

When you submit a DATA step for execution, SAS compiles the DATA step and then executes it.

During the compilation phase, SAS scans each statement for syntax errors. Most syntax errors prevent further processing of the DATA step. When the compilation phase is complete, the descriptor portion of the new data set is created.

If the DATA step compiles successfully, then the execution phase begins. During the execution phase, the DATA step reads and processes the input data. The DATA step executes once for each record in the input file, unless otherwise directed.

5.1   Compilation Phase

5.1.1   Input Buffer

During the compilation stage, after checking for syntax errors, SAS creates the input buffer, an area of memory to hold a record from the external file. The input buffer is a temporary holding place for a record of raw data as it is being read by SAS via the `input` statement. The input buffer refers to a logical concept; it is not a physical storage area.

The input buffer is created only when raw data is read, not when a SAS data set is read.

You can visualize the input buffer as consecutive blocks of memory to store a record of the raw input data:

```
Input Buffer
```

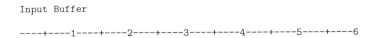

5.1.2   Program Data Vector

After the input buffer is created, SAS creates the PDV, an area of memory where SAS builds a table, one row at a time. Like the term input buffer, the term PDV refers to a logical concept.

```
PDV
----------------------------------------------------------
|  _N_  | _ERROR_ |  CustID  | OrderDate | Amount |  Tax  |
----------------------------------------------------------
|       |         |          |           |        |       |
----------------------------------------------------------
```

The `PDV` contains the variables that are named in the `input` statement as well as the variables created via the assignment statement. `_N_` and `_ERROR_` are automatically generated for every DATA step but are not written to the `Sales` table.

As the `input` statement is compiled, a slot is added to the PDV for each variable in the output table. Generally, variable attributes such as length and type are determined the first time a variable is encountered. Any variables created by an assignment statement in the DATA step are also added to the PDV.

5.1.3   Descriptor Portion

At the end of the DATA step (when the `run` statement is encountered in Program 5.0.3), the compilation phase is complete and the descriptor portion of the new SAS data set is created. The descriptor portion of the data set includes:

- the name of the data set

- the number of observations and variables

- the names and attributes of the variables

```
                      Data set descriptor

Data Set Name: WORK.SALES      Observations:          0
Member Type:   DATA            Variables:             4
Engine:        Vx              Indexes:               0
Created:        date time      Observation Length:    32
Last Modified: date time       Deleted Observations:  0
Protection:                    Compressed:            NO
Data Set Type:                 Sorted:                NO
Label:


-----Engine/Host Dependent Information-----

Data Set Page Size:          4096
Number of Data Set Pages:    1
First Data Page:             1
Max Obs per Page:            126
Obs in First Data Page:      3
Number of Data Set Repairs:  0
File Name:                   path\_TDxxxx\mynum.sas7bdat
Release Created:             release number
Host Created:                operating system info


-----Alphabetic List of Variables and Attributes-----

#     Variable     Type     Len     Pos
---------------------------------------
3     Amount       Num       8       8
1     CustID       Char      7      24
2     OrderDate    Num       8       0
4     Tax          Num       8      16
```

There are no observations because the DATA step has not yet executed. During execution, each raw data record is processed and written to the data set as an observation.

This is the state of the Sales table, the input buffer, and the PDV during the compilation phase:

```
WORK.SALES
----------------------------------------------
| CustID  |  OrderDate  | Amount  |  Tax    |
----------------------------------------------
|         |             |         |         |
----------------------------------------------


Input Buffer
----+----1----+----2----+----3----+----4----+----5----+----6


PDV
-----------------------------------------------------------------
| _N_ | _ERROR_ |  CustID  |  OrderDate  | Amount  |  Tax   |
-----------------------------------------------------------------
|     |         |          |             |         |        |
-----------------------------------------------------------------
```

5.2   Execution Phase

After the DATA step is compiled, it is ready for execution. During the execution phase, the data portion of the data set is created. The data portion contains the data values.

During execution, each record in the raw input file is read into the input buffer. The variable values are extracted from the input buffer into the PDV. Variables created via the assignment statement are also stored in the PDV. At the end of the DATA step iteration, user-created variables in the PDV are inserted to the output table as one row. The DATA step executes once for each record in the input file, unless otherwise directed by additional statements.

5.2.1   First Iteration of the DATA Step

When reading variables from raw data using the `input` statement, SAS sets the value of each variable in the DATA step to missing at the beginning of each cycle of execution, with these exceptions:

- variables named in a `retain` statement

- variables created via a `sum` statement

- data elements in a `_TEMPORARY_` array

- any variables created with options in the `file` or `infile` statements

- automatic variables `_N_` and `_ERROR_`

In contrast, when reading variables from a SAS data set, SAS sets the values to missing only before the first cycle of the execution of the DATA step.

During the execution phase, after reading the `data Sales` statement, SAS sets `_N_` to 1 and `_ERROR_` to 0 (since there are no data errors) and initializes four user-created variables to missing. A missing numeric value is represented by a period and a missing character value is represented by a blank.

This is the state of the PDV:

```
PDV
-----------------------------------------------------------------
|  _N_  |  _ERROR_ |  CustID  | OrderDate | Amount  |  Tax   |
-----------------------------------------------------------------
|  1    |    0    |          |     .     |    .    |    .   |
-----------------------------------------------------------------
```

Input data   Next, SAS reads the `infile` statement and finds the location of the text file. SAS places the first record of the text file into the input buffer:

```
Input buffer

----+----1----+----2----+----3----+----4----+----5----+----6
    104 01/01/2014  $2,245.08
```

Input Pointer   When an `input` statement begins to read raw data from a record held in the input buffer, it uses an input pointer to keep track of the position of the record held in the input buffer. The input pointer starts at column 1 of the record in the input buffer, unless otherwise directed. As the `input` statement executes, the raw data in columns 1–7 is read and assigned to `CustID` in the PDV:

```
PDV
----------------------------------------------------------
|  _N_  | _ERROR_|  CustID  | OrderDate | Amount |  Tax  |
----------------------------------------------------------
|  1  |    0   |   104    |     .     |    .   |   .  |
----------------------------------------------------------
```

Next, raw data in columns 9–18 is read and assigned to `OrderDate` in the PDV:

```
PDV
----------------------------------------------------------
|  _N_  |  _ERROR_  |  CustID  |  OrderDate  | Amount |  Tax  |
----------------------------------------------------------
|  1  |    0   |   104    |   19724   |    .   |   .  |
----------------------------------------------------------
```

19724 is the integer date for January 1, 2014.

Next, raw data in columns 20–29 is read and assigned to `Amount` in the PDV:

```
PDV
----------------------------------------------------------
|  _N_  |  _ERROR_  |  CustID  |  OrderDate  | Amount |  Tax  |
----------------------------------------------------------
|  1  |    0   |   104    |   19724   | 2245.08 |   .  |
----------------------------------------------------------
```

Next, the assignment statement executes. `Tax` is calculated and added to the PDV:

```
PDV
----------------------------------------------------------
|  _N_  |  _ERROR_  |  CustID  |  OrderDate  | Amount |  Tax  |
----------------------------------------------------------
|  1  |    0   |   104    |   19724   | 2245.08 | 67.3524 |
----------------------------------------------------------
```

End of the DATA step   The implied `output` statement and the implied `return` statement execute at the end of the DATA step iteration. The program automatically does the following:

- inserts values from the PDV to the `Sales` table as a new row
- loops back to the top of the DATA step to begin the next iteration
- increments the automatic variable `_N_` by 1

- resets the automatic variable _ERROR_ to 0

- sets the user-created variables to missing

This is the state of the Sales table, the input buffer, and the PDV at the end of the first iteration of the DATA step:

```
WORK.SALES
---------------------------------------------
| CustID | OrderDate | Amount  |   Tax    |
---------------------------------------------
|  104   |   19724    | 2245.08 |  67.3524 |
---------------------------------------------

Input buffer
----+----1----+----2----+----3----+----4----+----5----+----6
    104 01/01/2014  $2,245.08

PDV
-----------------------------------------------------------
| _N_ | _ERROR_ | CustID | OrderDate | Amount |   Tax    |
-----------------------------------------------------------
|  2  |    0    |        |     .     |    .   |    .     |
-----------------------------------------------------------
```

5.2.2   Second Iteration of the DATA Step

Execution continues. The input statement reads the second record into the input buffer:

```
Input buffer

----+----1----+----2----+----3----+----4----+----5----+----6
 590194 10/23/2014 $26,820.07
```

In the PDV, SAS assigns values to the variables and calculates the Tax value, building the second observation just as it did the first one.

```
PDV
-----------------------------------------------------------
| _N_ | _ERROR_ | CustID | OrderDate | Amount |   Tax    |
-----------------------------------------------------------
|  2  |    0    | 590194 |   20019   |26820.07| 804.6021 |
-----------------------------------------------------------
```

At the end of the iteration, the implied output statement executes. New data values from the PDV are inserted into the second row of the Sales table.

This is the state of the Sales table, the input buffer, and the PDV at the end of the second iteration of the DATA step:

```
WORK.SALES
-----------------------------------------------
| CustID  | OrderDate | Amount  |  Tax    |
-----------------------------------------------
|  104    |  19724    | 2245.08 | 67.3524 |
-----------------------------------------------
| 590194  |  20019    |26820.07|  804.6021 |
-----------------------------------------------

Input buffer
----+----1----+----2----+----3----+----4----+----5----+----6
 590194 10/23/2014 $26,820.07

PDV
---------------------------------------------------------
| _N_  | _ERROR_ | CustID  | OrderDate | Amount  |  Tax  |
---------------------------------------------------------
| 3   |   0    |        |     .    |    .   |   .  |
---------------------------------------------------------
```

Next, the implied **return** statement executes. The program loops back to the top of the DATA step to begin the third iteration.

5.2.3   Third Iteration of the DATA Step

Execution continues. The **input** statement reads the third record into the input buffer:

```
Input buffer

----+----1----+----2----+----3----+----4----+----5----+----6
1000000 05/11/2014      19.52
```

In the PDV, SAS assigns values to the variables and calculates the **Tax** value, building the third observation.

```
PDV
---------------------------------------------------------
| _N_  | _ERROR_ | CustID  | OrderDate | Amount  |  Tax   |
---------------------------------------------------------
| 3   |   0    | 1000000 |   19854   |  19.52  | 0.5856 |
---------------------------------------------------------
```

Then SAS encounters the implied **output** statement the third time, writing data values from the PDV as the third row into the **Sales** table.

This is the state of the **Sales** table, the input buffer, and the PDV at the end of the third iteration of the DATA step:

```
WORK.SALES
-----------------------------------------------
|  CustID  | OrderDate | Amount  |  Tax    |
-----------------------------------------------
```

```
|   104    |  19724    | 2245.08 |  67.3524 |
-------------------------------------------
| 590194   |  20019    |26820.07 | 804.6021 |
-------------------------------------------
| 1000000  |  19854    |  19.52  |   0.5856 |
-------------------------------------------
```

```
Input buffer
----+----1----+----2----+----3----+----4----+----5----+----6
1000000 05/11/2014       19.52
```

```
PDV
-----------------------------------------------------------
|  _N_  | _ERROR_ | CustID  | OrderDate | Amount  |  Tax  |
-----------------------------------------------------------
|  4    |   0     |         |     .     |    .    |   .   |
-----------------------------------------------------------
```

Next, the implied **return** statement executes. The program loops back to the top of the DATA step to begin the fourth iteration.

Execution continues. The **input** statement is executed the fourth time, but there's no more record in the input file. After detecting the end of the raw input text file, SAS terminates the DATA step and moves on to the next DATA step or the next PROC step.

5.3   Further Reading

How SAS Thinks or Why the DATA Step Does What It Does

http://www2.sas.com/proceedings/sugi29/252-29.pdf

Understanding the SAS DATA Step and the Program Data Vector

http://support.sas.com/resources/papers/proceedings09/136-2009.pdf

SAS DATA Step Compile, Execution, and the Program Data Vector

http://www.lexjansen.com/nesug/nesug11/ds/ds04.pdf

How to Think Through the SAS DATA Step

http://www2.sas.com/proceedings/sugi31/246-31.pdf

Chapter 6

Calculate a Performance-Based Raise

Instead of giving everyone a 10% raise as in Program 4.1.3, now you need to calculate the performance-based raise as follows:

```
                 Peformance based raise

               first                      raise_
Obs   id  sex  Name    lastName  salary  rating  percent  raise

 1     1   M   John    Smith     66000     9      0.10    6000
 2     2   F   Jane    Johnson   75600     7      0.08    5600
 3     5   F   Mary    Williams  88000    10      0.10    8000
 4    20   M   Robert  Walker    97200     8      0.08    7200
```

Program 6.0.1
workerRaiseDataStep.sas

```
1   dm log 'clear'; dm output 'clear';
2   data worker;
3   infile datalines firstobs=2 dsd;
4   input
5     id
6     sex $
7     firstName $
8     lastName $
9     salary
10    rating
11  ;
12  datalines;
13  id,sex,firstName,lastName,salary,rating
14  1,'M','John','Smith',60000,9
15  2,'F','Jane','Johnson',70000,7
16  5,'F','Mary','Williams',80000,10
17  20,'M','Robert','Walker',90000,8
18  ;
19  run;
20
21  data worker;
22  set worker;
23  select(rating);
24    when (10,9) raise_percent=0.1;
25    when (8,7)  raise_percent=0.08;
26    when (6,5)  raise_percent=0.06;
27    otherwise   raise_percent=0.02;
28  end;
29
30  raise = salary * raise_percent;
31  salary =salary + raise;
32  run;
33
34  options linesize=min nonumber nodate;
35  proc print data=worker;
36   title 'Peformance based raise';
37  run;
```

Output:

Peformance based raise

Obs	id	sex	first Name	lastName	salary	rating	raise_ percent	raise
1	1	M	John	Smith	66000	9	0.10	6000
2	2	F	Jane	Johnson	75600	7	0.08	5600
3	5	F	Mary	Williams	88000	10	0.10	8000
4	20	M	Robert	Walker	97200	8	0.08	7200

Compared with Program 4.1.3, Program 6.0.1 has a second DATA step (Lines 21–28). In this new DATA step, the **data** statement (Line 21) specifies the output table; the **set** statement (Line 22) specifies an existing SAS table as the incoming table. Typically, the output table is different from the incoming table. When the two tables are the same, the incoming table is overwritten.

While the INPUT statement reads in data from a raw external file, the SET statement reads in data from an existing SAS table.

The **select** group can be replaced by the following **if-then-else** statements:

```
      if rating>=9 then raise_percent=0.1;
else if rating>=7 then raise_percent=0.08;
else if rating>=5 then raise_percent=0.06;
else              raise_percent=0.02;
```

For a long list of mutually exclusive conditions, however, a `select` group is more efficient than a series of `if-then-else` statements.

Here's the PROC SQL counterpart to Program 6.0.1:

Program 6.0.2
workerRaiseSQL.sas

```
1   dm log 'clear'; dm output 'clear';
2   proc sql;
3   create table worker
4   (
5      id num,
6      sex char(1),
7      firstName char(12),
8      lastName char,
9      salary num,
10     rating num
11  );
12
13  insert into work.worker
14  values(1,'M','John','Smith',60000,9)
15  values(2,'F','Jane','Johnson',70000,7)
16  values(5,'F','Mary','Williams',80000,10)
17  values(20,'M','Robert','Walker',90000,8)
18  ;
19
20  alter table worker
21  add
22     raise num,
23     raise_percent num
24  ;
25
26  update worker
27  set raise_percent=
28    case
29      when rating>=9          then 0.10
30      when rating=8 or rating=7 then 0.08
31      when rating=6 or rating=5 then 0.06
32    else                      0.02
33  end;
34
35  update worker
36  set raise = salary * raise_percent;
37
38  update worker
39  set salary =salary + raise;
40
41  title 'Peformance based raise';
42  select * from worker;
43  quit;
```

Output:

Peformance based raise

id	sex	firstName	lastName	salary	rating	raise	raise_percent
1	M	John	Smith	66000	9	6000	0.1
2	F	Jane	Johnson	75600	7	5600	0.08
5	F	Mary	Williams	88000	10	8000	0.1
20	M	Robert	Walker	97200	8	7200	0.08

The DATA step Program 6.0.1 is simpler than Program 6.0.2. Program 6.0.1 resembles procedural programming.

However, be absolutely clear that a DATA step is not a procedural program like one in other languages such as C or Python. You've already seen some unique features of a DATA step program.

For example, a DATA step is an implicit loop to build a table one row a time. In addition, the conventional method to find the cumulative sum doesn't work in a DATA step.

6.1 Variables Read From an Existing SAS Table Are Automatically Retained

In the second DATA step of Program 6.0.1, during each iteration, the set statement reads in the next row from the source table worker. The total number of iterations in the second DATA step is equal to the number of rows in the source worker table plus 1. During the fifth iteration, the set statement attempts to read the next row from the source worker table but there's no more row to be read. The DATA step terminates.

There are two major differences between the input statement and the set statement. First, while the input statement loads one record from the raw input file into the input buffer, the set statement loads one record from an existing SAS table directly into the PDV. The data in an existing SAS table was most likely extracted from a raw input file and is considered in good shape and loaded directly into the PDV.

Here's the second major difference. Unlike variables read from a raw input file via the input statement, variables read from an existing SAS table via the set statement are retained in the PDV by default without you writing any explicit retain statement. Variables read from an existing SAS table via the set statement are initialized to missing only at the beginning of the first DATA step iteration. From this point on, they are retained in the PDV. Retaining the variables read from a SAS table makes many jobs easier.

Program 6.1.1

autoRetain.sas

```
1    dm log 'clear'; dm output 'clear';
2    data ten;
3    do i=1 to 10;
4    output;
5    end;
6    run;
7
8    data sumTen;
9    total=1+2+3+4+5+6+7+8+9+10;
10   run;
11
12   data ten2;
13   put 'before ' _all_;
14   lag=i;
15
16   set ten;
17   if _n_=1 then set sumTen;
18   weight= i/total;
19
20   put 'after ' _all_;
21   run;
22
23   options linesize=min nonumber nodate;
24   proc print data=ten2 noobs;
25   format weight percent8.2;
26   title  "Vars read from a SAS table are retained by default";
27   title2 "Vars created by assignment statement are not retained";
28   run;
```

Output:

Vars read from a SAS table are retained by default
Vars created by assignment statement are not retained

lag	i	total	weight
.	1	55	1.82%
1	2	55	3.64%
2	3	55	5.45%
3	4	55	7.27%
4	5	55	9.09%
5	6	55	10.91%
6	7	55	12.73%
7	8	55	14.55%
8	9	55	16.36%
9	10	55	18.18%

The third DATA step creates the ten2 table using two input tables, ten and sumTen. The set ten statement sequentially reads in one row from the table ten. The if _n_=1 then set sumTen statement reads in total=55 from the sumTen table only during the first iteration of the DATA step. However, total=55 is automatically retained in the PDV for the subsequent iterations of the DATA step. Hence the ten2 table contains 10 rows of total=55.

Here is how the third DATA step works in detail. At the beginning of the first iteration, lag, i, total, and weight are all set to missing in the PDV. Then the statement lag=i executes. At this point, i is still missing; the statement set ten hasn't been executed and the variable i hasn't been read into SAS yet. So lag remains missing during the first iteration of the DATA step.

The first iteration continues. The statement set ten executes, reading in the first row i=1 from the ten table. Since _n_=1 evaluates to true, set sumTen executes, reading in the first and only row total=55 from sumTen. Next, weight is calculated. At the end of the first iteration, only lag is missing; all the other variables have values. The data values are inserted as one row into the output table ten2.

Next, the second iteration of the DATA step begins. SAS initializes lag and weight to missing in the PDV because they are created via an assignment statement. However, i and total are read from existing SAS tables and their previous values i=1 and total=55 are automatically retained in the PDV. Next, the statement lag=i executes, updating lag from missing to the retained value of i=1. Next, the set ten statement executes, reading in the next row i=2 from the ten table, updating i=1 to i=2 in the PDV.

The condition _n_=1 evaluates to false. The set sum statement is not executed; SAS will not attempt to read the next row from the sumTen table. However, the previous value total=55 is retained in the PDV.

Next, SAS calculates weight. At the end of the second iteration, the following values are written as one row into the output table ten2:

lag=1; i=2; total=55; weight=0.03636;

The third iteration starts. The third iteration works just like the second iteration. The lag variable gets the previous value of i.

This process continues. At the end of the tenth iteration, the last row is created in the ten2 table. Then the eleventh iteration starts. The set ten statement executes, attempting to read the next row from the ten table. However, there's no more row to be read from the ten table. The DATA step terminates.

Here's the log:

```
before lag=. i=. total=. weight=. _ERROR_=0 _N_=1
after  lag=. i=1 total=55 weight=0.0181818182 _ERROR_=0 _N_=1
before lag=. i=1 total=55 weight=. _ERROR_=0 _N_=2
after  lag=1 i=2 total=55 weight=0.0363636364 _ERROR_=0 _N_=2
before lag=. i=2 total=55 weight=. _ERROR_=0 _N_=3
after  lag=2 i=3 total=55 weight=0.0545454545 _ERROR_=0 _N_=3
before lag=. i=3 total=55 weight=. _ERROR_=0 _N_=4
after  lag=3 i=4 total=55 weight=0.0727272727 _ERROR_=0 _N_=4
before lag=. i=4 total=55 weight=. _ERROR_=0 _N_=5
after  lag=4 i=5 total=55 weight=0.0909090909 _ERROR_=0 _N_=5
before lag=. i=5 total=55 weight=. _ERROR_=0 _N_=6
after  lag=5 i=6 total=55 weight=0.1090909091 _ERROR_=0 _N_=6
before lag=. i=6 total=55 weight=. _ERROR_=0 _N_=7
after  lag=6 i=7 total=55 weight=0.1272727273 _ERROR_=0 _N_=7
before lag=. i=7 total=55 weight=. _ERROR_=0 _N_=8
after  lag=7 i=8 total=55 weight=0.1454545455 _ERROR_=0 _N_=8
before lag=. i=8 total=55 weight=. _ERROR_=0 _N_=9
after  lag=8 i=9 total=55 weight=0.1636363636 _ERROR_=0 _N_=9
before lag=. i=9 total=55 weight=. _ERROR_=0 _N_=10
after  lag=9 i=10 total=55 weight=0.1818181818 _ERROR_=0 _N_=10
before lag=. i=10 total=55 weight=. _ERROR_=0 _N_=11
NOTE: There were 10 observations read from the dataset WORK.TEN.
NOTE: There were 1 observations read from the dataset WORK.SUMTEN.
NOTE: The data set WORK.TEN2 has 10 observations and 4 variables.
NOTE: DATA statement used:
      real time           0.01 seconds
      cpu time            0.01 seconds
```

The sumTen table is created in the second DATA step. However, the sumTen table could have been created from PROC SQL (see Program 1.9.1).

In case you are wondering what would happen to Program 6.1.1 if we change the statement from

if _n_=1 then set sumTen;

to

```
set sumTen;
```

Then Program 6.1.1 will generate the following output:

```
   Vars read from a SAS table are retained by default
  Vars created by assignment statement are not retained

         lag     i     total      weight

                 1      55        1.82%
```

When the `set sumTen` statement executes during the second iteration of the DATA step, SAS attempts to read the second row from the `sumTen` table but finds that there's no more row to be read. The DATA step terminates. The resulting `ten2` table has only one row.

Program 6.0.1 uses two DATA steps on the assumption that the workers input file was already read into a SAS table `worker` before we knew that we needed to calculate the raise. If the workers source data was not read into SAS yet, only one DATA step is necessary to calculate the raise.

Program 6.1.2
workerRaiseDataStep2.sas

```
1   dm log 'clear'; dm output 'clear';
2   data worker;
3   infile datalines firstobs=2 dsd;
4   input
5     id
6     sex $
7     firstName $
8     lastName $
9     salary
10    rating
11  ;
12
13  select(rating);
14    when (10,9) raise_percent=0.1;
15    when (8,7)  raise_percent=0.08;
16    when (6,5)  raise_percent=0.06;
17    otherwise   raise_percent=0.02;
18  end;
19
20  raise = salary * raise_percent;
21  salary =salary + raise;
22
23  datalines;
24  id,sex,firstName,lastName,salary,rating
25  1,'M','John','Smith',60000,9
26  2,'F','Jane','Johnson',70000,7
27  5,'F','Mary','Williams',80000,10
28  20,'M','Robert','Walker',90000,8
29  ;
30  run;
31
32  options linesize=min nonumber nodate;
33  proc print data=worker;
34    title 'Peformance based raise';
35  run;
```

Output:

Peformance based raise

Obs	id	sex	first Name	lastName	salary	rating	raise_ percent	raise
1	1	M	John	Smith	66000	9	0.10	6000
2	2	F	Jane	Johnson	75600	7	0.08	5600
3	5	F	Mary	Williams	88000	10	0.10	8000
4	20	M	Robert	Walker	97200	8	0.08	7200

6.2   Multiple INPUT Statements in a DATA Step

During one DATA step iteration, multiple lines of raw input data can be read in to create one single row in the output table.

Program 6.2.1

workerRaiseDataStep3.sas

```
1    dm log 'clear'; dm output 'clear';
2    data worker;
3    infile datalines firstobs=6 dsd;
4    input id sex $ firstName $;
5    input lastName $ salary rating;
6    input;
7
8    select(rating);
9      when (10,9) raise_percent=0.1;
10     when (8,7)  raise_percent=0.08;
11     when (6,5)  raise_percent=0.06;
12     otherwise   raise_percent=0.02;
13   end;
14
15   raise = salary * raise_percent;
16   salary =salary + raise;
17
18   datalines;
19   /* data structure:
20   id,sex,firstName
21   lastName,salary,rating
22
23   */
24   1,'M','John'
25   'Smith',60000,9
26
27   2,'F','Jane'
28   'Johnson',70000,7
29
30   5,'F','Mary'
31   'Williams',80000,10
32
33   20,'M','Robert'
34   'Walker',90000,8
35
36   ;
37   run;
38
39   options linesize=min nonumber nodate;
40   proc print data=worker noobs;
41    title 'Peformance based raise';
42   run;
```

Output:

Peformance based raise

id	sex	first Name	lastName	salary	rating	raise_ percent	raise
1	M	John	Smith	66000	9	0.10	6000
2	F	Jane	Johnson	75600	7	0.08	5600
5	F	Mary	Williams	88000	10	0.10	8000
20	M	Robert	Walker	97200	8	0.08	7200

During the first iteration, the first `input` statement reads id=1, sex='M', and firstName='John' into SAS.

When the second `input` statement executes, SAS moves the pointer to the beginning of the second line in the external data file (simulated by datalines) and reads lastName='Smith', salary=60000, and rating=9 into SAS.

When the third `input` statement executes, SAS moves the pointer to the beginning of the third line in the external data file. However, the third `input` statement is empty without an argument; no DATA from the third line of the external data file is read into SAS.

The raw data read by three `input` statements forms a single row to be processed further in the DATA step. This program produces the same output as does Program 6.1.2.

6.3 Multiple OUTPUT Statements in the Same DATA Step

You can use consecutive and identical `output` statements to write the same values from the PDV to multiple rows in the destination table so your destination table will have duplicate rows.

Program 6.3.1

workerRaiseDataStep4.sas

```
1   dm log 'clear'; dm output 'clear';
2   data worker;
3   infile datalines firstobs=2 dsd;
4   input
5     id
6     sex $
7     firstName $
8     lastName $
9     salary
10    rating
11  ;
12
13  select(rating);
14    when (10,9) raise_percent=0.1;
15    when (8,7)  raise_percent=0.08;
16    when (6,5)  raise_percent=0.06;
17    otherwise   raise_percent=0.02;
18  end;
19
20  raise = salary * raise_percent;
21  salary =salary + raise;
22
23  output;
24  output;
25  output;
26
27  datalines;
28  id,sex,firstName,lastName,salary,rating
29  1,'M','John','Smith',60000,9
30  2,'F','Jane','Johnson',70000,7
31  5,'F','Mary','Williams',80000,10
32  20,'M','Robert','Walker',90000,8
33  ;
34  run;
35
36  options linesize=min nonumber nodate;
37  proc print data=worker noobs;
38    title 'Peformance based raise';
39  run;
```

Output:

Peformance based raise

id	sex	first Name	lastName	salary	rating	raise_ percent	raise
1	M	John	Smith	66000	9	0.10	6000
1	M	John	Smith	66000	9	0.10	6000
1	M	John	Smith	66000	9	0.10	6000
2	F	Jane	Johnson	75600	7	0.08	5600
2	F	Jane	Johnson	75600	7	0.08	5600
2	F	Jane	Johnson	75600	7	0.08	5600
5	F	Mary	Williams	88000	10	0.10	8000
5	F	Mary	Williams	88000	10	0.10	8000
5	F	Mary	Williams	88000	10	0.10	8000
20	M	Robert	Walker	97200	8	0.08	7200
20	M	Robert	Walker	97200	8	0.08	7200
20	M	Robert	Walker	97200	8	0.08	7200

You can also strategically place `output` statements at different places in the same DATA step to generate different rows.

Program 6.3.2

workerRaiseDataStep4b.sas

```
1   dm log 'clear'; dm output 'clear';
2   data worker;
3   infile datalines firstobs=2 dsd;
4   input
5     id
6     sex $
7     firstName $
8     lastName $
9     salary
10    rating
11  ;
12  output;
13
14  select(rating);
15    when (10,9) raise_percent=0.1;
16    when (8,7)  raise_percent=0.08;
17    when (6,5)  raise_percent=0.06;
18    otherwise   raise_percent=0.02;
19  end;
20  output;
21
22  raise = salary * raise_percent;
23  salary =salary + raise;
24  output;
25
26  datalines;
27  id,sex,firstName,lastName,salary,rating
28  1,'M','John','Smith',60000,9
29  2,'F','Jane','Johnson',70000,7
30  5,'F','Mary','Williams',80000,10
31  20,'M','Robert','Walker',90000,8
32  ;
33  run;
34
35  options linesize=min nonumber nodate;
36  proc print data=worker noobs;
37   title 'Peformance based raise';
38  run;
```

Output:

Peformance based raise

id	sex	first Name	lastName	salary	rating	raise_ percent	raise
1	M	John	Smith	60000	9	.	.
1	M	John	Smith	60000	9	0.10	.
1	M	John	Smith	66000	9	0.10	6000
2	F	Jane	Johnson	70000	7	.	.
2	F	Jane	Johnson	70000	7	0.08	.
2	F	Jane	Johnson	75600	7	0.08	5600
5	F	Mary	Williams	80000	10	.	.
5	F	Mary	Williams	80000	10	0.10	.
5	F	Mary	Williams	88000	10	0.10	8000
20	M	Robert	Walker	90000	8	.	.
20	M	Robert	Walker	90000	8	0.08	.
20	M	Robert	Walker	97200	8	0.08	7200

In the output `worker` table, Rows 1, 4, 7, and 10 are created by the first `output` statement in the DATA step; Rows 2, 5, 8, and 11 by the second `output` statement; and Rows 3, 6, 9, and 12 by the third.

6.4 The Output Tables in the Same DATA Step Have the Same Columns

Here's another example of using multiple `output` statements in the same DATA step.

Program 6.4.1
workerRaiseDataStep5.sas

Output:

```
 1   dm log 'clear'; dm output 'clear';
 2   data  worker raise_pcnt raise_amt
 3     best better good other promotion;
 4   infile datalines firstobs=2 dsd;
 5   input
 6     id sex $ fName $ lName $
 7     salary rating;
 8   output worker;
 9
10   select(rating);
11     when (10,9) raise_percent=0.1;
12     when (8,7)  raise_percent=0.08;
13     when (6,5)  raise_percent=0.06;
14     otherwise   raise_percent=0.02;
15   end;
16   output raise_pcnt;
17
18   raise = salary * raise_percent;
19   salary =salary + raise;
20   output raise_amt;
21
22   select(rating);
23     when (10) output best;
24     when (9)  output better;
25     when (8)  output good;
26     otherwise output other;
27   end;
28
29   if rating=10 then promoted='Yes';
30   else promoted='No';
31   output promotion;
32
33   datalines;
34   id,sex,fName,lName,salary,rating
35   1,'M','John','Smith',60000,9
36   2,'F','Jane','Johnson',70000,7
37   5,'F','Mary','Williams',80000,10
38   20,'M','Robert','Walker',90000,8
39   ;
40   run;
41
42   options linesize=min nodate;
43   proc print data=worker noobs;
44    title 'worker table';
45   proc print data=raise_pcnt noobs;
46    title 'raise_pcnt table';
47   proc print data=raise_amt noobs;
48    title 'raise_amt table';
49   proc print data=best noobs;
50    title 'best table';
51   proc print data=better noobs;
52    title 'better table';
53   proc print data=good noobs;
54    title 'good table';
55   proc print data=other noobs;
56    title 'other table';
57   proc print data=promotion noobs;
58    title 'promotion table';
59   run;
```

worker table

id	sex	fName	lName	salary	rating	raise_percent	raise	promoted
1	M	John	Smith	60000	9	.	.	
2	F	Jane	Johnson	70000	7	.	.	
5	F	Mary	Williams	80000	10	.	.	
20	M	Robert	Walker	90000	8	.	.	

raise_pcnt table

id	sex	fName	lName	salary	rating	raise_percent	raise	promoted
1	M	John	Smith	60000	9	0.10	.	
2	F	Jane	Johnson	70000	7	0.08	.	
5	F	Mary	Williams	80000	10	0.10	.	
20	M	Robert	Walker	90000	8	0.08	.	

raise_amt table

id	sex	fName	lName	salary	rating	raise_percent	raise	promoted
1	M	John	Smith	66000	9	0.10	6000	
2	F	Jane	Johnson	75600	7	0.08	5600	
5	F	Mary	Williams	88000	10	0.10	8000	
20	M	Robert	Walker	97200	8	0.08	7200	

best table

id	sex	fName	lName	salary	rating	raise_percent	raise	promoted
5	F	Mary	Williams	88000	10	0.1	8000	

better table

id	sex	fName	lName	salary	rating	raise_percent	raise	promoted
1	M	John	Smith	66000	9	0.1	6000	

good table

id	sex	fName	lName	salary	rating	raise_percent	raise	promoted
20	M	Robert	Walker	97200	8	0.08	7200	

other table

id	sex	fName	lName	salary	rating	raise_percent	raise	promoted
2	F	Jane	Johnson	75600	7	0.08	5600	

promotion table

id	sex	fName	lName	salary	rating	raise_percent	raise	promoted
1	M	John	Smith	66000	9	0.10	6000	No
2	F	Jane	Johnson	75600	7	0.08	5600	No
5	F	Mary	Williams	88000	10	0.10	8000	Yes
20	M	Robert	Walker	97200	8	0.08	7200	No

The `data` statement specifies 8 tables to be created by the DATA step from the same input file simulated by `datalines`. Surprisingly, these 8 tables have the same columns. If you strip all the rows from each table and keep only the column header, these 8 tables will be identical.

Let's see how SAS determines which columns will be created in the destination table. Open a new enhanced editor window and type up the following test program:

Program 6.4.2 *xyzuvw.sas*   Output:

```
1   dm log 'clear'; dm output 'clear';
2   data xyzuvw;
3
4   x='a'; y='1'; z1=y+1; z2=x+1;
5   z3='text'; z3=1; output;
6
7   x='bcd'; output;
8
9   if x='efg' then u=1;output;
10
11  v=10; output;
12
13  w=20;
14  run;
15
16  proc print data=xyzuvw;
17   title 'table xyzuvw';
18  run;
19
20  proc contents data=xyzuvw;
21  run;
```

```
                       table xyzuvw

Obs   x    y    z1    z2    z3    u     v     w

 1    a    1    2     .     1     .     .     .
 2    b    1    2     .     1     .     .     .
 3    b    1    2     .     1     .     .     .
 4    b    1    2     .     1     .    10     .


-----Alphabetic List of Variables and Attributes-----

     #    Variable   Type    Len    Pos
     --------------------------------------
     6    u          Num      8      16
     7    v          Num      8      24
     8    w          Num      8      32
     1    x          Char     1      40
     2    y          Char     1      41
     3    z1         Num      8       0
     4    z2         Num      8       8
     5    z3         Char     4      42
```

When you submit Program 6.4.2 for execution, it is first compiled and then executed. During the compile phase, SAS checks the syntax of the SAS statements and compiles them, that is, translating the statements into machine code. SAS further processes the code, allocates memory for reading in and for storing one row of the raw input data, and allocates memory for building the results row to be inserted to the destination table. In addition, during the compile phase, SAS builds the attributes of all the variables in the DATA step.

During the compile phase, SAS reads the DATA step code in Program 6.4.2 and identifies all the variables in the DATA step in the order they appear in the code. If a variable's `type` and `length` are not explicitly defined, the `type` and the `length` are implicitly defined by their first occurrence in a DATA step.

At the end of the compile phase, SAS has identified `name`, `type`, and `length`, the three most important attributes of each variable in the DATA step Program 6.4.2:

Variable name	Type	Len
x	Char	1
y	Char	1
z1	Num	8
z2	Num	8
z3	Char	4
u	Num	8
v	Num	8
w	Num	8

The process of identifying the attributes of all the variables in a DATA step is called building the descriptor information of the destination table. If you run PROC CONTENTS, you'll get the alphabetic list of variables and attributes.

The attributes gathered at the end of the compile phase apply to all the destination tables in the DATA step. No matter where you place your `output` statements and no matter how many tables are created by a DATA step, all the tables created by the same DATA step will have the same columns.

The next program creates multiple destination tables.

Program 6.4.3 *T1T2T3T4.sas*

```
1   dm log 'clear'; dm output 'clear';
2   data t1 t2 t3 t4;
3
4   x='a'; y='1'; z1=y+1; z2=x+1;
5   z3='text'; z3=1; output t1;
6
7   x='bcd'; output t2;
8
9   if x='efg' then u=1; output t3;
10
11  v=10; output t4;
12
13  w=20;
14  run;
15
16  proc print data=t1;
17    title 'table t1';
18  run;
19
20  proc print data=t2;
21    title 'table t2';
22  run;
23
24  proc print data=t3;
25    title 'table t3';
26  run;
27
28  proc print data=t4;
29    title 'table t4';
30  run;
```

Output:

table t1

Obs	x	y	z1	z2	z3	u	v	w
1	a	1	2	.	1	.	.	.

table t2

Obs	x	y	z1	z2	z3	u	v	w
1	b	1	2	.	1	.	.	.

table t3

Obs	x	y	z1	z2	z3	u	v	w
1	b	1	2	.	1	.	.	.

table t4

Obs	x	y	z1	z2	z3	u	v	w
1	b	1	2	.	1	.	10	.

Verify for yourself that all the destination tables have the same columns and that all the same-named columns have the same data type and length.

Program 6.4.2 reveals several important points. First, the T1 table contains u, v, and w columns even though these three variables are introduced after the `output T1` statement. The existence of a variable and its attributes are determined at the DATA step compile time.

Similarly, even though x will never be 'efg', the u column is still created in each output table. Only during the execution phase will SAS actually evaluate x='efg' to false and assigns a missing value to u.

Second, the literal string '1' is assigned to y. As a result, SAS sets y to be a 1-byte character column. However, the next statement z1=y+1 attempts to perform a numeric calculation on y. This doesn't matter at compile time. SAS just sets z1 to numeric. Then at execution time, SAS converts the literal string stored in y to number 1 and sets z1=2. SAS writes this message to the log:

```
NOTE: Character values have been converted to numeric values ...
```

Similarly, z3 is initialized to a literal string 'text'. SAS at compile time sets z3 to a 4-byte character column. During the execution phase, the statement z3=1 executes. SAS converts the number 1 into the literal string '1' and resets z3='1'. Column z3 is still a character column. SAS writes the following message to the log:

```
NOTE: Numeric values have been converted to character values ...
```

However, the statement z2=x+1 isn't so lucky. At compile time, SAS sets z2 to numeric. At execution time, SAS tries but fails to convert the literal string 'a' stored in x to a numeric value. As a result, SAS converts 'a' to a missing value and performs the numeric calculation missing+1. Since a missing value plus 1 is still missing, z2 is set to missing. SAS issues the following error in the log:

```
NOTE: Invalid numeric data, x='a' , at line ... column ....
x=b y=1 z1=2 z2=. z3=1 u=. v=10 w=20 _ERROR_=1 _N_=1
NOTE: Missing values were generated as a result of performing
an operation on missing values.
```

Finally, w=20 is never written to the destination table. If a user writes one or more output statements in the DATA step, there will be no implicit output statement at the end of the DATA step. However, the implicit return statement at the end of the DATA step still executes. Program 6.4.2 is equivalent to:

Program 6.4.4 *xyzuvwEquivalent.sas*

```
1   dm log 'clear'; dm output 'clear';
2   data xyzuvw;
3
4   x='a'; y='1'; z1=y+1; z2=x+1; z3='text'; z3=1; output;
5
6   x='bcd'; output;
7
8   if x='efg' then u=1; output;
9
10  v=10; output;
11  w=20;
12  return;
13  run;
14
15  proc print data=xyzuvw;
16  run;
17
18  proc contents data=xyzuvw;
19  run;
```

6.5 Count Your Rows

Let's count the rows of the destination tables in Program 6.4.1. The DATA step uses four complete loops to read data from the `datalines`. These four tables `worker`, `worker_raise_pcnt`, `worker_raise_pcnt_amt`, and `promotion` each have four rows. The `output` statement corresponding to each of the four tables is unconditional. For one row in from the `datalines`, one row is out to each of the four tables.

However, the `output` statements that generate the `best`, `better`, `good`, and `other` tables are conditional. For each row read from the `datalines`, the mutually exclusive yet all-encompassing conditions in the `rating` SELECT group will write the values into only one of these four tables. After the DATA step ends, the total number of rows in these four tables should be four.

If, on the other hand, you purposely want duplicate rows among `best`, `better`, `good`, and `other`, here's an example of what you can do:

```
     if rating=10          then output best;
     if rating in (9,10) then output better;
else if rating=8          then output good;
else                            output other;
```

Now if an incoming row has `rating=10`, then the same values will be written to both the `best` table and `better` table.

6.6 Make the Destination Tables Have Different Columns

You can use KEEP and DROP statements or KEEP= and DROP= data set options to control the number of columns that appear in a destination table. KEEP will keep the variables listed; the variables not listed in KEEP will not be kept. DROP will drop the variables listed; the remaining variables will be kept. This will make more sense in the next example.

Program 6.6.1
workerRaiseDataStep6.sas

Output:

```
1   dm log 'clear'; dm output 'clear';
2   data worker(keep=keep=lName salary rating)
3    raise_pcnt(keep=lName salary raise_percent)
4    raise_amt(keep=raise_percent raise)
5    best   (drop=id sex fName promoted)
6    better (drop=id sex fName promoted)
7    good   (drop=id sex fName promoted)
8    other  (drop=id sex fName promoted)
9    promotion(keep=id rating promoted raise_percent)
10   ;
11   infile datalines firstobs=2 dsd;
12   input id sex$ fName$ lName$ salary rating;
13   output worker;
14
15   select(rating);
16     when (10,9) raise_percent=0.1;
17     when (8,7)  raise_percent=0.08;
18     when (6,5)  raise_percent=0.06;
19     otherwise   raise_percent=0.02;
20   end;
21   output raise_pcnt;
22
23   raise = salary * raise_percent;
24   salary =salary + raise;
25   output raise_amt;
26
27   select(rating);
28     when (10) output best;
29     when (9)  output better;
30     when (8)  output good;
31     otherwise output other;
32   end;
33
34   if rating=10 then promoted='Yes';
35   else promoted='No';
36   output promotion;
37
38   datalines;
39   id,sex,fName,lName,salary,rating
40   1,'M','John','Smith',60000,9
41   2,'F','Jane','Johnson',70000,7
42   5,'F','Mary','Williams',80000,10
43   20,'M','Robert','Walker',90000,8
44   ;
45   run;
46   options linesize=min nodate nonumber;
47   proc print data=worker noobs;
48     title 'worker table';
49   proc print data=raise_pcnt noobs;
50     title 'raise_pcnt table';
51   proc print data=raise_amt noobs;
52     title 'raise_amt table';
53   proc print data=best noobs;
54     title 'best table';
55   proc print data=better noobs;
56     title 'beter table';
57   proc print data=good noobs;
58     title 'good table';
59   proc print data=other noobs;
60     title 'other table';
61   proc print data=promotion noobs;
62     title 'promotion table';
63   run;
```

worker table

lName	salary	rating
Smith	60000	9
Johnson	70000	7
Williams	80000	10
Walker	90000	8

raise_pcnt table

lName	salary	raise_percent
Smith	60000	0.10
Johnson	70000	0.08
Williams	80000	0.10
Walker	90000	0.08

raise_amt table

raise_percent	raise
0.10	6000
0.08	5600
0.10	8000
0.08	7200

best table

lName	salary	rating	raise_percent	raise
Williams	88000	10	0.1	8000

beter table

lName	salary	rating	raise_percent	raise
Smith	66000	9	0.1	6000

good table

lName	salary	rating	raise_percent	raise
Walker	97200	8	0.08	7200

other table

lName	salary	rating	raise_percent	raise
Johnson	75600	7	0.08	5600

promotion table

id	rating	raise_percent	promoted
1	9	0.10	No
2	7	0.08	No
5	10	0.10	Yes
20	8	0.08	No

6.7   Reorder Variables Using RETAIN

Often we need to reorder variables. There are many ways to reorder variables in SAS. The `retain` statement is most often used to reorder variables already in a SAS dataset.

In a DATA step, the variables in the final output table are arranged in the order in which each variable first appears in the DATA step. To change the order of variables, one must change the order in which variables first appear in the DATA step.

In the next program, `myTable` has 5 columns in the order of *abcde*. The RETAIN statement causes the output table `myFinalTable` to arrange its columns in the order of *cdabe*.

Program 6.7.1 *reorder.sas*

```
1   data myFinalTable;
2   retain c d a b e;
3   set myTable;
4   run;
```

In Program 6.7.1, it is redundant to `retain` any variable from `myTable` because the variables read via the `set` statement are automatically retained. The `retain` statement merely reorders the variables; it has no side effect.

However, you should be aware of the danger of the `retain` statement on variables created in the DATA step via the assignment statement. Without a `retain` statement, a variable created via the assignment statement is not automatically retained; it is set to missing at the beginning of each DATA step iteration. If you `retain` this variable for the purpose of reordering it, when SAS can't find its value, it will use its last known value. This may not be what you want.

Suppose this is your current program:

Program 6.7.2
DangerOfRetainBefore.sas

```
1    dm log 'clear'; dm output 'clear';
2    data old;
3    a=10;   b=20;   output;
4    a=100; b=200; output;
5    run;
6
7    data new;
8    set old;
9    c=a+b;
10   if a=10 then d=a;
11   run;
12
13   proc print data=new;
14   run;
```

Output:

Obs	a	b	c	d
1	10	20	30	10
2	100	200	300	.

Now you want the columns to appear in the order of *dcba*:

Program 6.7.3 *DangerOfRetainAfter.sas*

```
dm log 'clear'; dm output 'clear';
data old;
a=10;   b=20;   output;
a=100; b=200; output;
run;

data new2;
retain d c b a; /*reorder variables*/
set old;
c=a+b;
if a=10 then d=a;
run;

proc print data=new2;
run;
```

Output:

Obs	d	c	b	a
1	10	30	20	10
2	10	300	200	100

The variables are indeed reordered, but the **retain** statement has a side effect: the *d* value in the second observation is changed from missing in Program 6.7.2 to 10 in Program 6.7.3.

If you want to use **retain** to reorder variables in a SAS table, do so in the last step, after all the calculation is done. First, calculate everything you need without worrying about reordering variables. Then use a final DATA step solely for reordering variables, without creating any new variables. In the final DATA step, you are free to use dataset options such as **drop**, **keep**, **rename**, **obs**, and **firstobs**. However, don't introduce any new calculation logic in the final step. This way, you can use **retain** to reorder your variables without accidentally creating wrong results.

6.8   More on RETAIN

While we are at it, let's solve a **retain** related puzzle. Can you explain the output?

Program 6.8.1 *PuzzleOnRetain.sas*

```
1   dm log 'clear'; dm output 'clear';
2   data ab;
3   a=1; b=2; output;
4   a=.; b=4; output;
5   a=.; b=6; output;
6   run;
7
8   data abc;
9   retain c;
10  set ab;
11  c=a+b;
12  run;
13
14  proc print data=abc;
15  run;
```

Output:

Obs	c	a	b
1	3	1	2
2	.	.	4
3	.	.	6

The **retain c**; statement preserves the value of *c* in the PDV from one DATA step iteration to the next. And the values of *a* and *b* are automatically preserved in the PDV since they are from an existing SAS table. If one iteration of the DATA step can't find any information about *a*, *b*, or *c*, it will assign that variable to its last known value from previous iterations.

In the second iteration of the DATA step, when SAS encounters $c = a + b$, it evaluates c to missing since a is missing; internally SAS assigns the negative infinity to both a and c. SAS knows about a and c, even though their values are missing. This is different from SAS not knowing anything about a or c. Hence both a and c are set to missing at the end of the second DATA step iteration; they will not retain the last nonmissing values from the previous DATA step iteration. The same is true for the third DATA step iteration.

The next program shows the effect of the **retain** statement:

Program 6.8.2 *PuzzleOnRetain2.sas*

```
1   dm log 'clear'; dm output 'clear';
2   data ab;
3   a=1; b=2; output;
4   a=.; b=4; output;
5   a=.; b=6; output;
6   run;
7
8   data abc2;
9   retain c;
10  set ab;
11  if a=1 then c=a+b;
12  run;
13
14  proc print data=abc2;
15  run;
```

Output:

Obs	c	a	b
1	3	1	2
2	3	.	4
3	3	.	6

In the second and third DATA step iterations, a is not equal to 1 and SAS knows nothing about c. SAS will set c to its last known value of 3.

6.9   Further Reading

Step-by-Step Programming with Base SAS Software, Chapter 3, *Starting with Raw Data: The Basics*; chapter 4, *Starting with Raw Data: Beyond the Basics*.

For more readings on using RETAIN to reorder variables in a DATA step, see `http://support.sas.com/kb/8/395.html` and `http://www.sascommunity.org/wiki/Re-ordering_variables`.

Chapter 7

Generate Prime Numbers

A prime number is a positive integer greater than 1 that has no divisors other than 1 and itself. A positive integer greater than 1 that has at least one divisor other than 1 and itself is called a composite number.

The first four prime numbers are 2, 3, 5, and 7. The first four composite numbers are 4, 6, 8, and 9.

Here's a simple method to test whether a positive integer $n > 2$ is a prime number. If n is a multiple of any integer between 2 and $\sqrt{n}$, then n is not a prime number; otherwise, it is.

7.1   DATA Step

7.1.1   Program 1

The next program generates the prime numbers less than 100.

Program 7.1.1 *primeGenerator1.sas*

```
1   dm log 'clear'; dm output 'clear';
2   data primeTest prime(keep=p);
3   upperBound=100;
4   do p=2, 3;
5     isPrime=1; output;
6   end;
7
8   /* skip even numbers (2 is the only even prime) */
9   do p=5 to upperBound by 2;
10    isPrime=1;
11    do divisor=3 to ceil(sqrt(p)) by 2;
12       remainder= mod(p,divisor);
13       if remainder=0 then do;
14          isPrime=0; leave;
15       end;
16    end;
17
18    output primeTest;
19    if isPrime then output prime;
```

```
20   end;
21   run;
22
23   proc print data=primeTest;
24     title 'Table primeTest: find prime numbers less than 100';
25   run;
26   proc print data=prime;
27     title 'Table prime: prime numbers less than 100';
28   run;
```

Table primeTest: find prime numbers less than 100

Obs	upper Bound	p	is Prime	divisor	remainder
1	100	2	1	.	.
2	100	3	1	.	.
3	100	5	1	5	2
4	100	7	1	5	1
5	100	9	0	3	0
6	100	11	1	5	2
7	100	13	1	5	1
8	100	15	0	3	0
9	100	17	1	7	2
10	100	19	1	7	4
11	100	21	0	3	0
12	100	23	1	7	3
13	100	25	0	5	0
14	100	27	0	3	0
15	100	29	1	7	4
16	100	31	1	7	1
17	100	33	0	3	0
18	100	35	0	5	0
19	100	37	1	9	2
20	100	39	0	3	0
21	100	41	1	9	6
22	100	43	1	9	1
23	100	45	0	3	0
24	100	47	1	9	5
25	100	49	0	7	0
26	100	51	0	3	0
27	100	53	1	9	4
28	100	55	0	5	0
29	100	57	0	3	0
30	100	59	1	9	3
31	100	61	1	9	5
32	100	63	0	3	0
33	100	65	0	5	0
34	100	67	1	11	4
35	100	69	0	3	0
36	100	71	1	11	8
37	100	73	1	11	1
38	100	75	0	3	0
39	100	77	0	7	0
40	100	79	1	11	7
41	100	81	0	3	0
42	100	83	1	11	2

43	100	85	0	5	0
44	100	87	0	3	0
45	100	89	1	11	8
46	100	91	0	7	0
47	100	93	0	3	0
48	100	95	0	5	0
49	100	97	1	11	7
50	100	99	0	3	0

Table prime: prime numbers less than 100

Obs	p
1	2
2	3
3	5
4	7
5	11
6	13
7	17
8	19
9	23
10	29
11	31
12	37
13	41
14	43
15	47
16	53
17	59
18	61
19	67
20	71
21	73
22	79
23	83
24	89
25	97

Lines 4–6 iterate through the first two prime numbers: 2 and 3. The **output** statement without an argument writes 2 and 3 to the **primeTest** table and the **prime** table.

Lines 9–20 iterate p through only the odd integers 5 to 99, skipping even numbers. The only even prime number is 2, which was already written to the two output tables. During each iteration of the do-loop, an inner do-loop (Lines 11–16) test whether p is a prime number by dividing p by the odd **divisor** ranging from 3 to $\text{ceil}(\sqrt{n})$.

The **ceil** function returns the smallest integer that is greater than or equal to the argument. For example, $\text{ceil}(-0.99) = 0$ and $\text{ceil}(3.14) = 4$.

For example, when p is 27, a test is conducted to divide 27 by 3. Since the remainder is 0, 27 is not a prime number. The variable **isPrime** is reset to 0. Next, the **leave** statement executes, immediately terminating the inner do-loop. No more test by division is to be conducted. p=27 is immediately written to the **primeTest** table, but not to the **prime** table. Next, the outer loop resumes with p=29.

In contrast, when p is 29, the inner do-loop iterates through three divisors, 3, 5, and 7. Since the remainder is greater than 0 in each iteration, 29 is found to be a prime number.

7.1.2 Program 2

Instead of using the `leave` statement, the next program uses a do-loop with a `while` condition.

Program 7.1.2 *primeGenerator2.sas*

```
1   dm log 'clear'; dm output 'clear';
2   data primeTest2 prime2(keep=p);
3   upperBound=100;
4   do p=2, 3;
5     isPrime=1;output;
6   end;
7
8   /* skip even numbers (2 is the only even prime) */
9   do p=5 to upperBound by 2;
10    isPrime=1;
11    do divisor=3 to ceil(sqrt(p)) by 2 while(isPrime=1);
12       remainder= mod(p,divisor);
13       if remainder=0 then isPrime=0;
14    end;
15
16    output primeTest2;
17    if isPrime then output prime2;
18  end;
19  run;
20
21  proc print data=primeTest2;
22   title 'Table primeTest2: find prime numbers less than 100';
23  run;
24  proc print data=prime2;
25   title 'Table prime2: prime numbers less than 100';
26  run;
```

This is the output:

Table primeTest2: find prime numbers less than 100

Obs	upper Bound	p	is Prime	divisor	remainder
1	100	2	1	.	.
2	100	3	1	.	.
3	100	5	1	5	2
4	100	7	1	5	1
5	100	9	0	5	0
6	100	11	1	5	2
7	100	13	1	5	1
8	100	15	0	5	0
9	100	17	1	7	2
10	100	19	1	7	4

11	100	21	0	5	0
12	100	23	1	7	3
13	100	25	0	7	0
14	100	27	0	5	0
15	100	29	1	7	4
16	100	31	1	7	1
17	100	33	0	5	0
18	100	35	0	7	0
19	100	37	1	9	2
20	100	39	0	5	0
21	100	41	1	9	6
22	100	43	1	9	1
23	100	45	0	5	0
24	100	47	1	9	5
25	100	49	0	9	0
26	100	51	0	5	0
27	100	53	1	9	4
28	100	55	0	7	0
29	100	57	0	5	0
30	100	59	1	9	3
31	100	61	1	9	5
32	100	63	0	5	0
33	100	65	0	7	0
34	100	67	1	11	4
35	100	69	0	5	0
36	100	71	1	11	8
37	100	73	1	11	1
38	100	75	0	5	0
39	100	77	0	9	0
40	100	79	1	11	7
41	100	81	0	5	0
42	100	83	1	11	2
43	100	85	0	7	0
44	100	87	0	5	0
45	100	89	1	11	8
46	100	91	0	9	0
47	100	93	0	5	0
48	100	95	0	7	0
49	100	97	1	11	7
50	100	99	0	5	0

Table prime2: prime numbers less than 100

Obs	p
1	2
2	3
3	5
4	7
5	11
6	13
7	17
8	19
9	23
10	29
11	31
12	37
13	41

14	43
15	47
16	53
17	59
18	61
19	67
20	71
21	73
22	79
23	83
24	89
25	97

The second do-loop immediately terminates if the condition `isPrime=1` evaluates to false, that is, if `isPrime=0`.

7.1.3 Compare Two Tables

Manually build a comparison table   We can manually build the following comparison table using Notepad or Excel.

Obs	upper Bound	p	is Prime	primeTest divisor	primeTest2 divisor
1	100	2	1	.	.
2	100	3	1	.	.
3	100	5	1	5	5
4	100	7	1	5	5
5	100	9	0	3	5
6	100	11	1	5	5
7	100	13	1	5	5
8	100	15	0	3	5
9	100	17	1	7	7
10	100	19	1	7	7
11	100	21	0	3	5
12	100	23	1	7	7
13	100	25	0	5	7
14	100	27	0	3	5
15	100	29	1	7	7
16	100	31	1	7	7
17	100	33	0	3	5
18	100	35	0	5	7
19	100	37	1	9	9
20	100	39	0	3	5
21	100	41	1	9	9
22	100	43	1	9	9
23	100	45	0	3	5
24	100	47	1	9	9
25	100	49	0	7	9
26	100	51	0	3	5
27	100	53	1	9	9
28	100	55	0	5	7
29	100	57	0	3	5
30	100	59	1	9	9
31	100	61	1	9	9

32	100	63	0	3	5
33	100	65	0	5	7
34	100	67	1	11	11
35	100	69	0	3	5
36	100	71	1	11	11
37	100	73	1	11	11
38	100	75	0	3	5
39	100	77	0	7	9
40	100	79	1	11	11
41	100	81	0	3	5
42	100	83	1	11	11
43	100	85	0	5	7
44	100	87	0	3	5
45	100	89	1	11	11
46	100	91	0	7	9
47	100	93	0	3	5
48	100	95	0	5	7
49	100	97	1	11	11
50	100	99	0	3	5

Notice that when isPrime=0 such as in Observations 5 and 8, the divisor column from the primeTest table (Column 5 of the comparison table) and the divisor column from the primeTest2 table (Column 6 of the comparison table) are different. As explained in Program 4.9.1, in a do-loop, the loop variable will be incremented one extra time. This is what happened to the inner loop variable divisor in Program 7.1.2. However, in Program 7.1.1, when a remainder of 0 is found, the leave statement immediately terminates the inner do-loop, stopping the loop variable divisor from being incremented one extra time.

Programmatically compare tables - PROC COMPARE

Program 7.1.3 *comparePrimeTest.sas*

```
1   dm log 'clear'; dm output 'clear';
2   proc compare base=primeTest compare=primeTest2 nosummary;
3     title 'Compare primeTest and primeTest2';
4   run;
```

The base= option specifies the data set to use as the base data set. The compare= option specifies the data set to use as the comparison data set. If the base= option is omitted, PROC COMPARE uses the most recently created SAS data set as the base.

If you want to compare variables in the base data set with variables that might have different names in the comparison data set, then specify the names of the variables in the base data set in the VAR statement and specify the names of the matching variables in the WITH statement. For example, this is how to compare the divisor variable between the two tables:

```
1   dm log 'clear'; dm output 'clear';
2   proc compare base=primeTest compare=primeTest2 nosummary;
3     var divisor;
4     with divisor;
5     title 'Compare primeTest and primeTest2';
6   run;
```

However, since `primeTest` and `primeTest2` have identical column names, we don't need to specify variable names for comparison. PROC COMPARE will compare all the variables in the two data sets.

Program 7.1.3 produces the following output:

```
                 Compare primeTest and primeTest2

                        COMPARE Procedure
           Comparison of WORK.PRIMETEST with WORK.PRIMETEST2
                         (Method=EXACT)

NOTE: Values of the following 1 variables compare unequal: divisor


            Value Comparison Results for Variables


   ---------------------------------------------------------
         ||     Base      Compare
    Obs  ||   divisor     divisor      Diff.     % Diff
   ------ ||   -------    --------    --------   --------
         ||
      5  ||   3.0000     5.0000      2.0000     66.6667
      8  ||   3.0000     5.0000      2.0000     66.6667
     11  ||   3.0000     5.0000      2.0000     66.6667
     13  ||   5.0000     7.0000      2.0000     40.0000
     14  ||   3.0000     5.0000      2.0000     66.6667
     17  ||   3.0000     5.0000      2.0000     66.6667
     18  ||   5.0000     7.0000      2.0000     40.0000
     20  ||   3.0000     5.0000      2.0000     66.6667
     23  ||   3.0000     5.0000      2.0000     66.6667
     25  ||   7.0000     9.0000      2.0000     28.5714
     26  ||   3.0000     5.0000      2.0000     66.6667
     28  ||   5.0000     7.0000      2.0000     40.0000
     29  ||   3.0000     5.0000      2.0000     66.6667
     32  ||   3.0000     5.0000      2.0000     66.6667
     33  ||   5.0000     7.0000      2.0000     40.0000
     35  ||   3.0000     5.0000      2.0000     66.6667
     38  ||   3.0000     5.0000      2.0000     66.6667
     39  ||   7.0000     9.0000      2.0000     28.5714
     41  ||   3.0000     5.0000      2.0000     66.6667
     43  ||   5.0000     7.0000      2.0000     40.0000
     44  ||   3.0000     5.0000      2.0000     66.6667
     46  ||   7.0000     9.0000      2.0000     28.5714
     47  ||   3.0000     5.0000      2.0000     66.6667
     48  ||   5.0000     7.0000      2.0000     40.0000
     50  ||   3.0000     5.0000      2.0000     66.6667

   ---------------------------------------------------------
```

7.2   Method 2 - PROC SQL

Program 7.2.1 *primeGenerator3.sas*

```
1   dm log 'clear'; dm output 'clear';
2   proc sql noprint;
3   create table ZeroToNine
4   (
5      N num
6   )
7   ;
8
9   insert into ZeroToNine
10  values ( 0 )
11  values ( 1 )
12  values ( 2 )
13  values ( 3 )
14  values ( 4 )
15  values ( 5 )
16  values ( 6 )
17  values ( 7 )
18  values ( 8 )
19  values ( 9 )
20  ;
21
22  create table num1to100 as
23   select 1 + 10*d1.N + d2.N as n
24   from ZeroToNine as d1, ZeroToNine as d2;
25
26  create table prime as
27   select * from num1to100
28   except
29   select d1.n * d2.n
30   from num1to100 d1, num1to100 d2
31   where d1.n>1 and d2.n>1;
32
33  delete from prime where n=1;
34  quit;
35
36  proc sql;
37   title "Prime numbers between integers 1 and 100";
38   select * from prime;
39  quit;
```

Output:

Prime numbers between integers 1 and 100

```
       n
    --------
       2
       3
       5
       7
      11
      13
      17
      19
      23
      29
      31
      37
      41
      43
      47
      53
      59
      61
      67
      71
      73
      79
      83
      89
      97
```

What just happened   This program finds prime numbers by excluding non-prime numbers from a number sequence. We create a table `num1to100` that contains integers 1 to 100. The `except` operator removes composite numbers `d1.n * d2.n` from the integer sequence. Next, the `delete` statement deletes number 1 from the `prime` table. What's left are prime numbers.

7.2.1   Join Two Tables

We could have easily created the `num1to100` table using a DATA step do-loop as follows, but we would have missed the fun of SQL joins.

Program 7.2.2 *num1to100.sas*

```
1   dm log 'clear'; dm output 'clear';
2   data num1to100;
3     do N=1 to 100;
4       output;
5     end;
6   run;
7
8   proc print data=num1to100;
9   run;
```

To understand how the num1to100 table is created in Program 7.2.1, open an enhanced editor window and type the following code:

Program 7.2.3 *Sequence1To100.sas*

```
1   dm log 'clear'; dm output 'clear';
2   proc sql;
3   create table ZeroToNine
4   (
5       N num
6   );
7
8   insert into ZeroToNine
9   values ( 0 )
10  values ( 1 )
11  values ( 2 )
12  values ( 3 )
13  values ( 4 )
14  values ( 5 )
15  values ( 6 )
16  values ( 7 )
17  values ( 8 )
18  values ( 9 )
19  ;
20
21  create table Sequence1To100 as
22  select
23      d1.n as n1
24      ,d2.n as n2
25      ,1 + 10*d1.n + d2.n as m
26    from ZeroToNine as d1, ZeroToNine as d2;
27  quit;
28
29  proc print data=Sequence1To100;
30    title 'Cartesian product with 100=100 rows';
31  run;
```

Output:

Cartesian produce with 10x10=100 rows

Obs	n1	n2	m
1	0	0	1
2	0	1	2
3	0	2	3
4	0	3	4
5	0	4	5
6	0	5	6
7	0	6	7
8	0	7	8
9	0	8	9
10	0	9	10
11	1	0	11
12	1	1	12
13	1	2	13
. . . .			
20	1	9	20
21	2	0	21
. . . .			
91	9	0	91
92	9	1	92
. . . .			
100	9	9	100

The from ZeroToNine as d1, ZeroToNine as d2 clause joins ZeroToNine and ZeroToNine tables. When you specify multiple tables in the from clause but do not include a where statement to subset data, PROC SQL returns the Cartesian product of the tables. In a Cartesian product, each row in the first table is combined with each row in the second table.

A table can be joined to itself in a self-join. Use a self-join when you want to create a query result that joins each row from one instance of the table with each row from another instance of the same table. To list a table twice in the same query, you must provide a table alias for at least one instance of the table name. This table alias helps SAS determine whether columns should present data from the right or left version of the table.

Program 7.2.3 uses two aliases, d1 and d2, to identify two instances of the ZeroToNine table.

The expression 1+10*d1.N+d2.N as m generates an integer m for each pair of d1.n and d2.n.

The next program uses a self-join to create an integer sequence from 0 to 1 million.

Program 7.2.4 *Sequence1To1M.sas*

```
1   dm log 'clear'; dm output 'clear';
2   proc sql;
3   create table ZeroToNine
4   (
5      N num
6   );
7
8   insert into ZeroToNine
9   values ( 0 )
10  values ( 1 )
11  values ( 2 )
12  values ( 3 )
13  values ( 4 )
14  values ( 5 )
15  values ( 6 )
16  values ( 7 )
17  values ( 8 )
18  values ( 9 )
19  ;
20
21  create table Sequence1To1M as
22  select
23     d1.n as n1
24    ,d2.n as n2
25    ,d3.n as n3
26    ,d4.n as n4
27    ,d5.n as n5
28    ,d6.n as n6
29    ,1+d1.n+10*d2.n+100*d3.n+1000*d4.n
30       +10000*d5.n+100000*d6.n as m
31  from ZeroToNine as d1, ZeroToNine as d2, ZeroToNine as d3,
32       ZeroToNine as d4, ZeroToNine as d5, ZeroToNine as d6
33  order by m;
34  quit;
35
36  proc print data=Sequence1To1M (firstobs=999991);
37   title 'Cartesian product with 10**6=1 million rows';
38  run;
```

Output:

Cartesian product with 10**6=1 million rows

Obs	n1	n2	n3	n4	n5	n6	m
999991	0	9	9	9	9	9	999991
999992	1	9	9	9	9	9	999992
999993	2	9	9	9	9	9	999993
999994	3	9	9	9	9	9	999994
999995	4	9	9	9	9	9	999995
999996	5	9	9	9	9	9	999996
999997	6	9	9	9	9	9	999997
999998	7	9	9	9	9	9	999998
999999	8	9	9	9	9	9	999999
1000000	9	9	9	9	9	9	1000000

The next program uses a self-join to create a dating table where a male is paired with a female. However, the result is not what we want.

Output:

Dating table not working yet

Name1	Name2
Jeff	Jeff
Jeff	John
Jeff	Mark
Jeff	Mary
Jeff	Rose
Jeff	Linda
John	Jeff
John	John
John	Mark
John	Mary
John	Rose
John	Linda
Mark	Jeff
Mark	John
Mark	Mark
Mark	Mary
Mark	Rose
Mark	Linda
Mary	Jeff
Mary	John
Mary	Mark
Mary	Mary
Mary	Rose
Mary	Linda
Rose	Jeff
Rose	John
Rose	Mark
Rose	Mary
Rose	Rose
Rose	Linda
Linda	Jeff
Linda	John
Linda	Mark
Linda	Mary
Linda	Rose
Linda	Linda

Program 7.2.5 *DatingTableNotWorking.sas*

```
1   dm log 'clear'; dm output 'clear';
2   proc sql noprint;
3   create table Singles
4   (
5      Sex char(1)
6      ,Name char(10)
7   )
8   ;
9
10  insert into  Singles
11  values ( 'M', 'Jeff' )
12  values ( 'M', 'John' )
13  values ( 'M', 'Mark' )
14  values ( 'F', 'Mary' )
15  values ( 'F', 'Rose' )
16  values ( 'F', 'Linda' )
17  ;
18
19  create table DatingPairs as
20   select
21     s1.name as Name1
22     ,s2.name as Name2
23   from
24     Singles as s1
25     ,Singles as s2
26   ;
27  quit;
28
29  proc sql;
30   title 'Dating table not working yet';
31   select * from DatingPairs;
32  quit;
```

Since there's no **where** clause to restrict the query result, the Cartesian product has extraneous results such as pairing one with oneself, pairing two people with the same sex, and duplicate pairings. The next query creates the desired result:

Program 7.2.6 *DatingTableWorking.sas*

```
1   dm log 'clear'; dm output 'clear';
2   proc sql noprint;
3   create table Singles
4   (
5      Sex char(1)
6     ,Name char(10)
7   )
8   ;
9
10  insert into  Singles
11  values ( 'M', 'Jeff' )
12  values ( 'M', 'John' )
13  values ( 'M', 'Mark' )
14  values ( 'F', 'Mary' )
15  values ( 'F', 'Rose' )
16  values ( 'F', 'Linda' )
17  ;
18
19  create table DatingPairs as
20   select
21     s1.name as Name1
22    ,s2.name as Name2
23   from
24     Singles as s1
25    ,Singles as s2
26   where s1.sex > s2.sex;
27   ;
28  quit;
29
30  proc sql;
31   title 'Dating table';
32   select * from DatingPairs;
33  quit;
```

Output:

```
          Dating table

Name1          Name2
---------------------------
Jeff           Mary
Jeff           Rose
Jeff           Linda
John           Mary
John           Rose
John           Linda
Mark           Mary
Mark           Rose
Mark           Linda
```

Why Program 7.2.6 works is explained in the next section.

7.2.2   SQL Logical Execution Sequence

While most programming languages execute code from top to bottom, the SQL code execution follows a special logical order. Even though select occurs first in the SQL code, it's logically executed the last.

This is the logical order in which the query is executed in Program 7.2.6:

1. The from clause executes first, returning the Cartesian product with $6 \times 6 = 36$ rows.

2. The where clause executes next. It filters out, from the 36 rows returned from Step 1, only the rows that meet the condition s1.sex > s2.sex. Since 'M'>'F' (e.g. the letter M comes after the letter F), the condition 'M'>'F' will pair a male from the first table with a female from the second table. Only 9 rows meet this condition.

3. The select clause executes last, returning the 9 rows generated from Step 2.

Bear in mind that this is the logical (conceptual) order of execution, not necessarily the physical order of execution. SAS is free to execute a query in whatever order it deems most efficient as long as the physical order of execution returns the same result as does the logical order of execution.

7.2.3 Calculate the Running Total

The next program calculates the running total of integers 1 to 10.

Program 7.2.7 *runningTotal.sas*

```
1   dm log 'clear'; dm output 'clear';
2   data oneToTen;
3     do N=1 to 10;
4       output;
5     end;
6   run;
7
8   proc sql;
9   create table myRunningTotal as
10  select
11    d1.N as N
12   ,sum(d2.N) as runningTotal
13
14  from oneToTen as d1, oneToTen as d2
15
16  where d2.N <= d1.N
17  group by d1.N
18  ;
19  quit;
20
21  proc print data=myRunningTotal;
22    title 'Running total: 1 to 10';
23  run;
```

Output:

Running total: 1 to 10

Obs	N	running Total
1	1	1
2	2	3
3	3	6
4	4	10
5	5	15
6	6	21
7	7	28
8	8	36
9	9	45
10	10	55

To understand this program, assume that the table **oneToTen** has only three rows:

```
N
1
2
3
```

The `from oneToTen as d1, oneToTen as d2` clause produces the following Cartesian product:

```
d1.N    d2.N
1       1
1       2
1       3
2       1
2       2
2       3
3       1
3       2
3       3
```

Next, `where d2.N <= d1.N` filters out only the rows that satisfy the condition `d2.N <= d1.N`:

```
d1.N      d2.N
1         1
2         1
2         2
3         1
3         2
3         3
```

From the above table, if we sum up d2.N by d1.N, we'll get the following running total:

```
N         RunningTotal
1              1
2              3
3              6
```

Program 7.2.7 can be rewritten as follows to ease your understanding:

Program 7.2.8 *runningTotal2.sas*

```
1   dm log 'clear'; dm output 'clear';
2   data oneToTen;
3     do N=1 to 10;
4       output;
5     end;
6   run;
7
8   proc sql;
9   /* Step 1 - create an interim table*/
10  create table N1N2 as
11  select d1.N as N1, d2.N as N2
12  from OneToTen as d1, OneToTen as d2
13  where d2.N <= d1.N
14  ;
15
16  /* Step 2 - calculate the running total */
17  create table myRunningTotal as
18  select N1 as N, sum(N2) as runningTotal
19  from N1N2
20  group by N1;
21
22  title 'myRunningTotal table';
23  select * from myRunningTotal;
24  quit;
```

Output:

myRunningTotal table

N	runningTotal
1	1
2	3
3	6
4	10
5	15
6	21
7	28
8	36
9	45
10	55

7.2.4   Calculate the Running Total by Subquery

Program 7.2.9

runningTotalSubQuery.sas

```
1    dm log 'clear'; dm output 'clear';
2    data oneToTen;
3      do N=1 to 10;                          Output:
4        output;
5      end;                                   Running total: 1 to 10
6    run;
7                                                               running
8    proc sql;                                Obs     N         Total
9    create table myRunningTotal as
10   select                                    1      1           1
11     d1.N as N                               2      2           3
12                                             3      3           6
13   ,(                                        4      4          10
14     select sum(d2.N)                        5      5          15
15     from OneToTen as d2                     6      6          21
16     where d2.N <= d1.N                      7      7          28
17   ) as runningTotal                         8      8          36
18                                             9      9          45
19   from OneToTen as d1                      10     10          55
20   group by d1.N
21   ;
22   quit;
23
24   proc print data=myRunningTotal;
25     title 'Running total: 1 to 10';
26   run;
```

This program has two **select** clauses, the outer and the inner. The inner **select** clause is called a subquery.

For each distinct **d1.N** value returned from the outer **select**, the inner **select** aggregates the corresponding **d2.N** values and returns their sum as a single row.

Here are the major rules for a subquery:

- You must enclose a subquery in parentheses.

- A subquery must include a **select** clause and a **from** clause.

- A subquery can include optional WHERE, GROUP BY, and HAVING clauses.

Many joins can be alternatively formulated as subqueries. In many cases, however, a join is faster than a subquery.

7.2.5   Calculate the Running Total by Group

In the next program, we want to calculate the running total separately for the even numbers and the odd numbers.

Program 7.2.10 *RunningTotalByEvenOddStepByStep.sas*

```
1   dm log 'clear'; dm output 'clear';
2   data oneToTen;
3    do N=1 to 10;
4      output;
5    end;
6   run;
7
8   proc sql;
9   /*Step 1 generate N1N2 table */
10  create table N1N2 as
11  select
12    d1.N as N1
13    ,d2.N as N2
14  from oneToTen as d1, oneToTen as d2
15  where d2.N <= d1.N and mod(d2.N,2)=mod(d1.N,2);
16
17  /*Step 2 get running total by even odd */
18  create table runningTotalByEvenOdd as
19  select
20    N1
21    ,sum(N2) as RunningTotal
22  from N1N2
23  group by
24    mod(N1,2)
25    ,N1
26  order by
27    mod(N1,2) desc
28    ,N1
29  ;
30  quit;
31
32  proc print data=RunningTotalByEvenOdd noobs;
33    title 'Running total by even/odd';
34  run;
```

Output:

Running total by even/odd

N1	Running Total
1	1
3	4
5	9
7	16
9	25
2	2
4	6
6	12
8	20
10	30

In Step 1, the `from OneToTen as d1, OneToTen as d2` clause generates a Cartesian product with $10 \times 10 = 100$ rows. Of these 100 rows, only the rows that satisfy the following condition will be retrieved:

`d2.N <= d1.N and mod(d2.N,2)=mod(d1.N,2)`

The result is the N1N2 table:

N1	N2
1	1
2	2
3	1
3	3
4	2
4	4
5	1
5	3
5	5
6	2

```
6      4
6      6
7      1
7      3
7      5
7      7
8      2
8      4
8      6
8      8
9      1
9      3
9      5
9      7
9      9
10     2
10     4
10     6
10     8
10     10
```

Next, Step 2 queries the N1N2 table and generates the running total by even and odd numbers.

In Program 7.2.10, Steps 1 and 2 can be combined as follows:

Program 7.2.11 *RunningTotalByEvenOdd.sas*

```
1   dm log 'clear'; dm output 'clear';
2   data oneToTen;
3     do N=1 to 10;
4       output;
5     end;
6   run;
7
8   proc sql;
9
10  create table RunningTotalByEvenOdd as
11  select
12    d1.N as N
13    ,sum(d2.N) as RunningTotal
14  from oneToTen as d1, oneToTen as d2
15  where d2.N <= d1.N and mod(d2.N,2)=mod(d1.N,2)
16  group by
17    mod(d1.N,2)
18    ,d1.N
19  order by
20    mod(d1.N,2) desc
21    ,d1.N
22  ;
23
24  quit;
25
26  proc print data=RunningTotalByEvenOdd;
27    title 'Running total by even/odd';
28  run;
```

Output:

Running total by even/odd

Obs	N	Running Total
1	1	1
2	3	4
3	5	9
4	7	16
5	9	25
6	2	2
7	4	6
8	6	12
9	8	20
10	10	30

7.2.6 Except and Except All

The next program uses the except operator to remove composite numbers from a sequence of integers.

The except operator returns rows that result from the first query but not from the second query. The except operator does not return duplicate rows that are unmatched by rows in the second query. Adding ALL keeps any duplicate rows that do not occur in the second query.

Program 7.2.12

exceptAndExceptAll.sas

```
1   dm log 'clear'; dm output 'clear';
2   data A;
3    do x=1 to 3;
4      output;output;
5    end;
6   run;
7
8   data B;
9    do x=1 to 2;
10     output;
11   end;
12  run;
13
14  proc sql;
15  create table C as
16   select * from A
17   except
18   select * from B;
19
20  create table D as
21   select * from A
22   except all
23   select * from B;
24  quit;
25
26  proc print data=A;
27   title 'Table A';
28  run;
29
30  proc print data=B;
31   title 'Table B';
32  run;
33
34  proc print data=C;
35   title 'A except B';
36  run;
37
38  proc print data=D;
39   title 'A except all B';
40  run;
```

Output:

```
          Table A

        Obs     x

         1      1
         2      1
         3      2
         4      2
         5      3
         6      3
          Table B

        Obs     x

         1      1
         2      2
        A except B

        Obs     x

         1      3
      A except all B

        Obs     x

         1      1
         2      2
         3      3
         4      3
```

7.3 Method 4 - the DATA Step and PROC SQL

Program 7.3.1 *primeGenerator4.sas*

```
1    dm log 'clear'; dm output 'clear';
2    data primeCandidate;
3    upperBound=100; p=2; output;
4
5    do p=3 to upperBound by 2;
6      output;
7    end;
8    run;
9
10   data composite;
11   upperBound=100;
12   do j=3 to ceil(upperBound/3) by 2;
13     do k=j to floor(upperBound/j) by 2;
14        multiple=j*k;
15        output;
16     end;
17   end;
18   run;
19
20   proc sql noprint;
21   create table prime as
22    select p from primeCandidate
23    except
24    select multiple from composite;
25   quit;
26
27   proc print data=composite;
28     title "odd composites between integers 1 and upperBound";
29   run;
30
31   proc print data=prime;
32     title "prime numbers between integers 1 and upperBound";
33   run;
```

odd composites between integers 1 and upperBound

Obs	upper Bound	j	k	multiple
1	100	3	3	9
2	100	3	5	15
3	100	3	7	21
4	100	3	9	27
5	100	3	11	33
6	100	3	13	39
7	100	3	15	45
8	100	3	17	51
9	100	3	19	57
10	100	3	21	63
11	100	3	23	69
12	100	3	25	75
13	100	3	27	81
14	100	3	29	87
15	100	3	31	93
16	100	3	33	99
17	100	5	5	25
18	100	5	7	35

19	100	5	9	45
20	100	5	11	55
21	100	5	13	65
22	100	5	15	75
23	100	5	17	85
24	100	5	19	95
25	100	7	7	49
26	100	7	9	63
27	100	7	11	77
28	100	7	13	91
29	100	9	9	81
30	100	9	11	99

prime numbers between integers 1 and upperBound

Obs	p
1	2
2	3
3	5
4	7
5	11
6	13
7	17
8	19
9	23
10	29
11	31
12	37
13	41
14	43
15	47
16	53
17	59
18	61
19	67
20	71
21	73
22	79
23	83
24	89
25	97

Program 7.3.1 is similar to Program 7.2.1 but is slightly more efficient.

7.4   Further Reading

SAS 9.3 SQL Procedure Users Guide, Chapter 3, *Retrieving Data from Multiple Tables.*

Dear Miss SASAnswers: A Guide to Efficient PROC SQL Coding https://support.sas.com/resources/papers/sgf09/336-2009.pdf

Chapter 8

Extract a Complex Text File

The Great Widget Co.'s old IT system generates a monthly year-to-date production report text file. At the end of each month, an employee manually converts the production text file into an Excel file. You are asked to write a SAS program to automate the conversion process. In the future an employee at the Great Widget Co. will use your SAS program to convert the production text file to a CSV file. Then he can open the CSV file with Excel and save it as an Excel file.

The following is the production text file as of the end of February, 2014. This file is saved as C:\LearnSAS\widgetFeb2014.txt. Line 1 of the text file is a ruler. The line numbers, however, are not in the text file but are added here to help illustrate the layout of the text file.

```
1     ----+----1----+----2----+----3----+----4----+----5----+----6----+----7
2          Great Widget Company
3                         Branch Office: North
4
5          MONTH OF Jan 2014
6     Factory: A
7                         No of Widgets produced        Success Rate
8                         1,234,567                     95.21%
9                         2,345,678                     90.68%
10                          456,789                     86.24%
11    subtotal            4,037,034                     91.56%
12
13    Factory: B
14                        No of Widgets produced        Success Rate
15                          666,666                     95.47%
16                        4,567,890                     97.36%
17    subtotal            5,234,556                                97.12%
18
19                MONTH OF Feb 2014
20    Factory: A
21                        No of Widgets produced        Success Rate
22                        2,345,678                     90.56%
23                        3,456,788                     94.40%
24                          567,890                     96.83%
25    subtotal            6,370,356                                93.20%
26
27    Factory: B
28                        No of Widgets produced        Success Rate
```

135

```
29                        777,777              89.45%
30                      5,678,901              85.00%
31    subtotal          6,456,678                       85.54%
32
33          Great Widget Company
34            Branch Office: South
35
36    MONTH OF Jan 2014
37    Factory: C
38                    No of Widgets produced    Success Rate
39                      4,567,890               95.21%
40                      6,789,012               90.68%
41                         11,111               86.24%
42    subtotal         11,368,013                       92.50%
43
44    Factory: D
45                    No of Widgets produced    Success Rate
46                        567,890               78.62%
47                        678,901               88.79%
48    subtotal          1,246,791                       84.16%
49
50                    MONTH OF Feb 2014
51    Factory: C
52                    No of Widgets produced    Success Rate
53                      1,111,111               82.34%
54                      2,222,222               93.57%
55                          3,333               86.40%
56    subtotal          3,336,666                       89.82%
57
58    Factory: D
59                    No of Widgets produced    Success Rate
60                        444,444               80.34%
61                        555,555               70.45%
62    subtotal            999,999                       74.85%
```

8.1   Version 1

Program 8.1.1 *widget.sas*

```
1   dm log 'clear'; dm output 'clear';
2   filename InFile 'C:\LearnSAS\widgetFeb2014.txt';
3
4   data widget;
5   retain Branch Month Factory;
6   infile InFile truncover;
7
8   input @1 content $char100. @;
9   /*charw. informat doesn't trim leading or trailing blanks*/
10  /* @ = hold the pointer */
11
12  if index(content,'MONTH OF Jan')>0 then Month='Jan';
13  else if index(content,'MONTH OF Feb')>0 then Month='Feb';
14
15  if index(content,'Branch Office: North')>0 then Branch='North';
16  else if index(content,'Branch Office: South')>0 then Branch='South';
17
```

```
18  if index(content,'Factory')>0 then input @10 factory $1. @;
19  if index(content,'%')>0 and index(content,'total')=0 then do;
20  input
21      @20 WidgetCount comma9.
22      @51 SuccessRate percent7.
23      ;
24  end;
25  Line+1;
26
27  run;
28  proc print data=widget (keep=content);
29  title 'This is the content';
30  run;
31
32  proc print data=widget (drop=content);
33  title 'These are the other variables';
34  run;
```

If you use SAS in the cloud, upload `widgetFeb2014.txt` to the following folder:

`/home/userid/myProgram`

Change the `filename` statement to:

`filename InFile '/home/userid/myProgram/widgetFeb2014.txt';`

Remember to replace `userid` with your ID for SAS in the cloud.

Submit Program 8.1.1 and you'll get the output generated by the two PROC PRINT steps. The first PROC PRINT displays the `content` column of the output table `work.widget`. The `content` column is a copy of the input text file.

```
                          This is the content

Obs                                  content
 1    ----+----1----+----2----+----3----+----4----+----5----+----6----+----7
 2          Great Widget Company
 3                        Branch Office: North
 4
 5          MONTH OF Jan 2014
 6    Factory: A
 7                        No of Widgets produced      Success Rate
 8                          1,234,567                 95.21%
 9                          2,345,678                 90.68%
10                            456,789                 86.24%
11    subtotal              4,037,034                 91.56%
12
13    Factory: B
14                        No of Widgets produced      Success Rate
15                            666,666                 95.47%
16                          4,567,890                 97.36%
17    subtotal              5,234,556                             97.12%
18
19                  MONTH OF Feb 2014
20    Factory: A
21                        No of Widgets produced      Success Rate
22                          2,345,678                 90.56%
```

```
23                          3,456,788              94.40%
24                            567,890              96.83%
25      subtotal            6,370,356                        93.20%
26
27      Factory: B
28                      No of Widgets produced     Success Rate
29                            777,777              89.45%
30                          5,678,901              85.00%
31      subtotal            6,456,678                        85.54%
32
33          Great Widget Company
34            Branch Office: South
35
36      MONTH OF Jan 2014
37      Factory: C
38                      No of Widgets produced     Success Rate
39                          4,567,890              95.21%
40                          6,789,012              90.68%
41                             11,111              86.24%
42      subtotal           11,368,013                        92.50%
43
44      Factory: D
45                      No of Widgets produced     Success Rate
46                            567,890              78.62%
47                            678,901              88.79%
48      subtotal            1,246,791                        84.16%
49
50                      MONTH OF Feb 2014
51      Factory: C
52                      No of Widgets produced     Success Rate
53                          1,111,111              82.34%
54                          2,222,222              93.57%
55                              3,333              86.40%
56      subtotal            3,336,666                        89.82%
57
58      Factory: D
59                      No of Widgets produced     Success Rate
60                            444,444              80.34%
61                            555,555              70.45%
62      subtotal              999,999                        74.85%
```

The second PROC PRINT lists the other columns of the output table `work.widget`.

```
                 These are the other variables
```

Obs	Branch	Month	Factory	Widget Count	Success Rate	Line
1				.	.	1
2				.	.	2
3	North			.	.	3
4	North			.	.	4
5	North	Jan		.	.	5
6	North	Jan	A	.	.	6
7	North	Jan	A	.	.	7
8	North	Jan	A	1234567	0.9521	8
9	North	Jan	A	2345678	0.9068	9
10	North	Jan	A	456789	0.8624	10

11	North	Jan	A	.	.	11
12	North	Jan	A	.	.	12
13	North	Jan	B	.	.	13
14	North	Jan	B	.	.	14
15	North	Jan	B	666666	0.9547	15
16	North	Jan	B	4567890	0.9736	16
17	North	Jan	B	.	.	17
18	North	Jan	B	.	.	18
19	North	Feb	B	.	.	19
20	North	Feb	A	.	.	20
21	North	Feb	A	.	.	21
22	North	Feb	A	2345678	0.9056	22
23	North	Feb	A	3456788	0.9440	23
24	North	Feb	A	567890	0.9683	24
25	North	Feb	A	.	.	25
26	North	Feb	A	.	.	26
27	North	Feb	B	.	.	27
28	North	Feb	B	.	.	28
29	North	Feb	B	777777	0.8945	29
30	North	Feb	B	5678901	0.8500	30
31	North	Feb	B	.	.	31
32	North	Feb	B	.	.	32
33	North	Feb	B	.	.	33
34	South	Feb	B	.	.	34
35	South	Feb	B	.	.	35
36	South	Jan	B	.	.	36
37	South	Jan	C	.	.	37
38	South	Jan	C	.	.	38
39	South	Jan	C	4567890	0.9521	39
40	South	Jan	C	6789012	0.9068	40
41	South	Jan	C	11111	0.8624	41
42	South	Jan	C	.	.	42
43	South	Jan	C	.	.	43
44	South	Jan	D	.	.	44
45	South	Jan	D	.	.	45
46	South	Jan	D	567890	0.7862	46
47	South	Jan	D	678901	0.8879	47
48	South	Jan	D	.	.	48
49	South	Jan	D	.	.	49
50	South	Feb	D	.	.	50
51	South	Feb	C	.	.	51
52	South	Feb	C	.	.	52
53	South	Feb	C	1111111	0.8234	53
54	South	Feb	C	2222222	0.9357	54
55	South	Feb	C	3333	0.8640	55
56	South	Feb	C	.	.	56
57	South	Feb	C	.	.	57
58	South	Feb	D	.	.	58
59	South	Feb	D	.	.	59
60	South	Feb	D	444444	0.8034	60
61	South	Feb	D	555555	0.7045	61
62	South	Feb	D	.	.	62

How it works The `filename` statement creates a file reference `InFile`, which points to the physical file `C:\LearnSAS\widgetFeb2014.txt`. Then in the DATA step, you can use the file reference `InFile` in the `infile` statement to indicate the file source.

By the way, there's nothing magical about the file reference name `InFile`. You can name the file reference `myfile` if you like:

```
filename myfile 'C:\LearnSAS\widgetFeb2014.txt';

data widget;
retain Branch Month Factory;
infile myfile truncover;
/*more statements*/
```

If you don't want to create a file reference, you can directly specify the incoming text file like this:

```
...
data widget;
retain Branch Month Factory;

infile 'C:\LearnSAS\widgetFeb2014.txt' truncover;
...
```

However, using a file reference makes your code more flexible. If your source file name or location is changed, you just need to point `InFile` to the new physical file in the `filename` statement without changing your DATA step.

Under the TRUNCOVER option, when the DATA step reaches the end of an input record but some variables don't have values, the variables will be assigned missing values for that observation.

Let's look at the `input @1 content $char100. @` statement. The `content` variable holds the content of the current line of the raw data in the input buffer. The `@1 content $char100.` expression tells SAS that the `content` variable starts from Position 1 and is 100 character long. The `$charw.` informat does not trim leading and trailing blanks or convert a single period in the input data field to a blank before storing values. We want to keep leading and trailing blanks so we can use absolute positioning in the `input` statement.

The ending @ sign in the `input` statement holds the pointer in the current line in the input buffer so the next `input` statement in the same iteration of the DATA step will read data from the same line in the input buffer. Here's the next `input` statement:

```
if index(content,'Factory')>0 then input @10 factory $1. @;
```

If `index(content,'Factory')>0` evaluates to true, SAS will extract the `factory` value from Positions 10 to 11 of the same line of the raw data in the input buffer from which the `content` is extracted.

If you omit the ending at-sign @ in the first `input` statement, then the next `input` statement in the same iteration of the DATA step will load the next line of the raw input file into the input buffer and extract data from that line, producing wrong data values.

Similarly, the ending @ sign in the second `input` statement causes the third `input statement` to extract `WidgetCount` and `SuccessRate` from the same line in the input buffer.

The index(target-expression, search-expression) function searches target-expression, from left to right, for the first occurrence of the string specified in search-expression, and returns the position in target-expression of the string's first character. If the string is not found in target-expression, the index function returns 0. If there are multiple occurrences of the string, the index function returns only the position of the first occurrence.

Let's look at this block of code:

```
if index(content,'%')>0 and index(content,'total')=0 then do;
input
    @20 WidgetCount comma9.
    @51 SuccessRate percent7.
    ;
end;
```

If the raw record contains the percent sign but doesn't contain the string total, SAS extracts the WidgetCount value from Positions 20 to 28 and the SuccessRate value from Positions 51 to 57.

The COMMAw.d informat reads numeric values and removes embedded commas, blanks, dollar signs, percent signs, dashes and close parentheses from the input data. COMMAw.d converts an open parenthesis at the beginning of a field to a minus sign.

The PERCENTw.d informat converts the numeric portion of the input data to a number using the same method as COMMAw.d informat. If a percent sign follows the number in the input field, PERCENTw.d divides the number by 100.

Finally, the sum statement Line+1 creates a line number counter for debugging our code.

Since not every line in the raw input text file contains Branch, Month, or Factory, these three variables need to be retained in the PDV. Due to the retain Branch Month Factory statement, if a raw input record is missing any of these three variables, that variable's last known value will be used.

To see the effect of the retain statement, comment out the retain Branch Month Factory statement from Program 8.1.1. Re-submit Program 8.1.1 and see what happens.

Program 8.1.1 works but the output table widget has many rows where WidgetCount and SuccessRate are both missing. We can add another DATA step to Program 8.1.1 to remove these rows:

```
data widgetFinal (drop=content line);
set widget;
where WidgetCount NE .;
run;
```

If you previously submitted Program 8.1.1 and the widget table was created, submit this new DATA step. The widgetFinal table will be created. In addition, you'll get this log:

```
NOTE: There were 20 observations read from the dataset WORK.WIDGET.
      WHERE WidgetCount not = .;
NOTE: The data set WORK.WIDGETFINAL has 20 observations and 5 variables.
```

20 out of 62 rows from the incoming table `widget` have nonmissing `WidgetCount` values and are read into the `widgetFinal` table.

The WHERE statement filters the rows from the input table `widget`. Only the rows with a nonmissing `WidgetCount` value will participate in the DATA step and be written to the output table `widgetFinal`.

The DROP= option prevents the `content` column and the `line` column in the input table `widget` from being written to the output table `widgetFinal`.

If instead of using a WHERE statement, you can use the WHERE= option to restrict which rows from the incoming table should participate in the DATA step. The new DATA step can be rewritten as:

```
data widgetFinal (drop=content line);
set widget (where=(WidgetCount NE .));
run;
```

Submit these three lines of code. A new `widgetFinal` table will be created, overwriting the existing one. And you'll get this log:

```
NOTE: There were 20 observations read from the dataset WORK.WIDGET.
      WHERE WidgetCount not = .;
NOTE: The data set WORK.WIDGETFINAL has 20 observations and 5 variables.
```

These two versions of the second DATA step are equivalent.

Here's the final SAS program:

Program 8.1.2 *widgetFinal.sas*

```
1   dm log 'clear'; dm output 'clear';
2   filename InFile 'C:\LearnSAS\widgetFeb2014.txt';
3
4   data widget;
5   retain Branch Month Factory;
6   infile InFile truncover;
7   input @1 content $char100. @;
8   /*charw. informat doesn't trim leading or trailing blanks*/
9   /* @ = hold the pointer */
10
11  if index(content,'MONTH OF Jan')>0 then Month='Jan';
12  else if index(content,'MONTH OF Feb')>0 then Month='Feb';
13
14  if index(content,'Branch Office: North')>0 then Branch='North';
15  else if index(content,'Branch Office: South')>0 then Branch='South';
16
17  if index(content,'Factory')>0 then input @10 factory $1. @;
18
19  if index(content,'%')>0 and index(content,'total')=0 then do;
20  input
21     @20 WidgetCount comma9.
```

```
22     @51 SuccessRate percent7.
23       ;
24   end;
25   Line+1;
26   run;
27
28   data widgetFinal (drop=content line);
29   set widget;
30   where WidgetCount NE .;
31   run;
32
33   proc sql;
34   create table widgetFinalSum as
35   select
36     Month
37     ,Branch
38     ,Factory
39     ,sum(widgetCount) as totalWidgetCount
40     ,ceil(sum(widgetCount * SuccessRate)) as goodWidgetCount
41
42   from widgetFinal
43
44   group by
45     Month
46     ,Branch
47     ,Factory
48     ;
49   quit;
50
51   proc export
52      data=widgetFinal
53      outfile='C:\LearnSAS\widgetFinal.csv'
54      dbms=csv
55      replace;
56   run;
57
58   proc export
59      data=widgetFinalSum
60      outfile='C:\LearnSAS\widgetFinalSum.csv'
61      dbms=csv
62      replace;
63   run;
```

If you use SAS in the cloud, you'll need to adjust the file path in the `infile` statement and in the two PROC EXPORTs (see Preface "Adjust the File Path for SAS in the Cloud").

The PROC SQL step calculates the total number of widgets by month, branch, and factory. It also calculates the total number of good widgets by month, branch, and factory.

Finally, the PROC EXPORT step exports the `widgetFinal` and `widgetFinalSum` tables to two CSV files.

This is the newly created `widgetFinalSum.csv` file:

Month	Branch	Factory	totalWidgetCount	goodWidgetCount
Feb	North	A	6370356	5937342
Feb	North	B	6456678	5522788
Feb	South	C	3336666	2997102
Feb	South	D	999999	748455
Jan	North	A	4037034	3696427
Jan	North	B	5234556	5083764
Jan	South	C	11368013	10514947
Jan	South	D	1246791	1049272

This is the newly created `widgetFinal.csv` file:

Branch	Month	Factory	WidgetCount	SuccessRate
North	Jan	A	1234567	0.9521
North	Jan	A	2345678	0.9068
North	Jan	A	456789	0.8624
North	Jan	B	666666	0.9547
North	Jan	B	4567890	0.9736
North	Feb	A	2345678	0.9056
North	Feb	A	3456788	0.944
North	Feb	A	567890	0.9683
North	Feb	B	777777	0.8945
North	Feb	B	5678901	0.85
South	Jan	C	4567890	0.9521
South	Jan	C	6789012	0.9068
South	Jan	C	11111	0.8624
South	Jan	D	567890	0.7862
South	Jan	D	678901	0.8879
South	Feb	C	1111111	0.8234
South	Feb	C	2222222	0.9357
South	Feb	C	3333	0.864
South	Feb	D	444444	0.8034
South	Feb	D	555555	0.7045

8.2 Version 2

Program 8.1.2 works but isn't very flexible. For example, if we were to convert the year-to-date December production report to a CSV file, we would have to use 12 `index` functions to extract the names of the twelve months. Similarly, if the production report has 1,000 branch offices, we have to use 1,000 `index` functions to extract the branch offices.

Here's our second program, but it only works in SAS version 9.1 or higher.

Program 8.2.1 *widgetSASv9.sas*

```
1   dm log 'clear'; dm output 'clear';
2   filename InFile 'C:\LearnSAS\widgetFeb2014.txt';
3
```

```
4   data widgetSASv9 (drop=content m n posBranch posMonth Line);
5   retain Branch Month Factory;
6   infile InFile truncover;
7   input @1 content $char100. @;
8
9   m=lengthc('Branch Office: ');
10  posBranch=find(content,'Branch Office: ');
11  if posBranch>0 then input @posBranch + m Branch $5. @;
12
13  n=lengthc('MONTH OF ');
14  posMonth=find(content,'MONTH OF ');
15  if posMonth>0 then input @posMonth + n Month $3. @;
16
17  if index(content,'Factory')>0 then input @10 factory $1. @;
18
19  if index(content,'%')>0 and index(content,'total')=0 then do;
20  input
21    @20 WidgetCount comma9.
22    @51 SuccessRate percent7.
23    ;
24  end;
25
26  if WidgetCount>0;
27
28  Line+1;
29  run;
30
31  proc sql;
32  create table widgetSASv9Sum as
33  select
34    Month
35   ,Branch
36   ,Factory
37   ,sum(widgetCount) as totalWidgetCount
38   ,ceil(sum(widgetCount * SuccessRate)) as goodWidgetCount
39
40  from widgetSASv9
41
42  group by
43    Month
44   ,Branch
45   ,Factory
46   ;
47  quit;
48
49  proc export
50     data=widgetSASv9
51     outfile='C:\LearnSAS\widgetSASv9.csv'
52     dbms=csv
53     replace;
54  run;
55
56  proc export
57     data=widgetSASv9Sum
58     outfile='C:\LearnSAS\widgetSASv9Sum.csv'
59     dbms=csv
60     replace;
61  run;
```

This program uses two new functions introduced in SAS 9.1, the `lengthc(string)` function and the `find(string,substring)` function.

The `lengthc(string)` function returns the number of characters, both blanks and non-blanks, in `string`. So m=lengthc('Branch Office: ') evaluates to m=15.

The `find(string,substring)` function searches `string` and returns the position of the first occurrence of `substring`. If `substring` is not found in `string`, `find` returns 0.

The statement `posBranch=find(content,'Branch Office:   ')` dynamically calculates the position of the substring 'Branch Office: ' in `content`. The next statement is the key:

```
if posBranch>0 then input @posBranch + m Branch $5. @;
```

If a raw record in the input buffer has the substring 'Branch Office: ', we move the pointer in the input buffer to the beginning of the substring 'Branch Office: ' and then move m columns right to extract the 5 column wide `Branch` value.

If the input text file is large, to make your SAS program more efficient, you can eliminate the variable `m` and write the following instead:

```
if posBranch>0 then input @posBranch + 15 Branch $5. @;
```

8.3 Subsetting IF

Look at Line 26 of Program 8.2.1:

```
if WidgetCount>0;
```

This is how the IF statement without THEN works in any DATA step. If the condition specified by the IF statement is not met, the current iteration of the DATA step will immediately end and the next iteration will start.

In Program 8.2.1, during each iteration of the DATA step, if the condition `WidgetCount>0` is met, the DATA step processing continues. The subsequent statement `Line+1` and the implicit `output` statement at the end of the DATA step will both be executed. The current observation will be written to the output table `widgetSASv9`.

However, if the condition `WidgetCount>0` is not met, the current iteration of the DATA step ends immediately and the next iteration starts. The subsequent statement `Line+1` will not be executed. The implicit `output` statement at the end of the DATA step will not be executed either and the observation will not be written to the output table `widgetSASv9`.

You might wonder whether the condition `WidgetCount>0` is satisfied if a record has a missing `WidgetCount`. The missing numeric value represented by a period is implemented as the negative infinity in SAS and will cause `WidgetCount>0` to fail. As a result, if a record is missing `WidgetCount`, that record is not written to the output table `widgetSASv9`.

You might wonder why I created the accumulator variable `line`, but only to drop it in the end. The `line` column is for debugging my code. When I was testing my code, I would keep all my variables. So my development code would look like this:

```
...
data widgetSASv9;
retain Branch Month Factory;
infile InFile truncover;
...
```

Once my code is working, I'll change my DATA statement to:

```
data widgetSASv9 (drop=content m n posBranch posMonth Line);
```

The five extraneous variables are dropped. The remaining variables are truly needed by end users and are kept.

8.4   IF versus WHERE

Now you have seen two methods to restrict the flow of the incoming data into the DATA step. The IF statement without THEN prevents an observation that doesn't meet the condition from being further processed in the subsequent statements in the DATA step. The WHERE statement or the equivalent WHERE= option prevents all the rows in the incoming table that don't meet the condition from participating in the DATA step at all.

Here's the major difference between the subsetting IF statement and the subsetting WHERE statement or WHERE= option. The subsetting condition in the WHERE statement or WHERE= option can include only the variables already existing in the input table; the subsetting condition in the IF statement can include any DATA step variables.

When a DATA step reads in data from an existing SAS table via the SET statement, you can use a WHERE statement or WHERE= option to test whether one or more existing variables from the incoming table meet a condition. If the condition is met, that row will be loaded into the PDV to participate in the DATA step. If the condition is not met, that row will not be loaded into the PDV and is excluded from DATA step processing.

When a DATA step reads in data from an existing SAS table via the SET statement, you can use the IF statement without THEN to test whether any DATA step variables meet the condition and determine whether a row from the incoming table should be processed further in the DATA step.

When a DATA step reads in raw data from an external file via the INPUT statement, the WHERE statement or the WHERE= option cannot be used to restrict the incoming data, but you can use an IF statement to control which observations will be further processed in a DATA step.

Program 8.4.1 *subsetIF.sas*

Output:

```
1   dm log 'clear';
2   dm output 'clear';
3   data demoIF;
4   put 'before ' _all_;
5
6   input x y$;
7   if x>3 and y>'f';
8
9   z=x*10;
10
11  put 'after  ' _all_;
12  datalines;
13  1 m
14  2 n
15  3 p
16  4 q
17  5 r
18  6 e
19  7 d
20  8 c
21  9 b
22  10 a
23  ;
24  run;
25
26  proc print;
27   title 'IF without THEN';
28  run;
```

```
              IF without THEN

Obs     x     y     z

 1      4     q     40
 2      5     r     50
```

Log:

```
before x=. y=  z=. _ERROR_=0 _N_=1
before x=. y=  z=. _ERROR_=0 _N_=2
before x=. y=  z=. _ERROR_=0 _N_=3
before x=. y=  z=. _ERROR_=0 _N_=4
after  x=4 y=q z=40 _ERROR_=0 _N_=4
before x=. y=  z=. _ERROR_=0 _N_=5
after  x=5 y=r z=50 _ERROR_=0 _N_=5
before x=. y=  z=. _ERROR_=0 _N_=6
before x=. y=  z=. _ERROR_=0 _N_=7
before x=. y=  z=. _ERROR_=0 _N_=8
before x=. y=  z=. _ERROR_=0 _N_=9
before x=. y=  z=. _ERROR_=0 _N_=10
before x=. y=  z=. _ERROR_=0 _N_=11
NOTE: The data set WORK.DEMOIF has 2 observations
      and 3 variables.
```

The variables x and y are created via the **input** statement. Only the IF statement without THEN can be used to subset the incoming raw input data. Neither the WHERE statement nor the WHERE= option can be used. All the records from the raw input file are sequentially read into the input buffer and loaded into the PDV, but only the observations that meet the condition x>3 and y>'f' are further processed by the second PUT statement and by the implicit **output** statement.

Next, let's look at using a WHERE statement to restrict rows from the input table. All the remaining SAS programs in this section will use the following table XY:

Program 8.4.2 *XYtable.sas*

```
1   data XY;
2   input x y$;
3   datalines;
4   1 m
5   2 n
6   3 p
7   4 q
8   5 r
9   6 e
10  7 d
11  8 c
12  9 b
13  10 a
```

```
14   ;
15   run;
```

Program 8.4.3
subsetWHERE.sas

```
dm log 'clear'; dm output 'clear';
data XY;
input x y$;
datalines;
1 m
2 n
3 p
4 q
5 r
6 e
7 d
8 c
9 b
10 a
;
run;

data demoWHERE;
put 'before ' _all_;

set XY (where=(x>3 and y>'f'));
z=x*10;

put 'after  ' _all_;
run;

proc print;
 title 'WHERE= option';
run;
```

Output:

```
        WHERE= option

Obs    x    y    z

 1     4    q    40
 2     5    r    50
```

Log:

```
before x=. y=  z=. _ERROR_=0 _N_=1
after  x=4 y=q z=40 _ERROR_=0 _N_=1
before x=4 y=q z=. _ERROR_=0 _N_=2
after  x=5 y=r z=50 _ERROR_=0 _N_=2
before x=5 y=r z=. _ERROR_=0 _N_=3
NOTE: There were 2 observations read from the dataset WORK.XY.
      WHERE (x>3) and (y>'f');
NOTE: The data set WORK.DEMOWHERE has 2 observations and
      3 variables.
```

Due to the WHERE= option, from the input table, only the observations that meet the condition x>3 and y>'f' will participate in the DATA step and be loaded into the PDV.

Program 8.4.3 is equivalent to:

Program 8.4.4

subsetWHERE2.sas

```
dm log 'clear';
dm output 'clear';
data XY;
input x y$;
datalines;
1 m
2 n
3 p
4 q
5 r
6 e
7 d
8 c
9 b
10 a
;
run;

data demoWHERE2;
put 'before ' _all_;

set XY;
where x>3 and y>'f';

z=x*10;

put 'after  ' _all_;
run;

proc print;
 title 'WHERE statement';
run;
```

Output:

```
   WHERE statement

Obs    x    y     z

 1     4    q    40
 2     5    r    50
```

Log:

```
before x=. y=  z=. _ERROR_=0 _N_=1
after  x=4 y=q z=40 _ERROR_=0 _N_=1
before x=4 y=q z=. _ERROR_=0 _N_=2
after  x=5 y=r z=50 _ERROR_=0 _N_=2
before x=5 y=r z=. _ERROR_=0 _N_=3
NOTE: There were 2 observations read from the dataset WORK.XY.
      WHERE (x>3) and (y>'f');
NOTE: The data set WORK.DEMOWHERE2 has 2 observations and
      3 variables.
```

Program 8.4.3 and Program 8.4.4 are equivalent to:

Program 8.4.5
subsetWHERE3.sas

```
dm log 'clear';
dm output 'clear';
data XY;
input x y$;
datalines;
1 m
2 n
3 p
4 q
5 r
6 e
7 d
8 c
9 b
10 a
;
run;

data demoWHERE3;
put 'before ' _all_;

set XY;

z=x*10;
where x>3 and y>'f';

put 'after  ' _all_;
run;

proc print;
 title 'WHERE statement';
run;
```

Output:

```
        WHERE statement

   Obs    x     y     z

    1     4     q     40
    2     5     r     50
```

Log:

```
before x=. y=  z=. _ERROR_=0 _N_=1
after   x=4 y=q z=40 _ERROR_=0 _N_=1
before x=4 y=q z=. _ERROR_=0 _N_=2
after   x=5 y=r z=50 _ERROR_=0 _N_=2
before x=5 y=r z=. _ERROR_=0 _N_=3
NOTE: There were 2 observations read from the dataset WORK.XY.
      WHERE (x>3) and (y>'f');
NOTE: The data set WORK.DEMOWHERE3 has 2 observations and 3
      variables.
```

Surprisingly, though the WHERE statement is placed toward the end of the DATA step, it is executed immediately after the **set** statement.

Program 8.4.6 *subsetIF2.sas*

```
dm log 'clear';
dm output 'clear';
data XY;
input x y$;
datalines;
1 m
2 n
3 p
4 q
5 r
6 e
7 d
8 c
9 b
10 a
;
run;

data demoIF2;
put 'before ' _all_;

set XY;
if x>3 and y>'f';

z=x*10;
put 'after  ' _all_;
run;

proc print;
 title 'IF on an existing table';
run;
```

Output:

IF on an existing table

```
 Obs     x      y      z

  1      4      q      40
  2      5      r      50
```

Log:

```
before x=. y=  z=. _ERROR_=0 _N_=1
before x=1 y=m z=. _ERROR_=0 _N_=2
before x=2 y=n z=. _ERROR_=0 _N_=3
before x=3 y=p z=. _ERROR_=0 _N_=4
after  x=4 y=q z=40 _ERROR_=0 _N_=4
before x=4 y=q z=. _ERROR_=0 _N_=5
after  x=5 y=r z=50 _ERROR_=0 _N_=5
before x=5 y=r z=. _ERROR_=0 _N_=6
before x=6 y=e z=. _ERROR_=0 _N_=7
before x=7 y=d z=. _ERROR_=0 _N_=8
before x=8 y=c z=. _ERROR_=0 _N_=9
before x=9 y=b z=. _ERROR_=0 _N_=10
before x=10 y=a z=. _ERROR_=0 _N_=11
NOTE: There were 10 observations read from
      the dataset WORK.XY.
NOTE: The data set WORK.DEMOIF2 has 2 observations
      and 3 variables.
```

Program 8.4.6 is less efficient than Program 8.4.3 and Program 8.4.4, though the three programs create the same output table. Program 8.4.6 loads all the observations from the input table into the PDV, whereas the other two programs load only the observations that satisfy the WHERE condition into the PDV.

In the next program, the IF statement without THEN uses the automatic variable _n_ to restrict the incoming rows.

Program 8.4.7 *subsetIF2b.sas*

Output:

```
dm log 'clear';
dm output 'clear';
data XY;
input x y$;
datalines;
1 m
2 n
3 p
4 q
5 r
6 e
7 d
8 c
9 b
10 a
;
run;

data demoIF2b;
put 'before ' _all_;

set XY;
if _n_>8;

z=x*10;
put 'after  ' _all_;
run;

proc print;
 title 'IF using _n_';
run;
```

```
        IF using _n_

 Obs     x     y      z

  1      9     b      90
  2     10     a     100
```

Log:

```
before x=. y=  z=. _ERROR_=0 _N_=1
before x=1 y=m z=. _ERROR_=0 _N_=2
before x=2 y=n z=. _ERROR_=0 _N_=3
before x=3 y=p z=. _ERROR_=0 _N_=4
before x=4 y=q z=. _ERROR_=0 _N_=5
before x=5 y=r z=. _ERROR_=0 _N_=6
before x=6 y=e z=. _ERROR_=0 _N_=7
before x=7 y=d z=. _ERROR_=0 _N_=8
before x=8 y=c z=. _ERROR_=0 _N_=9
after  x=9 y=b z=90 _ERROR_=0 _N_=9
before x=9 y=b z=. _ERROR_=0 _N_=10
after  x=10 y=a z=100 _ERROR_=0 _N_=10
before x=10 y=a z=. _ERROR_=0 _N_=11
NOTE: There were 10 observations read
      from the dataset WORK.XY.
NOTE: The data set WORK.DEMOIF2B has 2 observations
      and 3 variables.
```

The next program uses multiple subsetting IF statements to progressively filter rows to be further processed by subsequent statements in the DATA step.

Program 8.4.8

subsetIFandWHERE.sas

```
dm log 'clear';
dm output 'clear';
data XY;
input x y$;
datalines;
1 m
2 n
3 p
4 q
5 r
6 e
7 d
8 c
9 b
10 a
;
run;

data XYZU;
put 'before ' _all_;
set XY (where=(x>2));

z=x**2;
if z<80;

u=z+10;
if u>50;

put 'after  ' _all_;
run;

proc print;
 title 'Use WHERE and IF';
run;
```

Output:

```
        Use WHERE and IF

Obs    x     y     z     u

 1     7     d     49    59
 2     8     c     64    74
```

Log:

```
before x=. y=  z=. u=. _ERROR_=0 _N_=1
before x=3 y=p z=. u=. _ERROR_=0 _N_=2
before x=4 y=q z=. u=. _ERROR_=0 _N_=3
before x=5 y=r z=. u=. _ERROR_=0 _N_=4
before x=6 y=e z=. u=. _ERROR_=0 _N_=5
after  x=7 y=d z=49 u=59 _ERROR_=0 _N_=5
before x=7 y=d z=. u=. _ERROR_=0 _N_=6
after  x=8 y=c z=64 u=74 _ERROR_=0 _N_=6
before x=8 y=c z=. u=. _ERROR_=0 _N_=7
before x=9 y=b z=. u=. _ERROR_=0 _N_=8
before x=10 y=a z=. u=. _ERROR_=0 _N_=9
NOTE: There were 8 observations read from the dataset WORK.XY.
      WHERE x>2;
NOTE: The data set WORK.XYZU has 2 observations and 4 variables.
```

8.5 Further Reading

Step-by-Step Programming with Base SAS Software, Chapter 4, *Starting with Raw Data: Beyond the Basics*; Chapter 5, *Starting with SAS Data Sets*; and Chapter 10, *Creating Subsets of Observations*.

Reading Difficult Raw Data

http://www.lexjansen.com/nesug/nesug08/ff/ff01.pdf

Chapter 9

Calculate the Running Total and Find Duplicates

The following table lists different patients who visited their doctors during the first ten days of 1960. The first ten days of 1960 are chosen to keep the example simple; these dates are integers 0 to 9 in SAS.

ID	Sex	Date	fee
8	M	1/1/1960	20
4	F	1/2/1960	10
2	F	1/3/1960	30
10	M	1/4/1960	20
4	F	1/5/1960	10
3	F	1/6/1960	50
8	M	1/7/1960	40
4	F	1/8/1960	30
2	F	1/9/1960	20
2	F	1/10/1960	10

We want to find out

- which patients have multiple visits and which have only one visit

- the running total of the number of visits for each patient

- the running total of the fees for each patient

- the total number of visits for each patient

- the total fee for each patient

9.1 Method 1 - Use the First and the Last Variables

Program 9.1.1 *visits.sas*

```
1    dm log 'clear'; dm output 'clear';
2    data visits;
3    input ID sex $ date fee;
4    format date mmddyy10.;
5    datalines;
6     8  M  0 20
7     4  F  1 10
8     2  F  2 30
9    10  M  3 20
10    4  F  4 10
11    3  F  5 50
12    8  M  6 40
13    4  F  7 30
14    2  F  8 20
15    2  F  9 10
16   ;
17   run;
18
19   /*visitsSorted is ordered by ID ascending*/
20   proc sort data=visits out=visitsSorted;
21      by id;
22   run;
23
24   /* find idNoDup (patients with one doctor visit) and
25   idDup (patients with multiple doctor visits) */
26   data idNoDup idDup ;
27   set visitsSorted;
28   by id;
29
30   if first.id=1 and last.id=1 then output idNoDup;
31   else output idDup;
32   run;
33
34   /*find running total for each patient: count and fees*/
35   data runningTotalByPatient;
36   set visitsSorted;
37   by ID;
38
39   Count + 1; Fees + fee;
40   if first.ID=1 then do;
41     Count=1;
42     Fees=fee;
43   end;
44   run;
45
46   /*find total by patient: visit count and fees*/
47   data Total;
48   set visitsSorted;
49   by ID;
50
51   if first.ID=1 then do;
52      Count=0;
53      Fees=0;
54   end;
55
56   Count+1;
57   Fees+fee;
58
```

```
59  if last.ID then output;
60  run;
61
62  options linesize=min nonumber nodate;
63  %macro print(table);
64  proc print data=&table;
65     title "&table table";
66  run;
67  %mend;
68
69  %print(visits)
70  %print(visitsSorted)
71  %print(idNoDup)
72  %print(idDup)
73  %print(runningTotalByPatient)
74  %print(Total)
```

Submit the program. This is the output:

visits table

Obs	ID	sex	date	fee
1	8	M	01/01/1960	20
2	4	F	01/02/1960	10
3	2	F	01/03/1960	30
4	10	M	01/04/1960	20
5	4	F	01/05/1960	10
6	3	F	01/06/1960	50
7	8	M	01/07/1960	40
8	4	F	01/08/1960	30
9	2	F	01/09/1960	20
10	2	F	01/10/1960	10

visitsSorted table

Obs	ID	sex	date	fee
1	2	F	01/03/1960	30
2	2	F	01/09/1960	20
3	2	F	01/10/1960	10
4	3	F	01/06/1960	50
5	4	F	01/02/1960	10
6	4	F	01/05/1960	10
7	4	F	01/08/1960	30
8	8	M	01/01/1960	20
9	8	M	01/07/1960	40
10	10	M	01/04/1960	20

idNoDup table

Obs	ID	sex	date	fee
1	3	F	01/06/1960	50
2	10	M	01/04/1960	20

idDup table

Obs	ID	sex	date	fee

```
1    2    F    01/03/1960    30
2    2    F    01/09/1960    20
3    2    F    01/10/1960    10
4    4    F    01/02/1960    10
5    4    F    01/05/1960    10
6    4    F    01/08/1960    30
7    8    M    01/01/1960    20
8    8    M    01/07/1960    40
        runningTotalByPatient table
```

Obs	ID	sex	date	fee	Count	Fees
1	2	F	01/03/1960	30	1	30
2	2	F	01/09/1960	20	2	50
3	2	F	01/10/1960	10	3	60
4	3	F	01/06/1960	50	1	50
5	4	F	01/02/1960	10	1	10
6	4	F	01/05/1960	10	2	20
7	4	F	01/08/1960	30	3	50
8	8	M	01/01/1960	20	1	20
9	8	M	01/07/1960	40	2	60
10	10	M	01/04/1960	20	1	20

Total table

Obs	ID	sex	date	fee	Count	Fees
1	2	F	01/10/1960	10	3	60
2	3	F	01/06/1960	50	1	50
3	4	F	01/08/1960	30	3	50
4	8	M	01/07/1960	40	2	60
5	10	M	01/04/1960	20	1	20

`%macro print(table)` lets you call PROC PRINT using shorter syntax. For example, `%print(visits)` is equivalent to:

```
proc print data=visits;
   title "visits table";
run;
```

How a macro works in general is explained in Chapter 11.

To figure out how Program 9.1.1 works, write the next program:

Program 9.1.2 *byVariable.sas*

```
1   dm log 'clear'; dm output 'clear';
2   data visitsSorted;
3   set visitsSorted;
4   by id;
5
6   format date best12.;
7   put _all_;
8   run;
```

This program uses the `visitsSorted` table created by PROC SORT in Program 9.1.1 as the incoming table. It creates the output table with the same name, effectively overwriting the `visitsSorted` table.

What's new in Program 9.1.2 is the `by id` statement. If a DATA step has as BY statement after a SET statement and the table in the SET statement is pre-sorted by the variables listed in the BY statement, SAS creates two temporary variables FIRST and LAST to identify the first row and the last row of each unique occurrence of the BY variables.

First, submit Program 9.1.1 to create the `visitsSorted` table. Next, submit Program 9.1.2. This is the log:

```
ID=2 sex=F date=2 fee=30 FIRST.ID=1 LAST.ID=0 _ERROR_=0 _N_=1
ID=2 sex=F date=8 fee=20 FIRST.ID=0 LAST.ID=0 _ERROR_=0 _N_=2
ID=2 sex=F date=9 fee=10 FIRST.ID=0 LAST.ID=1 _ERROR_=0 _N_=3
ID=3 sex=F date=5 fee=50 FIRST.ID=1 LAST.ID=1 _ERROR_=0 _N_=4
ID=4 sex=F date=1 fee=10 FIRST.ID=1 LAST.ID=0 _ERROR_=0 _N_=5
ID=4 sex=F date=4 fee=10 FIRST.ID=0 LAST.ID=0 _ERROR_=0 _N_=6
ID=4 sex=F date=7 fee=30 FIRST.ID=0 LAST.ID=1 _ERROR_=0 _N_=7
ID=8 sex=M date=0 fee=20 FIRST.ID=1 LAST.ID=0 _ERROR_=0 _N_=8
ID=8 sex=M date=6 fee=40 FIRST.ID=0 LAST.ID=1 _ERROR_=0 _N_=9
ID=10 sex=M date=3 fee=20 FIRST.ID=1 LAST.ID=1 _ERROR_=0 _N_=10
```

The `date` value is displayed as an integer in the log due to the `format date best12.` statement in Program 9.1.2.

As shown in the log, SAS creates two variables in the PDV: `first.id` and `last.id`. These variables are available for DATA step programming but are not written to the output table. Their values indicate whether an observation is one of the following:

- the first one in an `id` group: `first.id=1`

- the last one in an `id` group: `last.id=1`

- neither the first nor the last in an `id` group: `first.id=0` and `last.id=0`

- both the first and the last, as is the case when there is only one observation in an `id` group: `first.id=1` and `last.id=1`

However, if the table in the SET statement is not pre-sorted by the BY variables in ascending order, adding a BY statement after the SET statement will generate an error in the log.

Program 9.1.3 *byVariableError.sas*

```
1   data visitsOut;
2   set visits;
3   by id;
4   run;
```

Because the incoming table `visits` is not pre-sorted by `id`, SAS writes the following error to the log:

```
ERROR: BY variables are not properly sorted on data set WORK.VISITS.

NOTE: The SAS System stopped processing this step because of errors.
```

Though the FIRST and the LAST variables are not written to the output table, you can pass these two temporary variables to new DATA step variables.

Program 9.1.4 *byVariable2.sas*

```
1    dm log 'clear'; dm output 'clear';
2    data visitsSorted2;
3    set visitsSorted;
4    by id;
5
6    firstID=first.id;
7    lastID=last.id;
8    run;
9
10   proc print data=visitsSorted2;
11     format date mmddyy10.;
12     title 'visitsSorted2 table';
13   run;
```

The temporary variables `first.id` and `last.id` are passed to `firstID` and `lastID`.

This is the output:

```
                    visitsSorted2 table

                                            first   last
        Obs   ID   sex       date    fee     ID      ID

          1    2    F    01/03/1960    30      1       0
          2    2    F    01/09/1960    20      0       0
          3    2    F    01/10/1960    10      0       1
          4    3    F    01/06/1960    50      1       1
          5    4    F    01/02/1960    10      1       0
          6    4    F    01/05/1960    10      0       0
          7    4    F    01/08/1960    30      0       1
          8    8    M    01/01/1960    20      1       0
          9    8    M    01/07/1960    40      0       1
         10   10    M    01/04/1960    20      1       1
```

The next program calculates the running total of the monthly sales.

Program 9.1.5
monthlySales.sas

```
1   dm log 'clear'; dm output 'clear';
2   data monthlySales;
3   input month sales;
4   datalines;
5   1 5
6   1 6
7   2 7
8   2 8
9   3 9
10  3 10
11  ;
12  run;
13
14  data TotalSales;
15  set monthlySales;
16  by month;
17
18  countByMonth + 1;
19  totalByMonth + sales;
20  count + 1;
21  total + sales;
22
23  if first.month=1 then do;
24     countByMonth=1;
25     totalByMonth=sales;
26  end;
27  run;
28
29  options linesize=min nonumber nodate;
30  proc print data=TotalSales noobs;
31   title 'Running totals';
32  run;
```

Output:

Running totals

month	sales	count ByMonth	total ByMonth	count	total
1	5	1	5	1	5
1	6	2	11	2	11
2	7	1	7	3	18
2	8	2	15	4	26
3	9	1	9	5	35
3	10	2	19	6	45

In the second DATA step, the four accumulator variables countByMonth, totalByMonth, count, and total keep incrementing across iterations of the DATA step. The BY statement creates two temporary variables first.month and last.month. When the DATA step encounters the first row of a unique month (e.g. first.month=1), countByMonth is reset to 1 and totalByMonth is reset to that month's sales.

The next program is similar to Program 9.1.5 except that the input table monthlySales is pre-sorted by month in descending order. In the second DATA step, the by descending month statement creates two temporary variables, first.month and last.month.

Program 9.1.6

monthlySales2.sas

```
1    dm log 'clear'; dm output 'clear';
2    data monthlySales;
3    input month sales;
4    datalines;
5    3 9
6    3 10
7    2 7
8    2 8
9    1 5
10   1 6
11   ;
12   run;
13
14   data TotalSales;
15   set monthlySales;
16   by descending month;
17
18   countByMonth + 1;
19   totalByMonth + sales;
20   count + 1;
21   total + sales;
22
23   if first.month=1 then do;
24      countByMonth=1;
25      totalByMonth=sales;
26   end;
27   run;
28
29   options linesize=min nonumber nodate;
30   proc print data=TotalSales noobs;
31    title 'Running totals';
32   run;
```

Output:

Running totals

month	sales	count ByMonth	total ByMonth	count	total
3	9	1	9	1	9
3	10	2	19	2	19
2	7	1	7	3	26
2	8	2	15	4	34
1	5	1	5	5	39
1	6	2	11	6	45

In Program 9.1.6, if you omit the `descending` option keyword in the BY statement, SAS will throw the following error in the log:

```
ERROR: BY variables are not properly sorted on data set WORK.MONTHLYSALES.
```

The next program is similar to Program 9.1.5 except that the input table `monthlySales` is not pre-sorted in either alphabetic or numeric order. The `notsorted` option in the BY statement specifies that observations that have the same BY value are grouped together but are not necessarily sorted in alphabetical or numeric order. SAS still creates two temporary variables: `first.month` and `last.month`.

Program 9.1.7
monthlySales3.sas

```
1   dm log 'clear'; dm output 'clear';
2   data monthlySales;
3   input month$ sales;
4   datalines;
5   Jan 5
6   Jan 6
7   Feb 7
8   Feb 8
9   Mar 9
10  Mar 10
11  ;
12  run;
13
14  data TotalSales;
15  set monthlySales;
16  by month notsorted;
17
18  countByMonth + 1;
19  totalByMonth + sales;
20  count + 1;
21  total + sales;
22
23  if first.month=1 then do;
24     countByMonth=1;
25     totalByMonth=sales;
26  end;
27  run;
28
29  options linesize=min nonumber nodate;
30  proc print data=TotalSales noobs;
31    title 'Running totals';
32  run;
```

Output:

Running totals

month	sales	count ByMonth	total ByMonth	count	total
Jan	5	1	5	1	5
Jan	6	2	11	2	11
Feb	7	1	7	3	18
Feb	8	2	15	4	26
Mar	9	1	9	5	35
Mar	10	2	19	6	45

In Program 9.1.7, if you omit the `notsorted` option keyword in the BY statement, SAS will throw the following error in the log:

```
ERROR: BY variables are not properly sorted on data set WORK.MONTHLYSALES.
```

The NOTSORTED option can appear anywhere in the BY statement and is useful if the incoming table is logically grouped. The NOTSORTED option works best when observations that have the same BY value are stored together.

In the next program, the incoming table is not pre-sorted or logically grouped. The `notsorted` option still works, but the output is less useful.

Program 9.1.8
monthlySales4.sas

```
1   dm log 'clear'; dm output 'clear';
2   data monthlySales;
3   input month$ sales;
4   datalines;
5   Jan 5
6   Jan 6
7   Feb 7
8   Mar 9
9   Feb 8
10  Mar 10
11  ;
12  run;
13
14  data TotalSales;
15  set monthlySales;
16  by month notsorted;
17
18  firstMonth=first.month;
19  lastMonth=last.month;
20
21  countByMonth + 1;
22  totalByMonth + sales;
23  count + 1;
24  total + sales;
25
26  if first.month=1 then do;
27     countByMonth=1;
28     totalByMonth=sales;
29  end;
30  run;
31
32  options linesize=min nonumber nodate;
33  proc print data=TotalSales noobs;
34    title 'Running totals';
35  run;
```

Output:

Running totals

month	sales	first Month	last Month	count ByMonth	total ByMonth	count	total
Jan	5	1	0	1	5	1	5
Jan	6	0	1	2	11	2	11
Feb	7	1	1	1	7	3	18
Mar	9	1	1	1	9	4	27
Feb	8	1	1	1	8	5	35
Mar	10	1	1	1	10	6	45

Once you understand the BY variables, you'll understand Program 9.1.1. Let's walk through the logic for finding which patients have multiple visits and which have only one visit:

```
data idNoDup idDup ;
set visitsSorted;
by id;
if first.id=1 and last.id=1 then output idNoDup;
else output idDup;
run;
```

The `idNoDup` and `idDup` tables are created off the incoming table `visitsSorted`. If `first.id=1` and `last.id=1`, then that observation has a unique ID and is written to the `idNoDup` table. Otherwise, that observation doesn't have a unique ID and is written to the `idDup` table.

`First.id` and `last.id` are either 1 or 0. Since 0 or a missing value evaluates to false and a non-zero and nonmissing value evaluates to true, the condition `if first.id=1 and last.id=1` can be simplified to `if first.id and last.id`.

Go through the remaining code in Program 9.1.1 and figure out why it works.

9.2 Method 2 - PROC SQL

Program 9.2.1 *visitsSQL.sas*

```
1   dm log 'clear'; dm output 'clear';
2   data visits;
3   input ID sex $ date fee;
4
5   datalines;
6    8  M  0 20
7    4  F  1 10
8    2  F  2 30
9   10  M  3 20
10   4  F  4 10
11   3  F  5 50
12   8  M  6 40
13   4  F  7 30
14   2  F  8 20
15   2  F  9 10
16   ;
17  run;
18
19  /* Find total count and fees by ID */
20  proc sql;
21  create table TotalByID as
22  select
23      ID
24     ,sex
25     ,date
26     ,fee
27     ,count(*) as TotalCount
28     ,sum(fee) as TotalFees
29  from visits
30  group by
31      ID
32  ;
33  quit;
34
35  /* method 1- find dup/nodup if you have count by ID*/
36  proc sql;
37  create table DupID as
38  select *
39  from TotalByID
40  where TotalCount>1;
41
42  create table UniqueID as
43  select *
44  from TotalByID
45  where TotalCount=1;
46  quit;
47
48  /* method 2- find dup/nodup if you have count by ID*/
49  data UniqueID DupID;
50  set TotalByID;
```

```
51  if TotalCount>1 then output DupID; else output UniqueID;
52  run;
53
54  /* Find running total. Step 1 - generate v1v2 table */
55  proc sql;
56  create table v1v2 as
57  select
58      v1.*
59      ,v2.fee as fee2
60  from visits as v1, visits as v2
61  where v1.id = v2.id and v1.fee>=v2.fee
62  order by
63      ID
64      ,fee
65      ,fee2
66  ;
67  quit;
68
69  /* Find running total. Step 2 - get running total */
70  proc sql;
71  create table ByPatientRunningTotal as
72  select
73      ID
74      ,fee
75      ,count(*)  as RunningCount
76      ,sum(fee2) as RunningTotal
77  from v1v2
78  group by
79      ID
80      ,fee
81  ;
82  quit;
83
84  options linesize=min nonumber nodate;
85  %macro print(table);
86  proc print data=&table;
87      title "&table table";
88  run;
89  %mend;
90
91  %print(visits)
92  %print(TotalByID)
93  %print(DupID)
94  %print(UniqueID)
95  %print(v1v2)
96  %print(ByPatientRunningTotal)
```

This is the output:

```
                visits table

        Obs    ID    sex    date    fee

         1      8     M       0      20
         2      4     F       1      10
         3      2     F       2      30
         4     10     M       3      20
```

```
        5     4     F      4     10
        6     3     F      5     50
        7     8     M      6     40
        8     4     F      7     30
        9     2     F      8     20
       10     2     F      9     10
              TotalByID table
```

Obs	ID	sex	date	fee	Total Count	Total Fees
1	2	F	2	30	3	60
2	2	F	8	20	3	60
3	2	F	9	10	3	60
4	3	F	5	50	1	50
5	4	F	4	10	3	50
6	4	F	1	10	3	50
7	4	F	7	30	3	50
8	8	M	6	40	2	60
9	8	M	0	20	2	60
10	10	M	3	20	1	20

DupID table

Obs	ID	sex	date	fee	Total Count	Total Fees
1	2	F	2	30	3	60
2	2	F	8	20	3	60
3	2	F	9	10	3	60
4	4	F	4	10	3	50
5	4	F	1	10	3	50
6	4	F	7	30	3	50
7	8	M	6	40	2	60
8	8	M	0	20	2	60

UniqueID table

Obs	ID	sex	date	fee	Total Count	Total Fees
1	3	F	5	50	1	50
2	10	M	3	20	1	20

v1v2 table

Obs	ID	sex	date	fee	fee2
1	2	F	9	10	10
2	2	F	8	20	10
3	2	F	8	20	20
4	2	F	2	30	10
5	2	F	2	30	20
6	2	F	2	30	30
7	3	F	5	50	50
8	4	F	1	10	10
9	4	F	1	10	10
10	4	F	4	10	10
11	4	F	4	10	10
12	4	F	7	30	10
13	4	F	7	30	10

```
            14    4    F    7    30    30
            15    8    M    0    20    20
            16    8    M    6    40    20
            17    8    M    6    40    40
            18   10    M    3    20    20
                 ByPatientRunningTotal table
```

Obs	ID	fee	Running Count	Running Total
1	2	10	1	10
2	2	20	2	30
3	2	30	3	60
4	3	50	1	50
5	4	10	4	40
6	4	30	3	50
7	8	20	1	20
8	8	40	2	60
9	10	20	1	20

There's nothing in Program 9.2.1 you haven't seen before. The most complex part of the program is calculating the running total. The running total logic is similar to that in Program 7.2.10.

9.3   Remerge Summary Statistics Back to the Original Table

Program 9.2.1 generates the following log:

```
NOTE: The query requires remerging summary statistics back with the original data.
NOTE: Table WORK.TOTALBYID created, with 10 rows and 6 columns.
```

Remerging occurs when any of the following conditions exist:

- The values returned by a summary function are used in a calculation.

- The `select` clause specifies a column that contains a summary function and other columns that are not listed in a `group by` clause.

- The `having` clause specifies one or more columns or column expressions that are not included in a subquery or a `group by` clause.

During remerging, `proc sql` makes two passes through the table:

- It calculates and returns the value of summary functions. It also groups data according to the `group by` clause.

- It retrieves any additional columns and rows that it needs to display in the output, and uses the result from the summary function to calculate any arithmetic expressions in which the summary function participates.

The following code block triggers the remerging log:

```
/* Find total count and fees by ID */
proc sql;
create table TotalByID as
select
   ID
  ,sex
  ,date
  ,fee
  ,count(*) as TotalCount
  ,sum(fee) as TotalFees
from visits
group by
   ID
;
quit;
```

This query returns the total row count and the total fee for each unique ID, yet it also returns all the individual rows for sex, date, and fee. This is typically not allowed in most other database engines. For example, Microsoft Transaction SQL will issue an error message similar to the following:

```
Column 'sex', 'date', 'fee' are invalid in the select list because they are
not contained in either an aggregate function or the GROUP BY clause.
```

This is the reason for the error message. The group by clause is evaluated before the select clause. It divides the rows from the incoming table into groups, with each group having a unique combination of the group by values. The select clause will query these groups, returning only one row for each group. The row returned consists of unique characteristics of that group, such as the group count, the group sum, and the group by values.

In most RDBMS, the select clause can not return values that are not the characteristics of a group. In Program 9.2.1, different values of sex, date, and fee may exist within each pID group. Since only one row is returned from each pID group, sex, date, or fee can not be returned.

However, as an enhancement, the SAS implementation of SQL allows you to select columns not listed in the group by clause when there's a summary function. Behind the scenes, SAS first returns the group characteristics specified by the summary function and the group by clause, as do most other database engines. While most other database engines stop here, SAS starts the second pass, retrieving additional columns not listed in the group by clause and merging these additional columns with the group characteristics retrieved from the first pass.

Even though SAS lets you remerge summary statistics to the original data, mixing the aggregate result with individual rows can generate misleading results.

Program 9.3.1 *remergePitfall.sas*

```
1    dm log 'clear'; dm output 'clear';
2    data sales;
3    employee='John'; sales=100; output;
4    employee='Mary'; sales=200; output;
5    employee='Mark'; sales=300; output;
6    employee='Jane'; sales=400; output;
7    run;
8
9    proc sql;
10     title 'Total sales by employee';
11     select
12       employee
13       ,sum(sales) as Sales
14   from sales;
15   quit;
```

Output:

Total sales by employee

employee	Sales
John	1000
Mary	1000
Mark	1000
Jane	1000

It appears that every employee has the same total sales amount. If your SQL generates a nonsensical result, one possible culprit is that you are combing the aggregate result with individual row values.

However, remerging the aggregate result with individual rows can be useful sometimes.

Program 9.3.2 *remergeUseful.sas*

```
1    dm log 'clear'; dm output 'clear';
2    data sales;
3    employee='John'; sales=100; output;
4    employee='Mary'; sales=200; output;
5    employee='Mark'; sales=300; output;
6    employee='Jane'; sales=400; output;
7    run;
8
9    proc sql;
10     title 'Total sales percentage by employee';
11     select
12       employee
13       ,sales/sum(sales) as SalesPercent
14   from sales;
15   quit;
```

Output:

Total sales percentage by employee

employee	SalesPercent
John	0.1
Mary	0.2
Mark	0.3
Jane	0.4

The next program also remerges summary statistics back to the original data:

Program 9.3.3 *remerge.sas*

```
1   dm log 'clear'; dm output 'clear';
2   data treatment;
3   /*pId=patient ID, dID=doctor ID */
4   input pID dID fee;
5   datalines;
6   1 10 1
7   1 10 5
8   1 20 3
9   2 10 2
10  2 10 6
11  2 20 4
12  3 10 1
13  ;
14  run;
15
16  proc sql;
17  create table treatmentSummary as
18  select
19   pID
20  ,dID
21  ,fee
22  ,sum(fee) as totalFee
23  from treatment
24  group by pID
25  order by pID, dID
26  ;
27  quit;
28
29  proc print data=treatmentSummary;
30   title 'treatmentSummary with remmerging';
31  run;
```

Output:

treatmentSummary with remmerging

Obs	pID	dID	fee	total Fee
1	1	10	5	9
2	1	10	1	9
3	1	20	3	9
4	2	10	2	12
5	2	10	6	12
6	2	20	4	12
7	3	10	1	1

The next program accomplishes the same without using remerging. This is what most other database engines will do.

Program 9.3.4 *remergeAlternative.sas*

```
1    dm log 'clear'; dm output 'clear';
2    data treatment;
3    /*pId=patient ID, dID=doctor ID */
4    input pID dID fee;
5    datalines;
6    1 10 1
7    2 10 2
8    1 20 3
9    2 20 4
10   1 10 5
11   2 10 6
12   3 10 1
13   ;
14   run;
15
16   /* Method 1 - use join*/
17   proc sql;
18   create table sumBYpID as
19   select
20    pID
21   ,sum(fee) as feeBYpID
22   from treatment
23   group by pID
24   ;
25
26   create table treatmentSummary2 as
27   select a.*, b.feeBYpID
28   from treatment a, sumBYpID b
29   where a.pID=b.pID
30   order by pID, dID
31   ;
32   quit;
33
34   /* Method 2- use subquery */
35   proc sql;
36   create table treatmentSummary3 as
37   select a.*, b.feeBYpID
38   from treatment a,
39   (
40     select
41     pID,sum(fee) as feeBYpID
42     from treatment
43     group by pID
44   )
45   as b
46   where a.pID=b.pID
47   order by pID, dID
48   ;
49   quit;
50
51   proc print data=treatmentSummary2;
52    title 'treatmentSummary2 without remmerging';
53   run;
54
55   proc print data=treatmentSummary3;
56    title 'treatmentSummary3 without remmerging';
57   run;
```

Output:

treatmentSummary2 without remmerging

Obs	pID	dID	fee	fee BYpID
1	1	10	5	9
2	1	10	1	9
3	1	20	3	9
4	2	10	6	12
5	2	10	2	12
6	2	20	4	12
7	3	10	1	1

treatmentSummary3 without remmerging

Obs	pID	dID	fee	fee BYpID
1	1	10	5	9
2	1	10	1	9
3	1	20	3	9
4	2	10	6	12
5	2	10	2	12
6	2	20	4	12
7	3	10	1	1

9.4   Method 3 - PROC SORT, PROC MEANS

SAS procedures can also be used to find subtotals and identify duplicates.

9.5   PROC SORT Nodupkey Dupout

SAS version 9 added the `dupout=` option to `proc sort`. Here's how to find the duplicate IDs using the `dupout=` option.

Program 9.5.1 *visitsSASv9.sas*

```
1   dm log 'clear'; dm output 'clear';
2   data visits;
3   input
4     ID
5     sex $
6     date
7   ;
8
9   datalines;
10   8   M   0
11   4   F   1
12   2   F   2
13   10  M   3
14   4   F   4
15   3   F   5
16   8   M   6
17   4   F   7
18   2   F   8
19   2   F   9
20   ;
21   run;
22
23   proc print data=visits;
24     title 'Patient visits in 1960';
25     format date mmddyy10.;
26   run;
27
28   proc sort data=visits out=IDfirstOccurrence nodupkey
29     dupout=IDotherOccurrence;
30     by id;
31   run;
32
33   proc print data=IDfirstOccurrence;
34     title 'Only 1st occurrence of an ID is kept';
35     format date mmddyy10.;
36   run;
37
38   proc print data=IDotherOccurrence;
39     title 'Other occurrence of an ID is kept';
40     format date mmddyy10.;
41   run;
```

Output:

Patient visits in 1960

Obs	ID	sex	date
1	8	M	01/01/1960
2	4	F	01/02/1960
3	2	F	01/03/1960
4	10	M	01/04/1960
5	4	F	01/05/1960
6	3	F	01/06/1960
7	8	M	01/07/1960
8	4	F	01/08/1960
9	2	F	01/09/1960
10	2	F	01/10/1960

Only 1st occurrence of an ID is kept

Obs	ID	sex	date
1	2	F	01/03/1960
2	3	F	01/06/1960
3	4	F	01/02/1960
4	8	M	01/01/1960
5	10	M	01/04/1960

Other occurrence of an ID is kept

Obs	ID	sex	date
1	2	F	01/09/1960
2	2	F	01/10/1960
3	4	F	01/05/1960
4	4	F	01/08/1960
5	8	M	01/07/1960

In the SORT procedure, the `nodupkey` option checks for and eliminates rows that have duplicate BY variable values (in this case the patient ID). If you specify this option, then PROC SORT compares all BY variable values for each row to those for the previous row written to the output table specified by the **out=** option. If an exact match is found, then the row is not written to the output table specified by the **out=** option but written to the table specified by the **dupout=** option. If the **dupout=** option is not used, then the match is not written to any output table.

If you don't specify the **out=** option, the **out=** option will point to the incoming table specified in the **data=** option, overwriting the incoming table.

Program 9.5.1 writes the following to the log:

```
NOTE: There were 10 observations read from the data set WORK.VISITS.
NOTE: 5 observations with duplicate key values were deleted.
NOTE: The data set WORK.IDFIRSTOCCURRENCE has 5 observations and 3 variables.
NOTE: The data set WORK.IDOTHEROCCURRENCE has 5 observations and 3 variables.
```

PROC SORT isn't perfect, though. The duplicate IDs are listed in two tables: **IDfirstOccurrence** and **IDotherOccurrence**.

9.6 PROC MEANS

Program 9.6.1 *visitsProcMeans.sas*

```
1   dm log 'clear'; dm output 'clear';
2   title;
3   data visits;
4   input ID sex $ date fee;
5
6   datalines;
7    8  M  0 20
8    4  F  1 10
9    2  F  2 30
10  10  M  3 20
11   4  F  4 10
12   3  F  5 50
13   8  M  6 40
14   4  F  7 30
15   2  F  8 20
16   2  F  9 10
17  ;
18  run;
19
20  proc means data=visits;
21  var fee;   /* variable to be analyzed*/
22  class ID;  /* similar to GROUP BY ID in SQL */
23  output out=visitsSummary; /*specifies the output table*/
24  run;
25
26  proc print data=visitsSummary;
27   title 'visits Summary';
28  run;
29
30  *not print result of proc means in the log;
31  proc means data=visits noprint;
32  var fee;
```

```
33   class ID;
34   output out=visitsSum sum=totalFee;
35   run;
36
37   proc print data=visitsSum;
38     title 'visitSum';
39   run;
```

This is the output:

The MEANS Procedure

Analysis Variable : fee

ID	N Obs	N	Mean	Std Dev	Minimum	Maximum
2	3	3	20.0000000	10.0000000	10.0000000	30.0000000
3	1	1	50.0000000	.	50.0000000	50.0000000
4	3	3	16.6666667	11.5470054	10.0000000	30.0000000
8	2	2	30.0000000	14.1421356	20.0000000	40.0000000
10	1	1	20.0000000	.	20.0000000	20.0000000

visits Summary

Obs	ID	_TYPE_	_FREQ_	_STAT_	fee
1	.	0	10	N	10.0000
2	.	0	10	MIN	10.0000
3	.	0	10	MAX	50.0000
4	.	0	10	MEAN	24.0000
5	.	0	10	STD	13.4990
6	2	1	3	N	3.0000
7	2	1	3	MIN	10.0000
8	2	1	3	MAX	30.0000
9	2	1	3	MEAN	20.0000
10	2	1	3	STD	10.0000
11	3	1	1	N	1.0000
12	3	1	1	MIN	50.0000
13	3	1	1	MAX	50.0000
14	3	1	1	MEAN	50.0000
15	3	1	1	STD	.
16	4	1	3	N	3.0000
17	4	1	3	MIN	10.0000
18	4	1	3	MAX	30.0000
19	4	1	3	MEAN	16.6667
20	4	1	3	STD	11.5470
21	8	1	2	N	2.0000
22	8	1	2	MIN	20.0000
23	8	1	2	MAX	40.0000
24	8	1	2	MEAN	30.0000
25	8	1	2	STD	14.1421

```
26    10    1    1    N      1.0000
27    10    1    1    MIN   20.0000
28    10    1    1    MAX   20.0000
29    10    1    1    MEAN  20.0000
30    10    1    1    STD      .
```

visits Sum

Obs	ID	_TYPE_	_FREQ_	total Fee
1	.	0	10	240
2	2	1	3	60
3	3	1	1	50
4	4	1	3	50
5	8	1	2	60
6	10	1	1	20

PROC MEANS creates the two special variables _TYPE_ and _STAT_. _TYPE_=0 gives us the summary statistics for the table as a whole. _TYPE_=1 gives us the summary statistics for each ID group. The _STAT_ variable indicates the types of summary statistics generated by MEANS procedure. N is the count; min is the minimum; max is the maximum; mean is the mean; and std is the standard deviation.

The visitsSum table generated by the MEANS procedure lists the count and the total fee by ID.

Proc sort and proc means are two of the most useful SAS procedures. With a few lines of code, you can generate many summary statistics about a table. The downside, however, is the complexity. This is especially true for proc means, which has a large number of options.

9.7   Find Duplicates and Running Subtotals by Two Variables

The following table lists patient visits to their doctors.

Fees of doct visits in 1960

patientID	sex	date	doctID	fee
8	M	01/01/1960	7	88
4	F	01/02/1960	6	67
2	F	01/03/1960	3	59
10	M	01/04/1960	1	96
4	F	01/05/1960	6	68
3	F	01/06/1960	4	62
8	M	01/07/1960	5	90
4	F	01/08/1960	6	70
2	F	01/09/1960	3	57
2	F	01/10/1960	4	60

We need to find:

- unique patients

- unique combinations of patients and doctors

- which patients have only one visit

- subtotal of visits and fees for visits, grouped by patient and by doctor

9.7.1 Method 1 - DATA step

Program 9.7.1 *visitFees.sas*

```
1   dm log 'clear'; dm output 'clear';
2   data visitFees;
3   input patientID sex $ date doctID fee;
4
5   datalines;
6    8   M   0   7   88
7    4   F   1   6   67
8    2   F   2   3   59
9   10   M   3   1   96
10   4   F   4   6   68
11   3   F   5   4   62
12   8   M   6   5   90
13   4   F   7   6   70
14   2   F   8   3   57
15   2   F   9   4   60
16   ;
17   run;
18
19   proc print data=visitFees;
20     title 'Fees of doct visits in 1960';
21     format date mmddyy10. fee dollar4.;
22   run;
23
24   proc sort data=visitFees out=visitFeesSorted;
25      by patientID doctID;
26   run;
27
28   /* visitFeesSorted2 stores first and last variables */
29   data visitFeesSorted2 (rename=(patientID=pID doctID=dID));
30
31   /* use retain to reorder variables*/
32   retain patientID doctID sex date fee
33          firstP lastP firstD lastD;
34
35   set visitFeesSorted;
36   by patientID doctID;
37
38   firstP=first.patientID; lastP=last.patientID;
39   firstD=first.doctID;    lastD=last.doctID;
40   run;
41
42   /* find count/fee by patient and by doctor*/
43   data VisitByPatientDoct;
44   retain patientID doctID sex date fee CountBy2IDs FeeBy2IDs;
45   set visitFeesSorted;
46
47   CountBy2IDs+1;
48   FeeBy2IDs + fee;
```

```
49   by patientID doctID;
50
51   if first.patientID=1 or first.doctID=1 then
52     do;
53       CountBy2IDs=1;
54       FeeBy2IDs=fee;
55     end;
56   run;
57
58   /* get distinct P, PDcombo (hard to find distinct D here)*/
59   data distinctP distinctPDcombo oneVisit;
60   set visitFeesSorted2;
61
62   if firstP=1              then output distinctP;
63   /* if lastP=1; will also retreive distinct patient IDs, but
64   the date and fee column might be different and that's OK. */
65
66   if firstD=1              then output distinctPDcombo;
67   /* if lastD=1; also yields distinct doct ID*/
68
69   if firstP=1 and lastP=1 then output oneVisit;
70   /* Patient has only 1 visit */
71   run;
72
73   %macro export2csv(sourceTable);
74   proc export
75   data=&sourceTable
76   outfile="C:\LearnSAS\&sourceTable..csv"
77   dbms=csv
78   replace
79   ;
80   run;
81   %mend;
82
83   %export2csv(visitFeesSorted2);
84   %export2csv(distinctP);
85   %export2csv(distinctPDcombo);
86   %export2csv(oneVisit);
87   %export2csv(VisitByPatientDoct);
```

If you use SAS in the cloud, change the `outfile` statement to:

`outfile="/home/userid/myProgram/&sourceTable..csv";`

In the second DATA step, the incoming table `visitFeesSorted` is pre-sorted by `patientID` and `doctID`. The `by patientID doctID` statement creates four temporary variables:

`first.patientID, last.patientID, first.doctID,` and `last.doctID`

These temporary variables are saved into four new DATA variables respectively:

`firstP, lastP, firstD,` and `lastD`

This program contains a macro `%export2csv(sourceTable)` to reduce the repetitive coding of PROC EXPORT. The macro is explained in Chapter 11.

Submit the program. This is the `visitFeesSorted2.csv` file. The `pID` column determines `firstP` and `lastP`. However, `firstD` and `lastD` are determined not by `dID` alone, but by `pID` and `dID` jointly.

pID	dID	sex	date	fee	firstP	lastP	firstD	lastD
2	3	F	2	59	1	0	1	0
2	3	F	8	57	0	0	0	1
2	4	F	9	60	0	1	1	1
3	4	F	5	62	1	1	1	1
4	6	F	1	67	1	0	1	0
4	6	F	4	68	0	0	0	0
4	6	F	7	70	0	1	0	1
8	5	M	6	90	1	0	1	1
8	7	M	0	88	0	1	1	1
10	1	M	3	96	1	1	1	1

This is the `distinctP.csv` file. The `pID` column has all the possible distinct values. The indicator is `firstP=1`. Alternatively, you can use the indicator `lastP=1` to get the same distinct combinations.

pID	dID	sex	date	fee	firstP	lastP	firstD	lastD
2	3	F	2	59	1	0	1	0
3	4	F	5	62	1	1	1	1
4	6	F	1	67	1	0	1	0
8	5	M	6	90	1	0	1	1
10	1	M	3	96	1	1	1	1

This is the `distinctPDcombo.csv` file listing the distinct patient/doctor combinations; the indicator is `firstD=1`. Alternatively, you can use the indicator `lastD=1` to get the same distinct doctor IDs.

pID	dID	sex	date	fee	firstP	lastP	firstD	lastD
2	3	F	2	59	1	0	1	0
2	4	F	9	60	0	1	1	1
3	4	F	5	62	1	1	1	1
4	6	F	1	67	1	0	1	0
8	5	M	6	90	1	0	1	1
8	7	M	0	88	0	1	1	1
10	1	M	3	96	1	1	1	1

This is the `oneVisit.csv` listing the patients with only 1 visit; the indicator is `firstP=1` and `lastP=1`:

pID	dID	sex	date	fee	firstP	lastP	firstD	lastD
3	4	F	5	62	1	1	1	1
10	1	M	3	96	1	1	1	1

This is the `VisitByPatientDoct.csv` listing the running total of the number of visits and of the fees by patient/doctor combination:

patientID	doctID	sex	date	fee	CountBy2IDs	FeeBy2IDs
2	3	F	2	59	1	59
2	3	F	8	57	2	116
2	4	F	9	60	1	60
3	4	F	5	62	1	62
4	6	F	1	67	1	67
4	6	F	4	68	2	135
4	6	F	7	70	3	205
8	5	M	6	90	1	90
8	7	M	0	88	1	88
10	1	M	3	96	1	96

9.7.2 Method 2 - PROC SQL

Program 9.7.2 *visitFeesSQL.sas*

```
1   dm log 'clear'; dm output 'clear';
2   data visitFees;
3   input patientID sex $ date doctID fee;
4
5   datalines;
6    8  M  0  7  88
7    4  F  1  6  67
8    2  F  2  3  59
9   10  M  3  1  96
10   4  F  4  6  68
11   3  F  5  4  62
12   8  M  6  5  90
13   4  F  7  6  70
14   2  F  8  3  57
15   2  F  9  4  60
16  ;
17  run;
18
19  /* Find total count and fees by patientID, doctID */
20  proc sql;
21  create table TotalBy2IDs as
22  select
23    patientID
24   ,doctID
25   ,sex
26   ,date
27   ,fee
28   ,count(*) as TotalCount
29   ,sum(fee) as TotalFees
30  from visitFees
31  group by
32    patientID
33   ,doctID
34  ;
```

```
35   quit;
36
37   /* method 1- find dup/nodup if you have count by 2 IDs*/
38   proc sql;
39   create table Dup2IDs as
40   select *
41   from TotalBy2IDs
42   where TotalCount>1;
43
44   create table Unique2IDs as
45   select *
46   from TotalBy2IDs
47   where TotalCount=1;
48   quit;
49
50   /* method 2- find dup/nodup if you have count by 2 IDs*/
51   data Unique2IDs  Dup2IDs;
52   set TotalBy2IDs;
53   if TotalCount>1 then output Dup2IDs;
54   else output Unique2IDs;
55   run;
56
57   /* Find running total. Step 1 - generate v1v2 table */
58   proc sql;
59   create table vf1vf2 as
60   select
61       vf1.*
62      ,vf2.fee as fee2
63   from visitFees as vf1, visitFees as vf2
64   where
65       vf1.patientID = vf2.patientID
66    and vf1.doctID = vf2.doctID
67    and vf1.fee >= vf2.fee
68
69   order by
70       patientID
71      ,doctID
72      ,fee
73      ,fee2
74   ;
75   quit;
76
77   /* Find running total. Step 2 - get running total */
78   proc sql;
79   create table By2IDsRTotal as
80   select
81       patientID
82      ,doctID
83      ,fee
84      ,count(*)  as RCount
85      ,sum(fee2) as RTotal
86   from vf1vf2
87   group by
88       patientID
89      ,doctID
90      ,fee
91   ;
92   quit;
```

Program 9.7.2 creates six tables in the work library. This is the visitFees table:

patientID	sex	date	doctID	fee
8	M	0	7	88
4	F	1	6	67
2	F	2	3	59
10	M	3	1	96
4	F	4	6	68
3	F	5	4	62
8	M	6	5	90
4	F	7	6	70
2	F	8	3	57
2	F	9	4	60

This is the TotalBy2IDs table:

patientID	doctID	sex	date	fee	TotalCount	TotalFees
2	3	F	2	59	2	116
2	3	F	8	57	2	116
2	4	F	9	60	1	60
3	4	F	5	62	1	62
4	6	F	4	68	3	205
4	6	F	1	67	3	205
4	6	F	7	70	3	205
8	5	M	6	90	1	90
8	7	M	0	88	1	88
10	1	M	3	96	1	96

This is the Unique2IDs table:

patientID	doctID	sex	date	fee	TotalCount	TotalFees
2	4	F	9	60	1	60
3	4	F	5	62	1	62
8	5	M	6	90	1	90
8	7	M	0	88	1	88
10	1	M	3	96	1	96

This is the Dup2IDs table:

patientID	doctID	sex	date	fee	TotalCount	TotalFees
2	3	F	2	59	2	116
2	3	F	8	57	2	116
4	6	F	4	68	3	205
4	6	F	1	67	3	205
4	6	F	7	70	3	205

This is the `vf1vf2` table:

patientID	sex	date	doctID	fee	fee2
2	F	8	3	57	57
2	F	2	3	59	57
2	F	2	3	59	59
2	F	9	4	60	60
3	F	5	4	62	62
4	F	1	6	67	67
4	F	4	6	68	67
4	F	4	6	68	68
4	F	7	6	70	67
4	F	7	6	70	68
4	F	7	6	70	70
8	M	6	5	90	90
8	M	0	7	88	88
10	M	3	1	96	96

This is the `By2IDsRTotal` table:

patientID	doctID	fee	RCount	RTotal
2	3	57	1	57
2	3	59	2	116
2	4	60	1	60
3	4	62	1	62
4	6	67	1	67
4	6	68	2	135
4	6	70	3	205
8	5	90	1	90
8	7	88	1	88
10	1	96	1	96

9.8   Further Reading

Step-by-Step Programming with Base SAS Software, Chapter 11, *Working with Grouped or Sorted Observations.*

SAS 9.3 SQL Procedure Users Guide, Chapter 6, *Chapter 6 Practical Problem-Solving with PROC SQL*

The Power of the BY Statement

`http://www2.sas.com/proceedings/forum2007/222-2007.pdf`

Dealing with Duplicates in Your Data

`http://www.mwsug.org/proceedings/2011/sas101/MWSUG-2011-S111.pdf`

Chapter 10

Combine Tables

In a real world project, often you need to combine multiple tables into one. The next program combines two tables P and T in different ways and creates three tables: PT, PTv2, and PTv3.

The PT table is created via two SET statements. This operation is called 1-to-1 read, which combines tables horizontally.

The PTv2 table is created via a SET list (e.g. multiple tables are listed in one SET statement). This operation is called concatenating tables, that is, appending one table to the end of another to produce a taller table.

The PTv3 table is created via a MERGE statement without a BY statement. This operation is called 1-to-1 merge. 1-to-1 merge works exactly the same as 1-to-1 read except that the output table created by 1-to-1 merge contains all the rows from all the participating tables.

Program 10.0.1 *combinePT.sas*

```
1   dm log 'clear'; dm output 'clear';
2   data P; /* Patient table */
3   input name$ sex$ @10 dob mmddyy10.;
4   format dob mmddyy10.;
5   datalines;
6   Adam    M 01/01/1994
7   Betty   F 04/18/1984
8   Carl    M 09/24/1987
9   Dennis F 03/25/1983
10  ;
11  run;
12
13  data T; /* Treatment table */
14  input name$ @8 date mmddyy10. fees;
15  format date mmddyy10.;
16  datalines;
17  Adam    04/15/2011 50
18  Easter 03/16/2011 60
19  Betty   10/08/2011 80
20  ;
21  run;
22
23  /* PT Table (set P; set T;) */
24  data PT;
25  set P;
26  set T;
27  if sex='M' then sex_id=1;
28  else sex_id=2;
29  run;
30
31  /* PTv2 Table (set P T;) */
32  data PTv2;
33  set P T;
34      if sex=' ' then sex_id=.;
35  else if sex='M' then sex_id=1;
36  else             sex_id=2;
37  run;
38
39  /* PTv3 Table (merge P T;) */
40  data PTv3;
41  merge P T;
42      if sex=' ' then sex_id=.;
43  else if sex='M' then sex_id=1;
44  else             sex_id=2;
45  run;
46
47  options linesize=min nonumber nodate;
48  proc print data=P noobs;
49   title 'P table';
50  proc print data=T noobs;
51   title 'T table';
52  proc print data=PT noobs;
53   title 'PT table (set P; set T;)';
54  proc print data=PTv2 noobs;
55   title 'PTv2 table (set P T;)';
56  proc print data=PTv3 noobs;
57   title 'PTv3 table (merge P T;)';
58   run;
```

Output:

P table

name	sex	dob
Adam	M	01/01/1994
Betty	F	04/18/1984
Carl	M	09/24/1987
Dennis	F	03/25/1983

T table

name	date	fees
Adam	04/15/2011	50
Easter	03/16/2011	60
Betty	10/08/2011	80

PT table (set P; set T;)

name	sex	dob	date	fees	sex_id
Adam	M	01/01/1994	04/15/2011	50	1
Easter	F	04/18/1984	03/16/2011	60	2
Betty	M	09/24/1987	10/08/2011	80	1

PTv2 table (set P T;)

name	sex	dob	date	fees	sex_id
Adam	M	01/01/1994			1
Betty	F	04/18/1984			2
Carl	M	09/24/1987			1
Dennis	F	03/25/1983			2
Adam			04/15/2011	50	.
Easter			03/16/2011	60	.
Betty			10/08/2011	80	.

PTv3 table (merge P T;)

name	sex	dob	date	fees	sex_id
Adam	M	01/01/1994	04/15/2011	50	1
Easter	F	04/18/1984	03/16/2011	60	2
Betty	M	09/24/1987	10/08/2011	80	1
Dennis	F	03/25/1983			2

10.1 Combine Tables Horizontally: 1-to-1 Read

You perform 1-to-1 read using the following DATA step template:

```
data widerShorterTable;
set dataSource1;
set dataSource2;
...
set dataSourceN;
/* additional processing */
run;
```

1-to-1 read combines the first row from each participating table into the first row in the new table, the second row from each participating table into the second row in the new table, and so on, till SAS has read in the last row from the smallest table. The DATA step stops after it has read the last row from the smallest table. The number of rows in the output table is equal to the smallest number of rows among all the contributing tables.

In 1-to-1 read, the output table contains all of the columns from each contributing table. If the contributing tables have a same-named column, the column value that is read from a later table overwrites the value that was read in from an earlier table.

During the compilation phase, SAS reads the descriptor information of each contributing table and creates the PDV that contains all the variables from each contributing table and the variables created in the DATA step:

```
-----------------------------------------------------------
|_N_ |_ERROR_| name | sex |  dob  | d  | fees | sex_id |
-----------------------------------------------------------
|    |       |      |     |       |    |      |        |
-----------------------------------------------------------
```

Next, the DATA step executes. During the first iteration of the DATA step, the `set P` statement reads the first row from P into the PDV. In addition, the assignment statement is executed, creating the variable `sex_id`.

```
-----------------------------------------------------------
|_N_ |_ERROR_| name | sex |  dob  | d  | fees | sex_id |
-----------------------------------------------------------
| 1  |   0   | Adam |  M  | 12419 | .  |  .   |   .    |
-----------------------------------------------------------
```

12419 is the SAS integer date for 01/01/1994.

Next, the `set T` statement reads the first row from T into PDV, with `Adam` read in from T overwriting `Adam` in the PDV:

```
-----------------------------------------------------------
|_N_ |_ERROR_| name | sex |  dob  |  d   | fees | sex_id |
-----------------------------------------------------------
| 1  |   0   | Adam |  M  | 12419 |18732 |  50  |   1    |
-----------------------------------------------------------
```

18732 is the SAS integer date for 4/15/2011.

At the end of the first iteration, variables in the PDV are written to the output table PT.

During the second iteration, the set P statement reads the second row from P into PDV. Next, the set T statement reads the second row from T into PDV, with Easter read from T overwriting Betty in the PDV.

During the third iteration, Betty read from T overwrites Carl read from P.

The fourth iteration starts. SAS detects that there's no more row to be read from T. The DATA step terminates.

Clearly, the second and third rows of PT contain wrong results.

1-to-1 read is best suited for the following situation. Table 1 Row 1 contains facts about a subject (we call Subject 1 for convenience). Table 2 Row 1 contains additional facts about Subject 1 that is not contained in Table 1 Row 1. Or Table 2 Row 1 corrects some mistakes in Table 1 Row 1 by providing updated facts. Similarly, Table 3 Row 1 contains additional facts about Subject 1 that is not contained in Table 1 or Table 2; or it corrects the mistakes in Table 1 or Table 2 by providing updated facts about Subject 1. And so on. Then 1-to-1 read will combine all the facts about the same subject from the same row from all the contributing tables into one row in the output table.

```
data totalFacts;
set Table1;
set Table2;
  ...
set TableN;
/* additional processing */
run;
```

If two participating tables have the same-named column, the table containing the newer fact should be listed after the table containing the outdated fact to allow the newer fact to overwrite the older fact in the combined table. If you reverse the order and place the older fact table after the newer fact table, the older fact will overwrite the newer fact in the combined table, generating wrong results.

1-to-1 read will also generate wrong results when the same row in multiple contributing tables contains facts about different subjects. This is the case in Program 10.0.1.

The next program illustrates another common mistake when 1-to-1 read is performed. The ID column is numeric in one contributing table but character in another. SAS generates an error log in the compilation phase and stops processing.

Program 10.1.1 *one2oneReadIncompatibleVar.sas*

```
1  dm log 'clear'; dm output 'clear';
2  data T1;
3  input ID var1$;
4  datalines;
5  1 a
6  2 b
```

```
7    ;
8    run;
9
10   data T2;
11   input ID$ var2$;
12   datalines;
13   1 aa
14   2 bb
15   ;
16   run;
17
18   data T1T2;
19   set T1;
20   set T2;
21   run;
```

SAS writes the following message to the log:

```
ERROR: Variable ID has been defined as both character and numeric.

NOTE: The SAS System stopped processing this step because of errors.

WARNING: The data set WORK.T1T2 may be incomplete.  When this step
         was stopped there were 0 observations and 3 variables.
```

In 1-to-1 read, if the same-named column has different lengths, labels, formats, or informats, SAS takes the attribute from the first contributing table that contains the column with that attribute.

Program 10.1.2

one2oneReadDiffAttribute.sas

```
1   dm log 'clear'; dm output 'clear';
2   data A;
3   label x ='VarX';
4   x='abc';
5   run;
6
7   data B;
8   label x ='Xvar';
9   x='vwxyz';
10  run;
11
12  data C1;
13  set A;
14  set B;
15  run;
16
17  data C2;
18  set B;
19  set A;
20  run;
21
22  proc print data=C1 label;
23    title 'C1 table';
24  run;
25
26  proc print data=C2 label;
27    title 'C2 table';
28  run;
29
30  proc contents data=C1;
31    title 'C1 table';
32  run;
33
34  proc contents data=C2;
35    title 'C2 table';
36  run;
```

Output:

```
                    C1 table
                Obs      VarX
                 1        vwx

                    C2 table
                Obs      Xvar
                 1        abc

                      C1 table
                 The CONTENTS Procedure
       -----Alphabetic List of Variables and Attributes-----
         #    Variable    Type    Len   Pos    Label
         ----------------------------------------------
         1    x           Char     3     0     VarX

                      C2 table
                 The CONTENTS Procedure
       -----Alphabetic List of Variables and Attributes-----
         #    Variable    Type    Len   Pos    Label
         ----------------------------------------------
         1    x           Char     5     0     Xvar
```

A and B have different lengths and labels for x. Column x is 3 character wide in A but 5 character wide in B; it is nicknamed VarX in A but Xvar in B.

In the 1-to-1 read to create the table C1, the set A statement appears before the set B statement. Hence A determines the length and the label of x in C1, causing x in C1 to have length 3 and be nicknamed VarX. The x value from B overwrites the x value from A. SAS truncates the string vwxyz to fit the length 3 of x in C1, producing a 3 character literal string vwx.

However, in the 1-to-1 read to create the table C2, the set B statement appears before the set A statement. Hence B determines the length and the label of x in C2, causing x in C2 to have length 5 and be nicknamed Xvar. The x value from B overwrites the x value from A. Though x in C2 appears to be a 3 character string abc, it is actually a 5 character string, consisting of abc and two trailing blanks.

10.2   Combine Tables Vertically: Concatenate Tables

You concatenate multiple tables using the following DATA step template:

```
data widerTallerTable;
set dataSource1
    dataSource2
      ...
    dataSourceN
    ;
/* additional processing */
run;
```

When you concatenate tables, you append the second table to the end of the first table, the third table to end of the second table, and so on, creating a wider and taller output table. Wider because the output table contains all of the columns from each contributing table. Taller because the number of rows in the output table is the sum of the number of rows in each contributing table.

The compilation phase in concatenation works exactly the same as in 1-to-1 read. During the compilation phase, SAS reads the descriptor information of the contributing table in the SET statement and creates a PDV that contains the variables from all the contributing tables as well as the variables created by the DATA step.

The execution phase in concatenation is different from that in 1-to-1 read. When you concatenate tables, during the execution phase, SAS reads the first row from the first contributing table into the PDV, executes all the statements in the DATA step, and writes the contents of the PDV to the output table. This process continues till there are no more rows to be read from the first participating table.

Next, SAS reads the first row from the second contributing table into the PDV, executes all the statements in the DATA step, and writes the contents of the PDV to the output table. This process continues till there are no more rows to be read from the second participating table.

This pattern continues till SAS reads in the last row from the last participating table.

Similar to when you perform 1-to-1 read, when you concatenate tables, if a same-named column is numeric in one participating table but character in another participating table, SAS stops processing the DATA step and issues an error message in the compile phase stating that the two columns are incompatible. In addition, if the same-named column has different lengths, labels, formats, or informats, SAS takes the attribute from the first contributing table that contains the column with that attribute.

Concatenating tables is frequently used in practice. For example, if you perform the same analysis each month throughout a year, you can create the annual result by concatenating the 12 monthly results:

```
data annualResult;
set JanResult
    FebResult
      ...
    DecResult
    ;
```

```
/* additional processing */
run;
```

Before you concatenate multiple tables, it's best that you make the all the contributing tables alike. The columns in one contributing table should exactly match the columns in any other contributing table in data type, length, and other attributes. This way, you don't have to worry about a common concatenation error that the same-named column is numeric in one table but character in another; nor do you need to worry about having a messy concatenation because the same-named columns have different lengths among different contributing tables.

10.3   1-to-1 Merge

You perform 1-to-1 merge using the following DATA step template:

```
data widerAsTallAsTheTallestTable;
merge dataSource1
      dataSource2
      ...
      dataSourceN
      ;
/* additional processing */
run;
```

1-to-1 merge combines the first row from all the tables in the MERGE statement into the first row in the new table, the second row from all the tables into the second row in the new table, and so on. In 1-to-1 merge, the number of rows in the new table equals the number of rows in the largest table in the MERGE statement.

1-to-1 merge works exactly the same as 1-to-1 read except for one difference. In 1-to-1 read, the DATA step stops processing after it has read in the last row from the smallest participating table. However, in 1-to-1 merge, the DATA step continues processing until it has read in all the rows from all the participating tables.

Similar to 1-to-1 read, in 1-to-1 merge, when a same-named column is numeric in one participating table but character in another, SAS stops processing the DATA step and issues an error message in the compile phase stating that the two columns are incompatible. If the same-named column has the same data type, the value read from a later table will overwrite the value read from an earlier table, possibly leading to wrong results. Finally, if the same-named column has different lengths, labels, formats, or informats, SAS takes the attribute from the first contributing table that contains the column with that attribute.

10.4   PROC APPEND as an Alternative to Concatenation

If two tables contain the same-named columns and the columns have the same attributes, you can use PROC APPEND as an alternative to the SET list.

Program 10.4.1 *procAppendTables.sas*

```
1    dm log 'clear'; dm output 'clear';
2    data P1; /*P=patient*/
3    input name $ sex $ @10 dob mmddyy10. ;
4    format dob mmddyy10.;
5    datalines;
6    Adam    M 01/01/1994
7    Betty   F 04/18/1984
8    ;
9    run;
10
11   proc print data=P1;
12     title 'This is the old P1.';
13   run;
14
15   data P2; /*P=patient*/
16   input name $ sex $ @10 dob mmddyy10. ;
17   format dob mmddyy10.;
18   datalines;
19   Carl    M 09/24/1987
20   Dennis F 03/25/1983
21   Mark    M 10/01/1989
22   ;
23   run;
24
25   proc print data=P2;
26     title 'This is P2.';
27   run;
28
29   proc append base=P1 data=P2;
30   run;
31   proc print data=P1;
32     title 'This is the new P1 (old P1 + P2).';
33   run;
```

Output:

This is the old P1.

Obs	name	sex	dob
1	Adam	M	01/01/1994
2	Betty	F	04/18/1984

This is P2.

Obs	name	sex	dob
1	Carl	M	09/24/1987
2	Dennis	F	03/25/1983
3	Mark	M	10/01/1989

This is the new P1 (old P1 + P2).

Obs	name	sex	dob
1	Adam	M	01/01/1994
2	Betty	F	04/18/1984
3	Carl	M	09/24/1987
4	Dennis	F	03/25/1983
5	Mark	M	10/01/1989

This is the log:

```
NOTE: Appending WORK.P2 to WORK.P1.
NOTE: There were 3 observations read from the dataset WORK.P2.
NOTE: 3 observations added.
NOTE: The data set WORK.P1 has 5 observations and 3 variables.
NOTE: PROCEDURE APPEND used:
      real time            0.01 seconds
      cpu time             0.01 seconds
```

The next program uses a SET list to concatenate P1 and P2:

Program 10.4.2 `concatenatTables.sas`

```
data P1P2;
set P1 P2;
run;

proc print data=P1P2;
 title 'Concatenate P1 and P2.';
run;
```

Output:

Concatenate P1 and P2.

Obs	name	sex	dob
1	Adam	M	01/01/1994
2	Betty	F	04/18/1984
3	Carl	M	09/24/1987
4	Dennis	F	03/25/1983
5	Mark	M	10/01/1989

This is the log:

```
NOTE: There were 2 observations read from the dataset WORK.P1.
NOTE: There were 3 observations read from the dataset WORK.P2.
NOTE: The data set WORK.P1P2 has 5 observations and 3 variables.
NOTE: DATA statement used:
      real time           0.01 seconds
      cpu time            0.01 seconds
```

The P1P2 table is identical to the updated P1 table generated by Program 10.4.1.

What's the advantage of PROC APPEND over a SET list? To concatenate two large tables, PROC APPEND can be much faster. This is because only the rows in the `data=` table are read and added to the end of the `base=` table. The rows in the `base=` table are not read at all.

In contrast, when encountering a SET list, SAS sequentially reads in each row from each contributing table into the PDV.

The difference is confirmed by the log generated by Program 10.4.1:

```
NOTE: There were 3 observations read from the dataset WORK.P2.
```

In contrast, the log generated by Program 10.4.2 says the following:

```
NOTE: There were 2 observations read from the dataset WORK.P1.
NOTE: There were 3 observations read from the dataset WORK.P2.
```

What's the downside of PROC APPEND? First, a SET list in a DATA step allows you to concatenate multiple tables, while PROC APPEND can concatenate only two tables at a time. Second, a SET list lets you do additional processing in the DATA step, while PROC APPEND only appends one table to the end of another.

If all the contributing tables have the same columns with the same attributes, then PROC APPEND and the SET list produce the same output table. However, when the columns in the two contributing tables are not alike, then the two methods may produce different results. One needs to understand the subtleties in each method to determine which method to use.

PROC APPEND has a FORCE option:

```
proc append base=baseTable data=tableToAdd force;
run;
```

You use the FORCE option when the DATA= table contains variables that

- are not in the BASE= table

- do not have the same type as the variables in the BASE= table

- are longer than the variables in the BASE= table

However, using the FORCE option can cause loss of data due to truncation or dropping of variables. Refer to the SAS documentation on the FORCE option.

Program 10.4.1 is efficient but it overwrites the P1 table. The next program uses PROC APPEND without overwriting any participating table.

Program 10.4.3 *procAppendTables2.sas*

Output:

```
1   proc sql;
2   create table P1P2 like P1;
3   quit;
4
5   proc append base=P1P2 data=P1;
6   run;
7
8   proc append base=P1P2 data=P2;
9   run;
10
11  proc print data=P1P2;
12    title 'P1P2 created by PROC APPEND.';
13  run;
```

```
P1P2 created by PROC APPEND.

Obs     name    sex       dob

 1      Adam     M     01/01/1994
 2      Betty    F     04/18/1984
 3      Carl     M     09/24/1987
 4      Dennis   F     03/25/1983
 5      Mark     M     10/01/1989
 6      Carl     M     09/24/1987
 7      Dennis   F     03/25/1983
 8      Mark     M     10/01/1989
```

The `create table P1P2 like P1` statement creates an empty P1P2 which is just like P1. The P1P2 table has the same column names and column attributes as the P1 table.

10.5 Concatenate Multiple Tables

You can use a SET list or PROC APPEND to concatenate many tables. If your participating tables have similar names like `table1`, `table2`,...,`tableN`, you can concatenate all your tables without manually listing all the participating tables.

The next program concatenates three tables A1, A2, and A3 using three methods. The first method uses a dataset list, which was introduced in SAS 9.2. The other two methods use SAS macros and are good for all SAS versions.

How a SAS macro works in general is to be explained in Chapter 11.

Program 10.5.1 *concatenateManyTables.sas*

```
1   dm log 'clear'; dm output 'clear';
2   data A1;
3   x=1;
4   run;
5
6   data A2;
7   x=2;
8   run;
9
10  data A3;
11  x=3;
12  run;
13
14  /*concatenate A1 A2 A3.*/
15  /* Method 1 - use dataset list -good for SAS 9.2+*/
16  data bigTable;
17  set A1-A3; /*dataset list new in SAS 9.2*/
18  run;
19
20  /* Method 2 - SET list and macro - for any SAS versions*/
21  %macro combine(N);
22  %do i=1 %to &N;
23    A&i
24  %end;
25  %mend;
26
27  data bigTable;
28  set %combine(3)
29  ;
30  run;
31
32  /* Method 3 - PROC APPEND and macro - for any SAS versions*/
33  proc sql;
34  create table bigTable like A1;
35  quit;
36
37  %macro appendMany(N);
38  %do i=1 %to &N;
39   proc append base=bigTable data=A&i;
40   run;
41  %end;
42  %mend;
43  %appendMany(3)
```

Newly created bigTable:

```
 x
---
 1
 2
 3
```

10.6   Interleave Tables

The next program illustrates two other ways to combine tables: interleaving and match merging.

Program 10.6.1
interleaveMatchMergePT.sas

```
1   dm log 'clear'; dm output 'clear';
2   data P; /* Patient table*/
3   input
4     name $ sex $
5     @10 dob mmddyy10.
6     ;
7   format dob mmddyy10.;
8   datalines;
9   Adam    M 01/01/1994
10  Betty   F 04/18/1984
11  Carl    M 09/24/1987
12  Dennis  F 03/25/1983
13  ;
14  run;
15
16  data T; /*Treatment table*/
17  input
18    name $
19    @8 date mmddyy10.
20    fees
21    ;
22  format date mmddyy10.;
23  datalines;
24  Adam    04/15/2011 50
25  Adam    05/08/2011 70
26  Adam    06/20/2011 60
27  Easter  03/16/2011 60
28  Betty   10/08/2011 80
29  ;
30  run;
31
32  proc sort data=P out=Psorted;
33    by name;
34  proc sort data=T out=Tsorted;
35    by name;
36  /* interleaving*/
37  data PTinterleave;
38  set Psorted Tsorted;
39  by name;
40      if sex=' ' then sex_id=.;
41  else if sex='M' then sex_id=1;
42  else            sex_id=2;
43  run;
44
45  /* match merge */
46  data PTmatchMerge;
47  merge Psorted Tsorted;
48  by name;
49      if sex=' ' then sex_id=.;
50  else if sex='M' then sex_id=1;
51  else            sex_id=2;
52  run;
53
54  options linesize=min nonumber nodate;
55  proc print data=Psorted noobs;
56   title 'Psorted table';
57  proc print data=Tsorted noobs;
58   title 'Tsorted table';
59  proc print data=PTinterleave noobs;
60   title 'PTinterleave table';
61  proc print data=PTmatchMerge noobs;
62   title 'PTmatchMerge table';
63  run;
```

Output:

Psorted table

name	sex	dob
Adam	M	01/01/1994
Betty	F	04/18/1984
Carl	M	09/24/1987
Dennis	F	03/25/1983

Tsorted table

name	date	fees
Adam	04/15/2011	50
Adam	05/08/2011	70
Adam	06/20/2011	60
Betty	10/08/2011	80
Easter	03/16/2011	60

PTinterleave table

name	sex	dob	date	fees	sex_id
Adam	M	01/01/1994	.	.	1
Adam		.	04/15/2011	50	.
Adam		.	05/08/2011	70	.
Adam		.	06/20/2011	60	.
Betty	F	04/18/1984	.	.	2
Betty			10/08/2011	80	.
Carl	M	09/24/1987	.	.	1
Dennis	F	03/25/1983	.	.	2
Easter			03/16/2011	60	.

PTmatchMerge table

name	sex	dob	date	fees	sex_id
Adam	M	01/01/1994	04/15/2011	50	1
Adam	M	01/01/1994	05/08/2011	70	1
Adam	M	01/01/1994	06/20/2011	60	1
Betty	F	04/18/1984	10/08/2011	80	2
Carl	M	09/24/1987	.	.	1
Dennis	F	03/25/1983	.	.	2
Easter			03/16/2011	60	.

The DATA step to create the `PTinterleave` table uses a SET list and a BY statement to interleave (e.g. intersperse) rows from two or more tables, based on the common BY variables.

You interleave multiple tables using the following DATA step template:

```
data mixRowsByCommonKey;
set    dataSource1sorted
       dataSource2sorted
       ...
       dataSourceNsorted
       ;
by     ...;
/* additional processing */
run;
```

Interleaving tables is similar to concatenating tables except the output table is already sorted by the BY variables. The number of rows in the new table created by interleaving is the sum of the number of rows in all the contributing tables.

Interleaving concatenates tables within each BY group. SAS chops up each participating table into BY groups and concatenates the same BY group rows from each table.

This is how interleaving works. Before executing the SET statement, SAS reads the descriptor portion of each table in the SET statement and creates a PDV that contains all the variables from all the participating tables as well as any variables created by the DATA step.

SAS sets the value of each variable to missing. It then looks at the first BY group in each table in the SET statement to determine which BY group should appear first in the output table. SAS copies to the output table all the rows in that BY group from each contributing table that contains rows in the BY group. SAS copies from the participating tables in the same order as they appear in the SET statement.

SAS looks at the next BY group in each table to determine which BY group should appear next in the output table. SAS sets the value of each variable in the PDV to missing.

This process continues until all the rows from all the participating tables are inserted to the output table.

Interleaving can be achieved by first concatenating the participating tables and then sorting the resulting table.

Program 10.6.2

concatenateAndSortPT.sas

Output:

```
1    data PT;
2    set P T;
3        if sex=' ' then sex_id=.;
4    else if sex='M' then sex_id=1;
5    else                sex_id=2;
6    run;
7
8    proc sort data=PT out=PTinterleave2;
9      by name;
10   run;
11
12   options linesize=min nonumber nodate;
13   proc print data=PTinterleave2 noobs;
14     title 'PTinterleave2 table';
15   run;
```

PTinterleave2 table

name	sex	dob	date	fees	sex_id
Adam	M	01/01/1994	.	.	1
Adam		.	04/15/2011	50	.
Adam		.	05/08/2011	70	.
Adam		.	06/20/2011	60	.
Betty	F	04/18/1984	.	.	2
Betty		.	10/08/2011	80	.
Carl	M	09/24/1987	.	.	1
Dennis	F	03/25/1983	.	.	2
Easter		.	03/16/2011	60	.

The `PTinterleave2` table created by Program 10.6.2 and the `PTinterleave` table created by Program 10.6.1 are identical.

What's the benefit of interleaving tables? If your participating tables are already sorted by a common key, interleaving will create a new table that is already sorted by the common key. This is more efficient than the concatenate-and-sort method.

10.7   Match-Merge

The last DATA step in Program 10.6.1 uses a match-merge.

A match-merge combines rows from two or more SAS tables into a single row in a new table. The number of rows in the new table is the sum of the largest number of rows in each BY group in all the participating tables.

To perform a match-merge, use the MERGE statement with a BY statement.

Before you can perform a match-merge, all the participating tables must be sorted by the variables that you specify in the BY statement or they must have an index.

Indexes are not covered in this book. Interested readers can consult the SAS documentation.

DATA step processing during a match-merge

Compilation phase   SAS reads the descriptor information of each table that is named in the MERGE statement and creates a PDV that contains all the variables from all the tables as well as the variables created by the DATA step. SAS creates the FIRST.variable and LAST.variable for each variable listed in the BY statement.

Execution - Step 1   SAS looks at the first BY group in each table named in the MERGE statement to determine which BY group should appear first in the new table. The DATA step reads into the PDV the first row in that BY group from each table. The tables are read in the order in which they appear in the MERGE statement. If a table does not have any rows in that BY group, the PDV contains missing values for the variables unique to that table.

Execution - Step 2   After processing the first row from the last table and executing other statements, SAS writes variables in the PDV to the new table. SAS retains the values of all the variables in the PDV except those created by the DATA step; SAS sets those values to missing. SAS continues to merge rows until it writes all the rows from the first BY group to the new table. When SAS has read all the rows in a BY group from all the tables, it sets all the variables in the PDV to missing. SAS looks at the next BY group in each table to determine which BY group should appear next in the new table.

Execution - Step 3   SAS repeats these steps until it reads all the rows from all the BY groups in all the tables.

To predict the number of rows in the new table created by a match-merge, you need to predict the number of rows in each BY group in the new table. The number of rows of a given BY group in the new table is the largest number of rows of that BY group in all the participating tables.

The total number of rows in the new table is the sum of the number of rows of all the BY groups in the new table.

Program 10.7.1 *matchMergeAB.sas*

```
1   dm log 'clear'; dm output 'clear';
2   data A;
3   input id var1$;
4   datalines;
5   1    a
6   1    b
7   2    c
8   3    d
9   4    e
10  5    f
11  ;
12  run;
13
14  data B;
15  input id var2$;
16  datalines;
17  1   aa
18  2   bb
19  3   cc
20  3   dd
21  4   ee
22  5   ff
23  ;
24  run;
25
26  /*A and B already sorted by ID*/
27  data AB;
28  merge A B;
29  by id;
30  run;
31
32  proc print data=AB;
33    title 'Match-merge A and B by id';
34  run;
```

Output:

Match-merge A and B by id

Obs	id	var1
1	1	aa
2	1	b
3	2	bb
4	3	cc
5	3	dd
6	4	ee
7	5	ff

In Program 10.7.1, A and B each have 5 rows, but AB has 7 rows. For id=1, A has a larger row count 2. For id=3, B has a larger row count 2. For id=1,4,5, A and B each have only one row. The total number of rows in AB is $2 + 2 + 1 + 1 + 1 = 7$.

10.8 Common Pitfalls in Match-Merge

Program 10.8.1 *matchMergePitfall.sas*

```
1   dm log 'clear'; dm output 'clear';
2   data one;
3   input id v1;
4   datalines;
5   1 10
6   2 20
7   ;
8   run;
9
10  data two;
11  input id v2;
12  datalines;
13  1 1
14  1 2
15  1 3
16  2 4
17  3 5
18  ;
19  run;
20
21  data three;
22  merge one two;
23  by id;
24
25  v1=v1*2;
26  run;
27
28  options linesize=min nonumber nodate;
29  proc print data=one;
30   title 'Table one';
31  run;
32  proc print data=two;
33   title 'Table two';
34  run;
35  proc print data=three;
36  title 'Table three (merge one two; by id;)';
37  run;
```

Output:

Table one

Obs	id	v1
1	1	10
2	2	20

Table two

Obs	id	v2
1	1	1
2	1	2
3	1	3
4	2	4
5	3	5

Table three (merge one two; by id;)

Obs	id	v1	v2
1	1	20	1
2	1	40	2
3	1	80	3
4	2	40	4
5	3	.	5

Surprisingly, the first three rows of v1 in the work.three table are 20, 40, and 80, not 20, 20, and 20. What happened?

For id=1, there exists a 1-to-3 relationship between work.one table and work.two table. When match-merging work.one and work.two for i=1, SAS reads in v1=10 only once into the PDV yet it has to build three rows of v1 in work.three. The only way for SAS to do this is to retain v1 in the PDV while it builds the first three rows of work.three.

Indeed, variables that are read by a match-merge are automatically retained across iterations of the DATA step within the same BY group. In the third DATA step in Program 10.8.1, during the first iteration, the statement v1=v1*2 executes and v1 is updated to 20. SAS writes v1=20 to the output table work.three and retains v1=20 in the PDV.

During the second iteration of the DATA step, the statement v1=v1*2 executes and v1 is updated to 40. SAS writes v1=40 to the output table work.three and retains v1=40 in the PDV.

During the third iteration of the DATA step, the statement v1=v1*2 executes and v1 is updated to 80. SAS writes v1=80 to the output table work.three.

The fourth iteration of the DATA step works on a new BY group, id=2. Since this is a new BY group, SAS reads in v1=20 from work.one into the PDV. The statement v1=v1*2 executes and v1 is updated to 40. SAS writes v1=40 to the output table work.three.

The fifth iteration of the DATA step works on a new BY group, id=3. Since this is a new BY group and there's no v1 variable in work.one, SAS sets v1 to missing.

The next match-merge program generates a surprising result too.

Program 10.8.2
matchMergePitfall2.sas

```
1   dm log 'clear'; dm output 'clear';
2   data one;
3   input id1 id2 v1;
4   datalines;
5   1 2 10
6   1 2 30
7   ;
8   run;
9
10  data two;
11  input id1 id2 v2;
12  datalines;
13  1 2 100
14  1 2 200
15  1 2 300
16  ;
17  run;
18
19  data three;
20  merge one two;
21  by id1 id2;
22
23  v1=v1*2;
24  run;
25
26  options linesize=min nonumber nodate;
27  proc print data=one;
28    title 'Table one';
29  run;
30  proc print data=two;
31    title 'Table two';
32  run;
33  proc print data=three;
34    title 'Table three (merge one two; by id;)';
35  run;
```

Output:

Table one

Obs	id1	id2	v1
1	1	2	10
2	1	2	30

Table two

Obs	id1	id2	v2
1	1	2	100
2	1	2	200
3	1	2	300

Table three (merge one two; by id;)

Obs	id1	id2	v1	v2
1	1	2	20	100
2	1	2	60	200
3	1	2	120	300

For the joint key id1=1 and id2 = 2, there exists a 2-to-3 relationship between work.one and work.two. The output table work.three created by the match-merge contains three rows of v1, yet only two rows of v1 exist in work.one. As a result, the ending value v1=60 during the second iteration of the DATA step becomes the beginning value of v1 during the third iteration. Then v1=60 is updated to v1=120 at the end of the third iteration of the DATA step.

When you perform an m-to-n match-merge (where $m < n$) by a common key between Table A (which has the key m times) and Table B (which has the key n times), a non-key variable v1 from A is read in m times yet SAS has to write v1 n times to the output table. If you have any DATA step statements that alters v1, then the $(m + 1)$-th, $(m + 2)$-th, ..., n-th values of v1 in the output table may be misleading because v1 is retained in the PDV. Understanding this pattern is key to avoiding the common pitfall seen in Programs 10.8.1 and 10.8.2.

One way to avoid such a pitfall is to avoid any additional processing in a match-merge and create a separate DATA step to perform any additional processing. This may seem drastic, but it's better to be verbose but correct than to be terse but wrong. For example, Program 10.8.1 can be correctly rewritten as:

Program 10.8.3
matchMergePitfallAvoided.sas

```
1   dm log 'clear'; dm output 'clear';
2   data one;
3   input id v1;
4   datalines;
5   1 10
6   2 20
7   ;
8   run;
9
10  data two;
11  input id v2;
12  datalines;
13  1 1
14  1 2
15  1 3
16  2 4
17  3 5
18  ;
19  run;
20
21  data three;
22  merge one two;
23  by id;
24  run;
25
26  data four;
27  set three;
28  v1=v1*2;
29  run;
30
31  options linesize=min nonumber nodate;
32  proc print data=one;
33    title 'Table one';
34  run;
35
36  proc print data=two;
37    title 'Table two';
38  run;
39
40  proc print data=three;
41    title 'Table three (merge one two; by id;)';
42  run;
43
44  proc print data=four;
45    title 'Table four';
46  run;
```

Output:

Table one

Obs	id	v1
1	1	10
2	2	20

Table two

Obs	id	v2
1	1	1
2	1	2
3	1	3
4	2	4
5	3	5

Table three (merge one two; by id;)

Obs	id	v1	v2
1	1	10	1
2	1	10	2
3	1	10	3
4	2	20	4
5	3	.	5

Table four

Obs	id	v1	v2
1	1	20	1
2	1	20	2
3	1	20	3
4	2	40	4
5	3	.	5

Another way to avoid the pitfall is to avoid directly manipulating any original variable that is read from any participating tables in a match-merge and create new variables for data manipulation. This works because variables created via the assignment statement are not retained in the PDV. Program 10.8.1 can be correctly rewritten as:

Program 10.8.4

matchMergePitfallAvoided2.sas

```
1    dm log 'clear'; dm output 'clear';
2    data one;
3    input id v1;
4    datalines;
5    1 10
6    2 20
7    ;
8    run;
9
10   data two;
11   input id v2;
12   datalines;
13   1 1
14   1 2
15   1 3
16   2 4
17   3 5
18   ;
19   run;
20
21   data three;
22   merge one two;
23   by id;
24   v3=v1;
25   v3=v3*2;
26   run;
27
28   options linesize=min nonumber nodate;
29   proc print data=one;
30    title 'Table one';
31   run;
32
33   proc print data=two;
34    title 'Table two';
35   run;
36
37   proc print data=three;
38    title 'Table three (merge one two; by id;)';
39   run;
```

Output:

Table one

Obs	id	v1
1	1	10
2	2	20

Table two

Obs	id	v2
1	1	1
2	1	2
3	1	3
4	2	4
5	3	5

Table three (merge one two; by id;)

Obs	id	v1	v2	v3
1	1	10	1	20
2	1	10	2	20
3	1	10	3	20
4	2	20	4	40
5	3	.	5	.

10.9   In A only, in B only, in A and in B

In practice often we encounter this situation. Two tables employee1 and employee2 have a common key, empID. We want to know whether an empID that exists in one table also exists in the other. Similarly, two Order Details tables have the same common composite key Order ID and Customer ID to uniquely identify each row of the two tables. We want to know whether a combination of an Order ID and a Customer ID that exists in one table also exists in the other.

Generally, A and B have a common key. We want to determine, for all the keys that exist in at least one of the two tables:

- which keys are in A but not in B

- which keys are in B but not in A

- which keys are in both A and B

There are at least two ways to do this, by a match-merge or by PROC SQL.

10.9.1   Method 1 - Match Merge

Program 10.9.1

compareABbyMatchMerge.sas

Output (reformatted to fit the page):

```
1   data A;
2   input id var1 $;
3   datalines;
4   4 d
5   5 e
6   9 f
7   1 a
8   1 b
9   2 b
10  3 c
11  ;
12  data B;
13  input id var2 $;
14  datalines;
15  5 ee
16  8 ff
17  2 bb
18  3 cc
19  3 dd
20  8 gg
21  ;
22
23  proc sort data=A; by id; run;
24  proc sort data=B; by id; run;
25
26  data ABmerged InAnotInB InBnotInA InAInB;
27  merge A(in=x) B(in=y); by id;
28  inA=x; inB=y; output ABmerged;
29  if inA=1 then
30   do;
31     if inB=1 then output inAInB;
32     else output inAnotInB;
33   end;
34  else output inBnotInA;
35  run;
36
37  options linesize=min nonumber nodate;
38  proc print data=A;
39   title 'A sorted by id';
40  proc print data=B;
41   title 'B sorted by id';
42  proc print data=ABmerged;
43   title 'A merge B by id';
44  proc print data=InAnotInB;
45   title 'ID in A but not B';
46  proc print data=InBnotInA;
47   title 'ID in B but not A';
48  proc print data=InAInB;
49   title 'ID in A and in B';
50  run;
```

A sorted by id

Obs	id	var1
1	1	a
2	1	b
3	2	b
4	3	c
5	4	d
6	5	e
7	9	f

B sorted by id

Obs	id	var2
1	2	bb
2	3	cc
3	3	dd
4	5	ee
5	8	ff
6	8	gg

A merge B by id

Obs	id	var1	var2	inA	inB
1	1	a		1	0
2	1	b		1	0
3	2	b	bb	1	1
4	3	c	cc	1	1
5	3	c	dd	1	1
6	4	d		1	0
7	5	e	ee	1	1
8	8		ff	0	1
9	8		gg	0	1
10	9	f		1	0

ID in A but not B

Obs	id	var1	var2	inA	inB
1	1	a		1	0
2	1	b		1	0
3	4	d		1	0
4	9	f		1	0

ID in B but not A

Obs	id	var1	var2	inA	inB
1	8		ff	0	1
2	8		gg	0	1

ID in A and in B

Obs	id	var1	var2	inA	inB
1	2	b	bb	1	1
2	3	c	cc	1	1
3	3	c	dd	1	1
4	5	e	ee	1	1

Look at the core logic where A and B are merged. Here's how the `in=` dataset option in parentheses after a SAS dataset name in MERGE statement works. Values of `in=` variables are available to program statements during the DATA step, but the variables are not included in the SAS dataset that is being created, unless they are assigned to new variables.

When you use `in=` with BY-group processing, the `in=` value is 1 if a dataset contributes an observation to the current BY group; the `in=` value is 0 if a data set does not contribute an observation to the current BY group. In addition, the `in=` value remains as long as that BY group is still being processed and the value is not reset by programming logic.

In the statement `merge A(in=x) B(in=y)`, the `in=` option creates two temporary DATA step variables `x` and `y` to keep track of whether the BY variable `id` is present in Table A and Table B. For a given `id`,

- If an `id` is in A and B, then `x=1;y=1`.

- If an `id` is in A but not in B, then `x=1;y=0`.

- If an `id` is not in A but in B, then `x=0;y=1`.

Though the temporary variables `x` and `y` are not written to any output table, we preserve their values by assigning them to two new variables `inA` and `inB`.

The next program finds which patient ID is in the P table or the T table or both.

Program 10.9.2
comparePTbyMatchMerge.sas

```
1   dm log 'clear'; dm output 'clear';
2   data P; /*P=patient*/
3   input id sex $ dob mmddyy10. ;
4   format dob mmddyy10.;
5   datalines;
6   7 M 02/02/1981
7   8 F 03/25/1983
8   1 F 04/26/1987
9   3 F 07/01/1991
10  ;
11  run;
12
13  data T; /*T=treatment*/
14  input id date mmddyy10.;
15  format date mmddyy10.;
16  datalines;
17  3 01/12/2011
18  7 11/24/2011
19  9 09/18/2011
20  7 12/20/2011
21  ;
22  run;
23
24  /*sort each table by common key*/
25  proc sort data=P; by id; run;
26  proc sort data=T; by id; run;
27
28  data PTmatchMerge Ponly Tonly Both;
29  merge P(in=a) T(in=b);
30  by id;
31
32  inP=a; inT=b;
33  output PTmatchMerge;
34
35  if inP=1 then do;
36     if inT=1 then output Both;
37     else          output Ponly;
38  end;
39
40  else output Tonly;
41  run;
42
43  option linesiz=min nonumber nodate;
44  proc print data=P noobs;
45    title 'Patient table sorted by ID';
46  proc print data=T noobs;
47    title 'Treatment table sorted by ID';
48  proc print data=PTmatchMerge noobs;
49    title 'P and T match-merge result';
50  proc print data=Ponly noobs;
51    title 'ID in P but not in T';
52  proc print data=Tonly noobs;
53    title 'ID in T but not in P';
54  proc print data=Both noobs;
55    title 'ID in P and in T';
56  run;
```

Output:

Patient table sorted by ID

id	sex	dob
1	F	04/26/1987
3	F	07/01/1991
7	M	02/02/1981
8	F	03/25/1983

Treatment table sorted by ID

id	date
3	01/12/2011
7	11/24/2011
7	12/20/2011
9	09/18/2011

P and T match-merge result

id	sex	dob	date	inP	inT
1	F	04/26/1987	.	1	0
3	F	07/01/1991	01/12/2011	1	1
7	M	02/02/1981	11/24/2011	1	1
7	M	02/02/1981	12/20/2011	1	1
8	F	03/25/1983	.	1	0
9		.	09/18/2011	0	1

ID in P but not in T

id	sex	dob	date	inP	inT
1	F	04/26/1987	.	1	0
8	F	03/25/1983	.	1	0

ID in T but not in P

id	sex	dob	date	inP	inT
9		.	09/18/2011	0	1

ID in P and in T

id	sex	dob	date	inP	inT
3	F	07/01/1991	01/12/2011	1	1
7	M	02/02/1981	11/24/2011	1	1
7	M	02/02/1981	12/20/2011	1	1

10.9.2   Method 2 - PROC SQL

Program 10.9.3 *ABcompareSQL.sas*

```
1   dm log 'clear'; dm output 'clear';
2   data A;
3   input id var1 $;
4   datalines;
5   4 d
6   5 e
7   9 f
8   1 a
9   1 b
10  2 b
11  3 c
12  ;
13
14  data B;
15  input id var2 $;
16  datalines;
17  5 ee
18  8 ff
19  2 bb
20  3 cc
21  3 dd
22  8 gg
23  ;
24
25  /* ID in A but not in B*/
26  proc sql;
27  title 'ID in A but not in B';
28  create table InANotInB as
29  select A.*
30  from A left join B on A.id=B.id
31  where B.id is missing;
32  select * from InANotInB;
33
34  /* ID in B but not in A*/
35  proc sql;
36  title 'Id in B but not in A';
37  create table InBNotInA as
38  select B.*
39  from B left join A on B.id=A.id
40  where A.id is missing;
41  select * from InBNotInA;
42
43  /* ID in B but not in A*/
44  title 'ID in A and in B';
45  create table InAInB as
46  select A.*, B.var2
47  from A, B
48  where A.id=B.id;
49  select * from InAInB;
50  quit;
```

Output:

```
ID in A but not in B
--------------------
      id   var1
       1   b
       1   a
       4   d
       9   f


ID in B but not in A
--------------------
      id   var2
       8   gg
       8   ff


 ID in A  and in B
------------------
id  var1      var2
 5   e         ee
 2   b         bb
 3   c         cc
 3   c         dd
```

Let's see how Program 10.9.3 finds the IDs that are in A but not in B. Run the following query:

Program 10.9.4 *ALeftJoinB.sas*

Output:

```
1  dm log 'clear'; dm output 'clear';
2  proc sql;
3  title;
4  select A.*, B.*
5  from A
6  left join B
7  on A.id=B.id
8  ;
9  quit;
```

id	var1	id	var2
1	a	.	
1	b	.	
2	b	2	bb
3	c	3	cc
3	c	3	dd
4	d	.	
5	e	5	ee
9	f	.	

A left join B returns all the rows from the left table A plus all the matching rows from the right table B. From this query result, filter out all the rows that don't have matches in B (e.g. all the rows where B.id is missing) and you'll get all the IDs that are in A but not in B.

The is null or is missing operator selects observations in which the value of a variable is missing.

Opposite to A left join B is A right join B, which returns all the rows from the right table B plus any matching rows from the left table A.

By the way, A left join B is equivalent to B right join A. We can also build InANotInB using the following right join:

```
/* find ID in A but not in B using right join*/
proc sql;
title 'find ID in A but not in B using right join';
create table InANotInB as
select A.*
from B
right join A
on B.id=A.id
where B.id is missing;
;

select * from InANotInB;
quit;
```

Output:

Find ID in A but not in B using right join

id	var1
1	a
1	b
4	d
9	f

Here's the SQL counterpart of Program 10.9.2:

Program 10.9.5 *comparePTsql.sas*

```
1   dm log 'clear'; dm output 'clear';
2   data P; /*P=patient*/
3   input id sex $ dob mmddyy10. ;
4   format dob mmddyy10.;
5   datalines;
6   7 M 02/02/1981
7   8 F 03/25/1983
8   1 F 04/26/1987
9   3 F 07/01/1991
10  ;
11  run;
12
13  data T; /*T=treatment*/
14  input id date mmddyy10.;
15  format date mmddyy10.;
16  datalines;
17  3 01/12/2011
18  7 11/24/2011
19  9 09/18/2011
20  7 12/20/2011
21  ;
22  run;
23
24  /*No need to pre-sort P or T if using SQL*/
25  /* ID in P but not in T*/
26  proc sql;
27  title 'ID in P but not in T';
28  create table Ponly as
29  select P.*
30  from P left join T on P.id=T.id
31  where T.id is missing;
32  select * from Ponly;
33
34  /* ID in T but not in P*/
35  title 'Id in T but not in P';
36  create table Tonly as
37  select T.*
38  from T
39  left join P on T.id=P.id
40  where P.id is missing;
41  select * from Tonly;
42
43  /* ID in T but not in P*/
44  proc sql;
45  title 'ID in P and in T';
46  create table Both as
47  select P.*, T.date
48  from P, T
49  where P.id=T.id;
50  select * from Both;
51  quit;
```

Output:

```
            ID in P but not in T

        id  sex            dob
     -------------------------------
          1   F         04/26/1987
          8   F         03/25/1983
          Id in T but not in P

              id       date
          --------------------
            9   09/18/2011
            ID in P and in T

     id  sex            dob        date
    ------------------------------------------
     7   M         02/02/1981  11/24/2011
     7   M         02/02/1981  12/20/2011
     3   F         07/01/1991  01/12/2011
```

10.9.3 More Ways to Find in A but not in B using SQL

Besides using `left join` or `right join`, we can use `where not exists`, `where not in`, and `except` to compare A and B.

Program 10.9.6

moreSQLwaysToFindAonly.sas

```
1   dm log 'clear'; dm output 'clear';
2   data A;
3   input id var1 $;
4   datalines;
5   4 d
6   5 e
7   9 f
8   1 a
9   1 b
10  2 b
11  3 c
12  ;
13  data B;
14  input id var2 $;
15  datalines;
16  5 ee
17  8 ff
18  2 bb
19  3 cc
20  3 dd
21  8 gg
22  ;
23  /*method 1 - probably the fastest method*/
24  proc sql;
25  title 'In A not in B - A left join B';
26  create table Aonly1 as
27  select A.* from A left join B on A.id=B.id
28  where B.id is missing;
29  select * from Aonly1;
30
31  /*method 2*/
32  title 'In A not in B - where not exists';
33  create table Aonly2 as
34  select A.* from A where not exists
35  (select * from B where A.id=B.id);
36  select * from Aonly2;
37
38  /*method 3*/
39  title 'In A not in B - where not in';
40  create table Aonly3 as
41  select A.* from A where A.id not in
42  (select id from B);
43  select * from Aonly3;
44
45  /*method 4, not as flexible as method 1, 2, 3*/
46  title 'In A not in B - Except all';
47  create table Aonly4 as
48  select A.id from A
49  except all  /*all will return duplicates*/
50  select B.id from B;
51  select * from Aonly4;
52  quit;
```

Output:

```
In A not in B - A left join B

         id  var1
       ------------------
          1   b
          1   a
          4   d
          9   f
In A not in B - where not exists

         id  var1
       ------------------
          4   d
          9   f
          1   a
          1   b
In A not in B - where not in

         id  var1
       ------------------
          4   d
          9   f
          1   a
          1   b
In A not in B - Except all

             id
           --------
              1
              1
              4
              9
```

In Method 2, the `exists` condition is an operator whose right operand is a subquery. The result of an `exists` condition is true if the subquery resolves to at least one row. The result of a **not** `exists` condition is true if the subquery resolves to zero row.

In Method 4, the `except` operator returns rows that result from the first query but not from the second query. `Except` does not return duplicate rows that are unmatched by rows in the second query. Adding `all` keeps any duplicate rows that do not occur in the second query.

If you omit `all` in Method 4, it will return the following result instead:

```
In A not in B - Except all
            id
       --------
             1
             4
             9
```

10.10   Further Reading

Step-by-Step Programming with Base SAS Software, Part 4, *Combining SAS Data Sets*, Chapter 15–18.

SAS 9.3 SQL Procedure Users Guide, Page 91, *Comparing DATA Step Match-Merges with PROC SQL Joins*

MERGING vs. JOINING: Comparing the DATA Step with SQL

http://www2.sas.com/proceedings/sugi30/249-30.pdf

Alternatives to Merging SAS Data Set ... But Be Careful

http://www.ats.ucla.edu/stat/sas/library/nesug99/bt150.pdf

SAS DATA Step Merge A Powerful Tool

http://www.lexjansen.com/nesug/nesug11/ds/ds03.pdf

Passing Along SAS Data SET, MERGE, and UPDATE

http://analytics.ncsu.edu/sesug/2003/IN09-Kuligowski.pdf

Chapter 11

Use the Macro Facility to Automate Repetitive Coding

Most SAS programmers start from DATA step programming and later journey into PROC SQL. However, sooner or later they'll encounter a situation where using the DATA step or PROC SQL requires excessively repetitive code. Reducing repetitive coding leads them to the macro facility.

11.1 Export a SAS Table to Excel

One of the recurring tasks you do as a SAS programmer is to export a SAS table to an Excel spreadsheet. Excel is everywhere. It is used by organizations large and small. End users often want the final result as an Excel file so they can play with the data using a pivot table or generate graphs to put in a PowerPoint presentation. Occasionally you may need to import a user's Excel spreadsheet into a SAS table as your program input.

There are many ways to read in or write to Excel files. If you have SAS/Access to PC Files installed on your computer and are running SAS 9.3 Maintenance Release 1 or higher, the following program is one way to read an Excel file into SAS or write a SAS table to an Excel file.

Program 11.1.1 *readWriteExcel.sas*

```
1   dm log 'clear'; dm output 'clear';
2   data A;
3   do i=1 to 10;
4     output;
5   end;
6   run;
7
8   data B;
9   do j=11 to 20;
10    output;
11  end;
12  run;
13
14  data C;
```

```
15   do k=21 to 30;
16     output;
17   end;
18   run;
19
20   /*
21   Always requires SAS/Access to PC Files module.
22
23   dbms=excel option is new in SAS 9.3M1 (maintenance relase 1).
24   This option doesn't need a driver.
25   Writes to Excel 2010 files. Works on Windows and Unix.
26   */
27   proc export
28   data=A
29   outfile='C:\learnSAS\myexcel.xlsx'
30   dbms=xlsx
31   replace;
32   sheet=A;
33   run;
34
35   proc export
36   data=B
37   outfile='C:\learnSAS\myexcel.xlsx'
38   dbms=xlsx
39   replace;
40   sheet=B;
41   run;
42
43   proc export
44   data=C
45   outfile='C:\learnSAS\myexcel.xlsx'
46   dbms=xlsx
47   replace;
48   sheet=C;
49   run;
50
51   /* Write excel to sas table
52   Always needs SAS/Access to PC Files module.
53   In addition, dbms=xlsx requres SAS 9.3M1
54   */
55   proc import
56   out=work.tableA
57   datafile='C:\learnSAS\myexcel.xlsx'
58   dbms=xlsx
59   replace;
60   sheet='A';
61   getnames=yes;
62   run;
63
64   proc import
65   out=work.tableB
66   datafile='C:\learnSAS\myexcel.xlsx'
67   dbms=xlsx
68   replace;
69   sheet='B';
70   getnames=yes;
71   run;
72
```

```
73  proc import
74  out=work.tableC
75  datafile='C:\learnSAS\myexcel.xlsx'
76  dbms=xlsx
77  replace;
78  sheet='C';
79  getnames=yes;
80  run;
```

If you don't have SAS/Access to PC Files or your SAS version is below 9.3 Maintenance Release 1, you can use SAS in the cloud. SAS in the cloud has the latest version of Base SAS. It also includes SAS/Access to PC Files.

To use SAS in the cloud for Program 11.1.1, change each `outfile` statement from

`outfile='C:\learnSAS\myexcel.xlsx'` to:

`outfile='/home/userid/myProgram/myexcel.xlsx'`

In addition, change each `datafile=` option from

`datafile='C:\learnSAS\myexcel.xlsx'` to

`datafile='/home/userid/myProgram/myexcel.xlsx'`

Remember to replace `userid` with your user ID for SAS in the cloud.

In PROC EXPORT, the `replace` option causes the newly created file to overwrite the existing file with the same name. The `getnames=yes` option specifies that SAS variable names should be generated from the first record in the input file. Use `getnames=no` if the first record in the input file contains data values instead of field names. If you don't specify the `getnames=` option, SAS will automatically set `getnames=yes`.

Under the `getnames=yes` option, if a variable name in the first record in the input file contains special characters that are not valid in a SAS name, such as a blank, SAS converts the character to an underscore.

Instead of exporting a SAS table to an Excel file directly, you can export a table to a plain CSV file and open and save the CSV file as an Excel file. There are many benefits when exporting a table to a CSV file. First, exporting a table is fast because a CSV file is just a plain text file delimited by commas. Secondly, it doesn't require SAS/Access to PC Files. And, finally, it works in all SAS versions so your program is portable.

If you export multiple SAS tables to separate CSV files, you can use non-SAS tools to convert multiple CSV files into separate sheets in one Excel file. You can easily find Perl, Python, or Microsoft PowerShell scripts from the internet that will convert CSV files to an Excel file.

However, if you use SAS to export many tables to CSV files or Excel files, your program will be cluttered with PROC EXPORT steps as shown in the next PC SAS program.

Program 11.1.2 *table2csv.sas*

```
1  dm log 'clear'; dm output 'clear';
2  data table1;
```

```
3    input var1 var2;
4    datalines;
5    1 2
6    3 4
7    5 6
8    ;
9    run;
10
11   data table2;
12   input var3 var4$;
13   datalines;
14   1 a
15   2 b
16   3 c
17   ;
18   run;
19
20   data table3;
21   input var5$ var6$;
22   datalines;
23   x aa
24   y bb
25   z cc
26   ;
27   run;
28
29   proc export
30   data=table1
31   outfile="C:/LearnSAS/table1.csv"
32   dbms=csv
33   replace
34   ;
35   run;
36
37   proc export
38   data=table2
39   outfile="C:/LearnSAS/table2.csv"
40   dbms=csv
41   replace
42   ;
43   run;
44
45   proc export
46   data=table3
47   outfile="C:/LearnSAS/table3.csv"
48   dbms=csv
49   replace
50   ;
51   run;
```

Instead of manually typing three PROC EXPORTs, you can let the macro facility write the SAS code for you.

Program 11.1.3 *table2csvMacro.sas*

```
1    dm log 'clear'; dm output 'clear';
2    data table1;
```

```
3   input var1 var2;
4   datalines;
5   1 2
6   3 4
7   5 6
8   ;
9   run;
10
11  data table2;
12  input var3 var4$;
13  datalines;
14  1 a
15  2 b
16  3 c
17  ;
18  run;
19
20  data table3;
21  input var5$ var6$;
22  datalines;
23  x aa
24  y bb
25  z cc
26  ;
27  run;
28
29  %macro export2csv(sourceTable);
30  proc export
31  data=&sourceTable
32  outfile="C:\LearnSAS\&sourceTable..csv"
33  dbms=csv
34  replace
35  ;
36  run;
37  %mend;
38
39  %export2csv(table1)
40  %export2csv(table2)
41  %export2csv(table3)
```

Program 11.1.3 is equivalent to 11.1.2 but is shorter. It defines a macro `export2csv(sourceTable)`, where the parameter `sourceTable` represents the name of the table to be converted to a CSV file. The ampersand in `&sourceTable` is the value-of operator and the expression `&sourceTable` retrieves the text stored in the macro variable `sourceTable`.

After the macro `export2csv(sourceTable)` is defined, to export Table `xyz` to a CSV file, you write the expression `%export2csv(xyz)` in your code instead of writing the full PROC EXPORT code.

11.2   Macros Generate SAS Source Code

You define a macro using one of the following structures:

```
1   %macro mymacro;
2     myReplacementText
3   %mend;
```

```
1   %macro mymacro;
2     myReplacementText
3   %mend mymacro;
```

The macro facility in SAS is smart text replacement, a scaled-up version of AutoText in Microsoft Word or find-and-replace in Notepad. If you have ever used the AutoText feature in a word processor, you know the convenience of the automatic string find-and-replace. If you find yourself repeatedly typing a block of text such as a long address or a difficult word like Mississippi, you can store the block of text in the word processor and give it a short name. Next time you just type the short name and the word processor automatically replaces the short name with the block of the text of your intention.

The SAS macro facility works the same way. Instead of directly typing myReplacementText, you use a short name mymacro to generate myReplacementText.

Caution. The %macro statement can appear anywhere in a SAS program, except within data lines. In addition, a macro definition cannot contain a CARDS statement, a DATALINES statement, a PARMCARDS statement, or data lines. Use an INFILE statement instead. For details, see http://support.sas.com/kb/43/902.html.

The next program uses the macro generateValuesClause to generate 1,000 values clauses to populate the myNum table.

Program 11.2.1

generateValuesClauseMacro.sas

```
1   dm log 'clear'; dm output 'clear';
2   proc sql;
3   create table myNum
4   (
5     N num
6   );
7   quit;
8
9   %macro generateValuesClause(k);
10    %do i=1 %to &k;
11      values(&i)
12    %end;
13  %mend;
14
15  proc sql;
16  insert into myNum
17  %generateValuesClause(1000)
18  ;
19  quit;
20
21  proc print data=myNum (firstobs=991 obs=1000);
22    title 'The last 10 rows of the myNum table.';
23  run;
```

Output:

The last 10 rows of the myNum table.

Obs	N
991	991
992	992
993	993
994	994
995	995
996	996
997	997
998	998
999	999
1000	1000

In Line 17, the expression %generateValuesClause(1000) generates 1,000 lines of source code:

```
values(1)
values(2)
values(3)
...
values(1000)
```

As the result, the second PROC SQL block (Lines 15–19) is equivalent to:

```
proc sql;
insert into myNum
values(1)
values(2)
values(3)
...
values(1000)
;
quit;
```

The semicolon in Line 18 adds a semicolon in the generated source code after the last values clause `values(1000)`. If you delete Line 18, the second PROC SQL block is equivalent to:

```
proc sql;
insert into myNum
values(1)
values(2)
values(3)
...
values(1000)
quit;
```

Now the `insert into myNum` statement is missing an ending semicolon. Program 11.2.1 will fail. SAS will throw an error in the log similar to this:

```
32    %macro generateValuesClause(k);
33       %do i=1 %to &k;
34          values(&i)
35       %end;
36    %mend;
37
38    proc sql;
39    insert into myNum
40    %generateValuesClause(1000)
NOTE: SCL source line.
41    quit;
      -----
      22  200
ERROR 22-322: Syntax error, expecting one of the following: ;, VALUES.

ERROR 200-322: The symbol is not recognized and will be ignored.

42
NOTE: The SAS System stopped processing this step because of errors.
```

The `quit` statement is underlined and identified as the source of the error. This is why. After the macro `%generateValuesClause(1000)` expands into 1000 value clauses, SAS looks for a semicolon at the end of the value clauses to close the `select into` statement but cannot find it. SAS then looks for a semicolon at the beginning of the next line of code, the `quit` statement. Since the `quit` statement doesn't begin with a semicolon, SAS is unable to close the `select into` statement.

By the way, Lines 17–18 in Program 11.2.1 can be combined into one line:

```
%generateValuesClause(1000);
```

11.2.1   How the Macro Facility Works

To understand how the macro facility works in SAS, let's go through a primitive text find-and-replace example in Notepad. Imagine you need to type the following text (source `http://www.history.com/topics/us-states/mississippi`) in a research paper:

> Mississippi joined the Union as the 20th state in 1817 and gets its name from the Mississippi River, which forms its western border. Early inhabitants of the area that became Mississippi included the Choctaw, Natchez and Chickasaw. Spanish explorers arrived in the region in 1540 but it was the French who established the first permanent settlement in present-day Mississippi in 1699. During the first half of the 19th century, Mississippi was the top cotton producer in the United States, and owners of large plantations depended on the labor of black slaves. Mississippi seceded from the Union in 1861 and suffered greatly during the American Civil War. Despite the abolition of slavery, racial discrimination endured in Mississippi, and the state was a battleground of the Civil Rights Movement in the mid-20th century. In the early 21st century, Mississippi ranked among America's poorest states.

Since the text has many occurrences of the word `Mississippi`, to reduce typing, you decide to use the text `zzz` to represent `Mississippi` and type the following in Notepad:

> zzz joined the Union as the 20th state in 1817 and gets its name from the zzz River, which forms its western border. Early inhabitants of the area that became zzz included the Choctaw, Natchez and Chickasaw. Spanish explorers arrived in the region in 1540 but it was the French who established the first permanent settlement in present-day zzz in 1699. During the first half of the 19th century, zzz was the top cotton producer in the United States, and owners of large plantations depended on the labor of black slaves. zzz seceded from the Union in 1861 and suffered greatly during the American Civil War. Despite the abolition of slavery, racial discrimination endured in zzz, and the state was a battleground of the Civil Rights Movement in the mid-20th century. In the early 21st century, zzz ranked among America's poorest states.

Next, you replace each occurrence of `zzz` with `Mississippi` and turn in your research paper. You have used the text find-and-replace to generate the source text of your research paper.

Similarly, you use the macro facility to generate SAS source code.

Program 11.2.2 *mississippi.sas*

```
590  dm log 'clear'; dm output 'clear';
591
592  %let state=Mississippi;
593  %let joinDate=1817;
594  %let spanishExplorerArrivalDate=1540;
595  %let settlementDate=1699;
596  %let secededDate=1861;
597
598  %macro generateSourceCode;
```

```
599
600   &state joined the Union as the 20th state in &joinDate and gets
601   its name from the &state River, which forms its western border.
602   Early inhabitants of the area that became &state included the
603   Choctaw, Natchez and Chickasaw. Spanish explorers arrived in
604   the region in &spanishExplorerArrivalDate but it was the French
605   who established the first permanent settlement in present-day
606   &state in &settlementDate. During the first half of the 19th
607   century, &state was the top cotton producer in the United
608   States, and owners of large plantations depended on the labor
609   of black slaves. &state seceded from the Union in &secededDate
610   and suffered greatly during the American Civil War. Despite the
611   abolition of slavery, racial discrimination endured in &state,
612   and the state was a battleground of the Civil Rights Movement in
613   the mid-20th century. In the early 21st century, &state ranked
614   among the poorest states in the America.
615
616   %mend;
617
618   %put &state;
Mississippi
619   %put &joinDate;
1817
620   %put &spanishExplorerArrivalDate;
1540
621   %put &settlementDate;
1699
622   %put &secededDate;
1861
623   %put %generateSourceCode
Mississippi joined the Union as the 20th state in 1817 and gets its
name from the Mississippi River, which forms its western border.
Early inhabitants of the area that became Mississippi included the
Choctaw, Natchez and Chickasaw. Spanish explorers arrived in the
region in 1540 but it was the French who established the first
permanent settlement in present-day Mississippi in 1699 During the
first half of the 19th century, Mississippi was the top cotton
producer in the United States, and owners of large plantations
depended on the labor of black slaves. Mississippi seceded from the
Union in 1861 and suffered greatly during the American Civil War.
Despite the abolition of slavery, racial discrimination endured in
Mississippi, and the state was a battleground of the Civil Rights
Movement in the mid-20th century. In the early 21st century,
Mississippi ranked among the poorest states in the America.
```

Line 592 creates a macro variable `state` and assigns it the string `Mississippi`. Since a macro variable holds only a string value, you don't need to enclose `Mississippi` in either single quotes or double quotes before assigning `Mississippi` to a macro variable.

Lines 593–596 create and initialize four additional macro variables.

Lines 598–616 create a macro called `generateSourceCode`.

Line 614. We change the phrase `among America's poorest states` to `among the poorest states in the America`. SAS treats the apostrophe as the single quotation mark and demands you add a matching single quotation mark. It's best to rewrite your code to avoid the apostrophe.

Line 618. The macro PUT statement writes the text stored in the macro variable `state` to the log.

Lines 619–622 write the text stored in the four macro variables to the log.

The macro variable `joinDate` stores the text `1817`, not the number 1817. The same is true for the other macro variables that store a date string.

Line 623. The `%generateSourceCode` expression invokes the macro and retrieves the text stored in the macro. The macro PUT statement writes the retrieved text to the log..

While a macro variable can only hold a constant string, a macro can do much more. It can accept inputs as parameters and generate an output as in Program 11.1.3. It can generate repetitive text using the macro DO-LOOP as in Program 11.2.1 or conditionally generate text using the macro IF-THEN statement as in Program 11.5.1.

While every SAS statement must end with a semicolon, the ending semicolon is optional when you invoke a macro. The two statements below invoke the macro `generateSourceCode`, but the second statement also adds a semicolon to the end of the generated source code:

```
%generateSourceCode
%generateSourceCode; /*adds a semicolon in the source code*/
```

The next program uses the macro facility to generate part of the source code, but the output and the log are surprising:

Program 11.2.3 *mississippi2.sas*

```
1   dm log 'clear'; dm output 'clear';
2
3   %let state=Mississippi;
4   %let secededDate=1861;
5
6   data &state;
7     stateName=&state;
8     whenSeceded=&secededDate;
9   run;
10
11  options nodate nonumber;
12  proc print data=&state;
13    title '&state facts';
14  run;
```

Output:

```
                            &state facts

                       state                      when
             Obs        Name      Mississippi    Seceded

              1           .            .          1861
```

This is part of the log:

```
NOTE: Variable Mississippi is uninitialized.
```

After you submit the program, the macro processor replaces each occurrence of the text `&state` in the code with the text `Mississippi` unless the text `&state` is enclosed in single quotes. SAS, as many other programming languages, uses single quotes to represent the literal string. `'&x'` is a literal ampersand followed by the letter `x`, not the value of the macro variable `x`. The expression `'&state'` means the literal ampersand followed by the text `state` and will not be replaced by the text 'Mississippi'.

However, the unquoted expression `&state` will be replaced by the text `Mississippi`; the double quoted expression `"&state"` will be replaced by `"Mississippi"`.

Similarly, the macro processor will replace each occurrence of the text `&secededDate` with the text `1861`. After the macro processor finishes the text find-and-replace, Program 11.2.3 becomes:

Program 11.2.4 *mississippi2Source.sas*

```
1   dm log 'clear'; dm output 'clear';
2
3   data Mississippi;
4    stateName=Mississippi;
5    whenSeceded=1861;
6   run;
7
8   options nodate nonumber;
9   proc print data=Mississippi;
10   title '&state facts';
11  run;
```

Next, Program 11.2.4 compiles and executes. The variable `stateName` is set to be equal to the value of the variable `Mississippi`, but the variable `Mississippi` is never defined in the DATA step. As a result, SAS defaults both `stateName` and `Mississippi` to be numeric variables and assigns them a missing value.

The next program generates the desired result:

Program 11.2.5 *mississippi3.sas*

```
1   dm log 'clear'; dm output 'clear';
2
3   %let state=Mississippi;
4   %let secededDate=1861;
5
6   data &state;
7    stateName="&state";
8    whenSeceded=&secededDate;
9   run;
10
11  options nodate nonumber;
12  proc print data=&state;
13   title "&state facts";
14  run;
```

Output:

```
               Mississippi facts

                              when
     Obs     stateName      Seceded

      1     Mississippi      1861
```

After you submit Program 11.2.5, the macro processor generates part of the source code. This is the full source code:

Program 11.2.6 *mississippi3Source.sas*

```
1   dm log 'clear'; dm output 'clear';
2
3   data Mississippi;
4    stateName="Mississippi";
```

```
5    whenSeceded=1861;
6    run;
7
8    options nodate nonumber;
9    proc print data=Mississippi;
10     title "Mississippi facts";
11   run;
```

Next, Program 11.2.6 compiles and executes, generating the output.

By the way, suppose Program 11.2.5 Line 8 is changed into:

```
whenSeceded="&secededDate";
```

Now whenSeceded will no longer be a numeric column with length 8 holding the number 1861, but a character column with length 4 holding the string 1861.

The next program uses the macro facility to generate part of the source code of the DATA step.

Program 11.2.7 *mississippi4.sas*

```
1    dm log 'clear'; dm output 'clear';
2
3    %let state=Mississippi;
4    %let joinDate=1817;
5    %let spanishExplorerArrivalDate=1540;
6    %let settlementDate=1699;
7    %let secededDate=1861;
8
9    %macro generateSourceCode;
10
11   &state joined the Union as the 20th state in &joinDate and gets
12   its name from the &state River, which forms its western border.
13   Early inhabitants of the area that became &state included the
14   Choctaw, Natchez and Chickasaw. Spanish explorers arrived in
15   the region in &spanishExplorerArrivalDate but it was the French
16   who established the first permanent settlement in present-day
17   &state in &settlementDate. During the first half of the 19th
18   century, &state was the top cotton producer in the United
19   States, and owners of large plantations depended on the labor
20   of black slaves. &state seceded from the Union in &secededDate
21   and suffered greatly during the American Civil War. Despite the
22   abolition of slavery, racial discrimination endured in &state,
23   and the state was a battleground of the Civil Rights Movement in
24   the mid-20th century. In the early 21st century, &state ranked
25   among the poorest states in the America.
26
27   %mend;
28
29   data factsAbout&state;
30     state="&state";
31     factTotal="%generateSourceCode";
32     fact1=scan("%generateSourceCode",1,'.')||'.';
33     fact2=scan("%generateSourceCode",2,'.')||'.';
```

```
34   fact3=scan("%generateSourceCode",3,'.')||'.';
35   fact4=scan("%generateSourceCode",4,'.')||'.';
36   fact5=scan("%generateSourceCode",5,'.')||'.';
37   fact6=scan("%generateSourceCode",6,'.')||'.';
38   run;
39
40   proc print;
41    title "factsAbout&state";
42   run;
```

Your output is similar to this (the ... symbol is not part of the output but is added here to reduce the text so the output will fit the page):

```
                       factsAboutMississippi

Obs    state

 1  Mississippi

Obs                     factTotal

 1  Mississippi joined the Union ... the Mississippi River, which form

Obs                     fact1

 1  Mississippi joined the Union ... the Mississippi River, which form

Obs                     fact2

 1  Early inhabitants of ... the Choctaw, Natchez and Chickasaw.

Obs                     fact3

 1  Spanish explorers arrived ... the first permanent settl

Obs                     fact4

 1  Mississippi seceded from ... during the American Civil War.

Obs                     fact5

 1  Despite the abolition of slavery, ... the state was a battlegroun

Obs                     fact6

 1  In the early 21st century, ... poorest states in the America.
```

In the output, some columns are truncated. SAS generates the following warnings in the log:

```
Data too long for column "factTotal"; truncated to xxx characters to fit.
Data too long for column "fact1"; truncated to xxx characters to fit.
Data too long for column "fact3"; truncated to xxx characters to fit.
Data too long for column "fact5"; truncated to xxx characters to fit
```

where the number xxx depends on your SAS version.

In addition, you'll get the following warning six times in the log:

```
The quoted string currently being processed has become more than 262
characters long.  You may have unbalanced quotation marks.
```

You get these warning messages because the string generated by the macro "%generateSourceCode" is too long. Your output table factsAboutMississippi, however, is correctly created.

After you submit Program 11.2.7, the macro processor does a series of string substitutions and generates part of the source code. This is the full source code at the end of the macro compilation:

Program 11.2.8 *mississippi4Source.sas*

```
1   dm log 'clear'; dm output 'clear';
2
3   data factsAboutMississippi;
4     state="Mississippi";
5     factTotal= "Mississippi joined...in the America.";
6     fact1=scan("Mississippi joined...in the America.",1,'.')||'.';
7     fact2=scan("Mississippi joined...in the America.",2,'.')||'.';
8     fact3=scan("Mississippi joined...in the America.",3,'.')||'.';
9     fact4=scan("Mississippi joined...in the America.",4,'.')||'.';
10    fact5=scan("Mississippi joined...in the America.",5,'.')||'.';
11    fact6=scan("Mississippi joined...in the America.",6,'.')||'.';
12  run;
13
14  proc print;
15    title "factsAboutMississippi";
16  run;
```

Next, Program 11.2.8 compiles and executes, generating the output.

The scan(string, n, charlist) function returns the n-th word from the string delimited by characters listed in the charlist.

11.3 The Period Symbol and Double Quotes Are Special

Let's go back to Program 11.1.3. Notice the two period symbols in the following statement:

```
outfile="C:\LearnSAS\&sourceTable..csv''
```

To see why you need two period symbols, delete one period so the outfile= expression becomes:

```
outfile="C:\LearnSAS\&sourceTable.csv''
```

Submit Program 11.1.3. Instead of getting Table1.csv, Table2.csv, and Table3.csv, you'll get the Table1csv, Table2csv, and Table3csv. If you open, for example, Table1csv with Notepad, you'll find that the content of the file is correct, though the file extension is missing.

Why didn't the period show up in the file name? Because a period immediately after a macro variable name means something special: it signals the end of that macro variable.

To see why we need to signal the end of a macro variable, imagine this. Instead of naming the CSV file as `xyz.csv`, you want to name it as `xyzfinal.csv`. You might be tempted to define the macro as follows:

```
%macro export2csv(sourceTable);
proc export
data=&sourceTable
outfile="C:\LearnSAS\&sourceTableFinal.csv"
dbms=csv
replace
;
run;
%mend
```

But this doesn't work. SAS thinks that you have a new macro variable called `sourceTableFinal`.

The solution is to add a period after the `&sourceTable` to signal the end of the macro variable. Immediately after the period, you are free to add the text `final` and `final` isn't part of the macro variable:

```
%macro export2csv(sourceTable);
proc export
data=&sourceTable
outfile="C:\LearnSAS\&sourceTable.Final.csv"
dbms=csv
replace
;
run;
%mend
```

In the expression `outfile="C:\LearnSAS\&sourceTable..csv"` in Program 11.1.3, the first period signals the end of the macro variable `sourceTable`; the second period is the literal period to show the CSV file extension.

Finally, notice that a pair of double quotes is used in the `outfile=` expression.

Remember that in PROC EXPORT the right-hand side of the `outfile=` expression needs to be in either single quotes or double quotes like this:

```
proc export
data=numOneToTen
outfile='C:\LearnSAS\numOneToTen.csv'

/* This works too */
/* outfile="C:\LearnSAS\numOneToTen.csv" */

/* This doesn't work;
the file's full path and name need to be in quotes */
/* outfile=C:\LearnSAS\numOneToTen.csv */

dbms=csv
```

```
replace
;
run;
```

So the full file path `C:\LearnSAS\&sourceTable..csv` needs to be in either single quotes or double quotes. Which quotes to use, single or double?

As explained earlier, in SAS, both single quotes and double quotes can represent a literal string, but only double quotes allow for variable substitution. When SAS encounters

```
"C:\LearnSAS\&sourceTable..csv"
```

it generates a quoted string `"C:\LearnSAS\xxx.csv"` where `xxx` is the value of the macro variable `sourceTable`.

This is what happens if you use single quotes instead:

```
outfile='C:\LearnSAS\&sourceTable..csv'
```

Each time `%export2csv` is called, SAS creates a CSV file with the literal name `&sourceTable..csv` in `C:\LearnSAS`, overwriting the previous file with the same name.

11.4   Avoid Two Types of Errors Related to the Macro Facility

New learners of SAS tend to make two types of mistakes when they start using the macro facility. The first type of error occurs when a programmer attempts to use the non-macro code to control the macro code. The second type of error occurs when a programmer attempts to reference a macro variable that was once created but doesn't exist any more.

11.4.1   Type I Error

In the next program, the programmer wants to save the four DATA step variables into four macro variables and later reference the macro variables in PROC PRINT.

Program 11.4.1
firstUSPresidentLegend.sas

```
1   dm log 'clear'; dm output 'clear';
2
3   data firstUSPresidentLegend;
4   Id=1;
5   Fname='George';
6   Lname='Washington';
7   Legend='Cherry Tree';
8
9   %let ID=Id;
10  %let Fname=Fname;
11  %let Lname=Lname;
12  %let unauthenticatedStory=Legend;
13
14  run;
15
16  proc print data=firstUSPresidentLegend;
17    title "Legend about US president No &ID: &FName &LName";
18    title2 "Many talked about &unauthenticatedStory";
19    title3 'Was it real?';
20  run;
```

Output:

```
Legend about US president No Id: Fname Lname
             Many talked about Legend
                    Was it real?

Obs      Id      Fname         Lname          Legend

1        1       George        Washington     Cherry Tree
```

This is the output he expects to get:

```
Legend about US president No 1: George Washington
        Many talked about Cherry Tree
                Was it real?

Obs   Id    Fname       Lname         Legend

1     1     George      Washington    Cherry Tree
```

To figure out what happened, add the **options symbolgen**; statement to the top of Program 11.4.1. Now the program should look like this:

```
options symbolgen;
dm log 'clear'; dm output 'clear';
data firstUSPresidentLegend;
...
```

SYMBOLGEN displays the results of resolving macro variable references. Re-submit the program. You'll get this log:

```
     proc print data=firstUSPresidentLegend;
SYMBOLGEN:  Macro variable ID resolves to ID
SYMBOLGEN:  Macro variable FNAME resolves to Fname
SYMBOLGEN:  Macro variable LNAME resolves to Lname
     title "Legend about US president No &ID: &FName &LName";
SYMBOLGEN:  Macro variable UNAUTHENTICATEDSTORY resolves to Legend
       title2 "Many talked about &unauthenticatedStory";
       title3 'Was it real?';
     run;
```

Surprisingly, the literal string ID, that is, the letter I followed by the letter D, not the number 1, is assigned to the macro variable ID. The literal string Fname is assigned to the macro variable Fname. The literal string Lname is assigned to the macro variable Lname. Finally, the literal string Legend is assigned to the macro variable unauthenticatedStory.

This is how a macro SAS program gets compiled and executed. If your SAS program doesn't have any macros or macro variables, the code will be compiled and executed in the order in which the code is written, from left to right and from top to bottom.

However, if a program has macro activities, conceptually, the macro processor first isolates the macro code (the code containing a percent sign or ampersand) and processes the macro code in the order in which the macro code is written, from left to right and from top to bottom. Finally, the macro processor converts the macro code into SAS source code.

Then the source code generated by the macro activities merges with the non-macro source code to build the full source code. Next, the full source is compiled and executed from left to right and from top to bottom.

Notice the word "conceptually." In the physical implementation, SAS can do whatever it wants as long as the physical implementation generates the same result as does the conceptual processing.

This is what happens conceptually after you submit Program 11.4.1. The macro processor isolates the macro activities:

```
%let ID=Id;
%let Fname=Fname;
%let Lname=Lname;
%let unauthenticatedStory=Legend;

title "Legend about US president No &ID: &FName &LName";
title2 "Many talked about &unauthenticatedStory";
```

Next, the macro processor converts the macro code into SAS source code. The four macro %let statements don't generate any source code; they merely create and initialize four macro variables. Only the title and title2 statements generate source code. This is the source code generated by the macro activities:

```
title "Legend about US president No ID: FName LName";
title2 "Many talked about the Legend";
```

This is the complete source code of Program 11.4.1:

Program 11.4.2 *firstUSPresidentLegendSource.sas*

```
1   dm log 'clear'; dm output 'clear';
2
3   data firstUSPresidentLegend;
4   Id=1;
5   Fname='George';
6   Lname='Washington';
```

```
7   Legend='Cherry Tree';
8   run;
9
10  proc print data=firstUSPresidentLegend;
11    title "Legend about US president No ID: FName LName";
12    title2 "Many talked about Legend";
13    title3 'Was it real?';
14  run;
```

Next, the source code is compiled and executed.

If a DATA step contains any macro activities, the macro activities will always be compiled and converted into source code before the DATA step logic is evaluated. This is why in Program 11.4.1 the DATA step variables are not passed to the macro variables.

To pass a DATA step variable to a macro variable, we need to resolve the macro variable at the DATA step execution time, not at the macro code compilation time. The CALL SYMPUT routine will resolve the macro variable at the DATA step execution time. Later we'll write Program 13.0.1 to fix the errors in Program 11.4.1.

The next program uses the DATA step to control the macro LET statement. However, it doesn't work.

Program 11.4.3 *twoStates.sas*

```
1   dm log 'clear'; dm output 'clear';
2
3   data twoStates;
4   length state $ %length(Mississippi);
5   input state;
6
7   if state='Mississippi' then %let abbreviation=MS;
8                           else %let abbreviation=LA;
9
10  stateAbbreviation="&abbreviation";
11
12  datalines;
13  Louisiana
14  Mississippi
15  ;
16  run;
```

Submit the program. The output table `twoStates` is empty. In addition, you'll get the following error in the log:

```
ERROR: No matching IF-THEN clause.
```

To debug the code, comment out the following macro code:

```
/*if state='Mississippi' then %let abbreviation=MS; */
/*                       else %let abbreviation=LA;*/

/*stateAbbreviation="&abbreviation";*/
```

Re-submit the program. It will run without errors, generating the following output table `twoStates`:

```
   state
-----------
Louisiana
Mississippi
```

The macro function `%length(Mississippi)` doesn't cause any trouble; it returns 11 at the macro compile time. It saves you from having to manually count the length of the string `Mississippi` in the `length` statement:

```
length state $ 11;
```

If the `length` statement is omitted from Program 11.4.3, the `input state $` statement will use the default 8 width to read in the character variable `state` and generate the following output table `twoStates`:

```
   state
-----------
Louisian
Mississi
```

`Louisiana` and `Mississippi` are truncated to 8 characters.

To figure out the `No matching IF-THEN` error, remember that the macro facility generates SAS source code. After you submit Program 11.4.3, the `%length(Mississippi)` expression is converted to 11. The macro statement `%let abbreviation=MS;` including the ending semicolon vanishes without generating any source code; it merely creates the macro variable `abbreviation` and assigns it the text `MS`.

Similarly, the macro statement `%let abbreviation=LA;` including the ending semicolon vanishes and generates no source code; it reassigns the text `LA` to the macro variable `abbreviation`.

Finally, `"&abbreviation"` is converted to `"LA"`.

This is the full source code of Program 11.4.3 at the end of the macro compilation:

Program 11.4.4 *twoStatesSource.sas*

```
1    dm log 'clear'; dm output 'clear';
2
3    data twoStates;
4    length state $ 11;
5    input state;
6
7    if state='Mississippi' then
8                           else
9
10   stateAbbreviation="LA";
11
12   datalines;
```

```
13   Louisiana
14   Mississippi
15   ;
16   run;
```

Lines 7–8 in Program 11.4.4 cause the `No matching IF-THEN` error.

The next program fixes the syntax error, but the output table `twoStates` is still wrong:

Program 11.4.5 *twoStates2.sas*

```
1    dm log 'clear'; dm output 'clear';
2
3    data twoStates;
4    length state $ %length(Mississippi);
5    input state;
6
7    if state='Mississippi' then %let abbreviation=MS;;
8                           else %let abbreviation=LA;;
9
10   stateAbbreviation="&abbreviation";
11
12   datalines;
13   Louisiana
14   Mississippi
15   ;
16   run;
```

Notice the extra semicolon in Lines 7 and 8.

This is the full source code of Program 11.4.5 at the end of the macro compilation:

Program 11.4.6 *twoStates2Source.sas*

```
1    dm log 'clear'; dm output 'clear';
2
3    data twoStates;
4    length state $ 11;
5    input state;
6
7    if state='Mississippi' then;
8                           else;
9
10   stateAbbreviation="LA";
11
12   datalines;
13   Louisiana
14   Mississippi
15   ;
16   run;
```

Lines 7–8 now have a correct IF-THEN statement, even though the IF-THEN statement does nothing. This is the newly created `twoStates` table:

```
    state       stateAbbreviation
-----------    -----------------
Louisiana          LA
Mississippi        LA
```

If a SAS program has macro code, the macro processor will first convert the macro code into source code before the non-macro code logic is evaluated. Hence it's impossible to use the DATA step logic to conditionally trigger macro activities.

11.4.2 Type II Error

The second common error is to reference a macro variable that was once created but does not exist any more.

Program 11.4.7 *macroScopeError.sas*

```
1    dm log 'clear'; dm output 'clear';
2    option mlogic mprint symbolgen;
3
4    %macro loop(start, end, step);
5    %do i=&start %to &end %by &step;
6       x=&i;
7       output;
8    %end;
9    %mend;
10
11   data mynum;
12      %loop(1,11,2)
13   run;
14
15   options linesize=min nonumber nodate;
16   proc print data=myNum;
17      title "myNum table";
18      title2 "The start is &start";
19      title3 "The end is &end";
20      title4 "The step is &step";
21      title5 "i has an extra loop; its ending value is &i";
22   run;
```

Output:

```
                  myNum table
            The start is &start
             The end is &end
             The step is &step
    i has an extra loop; its ending value is &i

            Obs        x

             1         1
             2         3
             3         5
             4         7
             5         9
             6        11
```

The `symbolgen`, `mlogic`, and `mprint` are three options to help you debug your macro code. Here's what each option does:

- `symbolgen` displays the results of resolving macro variable references.

- `mlogic` causes the macro processor to trace its execution and to write the trace information to the SAS log.

- `mprint` displays the SAS statements that are generated by macro execution.

The output table `myNum` is correctly generated, but the `title2` to `title5` statements are not working. In addition, you get the following warnings in the log:

```
WARNING: Apparent symbolic reference START not resolved.
WARNING: Apparent symbolic reference END not resolved.;
WARNING: Apparent symbolic reference STEP not resolved.
WARNING: Apparent symbolic reference I not resolved.
```

The 4 macro variables start, end, step, and i are local to the macro %loop. They exist during the interval when the macro loop is executed and are destroyed at the end of the macro execution. When the TITLE2 – TITLE5 statements reference these macro variables, the macro loop was already executed and the 4 macro variables no longer exist, hence SAS issues the warnings in the log.

The next program fixes the macro scope error by creating 4 global macro variables mystart, mystep, myend, and i via 4 macro LET statements in the open code. Then the same-named macro variables inside the macro loop refer to the global macro variables.

Program 11.4.8

macroScopeErrorFix.sas

```
1    dm log 'clear'; dm output 'clear';
2    option mlogic mprint symbolgen;
3
4    %let mystart=;
5    %let myend=;
6    %let mystep=;
7    %let i=;
8
9    %macro loop(start, end, step);
10   %let mystart=&start;
11   %let myend=&end;
12   %let mystep=&step;
13
14   %do i=&start %to &end %by &step;
15      x=&i;
16      output;
17   %end;
18
19   %mend;
20
21   data mynum;
22     %loop(1,11,2)
23   run;
24
25   options linesize=min nonumber nodate;
26   proc print data=myNum;
27      title "myNum table";
28      title2 "The start is &mystart";
29      title3 "The end is &myend";
30      title4 "The step is &mystep";
31      title5 "i has an extra loop; its ending value is &i";
32   run;
```

Output:

```
                 myNum table
              The start is 1
              The end is 11
              The step is 2
    i has an extra loop; its ending value is 13

                   Obs       x

                    1        1
                    2        3
                    3        5
                    4        7
                    5        9
                    6       11
```

In each macro LET statement, there's nothing after the equals sign except the ending semicolon. This initializes a macro variable to null.

The macro variables mystart, mystep, and myend are the three parameters of the macro %loop. The parameters of a macro are always local to the macro that creates them and cannot be made global. As a result, we have to create three global macro variables `mystart`, `mystep`, and `myend` and pass the three parameters of the macro `start`, `step`, and `end` to these three global macro variables.

However, the macro variable `i` inside the macro `loop` is not a parameter of the macro `loop`. Hence we can declare a global macro variable with the same name `i` in the open code. Then the macro variable `i` inside the macro `loop` refers to the global macro variable `i`.

The next program attempts to make the three parameters of the macro `loop` global but it doesn't work. The parameters of a macro are always local to the defining macro.

Program 11.4.9 *macroScopeError2.sas*

```
1   dm log 'clear'; dm output 'clear';
2   option mlogic mprint symbolgen;
3
4   %let start=;
5   %let end=;
6   %let step=;
7   %let i=;
8
9   %macro loop(start, end, step);
10  %do i=&start %to &end %by &step;
11      x=&i;
12      output;
13  %end;
14  %mend;
15
16  data mynum;
17    %loop(1,11,2)
18  run;
19
20  options linesize=min nonumber nodate;
21  proc print data=myNum;
22    title "myNum table";
23    title2 "The start is &start";
24    title3 "The end is &end";
25    title4 "The step is &step";
26    title5 "i has an extra loop; its ending value is &i";
27  run;
```

Output:

```
                    myNum table
                  The start is
                   The end is
                   The step is
        i has an extra loop; its ending value is 13

                    Obs      x

                     1       1
                     2       3
                     3       5
                     4       7
                     5       9
                     6      11
```

In the PROC PRINT, the 4 macro variables refer to the global macro variables `start`, `step`, `end`, and `i`. While the value of the macro variable `i` is updated when the macro `loop` finishes execution, the other three macro variables remain null. SAS has created two sets of macro variables. The first set consists of `start`, `step`, `end`, and `i`; they are global and can be referenced anywhere. The same-named macro variable `i` inside the macro `loop` refers to the global macro variable `i`.

The other set consists of the macro variables `start`, `step`, and `end` that are local to the macro `loop`. The macro `loop` doesn't know anything about the same-named global macro variables `start`, `step`, or `end`. As a result, after the macro `loop` is executed, the same-named global macro variables `start`, `step`, and `end` remain null.

Here's another way to fix the macro variable scope issue in Program 11.4.7. Inside a macro definition, you can use the `%global` statement to specify a global macro variable. The next program is functionally equivalent to Program 11.4.8.

Program 11.4.10 *macroScopeErrorFix2.sas*

```
1    dm log 'clear'; dm output 'clear';
2    option mlogic mprint symbolgen;
3
4    %macro loop(start, end, step);
5    %global mystart myend mystep i;
6
7    %let mystart=&start;
8    %let myend=&end;
9    %let mystep=&step;
10
11   %do i=&start %to &end %by &step;
12      x=&i;
13      output;
14   %end;
15
16   %mend;
17
18   data mynum;
19    %loop(1,11,2)
20   run;
21
22   options linesize=min nonumber nodate;
23   proc print data=myNum;
24     title "myNum table";
25     title2 "The start is &mystart";
26     title3 "The end is &myend";
27     title4 "The step is &mystep";
28     title5 "i has an extra loop; its ending value is &i";
29   run;
```

The `%global mystart myend mystep i` statement specifies that the macro variables `mystart`, `mystep`, `myend`, and `i` are global. Even though these 4 macro variables first appear inside a macro, they can be referenced anywhere after they are declared to be global.

11.4.3 More Examples on the Scope of a Macro Variable

Example 1 defines three global macro variables: `a`, `b`, and `c`. They are accessible anywhere in the same SAS session.

```
1    /*Example 1*/
2    dm log 'clear'; dm output 'clear';
3    options mlogic mprint symbolgen;
4
5    %let a=1;
6    %let b=2;
7    %let c=3;
8    %put &a &b &c;
SYMBOLGEN:  Macro variable A resolves to 1
SYMBOLGEN:  Macro variable B resolves to 2
SYMBOLGEN:  Macro variable C resolves to 3
 1 2 3
```

Example 2 creates three local macro variables a2, b2, and c2. They exist in the defining `macro2` and are destroyed after `macro2` finishes execution. The second macro PUT statement attempts to reference the three local macro variables at the end of the macro execution, causing SAS to throw a message in the log: `WARNING: Apparent symbolic reference ... not resolved.`

```
9    /*Example 2*/
10   dm log 'clear'; dm output 'clear';
11   options mlogic mprint symbolgen;
12
13   %macro macro2;
14   %let a2=1;
15   %let b2=2;
16   %let c2=3;
17   %put 'Inside the macro: ' &a2 &b2 &c2;
18   %mend;
19
20   %macro2
MLOGIC(MACRO2):  Beginning execution.
MLOGIC(MACRO2):  %LET (variable name is A2)
MLOGIC(MACRO2):  %LET (variable name is B2)
MLOGIC(MACRO2):  %LET (variable name is C2)
MLOGIC(MACRO2):  %PUT 'Inside the macro: ' &a2 &b2 &c2
SYMBOLGEN:  Macro variable A2 resolves to 1
SYMBOLGEN:  Macro variable B2 resolves to 2
SYMBOLGEN:  Macro variable C2 resolves to 3
'Inside the macro: ' 1 2 3
MLOGIC(MACRO2):  Ending execution.
21   %put 'After the macro executes: ' &a2 &b2 &c2;
WARNING: Apparent symbolic reference A2 not resolved.
WARNING: Apparent symbolic reference B2 not resolved.
WARNING: Apparent symbolic reference C2 not resolved.
'After the macro executes: ' &a2 &b2 &c2
```

Example 3 creates a global macro variable a3 and initializes it to 10. Inside `macro3`, the macro variable a3 refers to the global macro variable a3. If a macro variable inside a macro has the same name as a global macro variable, then the macro variable inside the macro is the global macro variable, unless you explicitly declare the same-named macro variable inside the macro to be a local macro variable using the `%local` expression (see Example 4).

When `macro3` executes, a3 is changed to 1. After `macro3` finishes execution, a3 is still 1.

```
22   /*Example 3*/
23   dm log 'clear'; dm output 'clear';
24   options mlogic mprint symbolgen;
25
26   %let a3=10;
27   %put 'Initial value: ' &a3;
SYMBOLGEN:  Macro variable A3 resolves to 10
'Initial value: ' 10
28
29   %macro macro3;
30   %let a3=1;
31   %put 'Inside the macro: ' &a3;
32   %mend;
33
```

```
34   %macro3
MLOGIC(MACRO3):  Beginning execution.
MLOGIC(MACRO3):  %LET (variable name is A3)
MLOGIC(MACRO3):  %PUT 'Inside the macro: ' &a3
SYMBOLGEN:  Macro variable A3 resolves to 1
'Inside the macro: ' 1
MLOGIC(MACRO3):  Ending execution.
35   %put 'After the macro executes: ' &a3;
SYMBOLGEN:  Macro variable A3 resolves to 1
'After the macro executes: ' 1
```

Example 4 creates a global macro variable `a4` and initializes it to 10. Then inside `macro4` another macro variable with the same name `a4` is declared to be a local macro variable and is set to 1. The local macro variable `a4` and the global macro variable `a4` are two different macro variables. SAS stores the global macro variable `a4` in a global symbol table for future lookup. SAS stores the local macro variable `a4` in a local symbol table for future lookup. After `macro4` finishes execution, the local macro variable `a4` is destroyed but the global macro variable `a4` remains and is still 10.

```
36   /*Example 4*/
37   dm log 'clear'; dm output 'clear';
38   options mlogic mprint symbolgen;
39
40   %let a4=10;
41   %put 'Initial value: ' &a4;
SYMBOLGEN:  Macro variable A4 resolves to 10
'Initial value: ' 10
42
43   %macro macro4;
44   %local a4;
45   %let a4=1;
46   %put 'Inside the macro: ' &a4;
47   %mend;
48
49   %macro4
MLOGIC(MACRO4):  Beginning execution.
MLOGIC(MACRO4):  %LOCAL  A4
MLOGIC(MACRO4):  %LET (variable name is A4)
MLOGIC(MACRO4):  %PUT 'Inside the macro: ' &a4
SYMBOLGEN:  Macro variable A4 resolves to 1
'Inside the macro: ' 1
MLOGIC(MACRO4):  Ending execution.
50   %put 'After the macro executes: ' &a4;
SYMBOLGEN:  Macro variable A4 resolves to 10
'After the macro executes: ' 10
```

In Example 5, the first macro PUT statement attempts to reference the macro variable `a5` but `a5` doesn't exist yet. SAS writes this warning to the log: `WARNING: Apparent symbolic reference A5 not resolved`.

Inside `macro5`, `a5` is declared to be a global variable and is set to 1. After `macro5` finishes execution, the global macro variable `a5` is still 1.

```
51   /*Example 5*/
52   dm log 'clear'; dm output 'clear';
```

```
53    options mlogic mprint symbolgen;
54
55    %put 'Initial value: ' &a5;
WARNING: Apparent symbolic reference A5 not resolved.
'Initial value: ' &a5
56
57    %macro macro5;
58    %global a5;
59    %let a5=1;
60    %put 'Inside the macro: ' &a5;
61    %mend;
62
63    %macro5
MLOGIC(MACRO5):  Beginning execution.
MLOGIC(MACRO5):  %GLOBAL  A5
MLOGIC(MACRO5):  %LET (variable name is A5)
MLOGIC(MACRO5):  %PUT 'Inside the macro: ' &a5
SYMBOLGEN:  Macro variable A5 resolves to 1
'Inside the macro: ' 1
MLOGIC(MACRO5):  Ending execution.
64    %put 'After the macro executes: ' &a5;
SYMBOLGEN:  Macro variable A5 resolves to 1
'After the macro executes: ' 1
```

11.4.4   Scope of a Macro Variable Created by **PROC SQL INSERT INTO**

A macro variable created by PROC SQL INSERT INTO can be either global or local.

Let's experiment. First, close your SAS software. This will destroy all the macro variables you created. Re-launch SAS from the START menu.

```
/* Proc SQL insert into macro var Example 1*/
dm log 'clear'; dm output 'clear';
options symbolgen mlogic mprint;

data ten;
do i=1 to 10;
  output;
end;
run;

proc sql;
select sum(i)
into :x1
from ten;
quit;

%put &x1;
```

The macro variable x1 is created in the open code (e.g. not inside a macro) and can be referenced anywhere in your code. This is the log:

```
SYMBOLGEN:  Macro variable X1 resolves to      55
16
17    %put &x1;
55
```

In the next example, x2 is a local macro variable inside `macro2`. The macro variable x2 exists during the short interval when `macro2` is executed. Once the execution is over, x2 is destroyed and not accessible to the second macro PUT statement.

```
18    /* Proc SQL insert into macro var Example 2*/
19    %macro macro2;
20    proc sql;
21    select sum(i)
22    into :x2
23    from ten;
24    quit;
25
26    %put 'During macro2 execution: x2=' &x2;
27    %mend;
28
29    %macro2
MLOGIC(MACRO2):  Beginning execution.
MPRINT(MACRO2):    proc sql;
MPRINT(MACRO2):    select sum(i) into :x2 from ten;
MPRINT(MACRO2):    quit;
NOTE: PROCEDURE SQL used:
      real time            0.00 seconds
      cpu time             0.00 seconds


MLOGIC(MACRO2):  %PUT 'During macro2 execution: x2=' &x2
SYMBOLGEN:  Macro variable X2 resolves to       55
'During macro2 execution: x2='       55
MLOGIC(MACRO2):  Ending execution.
WARNING: Apparent symbolic reference X2 not resolved.
30    %put 'At the end of macro2 execution: x2=' &x2;
'At the end of macro2 execution: x2=' &x2
```

In Example 3, a global macro variable x3 already exists before `macro3` executes. The x3 macro variable inside `macro3` refers to the global macro variable x3.

```
31    /* Proc SQL insert into macro var Example 3*/
32    %let x3=1;
33    %put 'Before macro3: x3=' &x3;
SYMBOLGEN:  Macro variable X3 resolves to 1
'Before macro3: x3=' 1
34
35    %macro macro3;
36    proc sql;
37    select sum(i)
38    into :x3
39    from ten;
40    quit;
41
42    %put 'During macro3 execution: x3=' &x3;
43    %mend;
44
45    %macro3
MLOGIC(MACRO3):  Beginning execution.
MPRINT(MACRO3):    proc sql;
```

```
MPRINT(MACRO3):    select sum(i) into :x3 from ten;
MPRINT(MACRO3):    quit;
NOTE: PROCEDURE SQL used:
      real time              0.01 seconds
      cpu time               0.01 seconds


MLOGIC(MACRO3):   %PUT 'During macro3 execution: x3=' &x3
SYMBOLGEN:  Macro variable X3 resolves to          55
'During macro3 execution: x3='          55
MLOGIC(MACRO3):   Ending execution.
SYMBOLGEN:  Macro variable X3 resolves to          55
46    %put 'At the end of macro3 execution: x3=' &x3;
'At the end of macro3 execution: x3='          55
```

11.4.5   Scope of a Macro Variable Created by Nested Macros

Now close your SAS software to destroy all the macro variables you created before. Re-launch SAS.

Program 11.4.11 *nestedMacroVar.sas*

```
1     dm log 'clear'; dm output 'clear';
2     options symbolgen mlogic mprint;
3
4     %let xxx=1;
5
6     %macro inner;
7       %put inner &xxx;
8       %let zzz=1;
9       %put inner &yyy;
10    %mend;
11
12    %macro outer;
13      %put outer &xxx;
14      %let yyy=2;
15
16      %inner
17      %put &zzz;
18    %mend;
19
20    %outer
MLOGIC(OUTER):  Beginning execution.
MLOGIC(OUTER):  %PUT outer &xxx
SYMBOLGEN:  Macro variable XXX resolves to 1
outer 1
MLOGIC(OUTER):  %LET (variable name is YYY)
MLOGIC(INNER):  Beginning execution.
MLOGIC(INNER):  %PUT inner &xxx
SYMBOLGEN:  Macro variable XXX resolves to 1
inner 1
MLOGIC(INNER):  %LET (variable name is ZZZ)
MLOGIC(INNER):  %PUT inner &yyy
SYMBOLGEN:  Macro variable YYY resolves to 2
inner 2
MLOGIC(INNER):  Ending execution.
MLOGIC(OUTER):  %PUT &zzz
```

```
WARNING: Apparent symbolic reference ZZZ not resolved.
&zzz
MLOGIC(OUTER):  Ending execution.
```

We define a global macro variable **xxx** and set it to 1. This macro variable is available anywhere in the program. The same-named macro variable **xxx** inside the **outer** macro and inside the **inner** macro refer to the global macro variable **xxx**. Therefore, SAS writes **outer** 1 and **inner** 1 to the log.

The macro variable **yyy** is defined and initialized to 2 inside the **outer** macro. **yyy** is available anywhere inside **outer**. Since **inner** is nested inside **outer**, **yyy** is available inside **inner**. SAS writes **inner** 2 to the log.

The macro variable **zzz** is defined and initialized to 3 inside **inner**. **zzz** exists only during the short duration when **inner** is executed and is destroyed after **inner** finishes execution. The second macro PUT statement inside **outer** attempts to access **zzz** after **inner** finishes execution, causing the error message `WARNING: Apparent symbolic reference ZZZ not resolved`.

11.5   Debug a Macro

Program 11.5.1 *bonus.sas*

```
1   dm log 'clear'; dm output 'clear';
2   options symbolgen mlogic mprint;
3
4   data pay;
5   input id salary rating;
6   datalines;
7   1 10000 10
8   2 20000 9
9   3 30000 8
10  4 40000 7
11  5 50000 6
12  ;
13  run;
14
15  %macro setBonus(bonusMethod);
16  %if &bonusMethod=PERFORMANCE %then
17     %do;
18        data bonusPerformance;
19        set pay;
20              if rating=10 then bonus=salary*0.10;
21        else if rating=9  then bonus=salary*0.09;
22        else if rating=8  then bonus=salary*0.08;
23        else                   bonus=salary*0.07;
24        run;
25     %end;
26  %else %if &bonusMethod=SAMEPCNT %then
27     %do;
28        data bonusSamePercent;
29        set pay;
30        bonus=salary*0.05;
31        run;
32     %end;
33  %mend;
34
35  %setBonus(PERFORMANCE)
36  proc print data=bonusPerformance;
37    title 'Bonus is based on performance rating.';
38  run;
39
40  %setBonus(SamePcnt)
41  proc print data=bonusSamePercent;
42    title 'Everyone gets the same percentage bonus.';
43  run;
```

Output:

Bonus is based on performance rating.

Obs	id	salary	rating	bonus
1	1	10000	10	1000
2	2	20000	9	1800
3	3	30000	8	2400
4	4	40000	7	2800
5	5	50000	6	3500

The macro setBonus(bonusMethod) conditionally generates the source code of the DATA step. If the parameter bonusMethod is PERFORMANCE, then the bonusPerformance table will be created using the performance-based raise percentage; if bonusMethod is SAMEPCNT, then the bonusSamePercent table will be created using a 5% raise for everyone.

The bonusSamePercent table is not created, even though the macro %setBonus(SamePcnt) is called.

To figure out what happened, let's read the log. This is the log generated when the macro setBonus(PERFORMANCE) is invoked:

```
169  %setBonus(PERFORMANCE)
MLOGIC(SETBONUS):  Beginning execution.
MLOGIC(SETBONUS):  Parameter BONUSMETHOD has value PERFORMANCE
SYMBOLGEN:  Macro variable BONUSMETHOD resolves to PERFORMANCE
MLOGIC(SETBONUS):  %IF condition &bonusMethod=PERFORMANCE is TRUE
MPRINT(SETBONUS):    data bonusPerformance;
MPRINT(SETBONUS):    set pay;
MPRINT(SETBONUS):    if rating=10 then bonus=salary*0.10;
MPRINT(SETBONUS):    else if rating=9 then bonus=salary*0.09;
MPRINT(SETBONUS):    else if rating=8 then bonus=salary*0.08;
MPRINT(SETBONUS):    else bonus=salary*0.07;
MPRINT(SETBONUS):    run;

NOTE: There were 5 observations read from the dataset WORK.PAY.
NOTE: The data set WORK.BONUSPERFORMANCE has 5 observations
      and 4 variables.
```

The seven `mprint` lines in the log confirm that the source code is generated correctly when the `setBonus(PERFORMANCE)` macro is called.

This is the log when the second macro `%setBonus(PERFORMANCE)` is called:

```
174  %setBonus(SamePcnt)
MLOGIC(SETBONUS):  Beginning execution.
MLOGIC(SETBONUS):  Parameter BONUSMETHOD has value SamePcnt
SYMBOLGEN:  Macro variable BONUSMETHOD resolves to SamePcnt
MLOGIC(SETBONUS):  %IF condition &bonusMethod=PERFORMANCE is FALSE
SYMBOLGEN:  Macro variable BONUSMETHOD resolves to SamePcnt
MLOGIC(SETBONUS):  %IF condition &bonusMethod=SAMEPCNT is FALSE
MLOGIC(SETBONUS):  Ending execution.
175  proc print data=bonusSamePercent;
ERROR: File WORK.BONUSSAMEPERCENT.DATA does not exist.
176    title 'Everyone gets the same percentage bonus.';
177  run;

NOTE: The SAS System stopped processing this step because of errors.
```

The fourth `mlogic` line in the log indicates that `&bonusMethod=SAMEPCNT` is evaluated to false.

A macro stores a literal string. All literal strings are case sensitive. Since the string `SamePcnt` is not equal to the string `SAMEPCNT`, the following condition evaluates to false:

`&bonusMethod=SAMEPCNT`

Had we invoked the macro `setBonus(SAMEPCNT)`, the `bonusSamePercent` table would have been correctly generated.

The next program makes the parameter `bonusMethod` case insensitive:

Program 11.5.2 *bonus2.sas*

```
1    dm log 'clear'; dm output 'clear';
2    options symbolgen mlogic mprint;
3
4    data pay;
5    input id salary rating;
6    datalines;
7    1 10000 10
8    2 20000 9
9    3 30000 8
10   4 40000 7
11   5 50000 6
12   ;
13   run;
14
15   %macro setBonus(bonusMethod);
16   %let method=%upcase(&bonusMethod);
17   %if &method=PERFORMANCE %then
18     %do;
19        data bonusPerformance;
20        set pay;
21             if rating=10 then bonus=salary*0.10;
22        else if rating=9  then bonus=salary*0.09;
23        else if rating=8  then bonus=salary*0.08;
24        else                   bonus=salary*0.07;
25        run;
26     %end;
27   %else %if &method=SAMEPCNT %then
28     %do;
29        data bonusSamePercent;
30        set pay;
31        bonus=salary*0.05;
32        run;
33     %end;
34   %mend;
35
36   %setBonus(performance)
37   proc print data=bonusPerformance;
38     title 'Bonus is based on performance rating.';
39   run;
40
41   %setBonus(samePcnt)
42   proc print data=bonusSamePercent;
43     title 'Everyone gets the same percentage bonus.';
44   run;
```

Output:

Bonus is based on performance rating.

Obs	id	salary	rating	bonus
1	1	10000	10	1000
2	2	20000	9	1800
3	3	30000	8	2400
4	4	40000	7	2800
5	5	50000	6	3500

Everyone gets the same percentage bonus.

Obs	id	salary	rating	bonus
1	1	10000	10	500
2	2	20000	9	1000
3	3	30000	8	1500
4	4	40000	7	2000
5	5	50000	6	2500

In Program 11.5.2, the symbolgen, mlogic, and mprint options are useful for debugging your macro code. However, once your code is working, you'll want to turn these options off using this statement so your program can run faster:

```
options nosymbolgen nomlogic nomprint;
```

11.6   Use Macros to Create a Generic Program

Suppose each week you need to write a similar SAS program. This is your program for Week 1.

Program 11.6.1 *num1to10step1.sas*

```
1   dm log 'clear'; dm output 'clear';
2   libname mylib 'C:\LearnSAS';
3
4   data mylib.num1to10step1;
5   do i=1 to 10 by 1;
6     output;
7   end;
8   run;
9
10  proc print data=mylib.num1to10step1;
11    title "num1to10step1";
12  run;
13
14  proc sql;
15  create table mylib.sum_num1to10step1 as
16  select
17     count(*) as count
18    ,sum(i)   as total
19  from mylib.num1to10step1;
20  quit;
21
22  proc export
23  data=mylib.sum_num1to10step1
24  outfile='C:\LearnSAS\sum_num1to10step1.csv'
25  dbms=csv
26  replace
27  ;
28  run;
```

This is your program for Week 2:

Program 11.6.2 *num2to8step2.sas*

```
1   dm log 'clear'; dm output 'clear';
2   libname mylib 'C:\LearnSAS';
3
4   data mylib.num2to8step2;
5   do i=2 to 8 by 2;
6     output;
7   end;
8   run;
9
10  proc print data=mylib.num2to8step2;
11    title "num2to8step2";
12  run;
13
14  proc sql;
15  create table mylib.sum_num2to8step2 as
16  select
17     count(*) as count
18    ,sum(i)   as total
19  from mylib.num2to8step2;
20  quit;
```

```
21
22   proc export
23   data=mylib.sum_num2to8step2
24   outfile='C:\LearnSAS\sum_num2to8step2.csv'
25   dbms=csv
26   replace
27   ;
28   run;
```

Since the two programs follow a similar pattern, let's write a generic program.

Program 11.6.3 *numXtoYstepZ.sas*

```
1    dm log 'clear'; dm output 'clear';
2    libname mylib 'C:\LearnSAS';
3
4    data mylib.num&X.to&Y.step&Z;
5    do i=&X to &Y by &Z;
6      output;
7    end;
8    run;
9
10   proc print data=mylib.num&X.to&Y.step&Z;
11     title "num&X.to&Y.step&Z";
12   run;
13
14   proc sql;
15   create table mylib.sum_num&X.to&Y.step&Z as
16   select
17     count(*) as count
18    ,sum(i)   as total
19   from mylib.num&X.to&Y.step&Z;
20   quit;
21
22   proc export
23   data=mylib.sum_num&X.to&Y.step&Z
24   outfile="C:\LearnSAS\sum_num&X.to&Y.step&Z..csv"
25   dbms=csv
26   replace
27   ;
28   run;
```

However, Program `numXtoYstepZ.sas` doesn't work yet. Submit it and you'll get the following error log:

```
WARNING: Apparent symbolic reference X not resolved.
WARNING: Apparent symbolic reference Y not resolved.
WARNING: Apparent symbolic reference Z not resolved.
```

Don't worry. Once we assign values to the macro variables X, Y, and Z, the error messages will disappear. Modify Program 11.6.3 as follows:

Program 11.6.4 *numXtoYstepZv2.sas*

```
1   dm log 'clear'; dm output 'clear';
2   libname mylib 'C:\LearnSAS';
3
4   %let X=1;
5   %let Y=10;
6   %let Z=1;
7
8   data mylib.num&X.to&Y.step&Z;
9   do i=&X to &Y by &Z;
10    output;
11  end;
12  run;
13
14  proc print data=mylib.num&X.to&Y.step&Z;
15    title "num&X.to&Y.step&Z";
16  run;
17
18  proc sql;
19  create table mylib.sum_num&X.to&Y.step&Z as
20  select
21    count(*) as count
22    ,sum(i)   as total
23  from mylib.num&X.to&Y.step&Z;
24  quit;
25
26  proc export
27  data=mylib.sum_num&X.to&Y.step&Z
28  outfile="C:\LearnSAS\sum_num&X.to&Y.step&Z..csv"
29  dbms=csv
30  replace
31  ;
32  run;
```

Now submit Program 11.6.4 and it will work.

To produce the Week 2 Program 11.6.2, in Program 11.6.4 just reset the macro variables to:

```
%let X=2;
%let Y=8;
%let Z=2;
```

If you use SAS in the cloud, you'll need to adjust the file paths in all the programs in this section according to Preface "Adjust the File Path for SAS in the Cloud."

11.6.1   Eval(), Sysevalf(), and Symbolgen

SAS macros are nothing more than string find-and-replace. A macro variable is always a string. You can't add one string to another or multiply one string by another. To perform arithmetic operations on macro variables, use either %eval() or %sysevalf().

Here's a log of a submitted program:

```
1   dm log 'clear'; dm output 'clear';
2   options nosymbolgen;
```

```
3
4     %let a=1;
5     %let b=2;
6     %let c=a+b;
7     %put &c;
a+b
8
9     %let d=&a+&b;
10    %put &d;
1+2
11
12    %let e=%eval(&a+&b);
13    %put &e;
3
14
15    %let g=1+2;
16    %let eval_g=%eval(&g);
17    %put &g is &eval_g;
1+2 is 3
18
19    %let h=11/3;
20    %let eval_h=%eval(&b);
21    %put &h is &eval_h;
11/3 is 2
22
23    %let i=5;
24    %let j=2;
25    %let k=&i*&j;
26    %let eval_k=%eval(&k);
27    %put &k is &eval_k;
5*2 is 10
28
29    %let m=1.25;
30    %let n=2;
31    %let p=&m*&n;
32    %let eval_p=%eval(&p);
ERROR: A character operand was found in the %EVAL function or %IF
condition where a numeric operand is required. The condition
was: 1.25*2
33    %put &p is &eval_p;
1.25*2 is
34
35    %let q=%sysevalf(&p);
36    %put &p is &q;
1.25*2 is 2.5
```

SAS evaluates &c to the literal string a+b and evaluates d=&a+&b to the literal string $1 + 2$.

The macro %eval() function converts its argument from a string to an integer or logical expression and then performs the evaluation, returning the result as a string. If all operands can be interpreted as integers, the expression is treated as arithmetic.

The statement %let eval_p=%eval(&p) generates an error log:

```
ERROR: A character operand was found in the %EVAL function or %IF
condition where a numeric operand is required. The condition was: 1.25*2
```

This is because &p evaluates to 1.25*2. %Eval() accepts only operands in arithmetic expressions that represent integers. Operands that contain a period character cause an error when they are part of an integer arithmetic expression; SAS will display an error message indicating that it has found a character operand where a numeric operand is required.

%Eval() performs only integer arithmetic. Use the %sysevalf() function to perform floating-point arithmetic. The statement %sysevalf(&p) evaluates to 2.5.

11.7 Export Multiple Tables to Separate Sheets in One Excel File

For simplicity, your SAS tables are named table1, table2,..., tableN. Assume you have SAS 9.3M1+ and SAS/ACCESS Interface installed on your computer. If not, you can use SAS in the cloud. The next program converts multiple SAS tables into separate sheets of one Excel file.

Program 11.7.1 *table2excelMacroGeneric.sas*

```
1   /* Assume your SAS tables are named table1, table2, ...*/
2   dm log 'clear'; dm output 'clear';
3
4   /*PC SAS*/
5   %let myfolder=C:\learnSAS;
6
7   /*uncomment next line if you use SAS in the cloud*/
8   /*%let myfolder=/home/userid/myProgram;*/
9
10  libname mylib "&myfolder";
11  data mylib.table1;
12  input var1 var2;
13  datalines;
14  1 2
15  3 4
16  5 6
17  ;
18  run;
19
20  data mylib.table2;
21  input var3 var4$;
22  datalines;
23  1 a
24  2 b
25  3 c
26  ;
27  run;
28
29  data mylib.table3;
30  input var5$ var6$;
31  datalines;
32  x aa
33  y bb
34  z cc
35  ;
36  run;
37
38  %macro convertTablesToOneExcel;
```

```
39   %do i=1 %to 3;
40         proc export
41         data=mylib.table&i
42         outfile="&myfolder/mytables.xlsx"
43         dbms=xlsx
44         replace;
45
46         sheet=table&i;
47         run;
48   %end;
49  %mend;
50  %convertTablesToOneExcel
```

11.8   Further Reading

How do I export from SAS to Excel files: Let me count the ways

`http://blogs.sas.com/content/sasdummy/2012/02/11/export-excel-methods/`

The *SAS 9.3 Macro Language Reference* pdf, Chapter 3, *Macro Variables*; Chapter 4, *Macro Processing*; Chapter 5, *Scopes of Macro Variables*.

Troubleshooting Your Macros

`http://v8doc.sas.com/sashtml/macro/z1302436.htm`

Macro Bugs - How to Create, Avoid and Destroy Them

`http://www2.sas.com/proceedings/sugi30/252-30.pdf`

Improving Program Efficiency with Macro Variables

`http://web.utk.edu/sas/OnlineTutor/1.2/en/60476/m32/m32_1.htm`

Global Macro Variables

`https://v8doc.sas.com/sashtml/macro/z1072159.htm`

Chapter 12

Generate Fibonacci Numbers

You need to write a program to generate Fibonacci numbers. The Fibonacci numbers are 0, 1, 1, 2, 3, 5, 8, 13, 21, ... The first two numbers are 0 and 1. Each subsequent number is the sum of the previous two.

$$f(n) = \begin{cases} 0 & n = 0 \\ 1 & n = 1 \\ f(n-1) + f(n-2) & n = 2, 3, ... \end{cases}$$

12.1 Program 1

Program 12.1.1 *FibonacciGenerator1.sas*

```
1   dm log 'clear'; dm output 'clear';
2
3   /*create fibonacci table; create first 2 Fibonacci numbers */
4   proc sql;
5   create table fibonacci (n num,f num);
6
7   insert into fibonacci
8   values (0,0)
9   values (1,1);
10  quit;
11
12  /* get the last 2 Fibonacci numbers*/
13  proc sql outobs=2;
14    create table last2 as
15    select * from fibonacci order by n descending;
16  quit;
17
18  /* generate the third Fibonacci number (n=2, f=1)*/
19  proc sql;
20    insert into fibonacci
21    select max(n)+1, sum(f) from last2;
22  quit;
23
24  /*Once again, get the last 2 Fibonacci numbers */
25  proc sql outobs=2;
26    create table last2 as
27    select * from fibonacci order by n descending;
28  quit;
29
30  /* generate the fourth Fibonacci number (n=3, f=2)*/
31  proc sql;
32    insert into fibonacci
33    select max(n)+1, sum(f) from last2;
34  quit;
35
36  /*print first 4 Fibonacci numbers*/
37  proc sql;
38    title 'first 4 Fibonacci sequences';
39    select * from fibonacci;
40  quit;
```

Output:

first 4 Fibonacci sequences

n	f
0	0
1	1
2	1
3	2

Here's how Program 12.1.1 works. First, we create the `fibonacci` table with two numeric columns, the counter n and the Fibonacci number $f(n)$. We insert the first two Fibonacci numbers into the `fibonacci` table. This is the `fibonacci` table:

```
work.fibonacci
n          f
-----------
0          0
1          1
```

Next, we query the `fibonacci` table and write the query result into a new table called `last2`. The `order by n descending` clause returns the query result in descending order of n. The `outobs=2` option restricts the query result to only the first 2 rows. Together, `order by n descending` and `outobs=2` retrieve the two rows with the highest n values from the `fibonacci` table.

This is the `work.last2` table:

```
work.last2
n          f
-----------
1          1
0          0
```

Next, from the `last2` table we retrieve `Max(n)+1=1+1=2` and `sum(f)=0+1=1` and insert the query result `n=2`, `f=1` into the `fibonacci` table. The query result is the third Fibonacci number. This is the updated `fibonacci` table:

```
work.fibonacci
n          f
-----------
0          0
1          1
2          1
```

Next, we create the fourth Fibonacci number as we did the third. The newly created `last2` table overwrites the previously generated `last2` table. This is the new `last2` table and the updated `fibonacci` table:

```
work.last2          work.fibonacci
n          f        n          f
-----------         -----------
2          1        0          0
1          1        1          1
                    2          1
                    3          2
```

12.2   Program 2 - Use a Macro

The next program uses a macro to automate the repetitive process in Program 12.1.1.

Program 12.2.1 *FibonacciGenerator2.sas*

```
1   dm log 'clear'; dm output 'clear';
2   /*create fibonacci table; create first 2 Fibonacci numbers */
3   proc sql;
4   create table fibonacci (n num,f num);
5
6   insert into fibonacci
7   values (0,0)
8   values (1,1);
9   quit;
10
11  %macro generate_next_fib;
12  proc sql outobs=2;
13    create table last2 as
14    select * from fibonacci order by n descending;
15  quit;
16
17  proc sql;
18    insert into fibonacci
19    select max(n)+1, sum(f) from last2;
20  quit;
21  %mend;
22
23  /*generate 3 more Fibonacci numbers*/
24  %generate_next_fib
25  %generate_next_fib
26  %generate_next_fib
27
28  proc sql;
29    title 'first 5 Fibonacci sequences';
30    select * from fibonacci;
31  quit;
```

Output:

```
first 5 Fibonacci sequences

        n        f
     ------------------
        0        0
        1        1
        2        1
        3        2
        4        3
```

12.3 Program 3 - A Better Macro

Program 12.3.1 *FibonacciGenerator3.sas*

```
1    dm log 'clear'; dm output 'clear';
2
3    /*create fibonacci table; create first 2 Fibonacci numbers */
4    proc sql;
5    create table fibonacci (n num,f num);
6
7    insert into fibonacci
8    values (0,0)
9    values (1,1);
10   quit;
11
12   %macro generate_next_fib;
13   proc sql outobs=2;
14     create table last2 as
15     select * from fibonacci order by n descending;
16   quit;
17
18   proc sql;
19     insert into fibonacci
20     select max(n)+1, sum(f) from last2;
21   quit;
22   %mend;
23
24   %macro generate_next_n_beyond_first_two(n);
25     %do i=1 %to &n;
26        %generate_next_fib
27     %end;
28   %mend;
29   %generate_next_n_beyond_first_two(10)
30
31   proc sql noprint;
32   select max(n)+1 into :N
33   from fibonacci;
34   quit;
35
36   proc sql;
37   title "first %trim(&N) Fibonacci numbers";
38   select * from fibonacci;
39   quit;
```

Output:

first 12 Fibonacci numbers

n	f
0	0
1	1
2	1
3	2
4	3
5	5
6	8
7	13
8	21
9	34
10	55
11	89

Line 32 creates a macro N, which is used in the `title` statement in Line 37. The `select into` clause is explained in Chapter 14.

12.4 Program 4 - DATA Step Program

Program 12.4.1

FibonacciGenerator4.sas

Output:

```
 1  dm log 'clear'; dm output 'clear';
 2  data fibonacci;
 3
 4  n=0; current_f=0; next_f=1; output;
 5  do n=1 to 10;
 6    last_f =current_f;
 7    current_f =next_f;
 8    next_f =last_f + next_f;
 9    output;
10  end;
11
12  run;
13
14  proc print data=fibonacci;
15  run;
```

Obs	n	f	next_f	last_f
1	0	0	1	.
2	1	1	1	0
3	2	1	2	1
4	3	2	3	1
5	4	3	5	2
6	5	5	8	3
7	6	8	13	5
8	7	13	21	8
9	8	21	34	13
10	9	34	55	21
11	10	55	89	34

12.5 Program 5 - Use the Lag Function

Output:

Program 12.5.1

FibonacciGenerator5.sas

```
 1  dm log 'clear'; dm output 'clear';
 2  data fibonacci;
 3
 4  n=0; f=0; output;
 5  n=1; f=1; output;
 6
 7  do n=2 to 20;
 8    f+lag(f);
 9    output;
10  end;
11
12  run;
13
14  proc print data=fibonacci;
15  run;
```

Obs	n	f
1	0	0
2	1	1
3	2	1
4	3	2
5	4	3
6	5	5
7	6	8
8	7	13
9	8	21
10	9	34
11	10	55
12	11	89
13	12	144
14	13	233
15	14	377
16	15	610
17	16	987
18	17	1597
19	18	2584
20	19	4181
21	20	6765

The lag functions, lag1, lag2, ..., lagN, return values from a queue using FIFO (first in, first out). The queue for each occurrence of lagN is initialized with N missing values. A lagN function stores a value in a queue and returns a value stored previously in that queue using FIFO. Each occurrence of a lagN function in a program generates its own queue of values. When an occurrence of lagN is executed, the value at the top of its queue pops out and gets returned, the remaining values move up, and the new value of the argument is placed at the bottom of the queue. Lag1 can be shortened as `lag`. The next program illustrates the lag*N* function.

Program 12.5.2 *lagDemo.sas*

Output:

```
1  dm log 'clear'; dm output 'clear';
2  data lagDemo;
3
4  do m=1 to 10;
5    m1=lag(m);
6    m2=lag2(m);
7    m3=lag3(m);
8    output;
9  end;
10
11 run;
12
13 proc print data=lagDemo;
14 run;
```

Obs	m	m1	m2	m3
1	1	.	.	.
2	2	1	.	.
3	3	2	1	.
4	4	3	2	1
5	5	4	3	2
6	6	5	4	3
7	7	6	5	4
8	8	7	6	5
9	9	8	7	6
10	10	9	8	7

The variables m1, m2, and m3 return the lagged values of n.

12.6   Program 6 - Use the Lag Function and a Macro

Program 12.6.1 *FibonacciDataStepLag.sas*

Output:

```
1  dm log 'clear'; dm output 'clear';
2
3  /* Specify how many Fibonacci numbers to generate */
4  %let howMany=20;
5
6  data fibonacci;
7  length n 8;
8  /* This merely makes n appear before f in the output table;
9   Even if you don't specify length, n gets default length 8
10 */
11
12 n=0; f=0; output;
13 n=1; f=1; output;
14
15 do n=2 to &howMany-1;
16   f+lag(f);
17   output;
18 end;
19
20 run;
21
22 proc print data=fibonacci;
23  title "First &howMany Fibonacci numbers";
24 run;
```

First 20 Fibonacci numbers

Obs	n	f
1	0	0
2	1	1
3	2	1
4	3	2
5	4	3
6	5	5
7	6	8
8	7	13
9	8	21
10	9	34
11	10	55
12	11	89
13	12	144
14	13	233
15	14	377
16	15	610
17	16	987
18	17	1597
19	18	2584
20	19	4181

12.7 Program 6 - Use Binet's Formula

Based on `http://mathworld.wolfram.com/BinetsFibonacciNumberFormula.html`, here's Binet's Fibonacci Number Formula: $f(n) = \dfrac{(1+\sqrt{5})^n - (1-\sqrt{5})^n}{2^n\sqrt{5}}$, where $n = 0, 1, 2, ...$

Output:

Obs	n	f
1	0	0
2	1	1
3	2	1
4	3	2
5	4	3
6	5	5
7	6	8
8	7	13
9	8	21
10	9	34
11	10	55
12	11	89
13	12	144
14	13	233
15	14	377
16	15	610
17	16	987
18	17	1597
19	18	2584
20	19	4181
21	20	6765

Program 12.7.1 *FibonacciGeneratorUseFormula.sas*

```
1   dm log 'clear'; dm output 'clear';
2   data fibonacci;
3   do n=0 to 20;
4     f=((1+sqrt(5))**n - (1-sqrt(5))**n) /(2**n*sqrt(5));
5     output;
6   end;
7   run;
8
9   proc print data=fibonacci;
10  run;
```

12.8 Further Reading

SAS Talk: LAG Lead

`http://www.sesug.org/SESUGOrganization/newsletters/fall2008/Ian_Whitlock_200809.pdf`

Pitfalls of the LAG function

`http://blogs.sas.com/content/sasdummy/2012/01/03/pitfalls-of-the-lag-function/`

RETAIN or NOT? Is LAG Far Behind?

`http://www.lexjansen.com/pharmasug/2005/CodersCorner/cc19.pdf`

Chapter 13

Call Symput Routine

Recall that Program 11.4.1 attempts to pass DATA step variables to macro variables using the macro LET statement, but it doesn't work. Any macro code is evaluated before the non-macro code is evaluated. To pass a DATA step variable to a macro variable, we need to resolve the macro variable at the DATA step execution time, not at the macro code compilation time. The `call symput` routine does just that.

Program 13.0.1

firstUSPresidentLegendWorking.sas

```
1    dm log 'clear'; dm output 'clear';
2
3    data firstUSPresidentLegend;
4    Id=1;                            Output:
5    Fname='George';
6    Lname='Washington';
7    Legend='Cherry Tree';      Legend about US president No        1: George Washington
8                                       Many talked about Cherry Tree
9    call symput('ID',Id);                         Was it real?
10   call symput('Fname',Fname);
11   call symput('Lname',Lname);     Obs    Id    Fname      Lname        Legend
12   call symput('unauthenticatedStory',Legend);
13                                    1      1    George    Washington   Cherry Tree
14   run;
15
16   options linesize=min nonumber nodate;
17   proc print data=firstUSPresidentLegend;
18    title "Legend about US president No &ID: &FName &LName";
19    title2 "Many talked about &unauthenticatedStory";
20    title3 'Was it real?';
21   run;
```

The output is almost what we want.

The `call symput` routine lets you transfer information between an executing DATA step and the macro processor. You use this routine to create a macro variable and to assign to it any value that is available in the DATA step.

A CALL routine in SAS is similar to a SAS function except it doesn't return a value. While a SAS function returns a value that can be used in an assignment statement or elsewhere in an expression, a CALL routine doesn't return a value and cannot be used in an assignment statements or expression. You invoke a CALL routine for its side effect.

You must use the word CALL to invoke a CALL routine. This gets annoying initially, but you'll gradually get used to it. Having to type the word CALL in your code reminds you that you can't assign a CALL routine to a variable or use a CALL routine in an expression.

`Call symput(macro-variable,text)` assigns the character value of `text` to `macro-variable`. `text` and `macro-variable` can each be specified as

- a literal, enclosed in quotation marks

- a DATA step variable

- a DATA step expression

If `macro-variable` already exists, the value of `text` replaces the former value.

Program 13.0.1 works, but the first line of the output looks ugly. There are 12 blanks between the string No and the literal string 1. Though the first blank is automatically added by SAS to separate two consecutive strings, the remaining 11 blanks are a mystery to be explained in the next section. However, we'll remove the 11 blanks now.

There are two ways to remove the 11 blanks from the printed TITLE statement. One is to remove the leading blanks before the value of Id is stored in the macro variable ID. To use this method, change the CALL SYMPUT statement from

```
call symput('ID',Id);
```

to

```
call symput('ID',trim(left(ID)));
```

The second method is to remove the leading blanks after you retrieve the value stored in the macro variable ID. To use this method, change the TITLE statement from

```
title "Legend about US president No &ID: &FName &LName";
```

to one of the following:

```
title "Legend about US president No %trim(&ID): &FName &LName";
title "Legend about US president No %left(&ID): &FName &LName";
```

While the first method alters the value stored in the macro variable ID, the second method doesn't. The second method creates a copy of the value of the macro variable ID and manipulates the copy. Either way will produce the following output:

```
Legend about US president No 1: George Washington
        Many talked about Cherry Tree
                Was it real?

Obs    Id    Fname        Lname          Legend

1      1     George     Washington     Cherry Tree
```

You might be tempted to use `%trim(%left(&ID))`, but `%left(&ID)` or `%trim(&ID)` is sufficient.

Though the SAS documentation indicates that `%left` left-aligns an argument by removing leading blanks and that `%trim` trims trailing blanks, the next program shows that these two macro functions generate an identical result by removing leading and trailing blanks.

Program 13.0.2 *macroLeftTrim.sas*

```
1    %let x=  abcdefgh  ;
2    %let y=%str(  abcdefgh  );
3    %put %length(&x) %length(&y);
8 12
4    %put |&x| |&y|;
|abcdefgh| |  abcdefgh  |
5    %let y2=%left(&y);
6    %let y3=%trim(&y);
7    %let y4=%trim(%left(&y));
8
9    %put |&y2| |&y3| |&y4|;
|abcdefgh| |abcdefgh| |abcdefgh|
10
11   %macro testEquality;
12     %if &y2=&y3 %then %put y2 and y3 are equal;
13     %if &y2=&y4 %then %put y2 and y4 are equal;
14   %mend;
15
16   %testEquality
y2 and y3 are equal
y2 and y4 are equal
```

The length of the macro variable x is 8, not 12. If a macro variable is assigned a value that has leading or trailing blanks, the leading and trailing blanks are not stored in the macro variable.

However, the length of the macro variable y is 12. The macro function `%str(  abcdefgh  )` creates a literal string consisting of 2 leading blanks followed by the string `abcdefgh` and ending with 2 blanks.

The logs generated by Lines 9 and 16 indicate that the macro variables y2, y3, and y4 are identical.

13.1 Formatting Rules for Assigning Values

If you don't want to get bogged down by the details of why there are 11 extra blanks in the TITLE statement, skip this section for now but do come back later.

Assigning numeric values When you use `call symput(x,n)` to pass a DATA step numeric variable `n` to the macro variable `x`, SAS automatically converts `n` to a string and assigns the converted string to the macro variable `x`. SAS writes a message to the log indicating that a numeric-to-string conversion has occurred.

Automatic numeric-to-string conversions always use the `best12.` format on any numeric value assigned to the macro variable. The resulting macro variable `x` is a 12-column wide, right-justified string with leading blanks if necessary to occupy the 12 width.

In Program 13.0.1, the macro variable `ID` contains a 12-byte string consisting of the string 1 preceded by 11 leading blanks. And you'll see this in the log:

```
NOTE: Numeric values have been converted to character values
at the places given by: (Line):(Column).
```

To remove the 11 leading blanks, change the first CALL SYMPUT statement into:

```
call symput('ID',trim(left(ID)));
```

The `left()` function shifts the left blanks to the right. The `trim()` function removes the trailing blanks.

The next program illustrates different ways of using `call symput(x,n)` to pass a DATA step numeric variable `n` to the macro variable `x`

Program 13.1.1 *symputFormatPassNumToMacroVar.sas*

```
71   dm log 'clear'; dm output 'clear';
72
73   data _null_;
74   n=1;
75
76   /*implicit number-to-string convertion;
77   cause nummeric-to-string conversion message in log*/
78   call symput('x1',n);
79   call symput('x2',left(n));
80   call symput('x3',trim(left(n)));
81
82   /*PUT explicitly converts n to string;
83   No nummeric-to-string conversion message in log */
84   call symput('x4',trim(left(put(n,8.))));
85   run;
```

```
NOTE: Numeric values have been converted to character values
 at the places given by: (Line):(Column).
     78:18    79:23    80:28
NOTE: DATA statement used:
     real time              0.00 seconds
     cpu time               0.00 seconds
```

```
87    %put x1 = |&x1|;
x1 = |            1|
88    %put x2 = |&x2|;
x2 = |1              |
89    %put x3 = |&x3|;
x3 = |1|
90    %put x4 = |&x4|;
x4 = |1|
```

The `data _null_` statement causes SAS to execute the DATA step without creating a new data set. This is efficient because the purpose of Program 13.1.1 is to create macro variables, not to create a data set.

Each of the first three CALL SYMPUT statements implicitly converts the numeric n to a string and assigns the converted string to a macro variable, generating a message in the log indicating that such a conversion has occurred.

In the final CALL SYMPUT statement, the PUT function explicitly converts n to a string and then the converted string is assigned to the macro variable x4. No numeric-to-string message is written to in the log. This is the preferred method to pass a numeric DATA step variable to a macro variable because the numeric-to-string conversion is explicit.

Assigning character values   When you use `call symput(x,u)` to pass a DATA step character variable u whose length is w to a macro variable x, the resulting macro variable x is a w-column wide, left-justified string, with trailing blanks if necessary to occupy the width w.

Program 13.1.2 *symputFormatPassStringToMacroVar.sas*

```
144   dm log 'clear'; dm output 'clear';
145
146   data _null_;
147   length u $5;
148   u='abc';
149
150   call symput('x1',u);
151   call symput('x2',trim(left(u)));
152   run;

NOTE: DATA statement used:
      real time          0.00 seconds
      cpu time           0.00 seconds


153
154   %put x1 = |&x1|;
x1 = |abc  |
155   %put x2 = |&x2|;
x2 = |abc|
```

13.2   Be Careful When Macro Variable Names Use Concatenation

Understanding this section will save you hours of frustration trying to figure out why your concatenated macro variable names don't work.

Often we need to create a series of macro variables using concatenation. The next program tries to do just that, but it doesn't work.

Program 13.2.1 *tenMacroVars.sas*   Output:

```
1   dm log 'clear'; dm output 'clear';
2
3   data tenMacroVars;
4   do n=1 to 10;
5   u='x'||n;
6   call symput(u,n);
7   output;
8   end;
9   run;
10
11  proc print data=tenMacroVars;
12   title 'Macro not working yet';
13  run;
```

```
            Macro not working yet

        Obs       n          u

         1        1     x         1
         2        2     x         2
         3        3     x         3
         4        4     x         4
         5        5     x         5
         6        6     x         6
         7        7     x         7
         8        8     x         8
         9        9     x         9
        10       10     x        10
```

This is the log:

```
164   dm log 'clear'; dm output 'clear';
165
166   data tenMacroVars;
167   do n=1 to 10;
168   u='x'||n;
169   call symput(u,n);
170   output;
171   end;
172   run;

NOTE: Numeric values have been converted to character values
at the places given by: (Line):(Column).
      168:8    169:15
ERROR: Symbolic variable name X          1 must contain
 only letters, digits, and underscores.
NOTE: Invalid argument to function SYMPUT at line 169 column 6.
ERROR: Symbolic variable name X          2 must contain
 only letters, digits, and underscores.

   ...

ERROR: Symbolic variable name X          10 must contain
 only letters, digits, and underscores.
NOTE: Invalid argument to function SYMPUT at line 169 column 6.
n=11 u=x          10 _ERROR_=1 _N_=1
NOTE: The SAS System stopped processing this step because of errors.
WARNING: The data set WORK.TENMACROVARS may be incomplete.
 When this step was stopped there were 10 observations and 2 variables.
```

In SAS, a numeric value is always right-justified; a character value is always left-justified. In Program 13.2.1, the DATA step variable u is created by concatenating the string x and the numeric value n. When a numeric value is concatenated with the string, the numeric value is first converted to a string. The automatic numeric-to-string conversion uses the default best12. format. The converted string n is right-justified occupying 12 columns and the resulting x variable contains 11 blanks.

Since a macro variable name cannot contain blanks, Program 13.2.1 fails. The cure is to use the `trim()` function and the `left()` function to remove the leading blanks from the value of n. The following shows the log of an executed SAS program:

Program 13.2.2 *twentyMacroVars.sas*

```
1     dm log 'clear'; dm output 'clear';
2
3     data tenMacroVars2;
4     do n=1 to 10;
5       u='x'||trim(left(put(n, 2.)));
6       v='y'||trim(left(put(n, 2.)));
7
8       call symput(u,n);
9       call symput(v,trim(left(n)));
10
11      output;
12    end;
13    run;
```

```
NOTE: Numeric values have been converted to character values at the places
      given by: (Line):(Column).
      8:17   9:27
NOTE: The data set WORK.TENMACROVARS2 has 10 observations and 3 variables.
NOTE: DATA statement used:
      real time            0.00 seconds
      cpu time             0.00 seconds
```

```
14
15    proc print data=tenMacroVars2;
16    title 'tenMacroVars2 working';
17    run;
```

```
NOTE: There were 10 observations read from the dataset WORK.TENMACROVARS2.
NOTE: PROCEDURE PRINT used:
      real time            0.01 seconds
      cpu time             0.01 seconds
```

```
18
19    %macro loop(k);
20    %do i=1 %to &k;
21      %put |x&i=&&x&i|;
22    %end;
23    %mend;
24    %loop(10)
|x1=          1|
|x2=          2|
|x3=          3|
|x4=          4|
|x5=          5|
|x6=          6|
|x7=          7|
|x8=          8|
|x9=          9|
```

```
|x10=            10|
25
26   %macro loop2(k);
27   %do i=1 %to &k;
28      %put |x&i=%trim(%left(&&x&i))|;
29   %end;
30   %mend;
31   %loop2(10)
|x1=1|
|x2=2|
|x3=3|
|x4=4|
|x5=5|
|x6=6|
|x7=7|
|x8=8|
|x9=9|
|x10=10|
32
33   %macro loop3(k);
34   %do i=1 %to &k;
35      %put |y&i=&&y&i|;
36   %end;
37   %mend;
38   %loop3(10)
|y1=1|
|y2=2|
|y3=3|
|y4=4|
|y5=5|
|y6=6|
|y7=7|
|y8=8|
|y9=9|
|y10=10|
```

Only the two CALL SYMPUT statements generate the numeric-to-string conversion message in the log. The two concatenation statements don't generate the numeric-to-string conversion message in the log because the PUT statement explicitly converts **n** to string before concatenation occurs.

This is the output:

```
tenMacroVars2 working

Obs     n     u       v

 1      1     x1      y1
 2      2     x2      y2
 3      3     x3      y3
 4      4     x4      y4
 5      5     x5      y5
 6      6     x6      y6
 7      7     x7      y7
 8      8     x8      y8
 9      9     x9      y9
10     10     x10     y10
```

Suppose we drop the PUT function and rewrite Program 13.2.2 Lines 5–6 as follows:

```
u='x'||trim(left(n));
v='y'||trim(left(n));
```

Submit the program. You'll get the same output table **tenMacroVars2** and the same macro variables **x1** to **x10** and **y1** to **y10**. However, your log will look different:

```
701  dm log 'clear'; dm output 'clear';
702
703  data tenMacroVars2;
704  do n=1 to 10;
705    u='x'||trim(left(n));
706    v='y'||trim(left(n));
707
708    call symput(u,n);
709    call symput(v,trim(left(n)));
710
711    output;
712  end;
713  run;
```

```
NOTE: Numeric values have been converted to character values at the places
      given by: (Line):(Column).
      705:20    706:20    708:17    709:27
NOTE: The data set WORK.TENMACROVARS2 has 10 observations and 3 variables.
```

Now the two concatenation statements and the two CALL SYMPUT statements all generate a numeric-to-string conversion message in the log.

Finally, rewrite Lines 5–6 and Lines 7–9 as follows:

```
u='x'||trim(left(put(n, 2.)));
v='y'||trim(left(put(n, 2.)));

call symput(u,put(n, 2.));
call symput(v,trim(left(put(n, 2.))));
```

Once again, you'll get the same output table **tenMacroVars2** and same macro variables **x1** to **x10** and **y1** to **y10**. However, your log will look different:

```
741  data tenMacroVars2;
742  do n=1 to 10;
743    u='x'||trim(left(put(n, 2.)));
744    v='y'||trim(left(put(n, 2.)));
745
746    call symput(u,put(n, 2.));
747    call symput(v,trim(left(put(n, 2.))));
748
749    output;
750  end;
751  run;
```

```
NOTE: The data set WORK.TENMACROVARS2 has 10 observations and 3 variables.
```

Now the numeric-to-string conversion message disappears from the log. The numeric value **n** is explicitly converted to a string via a PUT statement before **n** is concatenated with a string and before **n** is assigned to a macro variable.

In Program 13.2.2, the first CALL SYMPUT statement (Line 8) saves the untrimmed, right-justified value of **n** into the macro variable **u**.

The `loop` macro contains the symbol **&&x&i**. It takes the macro processor two passes to resolve **&&x&i**. Take $i = 1$ for example. In the first pass, **&&x** resolves to **&x** (two ampersands evaluate to one ampersand) and **&i** resolves to 1, resulting **&x1**. In the second pass, **&x1** resolves to 1.

If you have SAS 9.0+, you can use the new `cat` and the `call symputx` routine.

Program 13.2.3 *fortyMacroVarsSASv9.sas*

```
1    dm log 'clear'; dm output 'clear';
2
3    data _null_;
4    do n=1 to 10;
5
6    /*cat, cats, symputx functions in SAS v9 and above*/
7    call symput(cat('x',n),n);
8    call symput(cat('y',n),n);
9
10   call symputx(cat('u',n),n);
11   call symputx(cat('v',n),n);
12
13   end;
14   run;
15
16   %macro loop(n);
17   %do i=1 %to &n;
18   %put x(&i)= &&x&i y(&i)= &&y&i u(&i)= &&u&i v(&i)= &&v&i;
19   %end;
20   %mend;
21
22   %loop(10)
```

Submit the program. You'll get this log:

```
        %loop(10);
x(1)=           1 y(1)=        1 u(1)= 1 v(1)= 1
x(2)=           2 y(2)=        2 u(2)= 2 v(2)= 2
x(3)=           3 y(3)=        3 u(3)= 3 v(3)= 3
x(4)=           4 y(4)=        4 u(4)= 4 v(4)= 4
x(5)=           5 y(5)=        5 u(5)= 5 v(5)= 5
x(6)=           6 y(6)=        6 u(6)= 6 v(6)= 6
x(7)=           7 y(7)=        7 u(7)= 7 v(7)= 7
x(8)=           8 y(8)=        8 u(8)= 8 v(8)= 8
x(9)=           9 y(9)=        9 u(9)= 9 v(9)= 9
x(10)=         10 y(10)=      10 u(10)= 10 v(10)= 10
```

SAS 9.0 introduced several similar concatenation functions, `cat`, `cats`, `catx`, and `catt`. SAS 9.2 introduced `catq`. SAS 9.0 also introduced the `call symputx` routine. This routine, among other things, left-justifies both arguments and trims trailing blanks. In contrast, `call symput` does not left-justify the arguments or trim trailing blanks from the first argument only. If you have SAS version 9.0 or above, you can use the `call symputx` routine to simplify your code.

What does the next program do?

Program 13.2.4 *symputOneMaroVar.sas*

```
1   dm log 'clear'; dm output 'clear';
2   data oneTwoThree;
3   input m;
4   datalines;
5   1
6   2
7   3
8   ;
9   data _null_;
10  set oneTwoThree;
11  call symput('x', trim(left(put(m,2.))) );
12  run;
13  %put |&x|;
```

Let's look at the second DATA step. During its first iteration, the **set** statement reads in the first row m=1 from the input table **oneTwoThree**; the CALL SYMPUT statement assigns the string 1 to the macro variable x.

Similarly, the second iteration reads in **m=2** and reassigns the macro variable x the string 2. Finally, the third iteration reads in the last row **m=3** from the input table **oneTwoThree** and reassigns the macro variable x the string 3.

Submit the program and you'll get this log:

```
   %put |&x|;
|3|
```

Program 13.2.4 is equivalent to:

Program 13.2.5 *symputOneMacroVar2.sas*

```
1   dm log 'clear'; dm output 'clear';
2   data oneTwoThree;
3   input m;
4   datalines;
5   1
6   2
7   3
8   ;
9   data _null_;
10  set oneTwoThree end=EOF;
11  if EOF then call symput('x', trim(left(put(m,2.))) );
12  run;
13  %put |&x|;
```

Program 13.2.4 and 13.2.5 are equivalent to:

Program 13.2.6 *symputOneMacroVar3.sas*

```
1   dm log 'clear'; dm output 'clear';
2   data oneTwoThree;
3   input m;
4   datalines;
5   1
6   2
7   3
8   ;
9   data _null_;
10  set oneTwoThree;
11  if _n_=3 then call symput('x',trim(left(put(m,2.))));
12  run;
13  %put |&x|;
```

What does the next program do?

Program 13.2.7 *symputThreeMacroVars.sas*

```
1   dm log 'clear'; dm output 'clear';
2   data oneTwoThree;
3   input m;
4   datalines;
5   1
6   2
7   3
8   ;
9   data _null_;
10  set oneTwoThree;
11  call symput('x'||trim(left(put(_n_,2.))), trim(left(put(m,2.))));
12  run;
13  %put |&x1| |&x2| |&x3|;
```

This is the log:

```
   %put |&x1| |&x2| |&x3|;
|1| |2| |3|
```

When you use **call symput** to create a macro variable in a DATA step, the macro variable is not actually created or assigned a value until the DATA step is executed. Therefore, you cannot reference a macro variable that is created with the **call symput** routine by preceding its name with an ampersand within the same DATA step in which it is created, as illustrated by a log of an executed SAS program:

Program 13.2.8 *notRefMacroVarSameDataStep.sas*

```
1    dm log 'clear'; dm output 'clear';
2    data _null_;
3    x=1; y='a';
4    call symput('m1',x);
5    call symput('m2',y);
6    %put m1=&m1 m2=&m2;
WARNING: Apparent symbolic reference M1 not resolved.
WARNING: Apparent symbolic reference M2 not resolved.
m1=&m1 m2=&m2
7    run;

NOTE: Numeric values have been converted to character values at the places
given by: (Line):(Column).
      4:18
NOTE: DATA statement used:
      real time           0.00 seconds
      cpu time            0.00 seconds
```

The next program fixes the error. In this program, Line 14 references the macro variables m1 and m2 after the DATA step that creates these two macro variables via the `call symput` routine has executed.

Program 13.2.9 *refMacroVarNextDataStep.sas*

```
8    dm log 'clear'; dm output 'clear';
9    data _null_;
10   x=1; y='a';
11   call symput('m1',x);
12   call symput('m2',y);
13   run;

NOTE: Numeric values have been converted to character values at the places
given by: (Line):(Column).
      11:18
NOTE: DATA statement used:
      real time           0.00 seconds
      cpu time            0.00 seconds


14   %put m1=&m1 m2=&m2;
m1=          1 m2=a
```

13.3 Further Reading

The Power of CALL SYMPUT DATA Step Interface by Examples

http://www2.sas.com/proceedings/sugi29/052-29.pdf

Improving Program Efficiency with Macro Variables

http://web.utk.edu/sas/OnlineTutor/1.2/en/60476/m32/m32_33.htm

Character Functions

http://support.sas.com/publishing/pubcat/chaps/59343.pdf

Let the CAT Out of the Bag: String Concatenation in SAS 9

http://www.mwsug.org/proceedings/2013/S1/MWSUG-2013-S108.pdf

Tips:Using the SAS V9 CALL SYMPUTX Routine

http://www.sascommunity.org/wiki/Tips:Using_the_SAS_V9_CALL_SYMPUTX_Routine

Sample 24589: Concatenation functions in SAS 9.0 and above

http://support.sas.com/kb/24/589.html

Chapter 14

PROC SQL Macro Facility

Often we need to query a table and store the query result in macro variables.

14.1 Create Macro Variables from the First Row of a Query Result

If you specify a single macro variable in the INTO clause, then PROC SQL assigns to the single macro variable the value from only the first row of the appropriate column in the SELECT list.

In the next program, the SELECT statement (Line 18) returns all five rows of x and y from the source table work.test. However, only the first row of x (the number 1) is stored in the macro variable m1; only the first row of y (the string a) is stored in the macro variable m2.

Program 14.1.1 *procSqlMacroFacility1.sas*

```
1   dm log 'clear'; dm output 'clear';
2   options mprint mlogic symbolgen;
3   data test;
4   input x y$;
5   datalines;
6   1 a
7   2 b
8   3 c
9   4 d
10  5 a
11  ;
12  run;
13
14  proc sql;
15  title '5 rows are retrieved from work.test';
16  title2 'Only 1st row results are stored in m1 and m2';
17
18  select x,y into :m1,:m2 from test;
19  quit;
20
21  %put &m1 &m2;
22  data test1;
23    a=10; x=&m1; y="&m2"; z=&m2;
```

```
24   run;
25
26   proc print data=test1;
27     title 'Table test1';
28   run;
```

This is the log generated by the macro PUT statement:

```
     %put &m1 &m2;
1 a
```

This is the output:

```
     5 rows are retrieved from work.test
Only 1st row results are stored in m1 and m2

                    x   y
          ------------------
                    1   a
                    2   b
                    3   c
                    4   d
                    5   a
               Table test1

     Obs     a     x     y     z

      1     10     1     a     10
```

The top part of the output is generated by the SELECT statement. The remaining output is generated by PROC PRINT. This is the source code of the second DATA step:

```
data test1;
   a=10; x=1; y="a"; z=a;
run;
```

The literal string a is assigned to y. The variable z is set equal to the variable a.

14.2 Create Macro Variables from the Result of an Aggregate Function

The next program queries the total row count, the sum of x, and the count of the number of the unique values of y from the test table. It then stores the query result into three macro variables, m3, m4, and m5 respectively. Finally, it passes the values of the macro variables to the DATA step variables numX, totalX, and numUniqueY.

Program 14.2.1 *procSqlMacroFacility2.sas*

```
1    dm log 'clear'; dm output 'clear';
2    data test;
3    input x y$;
4    datalines;
5    1 a
6    2 b
7    3 c
8    4 d
9    5 a
10   ;
11   run;
12
13   proc sql;
14   title 'Store aggregate result into macro vars';
15
16   select count(*),sum(x),count(distinct y) into :m3,:m4,:m5 from test;
17   quit;
18
19   %put &m3 &m4 &m5;
20   data test2;
21     numX=&m3; totalX=&m4; numUniqueY=&m5;
22   run;
23
24   proc print data=test2;
25     title 'Table test2';
26   run;
```

This is the log generated by the macro PUT statement:

```
     %put &m3 &m4 &m5;
5       15      4
```

This is the output:

```
Store aggregate result into macro vars


        ----------------------------
            5        15         4
              Table test2

                          num
                 total   Unique
     Obs    numX    X       Y

      1      5     15       4
```

14.3   Create Multiple Macro Variables

In the next program, the SELECT statement retrieves all the five rows of x and y from the `testData` table. The `order by x descending` clause orders the query result by descending order of x. As the result, the first row of the query result is x=5; y=e; The second row of the query result is x=4; y=d; and so on.

The first two rows of x returned by the SELECT statement are stored in the macro variables u1 and u2 respectively. The five rows of y returned by the SELECT statement are stored in the macro variables v1 through v5 respectively.

The `create table TestData2 like testData` statement creates an empty table TestData2 which is just like the testData table. The TestData2 table has the same column names and column attributes as the testData table. Next, the `insert into TestData2` statement writes new rows into the TestData2 table.

Program 14.3.1 *procSqlMacroFacility3.sas*

```
1    dm log 'clear'; dm output 'clear';
2    data testData;
3    input x y$;
4    datalines;
5    1 a
6    2 b
7    3 c
8    4 d
9    5 e
10   ;
11   run;
12
13   proc sql noprint;
14   select x,y into :u1-:u2, :v1-:v5
15   from testData
16   order by x descending;
17   quit;
18
19   %put &u1 &u2 &v1 &v2 &v3 &v4 &v5;
20   proc sql;
21   create table TestData2 like testData;
22   insert into TestData2
23   values(&u1, "&v1")
24   values(&u1, "&v1")
25   values(&u2, "&v2")
26   values(&u2, "&v2")
27   ;
28   title 'TestData2';
29   select * from TestData2;
30   quit;
```

This is the log generated by the macro PUT statement:

```
    %put &u1 &u2 &v1 &v2 &v3 &v4 &v5;
1 2 a b c d a
```

This is the source code generated by Lines 23–26:

```
values(5, "e")
values(5, "e")
values(4, "d")
values(4, "d")
```

This is the output generated by Lines 28–29 :

```
    TestData2

      x   y
    ------------------
      5   e
      4   d
      3   c
      2   b
      1   a
```

The `noprint` option in Line 13 prevents SAS from writing the query result to the output window. If you remove the `noprint` option from Line 13 and resubmit Program 14.3.1, you'll get this output:

```
    TestData2

      x   y
    ------------------
      5   e
      4   d
      3   c
      2   b
      1   a
    TestData2

      x   y
    ------------------
      5   e
      5   e
      4   d
      4   d
```

In the next program, the SELECT statement returns all the five rows of the x column from the test table. It then attempts to store the five rows of the query result into seven macro variables, w1 to w7. As a result, only the first five macro variables, from w1 to w5, are created. SAS warns you in the log that w6 and w7 are not resolved.

Program 14.3.2 *procSqlMacroFacility4.sas*

```
1    dm log 'clear'; dm output 'clear';
2    data test;
3    input x y$;
4    datalines;
5    1 a
6    2 b
7    3 c
8    4 d
9    5 a
10   ;
11   run;
12
13   proc sql;
```

```
14    select
15       x
16    into
17       :w1-:w7
18
19    from test;
20    quit;
21
22    %put &w1 &w2 &w3 &w4 &w5 &w6 &w7;
23    %put &sqlobs;
```

This is the log generated by the two macro PUT statements:

```
     %put &w1 &w2 &w3 &w4 &w5 &w6 &w7;
WARNING: Apparent symbolic reference W6 not resolved.
WARNING: Apparent symbolic reference W7 not resolved.
1 2 3 4 5 &w6 &w7
     %put &sqlobs;
5
```

The macro variable, `sqlobs`, was automatically created by SAS. It stores the number of the rows that were processed by an SQL procedure statement.

The query result generated by the SELECT statement is written to the output window:

```
The SAS System

          x
    --------
          1
          2
          3
          4
          5
```

14.4   Chain Query Results into a Macro Variable List

Program 14.4.1 *procSqlMacroFacility5.sas*

```
1    dm log 'clear'; dm output 'clear';
2    data testData;
3    input x y$;
4    datalines;
5    1 a
6    2 b
7    3 c
8    4 d
9    5 e
10   ;
11   run;
12
13   proc sql;
14   select
```

```
15    x
16    ,x
17    ,y
18    ,y
19    ,put(x,1.)||y
20    ,put(x,1.)||y
21
22 into
23    :xlist1 separated by '*'
24    ,:xlist2 separated by '*' notrim
25    ,:ylist1 separated by '*'
26    ,:ylist2 separated by '*' notrim
27    ,:zlist1 separated by '*'
28    ,:zlist2 separated by '*' notrim
29
30 from testData;
31 quit;
32
33 %put &xlist1;
34 %put &xlist2;
35 %put &ylist1;
36 %put &ylist2;
37 %put &zlist1;
38 %put &zlist2;
```

This is the log generated by the six macro PUT statements:

```
    %put &xlist1;
1*2*3*4*5
    %put &xlist2;
1*        2*        3*        4*        5
    %put &ylist1;
a*b*c*d*e
    %put &ylist2;
a         *b        *c        *d        *e
    %put &zlist1;
1a*2b*3c*4d*5e
    %put &zlist2;
1a        *2b       *3c       *4d       *5e
```

The query result generated by the SELECT statement is written to the output window:

```
                    The SAS System

      x         x   y         y
    ------------------------------------------------------------
          1     1   a         a         1a        1a
          2     2   b         b         2b        2b
          3     3   c         c         3c        3c
          4     4   d         d         4d        4d
          5     5   e         e         5e        5e
```

Line 15 corresponds to Line 23. `Into :xlist1 separated by '*'` in Line 23 chains the five values of x returned by Line 15 into one macro variable xlist1 and uses an asterisk as the delimiter to separate two consecutive values of x. By default, the expression `into :xlist1 separated by '*'` removes the leading and trailing blanks from each value returned by the SELECT statement before the value is chained. The log generated by Line 33 indicates that xlist1 contains the text 1*2*3*4*5, which doesn't contain any blanks and uses an asterisk as the delimiter.

Line 16 corresponds to Line 24. The notrim option in Line 24 preserves the leading and trailing blanks of each x value. The log generated by Line 34 confirms that xlist2 contains blanks and is delimited by an asterisk:

```
1*       2*       3*       4*        5
```

You can use a different delimiter. Select x into :xlist1 separated by ',' assigns 1,2,3,4,5 to xlist1. Similarly, select x into :xlist1 separated by ' ' assigns 1 2 3 4 5 to xlist1.

Line 19 corresponds to Line 27. Line 19 generates five concatenated pairs of x and y. The put(x,1.) function converts the numeric variable x into a 1-column wide string. Then the converted string is concatenated with y. The five concatenated pairs are stored in the macro variable zlist1. The log generated by Line 37 indicates that zlist1 contains the text 1a*2b*3c*4d*5e.

In Line 19, if you concatenate x and y using x||y without first converting x to string, you'll get the following error in the log:

```
ERROR: Concatenation (||) requires character operands.
```

14.5 Search Words in a Macro Variable List

The next program retrieves the individual words from a macro variable list.

Program 14.5.1 *macroScanFunc1.sas*

```
1   dm log 'clear'; dm output 'clear';
2   %let x1=%scan(1*2*3*4*5, 1, *);
3   %let x2=%scan(1*2*3*4*5, 2, *);
4   %let x3=%scan(1*2*3*4*5, 3, *);
5   %let x4=%scan(1*2*3*4*5, 4, *);
6   %let x5=%scan(1*2*3*4*5, 5, *);
7   %let x6=%scan(1*2*3*4*5, 6, *);
8
9   %put &x1 &x2 &x3 &x4 &x5 &x6;
10
11  %macro testNull;
12    %if &x6= %then %put x6 is null and stores nothing;
13    %else %put x6 is not null;
14  %mend;
15  %testNull
```

This is the log:

```
    %put &x1 &x2 &x3 &x4 &x5 &x6;
1 2 3 4 5

    %testNull
x6 is null and stores nothing
```

The macro scan function %scan(text, n, charlist) searches text and returns the n-th word. A word is one or more characters separated by one or more delimiters. The optional charlist specifies a list of one or more characters that separate "words" in the text. Since the text 1*2*3*4*5 has five words, the macro variable x6 is set to null and contains nothing.

If the argument charlist is omitted, then the default delimiters depend on whether your computer uses ASCII or EBCDIC characters. If your computer uses ASCII characters, then the default delimiters are:

```
blank ! $ % & ( ) * + , - . / ; < ^
```

If your computer uses EBCDIC characters, then the default delimiters are:

```
blank ! $ % & ( ) * + , - . / ; < |
```

EBCDIC is the character encoding system of mainframes and ASCII is the encoding system of other operating systems such as VAX, PC, UNIX, and Macintosh. These two character sets represent the same data differently.

The default delimiter list contains an asterisk *. Program 14.5.1 can be rewritten to:

Program 14.5.2 *macroScanFunc2.sas*

```
1    dm log 'clear'; dm output 'clear';
2    %let x1=%scan(1*2*3*4*5, 1);
3    %let x2=%scan(1*2*3*4*5, 2);
4    %let x3=%scan(1*2*3*4*5, 3);
5    %let x4=%scan(1*2*3*4*5, 4);
6    %let x5=%scan(1*2*3*4*5, 5);
7    %let x6=%scan(1*2*3*4*5, 6);
8
9    %put &x1 &x2 &x3 &x4 &x5 &x6;
10
11   %macro testNull;
12     %if &x6= %then %put x6 is null and stores nothing;
13     %else %put x6 is not null;
14   %mend;
15   %testNull
```

14.5.1 Test Whether a Macro Variable Equals null

Often we need to test whether a macro variable was assigned a null string.

Program 14.5.3 *testMacroNull.sas*

```
1    %let x1=;
2    %put length of macro var x1 is %length(&x1);
length of macro var x1 is 0
3
4    %let x2='';
```

```
5    %put length of macro x2 is %length(&x2);
length of macro x2 is 2
6
7    %let x3=' ';
8    %put length of macro x3 is %length(&x3);
length of macro x3 is 3
9
10   %let x4=%str();
11   %put length of macro var x4 is %length(&x4);
length of macro var x4 is 0
12
13   %let x5=%str( );
14   %put length of macro var x5 is %length(&x5);
length of macro var x5 is 1
15
16   %let x6=%str(  );
17   %put length of macro var x6 is %length(&x6);
length of macro var x6 is 2
18
19   %macro test;
20   %if &x1=      %then %let y1=1; %else %let y1=0;
21   %if &x1=&x2  %then %let y2=1; %else %let y2=0;
22   %if &x1=&x3  %then %let y3=1; %else %let y3=0;
23   %if &x1=&x4  %then %let y4=1; %else %let y4=0;
24   %if &x1=&x5  %then %let y5=1; %else %let y5=0;
25   %if &x1=&x6  %then %let y6=1; %else %let y6=0;
26
27   %put |&x1| |&x2| |&x3| |&x4| |&x5| |&x6|;
28   %put |&y1| |&y2| |&y3| |&y4| |&y5| |&y6|;
29
30   %mend;
31
32   %test
|| |''| |' '| || | | |  |
|1| |0| |0| |1| |1| |1|
```

Line 1. The equals sign without an argument assigns a null string to the macro variable x1.

Line 4. The macro variable x2 is assigned a string of two single quotation marks.

Line 10. The %str() creates an empty string with 0 length.

Line 13. The %str( ) creates a string of 1 blank.

Line 16. The %str( ) creates a string of 2 blanks.

The two lines after Line 32 are the log generated when the macro %test is called. From the log, you see that the macro variables y1, y4, y5, and y6 are each assigned the string 1 and that the macro variables y2 and y3 are each assigned the string 0. This indicates that you can test whether a macro variable x has been assigned a null using one of the following methods:

```
/*equals sign without argument*/
%if &x= %then ... ;

/*there can be zero to many blanks inside the parenthesis*/
%if &x=%str() %then ... ;
%if &x=%str( ) %then ... ;
```

```
%if &x=%str(  ) %then ... ;
%if &x=%str(   ) %then ... ;
...
```

However, &x is not equal to '' because the latter consists of two single quotation marks.

Similarly, you can use one of the following methods to test whether the macro variable x has not been assigned a null string:

```
/*not equal operator without argument*/
%if &x NE  %then ... ;

/*there can be zero to many blanks inside the parenthesis*/
%if &x NE %str() %then ... ;
%if &x NE %str( ) %then ... ;
%if &x NE %str(  ) %then ... ;
%if &x NE %str(   ) %then ... ;
...
```

The **ne** is the not equal operator.

14.5.2   DATA Step Scan Function

The next program demonstrates the DATA step `scan()` function.

Program 14.5.4 *ScanFunc1.sas*

```
1    dm log 'clear'; dm output 'clear';
2    data testScan;
3    x1=scan('1*2*3*4*5', 1, '*');
4    x2=scan('1*2*3*4*5', 2, '*');
5    x3=scan('1*2*3*4*5', 3, '*');
6    x4=scan('1*2*3*4*5', 4, '*');
7    x5=scan('1*2*3*4*5', 5, '*');
8    x6=scan('1*2*3*4*5', 6, '*');
9
10   if x6=' ' then put 'x6 is null';
11   else put 'x6 is not null';
12   run;
13
14   proc print data=testScan;
15     title 'Result of scan function in a DATA step';
16   run;
```

This is the output:

```
Result of scan function in a DATA step

Obs    x1    x2    x3    x4    x5    x6

 1     1     2     3     4     5
```

This is the log generated by the PUT statement:

```
x6 is null
```

Program 14.5.4 can be shortened to:

Program 14.5.5 *ScanFunc2.sas*

```
1   dm log 'clear'; dm output 'clear';
2   data testScan;
3   x1=scan('1*2*3*4*5', 1);
4   x2=scan('1*2*3*4*5', 2);
5   x3=scan('1*2*3*4*5', 3);
6   x4=scan('1*2*3*4*5', 4);
7   x5=scan('1*2*3*4*5', 5);
8   x6=scan('1*2*3*4*5', 6);
9
10  if x6=' ' then put 'x6 is null';
11  else put 'x6 is not null';
12  run;
13
14  proc print data=testScan;
15   title 'Result of scan function in a DATA step';
16  run;
```

14.5.3   Quotation Marks often Can Be Omitted in the Macro Scan Function

Compare Program 14.5.4 and Program 14.5.1. In the scan function in Program 14.5.4, the first parameter (the string to be searched) and the third parameter (the list of delimiters) are in quotation marks. However, in the %scan function in Program 14.5.1, the first parameter and the third parameter are not enclosed in quotation marks.

If you insist, you can enclose the first and the third parameters of the %scan function in quotation marks and rewrite Program 14.5.1 as:

Program 14.5.6 *macroScanFunc3.sas*

```
1   dm log 'clear'; dm output 'clear';
2   %let x1=%scan('1*2*3*4*5', 1, '*');
3   %let x2=%scan('1*2*3*4*5', 2, '*');
4   %let x3=%scan('1*2*3*4*5', 3, '*');
5   %let x4=%scan('1*2*3*4*5', 4, '*');
6   %let x5=%scan('1*2*3*4*5', 5, '*');
7   %let x6=%scan('1*2*3*4*5', 6, '*');
8
9   %put &x1 &x2 &x3 &x4 &x5 &x6;
10
11  %macro testNull;
12    %if &x6= %then %put x6 is null and stores nothing;
13    %else %put x6 is not null;
14  %mend;
15  %testNull
```

In some cases, however, omitting quotation marks in the `%scan` function can create ambiguity. For example, the following statement is invalid:

```
%let x1=%scan(1,2,3,4,5, 1, ',');
```

The macro processor can't identify the first parameter (the string to be searched) and the third parameter (the list of delimiters) of the `%scan` function. The statement should be rewritten as:

```
%let x1=%scan('1,2,3,4,5', 1, ',');
```

14.5.4   Macro Scan Function - Some Special Cases

A comma has a double meaning. It can mean a literal comma or the comma as the delimiter to mark a word boundary. If the search string parameter contains one or more commas, SAS can't tell whether the comma is a literal string or the delimiter. You can use the macro string function `%str(,)` to specify a comma as a literal string, not a delimiter.

Program 14.5.7 *macroScanFunc4.sas*

```
1   dm log 'clear'; dm output 'clear';
2   options symbolgen;
3
4   /* This doesn't work */
5   /*
6   %let a1=%scan('1 , 2 , 3', 1);
7   %let a2=%scan('1 , 2 , 3', 2);
8   %let a3=%scan('1 , 2 , 3', 3);
9   */
10
11  /* This works */
12  %let a1=%scan(%str(1 , 2 , 3), 1, ',');
13  %let a2=%scan(%str(1 , 2 , 3), 2, ',');
14  %let a3=%scan(%str(1 , 2 , 3), 3, ',');
15
16  /* This works too */
17  %let b1=%scan(%str(1 , 2 , 3), 1, %str(,));
18  %let b2=%scan(%str(1 , 2 , 3), 2, %str(,));
19  %let b3=%scan(%str(1 , 2 , 3), 3, %str(,));
20
21  /* This works too */
22  %let c1=%scan(%str(1 , 2 , 3), 1);
23  %let c2=%scan(%str(1 , 2 , 3), 2);
24  %let c3=%scan(%str(1 , 2 , 3), 3);
25
26  %put &a1 &a2 &a3;
27  %put &b1 &b2 &b3;
28  %put &c1 &c2 &c3;
```

This is the output:

```
     %put &a1 &a2 &a3;
SYMBOLGEN:  Macro variable A1 resolves to 1
SYMBOLGEN:  Macro variable A2 resolves to 2
SYMBOLGEN:  Macro variable A3 resolves to 3
1 2 3
     %put &b1 &b2 &b3;
SYMBOLGEN:  Macro variable B1 resolves to 1
SYMBOLGEN:  Macro variable B2 resolves to 2
SYMBOLGEN:  Macro variable B3 resolves to 3
1 2 3
     %put &c1 &c2 &c3;
SYMBOLGEN:  Macro variable C1 resolves to 1
SYMBOLGEN:  Macro variable C2 resolves to 2
SYMBOLGEN:  Macro variable C3 resolves to 3
1 2 3
```

The macro string function %str(,) returns a literal comma. Similarly, %str(1 , 2 , 3) returns a literal string 1 , 2 , 3.

A comma is not the only symbol with double meanings. Parentheses, the plus sign +, single and double quotation marks, eq (a shorthand for the equals sign =), ne (a shorthand for not equal), ge (a shorthand for $\geq$), and some other symbols can mean a literal string or something special. You can use the macro string function to specify that the appearance of any of these symbols means nothing more than a literal string. For example, %str(ge) returns the literal string ge, the letter g followed by the letter e, not the greater-than-or-equal-to operator $\geq$.

A similar macro function %nstr() does everything that %str() does. In addition, it hides the special meaning of two more characters, the dollar sign $ and the percent sign %.

Similar to using %str(,) to create a literal comma, you can use %str( ) or ' ' to create a blank as the delimiter as shown in the next program.

Program 14.5.8 *macroScanFunc5.sas*

```
1   dm log 'clear'; dm output 'clear';
2   options symbolgen;
3
4   %let c1=%scan(1     2  3, 1, ' ');
5   %let c2=%scan(1     2  3, 2, ' ');
6   %let c3=%scan(1     2  3, 3, ' ');
7
8   %let d1=%scan(1     2  3, 1, %str(' '));
9   %let d2=%scan(1     2  3, 2, %str(' '));
10  %let d3=%scan(1     2  3, 3, %str(' '));
11
12  %let e1=%scan(1     2  3, 1);
13  %let e2=%scan(1     2  3, 2);
14  %let e3=%scan(1     2  3, 3);
15
16  %put &c1 &c2 &c3;
17  %put &d1 &d2 &d3;
18  %put &e1 &e2 &e3;
```

This is the output:

```
        %put &c1 &c2 &c3;
SYMBOLGEN:  Macro variable C1 resolves to 1
SYMBOLGEN:  Macro variable C2 resolves to 2
SYMBOLGEN:  Macro variable C3 resolves to 3
1 2 3
        %put &d1 &d2 &d3;
SYMBOLGEN:  Macro variable D1 resolves to 1
SYMBOLGEN:  Macro variable D2 resolves to 2
SYMBOLGEN:  Macro variable D3 resolves to 3
1 2 3
        %put &e1 &e2 &e3;
SYMBOLGEN:  Macro variable E1 resolves to 1
SYMBOLGEN:  Macro variable E2 resolves to 2
SYMBOLGEN:  Macro variable E3 resolves to 3
1 2 3
```

14.5.5   Pass and Parse a Macro Variable List

Rarely do you need to hard code the search string in the macro **scan** function or in the DATA step **scan** function. The next program illustrates how to pass a macro variable list from PROC SQL to a DATA step and how to parse a macro variable list in the DATA step.

Program 14.5.9 *passAndParseMacroVarList.sas*

```
1   dm log 'clear'; dm output 'clear';
2   options mprint mlogic symbolgen;
3
4   data one2five;
5   input x;
6   datalines;
7   1
8   2
9   3
10  4
11  5
12  ;
13  run;
14
15  proc sql;
16  title "Retrieve all x's from one2five";
17  title2 "Chain the 5 x's into the macro variable xlist";
18  select x into :xlist separated by ' ' from one2five;
19  quit;
20
21  %let x1=%scan(&xlist,1);
22  %let x2=%scan(&xlist,2);
23  %let x3=%scan(&xlist,3);
24  %let x4=%scan(&xlist,4);
25  %let x5=%scan(&xlist,5);
26
27  data myData;
28  xlist="&xlist";
29  x1=scan(xlist,1);
30  x2=scan(xlist,2);
31  x3=scan(xlist,3);
```

```
32   x4=scan(xlist,4);
33   x5=scan(xlist,5);
34   run;
35
36   proc print data=myData noobs;
37     title "xlist is &xlist";
38     title2 "The values are &x1, &x2, &x3, &x4, and &x5";
39   run;
```

This is the output:

```
        Retrieve all x's from one2five
Chain the 5 x's into the macro variable xlist


                         x
                     --------
                         1
                         2
                         3
                         4
                         5
            xlist is 1 2 3 4 5
      The values are 1, 2, 3, 4, and 5

    xlist        x1     x2     x3     x4     x5

    1 2 3 4 5     1      2      3      4      5
```

14.6 Count the Number of Words in a Macro Variable List

In this section, we'll write a macro to calculate the number of values in a macro variable list.

First, let's write a non-macro program to count the number of words in a string. Then we'll use the same logic to create a macro that counts how many words there are in a macro variable list.

14.6.1 Count Words in a DATA Step

Program 14.6.1 *countWord.sas*

```
1    dm log 'clear'; dm output 'clear';
2    data countWord;
3    string='It was the best of times, it was the worst of times,';
4
5    length word $10;  count=0;
6    do while(scan(string,count+1,' ') ne ' ');
7      count = count +1;
8      word = scan(string,count,' ');
9      output;
10   end;
11   run;
12
13   proc print noobs;
14     title 'countWord table';
15   run;
```

This is the output:

```
                        countWord table

                string                        word      count

It was the best of times, it was the worst of times,    It         1
It was the best of times, it was the worst of times,    was        2
It was the best of times, it was the worst of times,    the        3
It was the best of times, it was the worst of times,    best       4
It was the best of times, it was the worst of times,    of         5
It was the best of times, it was the worst of times,    times,     6
It was the best of times, it was the worst of times,    it         7
It was the best of times, it was the worst of times,    was        8
It was the best of times, it was the worst of times,    the        9
It was the best of times, it was the worst of times,    worst     10
It was the best of times, it was the worst of times,    of        11
It was the best of times, it was the worst of times,    times,    12
```

The LENGTH statement sets word to be 10 character wide. In a DATA step, if the scan function returns a value to a variable that has not yet been given a length, then that variable is given a length of 200 characters. Without the LENGTH statement, word will be 200 character wide.

The WHILE condition checks whether the next word delimited by blanks exists. If the next word exits, the SCAN function retrieves the next word. The Do-While statement can be rewritten as:

```
do while(not missing(scan(string,count+1,' ')));
```

The missing function checks a numeric or character expression for a missing value, and returns a numeric result. If the argument does not contain a missing value, SAS returns a value of 0. If the argument contains a missing value, SAS returns a value of 1.

In SAS, there are at least three ways to check whether a variable contains a missing value:

```
1   if x ne ' ' then ...;
2   if x ne . then ...;
3   if not missing(x) then ...;
```

Line 1 checks whether a character variable x has a missing value. Line 2 checks whether a numeric variable x has a missing value. Line 3 checks whether the variable x, be it character or numeric, has a missing value. Line 3 is more flexible because it works whether x is character or numeric.

The next program counts the number of words in a string using the countw function available in SAS 9.2 or above.

Program 14.6.2 *countWord2.sas*

```
1   /* countw function is available in SAS 9.2+ */
2   data countWord2;
3   string='It was the best of times, it was the worst of times,';
4   count=countw(string);
```

```
5   run;
6
7   proc print noobs;
8     title 'countWord2';
9   run;
```

This is the log:

```
                        countWord2

                string                                  count

      It was the best of times, it was the worst of times,      12
```

Please refer to the SAS documentation on the `countw` function.

14.6.2   Word-Counting Macro

Program 14.6.3 *countWordMacro.sas*

```
1   dm log 'clear'; dm output 'clear';
2
3   %macro countWord(text, delimiter=%str( ));
4   %local count;
5   %let count=0;
6
7   %do %while(%scan(&text,&count+1,&delimiter) ne);
8     %let count=%eval(&count+1);
9     /* %let word=%scan(&text,&count,&delimiter);*/
10     /* %put word;*/
11   %end;
12
13   &count
14   %mend;
15
16   %let s1=%str(It was the best of times, it was the worst of times,);
17   %let s2=a * b * c * d;
18   %let s3=a xxx b xxx c xxx d;
19
20   %put "&s1" has %countWord(&s1) words;
21   %put "&s2" has %countWord(&s2,delimiter=*) words;
22   %put "&s3" has %countWord(&s3,delimiter=xxx) words;
```

This is the log:

```
1     dm log 'clear'; dm output 'clear';
2
3     %macro countWord(text, delimiter=%str( ));
4     %local count;
5     %let count=0;
6
7     %do %while(%scan(&text,&count+1,&delimiter) ne);
8       %let count=%eval(&count+1);
```

```
9       /* %let word=%scan(&text,&count,&delimiter);*/
10      /* %put word;*/
11   %end;
12
13   &count
14   %mend;
15
16   %let s1=%str(It was the best of times, it was the worst of times,);
17   %let s2=a * b * c * d;
18   %let s3=a xxx b xxx c xxx d;
19
20   %put "&s1" has %countWord(&s1) words;
"It was the best of times, it was the worst of times," has 12 words
21   %put "&s2" has %countWord(&s2,delimiter=*) words;
"a * b * c * d" has 4 words
22   %put "&s3" has %countWord(&s3,delimiter=xxx) words;
"a xxx b xxx c xxx d" has 4 words
```

Line 4 declares a local macro variable `count`. By making `count` local to the macro `countWord`, you can freely create a global macro variable with the same name `count` without worrying that the `countWord` macro will ever overwrite the global macro variable `count`. The global macro variable `count` and the local macro variable `count` are two different macro variables.

The macro `countWord` has a default parameter value `delimiter=%str( )`. Line 20 invokes the `countWord` macro without specifying the second parameter `delimiter`. As the result, the `countWord` macro uses the default parameter `delimiter=%str( )`. The macro scan function inside the `countWord` macro uses blanks as the delimiter.

Line 21 invokes the `countWord` macro and specifies the second parameter `delimiter=*`. As the result, the macro scan function inside the `countWord` macro will use an asterisk as the delimiter. Similarly, Line 22 instructs the `countWord` macro to use `xxx` as the delimiter for the macro scan function.

Line 13 doesn't have an ending semicolon. This is the source code generated by Line 20:

```
%put "It was the best of times, it was the worst of times," has 12 words;
```

The above source code will execute without error. However, if you add an ending semicolon to Line 13 so it becomes `&count;`, the macro PUT statements in Lines 20–22 will fail and SAS will write the following message to the log:

```
ERROR 180-322: Statement is not valid or it is used out of proper order.
```

We'll just examine why Line 20 is wrong. If you add a semicolon at the end of Line 13, then Line 20 generates the following source code:

```
%put "It was the best of times, it was the worst of times," has 12; words;
```

There's a semicolon after the number 12. This semicolon marks the ending of the `%put` statement. SAS doesn't know what to do with the remaining statement `words`.

If you must add an ending semicolon to Line 13, then change Lines 20–22 into the following and the program will execute without errors:

```
20  %put "&s1" has %countWord(&s1); %put words;
21  %put "&s2" has %countWord(&s2,delimiter=*); %put words;
22  %put "&s3" has %countWord(&s3,delimiter=xxx); %put words;
```

Program 14.6.3 is one method to count the number of words in a macro variable. For different methods, see *Sample 26152: Retrieving the number of words in a macro variable* at `http://support.sas.com/kb/26/152.html`.

14.7 Iterate Through Values in a Macro Variable List

The next macro is similar to Program 14.6.3.

Program 14.7.1 *loopThruMacroVarList.sas*

```
1   dm log 'clear'; dm output 'clear';
2
3   %macro loopThruMacroVarList(text,delimiter=%str( ));
4   %local count;
5   %let count=0;
6
7   %do %while(%scan(&text,&count+1,&delimiter) ne);
8     %let count=%eval(&count+1);
9     %let word=%scan(&text,&count,&delimiter);
10
11    %put &word; /* sample action */
12    /*do more actions on &word */
13
14  %end;
15  %mend;
16
17  %let s1=%str(It was the best of times, it was the worst of times,);
18  %let s2=a * b * c * d;
19  %let s3=a xxx b xxx c xxx d;
20
21  %loopThruMacroVarList(&s1)
22  %loopThruMacroVarList(&s2,delimiter=*)
23  %loopThruMacroVarList(&s3,delimiter=xxx)
```

Submit the program and you'll get this log:

```
1    dm log 'clear'; dm output 'clear';
2
3    %macro loopThruMacroVarList(text,delimiter=%str( ));
4    %local count;
5    %let count=0;
6
7    %do %while(%scan(&text,&count+1,&delimiter) ne);
8      %let count=%eval(&count+1);
```

```
9        %let word=%scan(&text,&count,&delimiter);
10
11       %put &word; /* sample action */
12       /*do more actions on &word */
13
14    %end;
15    %mend;
16
17    %let s1=%str(It was the best of times, it was the worst of times,);
18    %let s2=a * b * c * d;
19    %let s3=a xxx b xxx c xxx d;
20
21    %loopThruMacroVarList(&s1)
It
was
the
best
of
times,
it
was
the
worst
of
times,
22    %loopThruMacroVarList(&s2,delimiter=*)
a
b
c
d
23    %loopThruMacroVarList(&s3,delimiter=xxx)
a
b
c
d
```

14.8   Further Reading

SAS 9.3 Macro Language Reference pdf, Chapter 6 *Macro Expressions*; Chapter 8 *Interfaces with the Macro Facility.*

Chapter 15

Allocate Cost Proportionally to Sales

15.1 Objective

You are given two tables: the revenue table, which lists the sales by department and by product, and the quarterly cost table. You need to allocate the total cost by department, with each department sharing the cost proportionally to its sales as follows:

```
     revenue              cost                    allocation
dept product sales   quarter cost     dept     percent        cost
1      a      100       1     100      1     300/2000=0.15     150
1      b      200       2     200      2     700/2000=0.35     350
2      c      300       3     300      3    1000/2000=0.50     500
2      d      400       4     400
3      e      500
3      f      500
---------------       -------------    -----------------------
total          2000   total  1000                   1.00 1000
```

For example, Department 1 has a total sales amount 300, which is 15% of the total sales for all the departments combined (2000). Hence Department 1 needs to share 15% of the total cost 1000.

The next program reads in the sales data and the quarterly cost data. It then calculates each department's cost allocation percentage and cost allocation amount.

Program 15.1.1 *allocateCostBySales.sas*

```
1   dm log 'clear';   dm output 'clear';
2
3   data revenue;
4   input dept product$ sales;
5   datalines;
6   1 a 100
7   1 b 200
8   2 c 300
9   2 d 400
10  3 e 500
11  3 f 500
```

299

```
12   ;
13   run;
14
15   data quarterlyCost;
16   input cost @@;
17   datalines;
18   100 200 300 400
19   ;
20   run;
21
22   proc sql noprint;
23   select
24    count(distinct dept)
25   ,sum(sales)
26
27   into
28    :n
29   ,:CompanySales
30   from revenue;
31
32   select
33    dept
34   ,sum(sales)
35
36   into
37    :dept1 - :dept%trim(&n),
38    :sales1 - :sales%trim(&n)
39
40   from revenue
41   group by dept
42   order by dept
43   ;
44
45   select
46   sum(cost) into :CompanyCost
47   from quarterlyCost;
48
49   quit;
50
51   %put _user_;
52
53   %macro allocateCostByDept;
54   %do i=1 %to &n;
55    dept=&&dept&i;
56    sales=&&sales&i;
57    allocationPcnt=sales / &CompanySales;
58    allocatedCost=CompanyCost * allocationPcnt;
59    output;
60   %end;
61   %mend;
62
63   data costAllocation;
64   retain CompanyCost &CompanyCost CompanySales &CompanySales;
65   %allocateCostByDept
66   run;
67
68   options linesize=min nonumber nodate;
69   proc print data=revenue;
```

```
70    title "revenue table";
71   run;
72
73   proc print data=quarterlyCost;
74    title "quarterlyCost table";
75   run;
76
77   proc print data=costAllocation;
78    title "Cost allocation among %trim(&n) departments";
79   run;
```

This is the output:

```
                        revenue table

              Obs    dept    product    sales

               1      1         a        100
               2      1         b        200
               3      2         c        300
               4      2         d        400
               5      3         e        500
               6      3         f        500
                     quarterlyCost table

                      Obs     cost

                       1      100
                       2      200
                       3      300
                       4      400
              Cost allocation among 3 departments

         Company   Company                 allocation   allocated
  Obs      Cost      Sales    dept   sales     Pcnt        Cost

   1       1000      2000      1      300      0.15        150
   2       1000      2000      2      700      0.35        350
   3       1000      2000      3     1000      0.50        500
```

15.2 Program Walkthrough

In the second DATA step of Program 15.1.1, the `input cost @@` statement uses the double at signs to read multiple observations from a single raw input line.

In the PROC SQL block, the number of departments and the total sales are saved into two macro variables, n and `CompanySales`. Next, the department IDs are saved into n macro variables, `dept1` through `deptn`. And the department sales are saved into n macro variables `sales1` through `salesn`. We use a hyphen in the INTO clause to specify a range of macro variables. The macro TRIM function removes leading and trailing blanks from the value of the macro variable n.

If you have SAS version 9, you can create a range of macro variables in the INTO clause without specifying the upper bound. Instead of

```
into
 :dept1 - :dept%trim(&n),
 :sales1 - :sales%trim(&n)
```

you can simply write:

```
/*require SAS v9 */
into
 :dept1 - ,
 :sales1 -
```

To understand the macro `%allocateCostByDept`, let's walk through its first iteration where `i=1`. The macro processor makes two passes to convert the expression `&&dept&i` into text. The first pass converts a double ampersand to a single ampersand sign, changing `&&dept&i` to `&dept1`. The second pass retrieves the value of the macro variable `dept1`. Similarly, the macro processor first converts `&&sales&i` to `&sales1` and then retrieves the value of the macro variable `sales1`.

The `%put _user_` statement is for debugging your macro code and can be removed once your program is working. This statement writes the user generated macro variables to the log. If your program doesn't have any errors, you should get a log similar to this:

```
    %put _user_;
GLOBAL SQLOBS 1
GLOBAL SALES3 1000
GLOBAL SQLOOPS 26
GLOBAL SALES2 700
GLOBAL DEPT1 1
GLOBAL DEPT2 2
GLOBAL DEPT3 3
GLOBAL N        3
GLOBAL COMPANYCOST    1000
GLOBAL COMPANYSALES   2000
GLOBAL SQLRC 0
GLOBAL SALES1 300
```

The macro variables you just created should be in the log. Also in the log are the automatic macro variables generated by the PROC SQL in Program 15.1.1. PROC SQL sets up macro variables which certain values after it executes each statement. After each PROC SQL statement has executed, the values of these macro variables are updated.

Here are the major automatic macro variables in the log. SQLOBS contains the number of rows or observations produced by a SELECT statement. SQLOOPS contains the number of iterations that the inner loop of PROC SQL processes. SQLRC contains the return code from an SQL statement. SQLRC=0 means that an SQL statement completed successfully with no errors; SQLRC=4 means that an SQL statement encountered a situation for which it issued a warning; and other values indicate that an SQL statement has encountered an error.

This is the source code generated by the macro activities:

Program 15.2.1 *allocateCostBySalesSource.sas*

```
1    data costAllocation;
2    retain CompanyCost 1000 CompanySales 2000;
3
4    dept=1;
5    sales=300;
6    allocationPcnt=sales / 2000;
7    allocatedCost=CompanyCost * allocationPcnt;
8    output;
9
10   dept=2;
11   sales=700;
12   allocationPcnt=sales / 2000;
13   allocatedCost=CompanyCost * allocationPcnt;
14   output;
15
16   dept=3;
17   sales=1000;
18   allocationPcnt=sales / 2000;
19   allocatedCost=CompanyCost * allocationPcnt;
20   output;
21
22   run;
23
24   proc print data=costAllocation;
25     title "Cost allocation among 3 departments";
26   run;
```

In Program 15.1.1, n is not hard coded as 3. You can use Program 15.1.1 to allocate cost proportionally to sales among more departments. The next program allocates the cost among five departments without you modifying the core program code.

Program 15.2.2 *allocateCostBySales2.sas*

```
1    dm log 'clear';   dm output 'clear';
2
3    data revenue;
4    input dept product$ sales;
5    datalines;
6    1 a 100
7    1 b 200
8    2 c 300
9    2 d 400
10   3 e 500
11   3 f 500
12   4 g 600
13   4 h 800
14   5 k 900
15   ;
16   run;
17
18   data quarterlyCost;
19   input cost @@;
20   datalines;
21   100 200 300 400 500
22   ;
```

```
23    run;
24
25    proc sql noprint;
26    select
27      count(distinct dept)
28    ,sum(sales)
29
30    into
31     :n
32    ,:CompanySales
33    from revenue;
34
35    select
36      dept
37    ,sum(sales)
38
39    into
40     :dept1 - :dept%trim(&n),
41     :sales1 - :sales%trim(&n)
42
43    from revenue
44    group by dept
45    order by dept
46    ;
47
48    select
49    sum(cost) into :CompanyCost
50    from quarterlyCost;
51
52    quit;
53
54    %put _user_;
55
56    %macro allocateCostByDept;
57    %do i=1 %to &n;
58      dept=&&dept&i;
59      sales=&&sales&i;
60      allocationPcnt=sales / &CompanySales;
61      allocatedCost=CompanyCost * allocationPcnt;
62      output;
63    %end;
64    %mend;
65
66    data costAllocation;
67    retain CompanyCost &CompanyCost CompanySales &CompanySales;
68    %allocateCostByDept
69    run;
70
71    options linesize=min nonumber nodate;
72    proc print data=revenue;
73      title "revenue table";
74    run;
75
76    proc print data=quarterlyCost;
77      title "quarterlyCost table";
78    run;
79
80    proc print data=costAllocation;
```

```
81    title "Cost allocation among %trim(&n) departments";
82  run;
```

This is the output:

```
                        revenue table

            Obs    dept    product    sales

             1      1        a         100
             2      1        b         200
             3      2        c         300
             4      2        d         400
             5      3        e         500
             6      3        f         500
             7      4        g         600
             8      4        h         800
             9      5        k         900
                 quarterlyCost table

                    Obs     cost

                     1      100
                     2      200
                     3      300
                     4      400
                     5      500
            Cost allocation among 5 departments

       Company   Company                   allocation   allocated
Obs      Cost      Sales    dept   sales       Pcnt        Cost

 1       1500      4300      1      300       0.06977     104.651
 2       1500      4300      2      700       0.16279     244.186
 3       1500      4300      3     1000       0.23256     348.837
 4       1500      4300      4     1400       0.32558     488.372
 5       1500      4300      5      900       0.20930     313.953
```

15.3   Further Reading

Step-by-Step Programming with Base SAS Software, Chapter 4, *Starting with Raw Data: Beyond the Basics.*

Using the Magical Keyword "INTO:" in PROC SQL

http://www2.sas.com/proceedings/sugi27/p071-27.pdf

Getting More Out of "INTO" in PROC SQL: An Example for Creating Macro Variables

http://www.lexjansen.com/nesug/nesug97/coders/eddlesto.pdf

Chapter 16

SAS Arrays

In a DATA step, you often need to perform the same action on many variables. Although you can apply the same logic to each variable individually, it is far easier to process all the variables as one group using an array.

16.1   Conventional Approach

The next program reads in daily average temperatures in Fahrenheit from datalines and converts the temperatures to Celsius.

Program 16.1.1 *TemperatureFtoC.sas*

```
1   dm log 'clear'; dm output 'clear';
2   data TemperatureF2C;
3   input M T W TH F Sa Su;
4
5   week+1;
6   M=5*(M-32)/9;
7   T=5*(T-32)/9;
8   W=5*(W-32)/9;
9   TH=5*(TH-32)/9;
10  F=5*(F-32)/9;
11  Sa=5*(Sa-32)/9;
12  Su=5*(Su-32)/9;
13
14  datalines;
15  60      69      68      62      69      60      69
16  66      60      64      60      64      64      70
17  60      69      60      68      63      62      66
18  68      70      70      60      68      70      68
19  62      69      62      70      67      70      62
20  64      62      65      69      70      65      65
21  68      69      62      61      63      63      68
22  66      62      62      70      65      67      62
23  61      62      69      61      61      64      68
24  64      64      66      66      65      65      66
25  62      67      63      68      65      70      66
```

```
26   64      69      67      60      62      68      67
27   ;
28   run;
29
30   option linesize=min nonumber nodate;
31   proc print data=TemperatureF2C;
32    title 'Temperatures in Celsius';
33    format M T W TH F Sa Su best4.;
34   run;
```

The same conversion logic is performed individually over 7 daily temperature variables from M to Su. This is the output:

```
                    Temperatures in Celsius

    Obs     M       T       W      TH       F      Sa      Su     week

     1    15.6    20.6      20    16.7    20.6    15.6    20.6      1
     2    18.9    15.6    17.8    15.6    17.8    17.8    21.1      2
     3    15.6    20.6    15.6      20    17.2    16.7    18.9      3
     4      20    21.1    21.1    15.6      20    21.1      20      4
     5    16.7    20.6    16.7    21.1    19.4    21.1    16.7      5
     6    17.8    16.7    18.3    20.6    21.1    18.3    18.3      6
     7      20    20.6    16.7    16.1    17.2    17.2      20      7
     8    18.9    16.7    16.7    21.1    18.3    19.4    16.7      8
     9    16.1    16.7    20.6    16.1    16.1    17.8      20      9
    10    17.8    17.8    18.9    18.9    18.3    18.3    18.9     10
    11    16.7    19.4    17.2      20    18.3    21.1    18.9     11
    12    17.8    20.6    19.4    15.6    16.7      20    19.4     12
```

16.2 Arrays in a DATA Step

The next program does the same as Program 16.1.1 but with an array. The array lets you access the 7 daily temperature variables via a common name `Temperature[i]`.

Program 16.2.1 *TemperatureFtoC2.sas*

```
1    dm log 'clear'; dm output 'clear';
2    data TemperatureFtoC (drop=i);
3    input M T W TH F Sa Su;
4
5    week+1;
6    array Temperature[7] 8 M T W TH F Sa Su;
7    do i=1 to 7;
8      Temperature[i] = 5*(Temperature[i]-32)/9;
9    end;
10
11   datalines;
12   60      69      68      62      69      60      69
13   66      60      64      60      64      64      70
14   60      69      60      68      63      62      66
15   68      70      70      60      68      70      68
16   62      69      62      70      67      70      62
17   64      62      65      69      70      65      65
```

18	68	69	62	61	63	63	68
19	66	62	62	70	65	67	62
20	61	62	69	61	61	64	68
21	64	64	66	66	65	65	66
22	62	67	63	68	65	70	66
23	64	69	67	60	62	68	67

```
24  ;
25  run;
26
27  option linesize=min nonumber nodate;
28  proc print data=TemperatureFtoC;
29   title 'Temperatures in Celsius';
30   format M T W TH F Sa Su best4.;
31  run;
```

Program 16.1.1 and 16.2.1 are equivalent.

16.3 SAS Arrays Are Unique

Arrays in SAS are different from arrays in most other languages. In almost all other programming languages, an array is a data structure similar to a matrix. In SAS, however, an array is just a group of DATA step variables with one common name.

The statement `array Temperature[7] 8 M T W TH F Sa Su` does the following for you:

- If the DATA step doesn't already have any of the numeric variables named M, T, . . . , Su, SAS will create them from scratch, with each variable having a length of 8 bytes.

- However, if the DATA step already has one or more numeric variables named M, T, . . . , Su, the ARRAY statement will use the existing DATA step variables with the same names; the same-named variables will not be recreated. Only the variables that appear in the ARRAY statement but are not already existing in the DATA step are created.

- Regardless of whether a variable in the ARRAY statement already exists in the DATA step, the ARRAY statement creates the following variable name aliases:

  - `Temperature[1]` is the alias of the variable M.
  - `Temperature[2]` is the alias of the variable T.
  - . . .
  - `Temperature[7]` is the alias of the variable Su.

- The array name `Temperature` does not become part of the output table.

Here are some limitations of a SAS array:

- The array name cannot be the name of a variable in the same DATA step.

- Avoid using a SAS function name as the name of your array. If your array happens to be a SAS function name, your array will still be correct, but you won't be able to use the function in the same DATA step and a warning message will appear in the SAS log.

- You cannot use array names in LABEL, FORMAT, DROP, KEEP, or LENGTH statements.

- Arrays exist only for the duration of the DATA step.

In Program 16.2.1, since all the variables in the ARRAY statement were already created via the INPUT statement, the ARRAY statement doesn't create any new DATA step variables; it merely creates aliases of the existing DATA step variables.

Since `Temperature[1]` is the alias of the variable M, the following statements are equivalent :

```
M=5*(M-32)/9;
Temperature[1]=5*(Temperature[1]-32)/9;
M=5*(Temperature[1]-32)/9;
Temperature[1]=5*(M-32)/9;
```

16.4   More Examples

Can you guess the output of the next program?

Program 16.4.1 *TemperatureFtoC3.sas*

```
1   dm log 'clear'; dm output 'clear';
2   data TemperatureFtoC3 (drop=i);
3   input M T W TH F Sa Su;
4
5   week+1;
6   array Temperature[7] 8 M T Wed TH F Sa Sun;
7
8   do i=1 to 7;
9      Temperature[i] = 5*(Temperature[i]-32)/9;
10   end;
11
12   datalines;
13   60      69      68      62      69      60      69
14   66      60      64      60      64      64      70
15   60      69      60      68      63      62      66
16   68      70      70      60      68      70      68
17   62      69      62      70      67      70      62
18   64      62      65      69      70      65      65
19   68      69      62      61      63      63      68
20   66      62      62      70      65      67      62
21   61      62      69      61      61      64      68
22   64      64      66      66      65      65      66
23   62      67      63      68      65      70      66
24   64      69      67      60      62      68      67
25   ;
26   run;
27
28   option linesize=min nonumber nodate;
29   proc print data=TemperatureFtoC3;
30     title 'TemperatureFtoC3 table';
31     title2 'Temperatures in Celsius';
32     format M T W TH F Sa Su best4.;
33   run;
```

In this program, the ARRAY statement contains two numeric variables, Wed and Sun, which are not existing in the DATA step. As a result, SAS creates these two variables. The other five variables listed in the ARRAY statement refer to the existing variables in the DATA step.

In addition, SAS creates an alias of each variable listed in the ARRAY statement. Since Wed (e.g. Temperature[3]) and Sun (e.g. Temperature[7]) don't have any values, the following statements will update Wed and Sun but their updated values are still missing:

```
Temperature[3]=5*(Temperature[3]-32)/9;
Temperature[7]=5*(Temperature[7]-32)/9;
```

The variables W and Su are not listed in the ARRAY statement and no aliases are created for them. As a result, they are not processed by the DO-LOOP. Their values are not converted to Celsius.

This is the output:

```
               TemperatureFtoC3 table
               Temperatures in Celsius

Obs     M     T     W    TH     F    Sa    Su   week  Wed  Sun

  1   15.6  20.6   68  16.7  20.6  15.6   69    1     .    .
  2   18.9  15.6   64  15.6  17.8  17.8   70    2     .    .
  3   15.6  20.6   60    20  17.2  16.7   66    3     .    .
  4     20  21.1   70  15.6    20  21.1   68    4     .    .
  5   16.7  20.6   62  21.1  19.4  21.1   62    5     .    .
  6   17.8  16.7   65  20.6  21.1  18.3   65    6     .    .
  7     20  20.6   62  16.1  17.2  17.2   68    7     .    .
  8   18.9  16.7   62  21.1  18.3  19.4   62    8     .    .
  9   16.1  16.7   69  16.1  16.1  17.8   68    9     .    .
 10   17.8  17.8   66  18.9  18.3  18.3   66   10     .    .
 11   16.7  19.4   63    20  18.3  21.1   66   11     .    .
 12   17.8  20.6   67  15.6  16.7    20   67   12     .    .
```

By the way, Program 16.2.1 can be rewritten as:

Program 16.4.2 *TemperatureFtoC4.sas*

```
1   dm log 'clear'; dm output 'clear';
2   data TemperatureFtoC4 (drop=i);
3   array Temperature[7] 8 M T W TH F Sa Su;
4   input Temperature[*];
5
6   week+1;
7   do i=1 to 7;
8     Temperature[i] = 5*(Temperature[i]-32)/9;
9   end;
10
11  datalines;
12  60      69      68      62      69      60      69
13  66      60      64      60      64      64      70
14  60      69      60      68      63      62      66
15  68      70      70      60      68      70      68
```

```
16   62    69    62    70    67    70    62
17   64    62    65    69    70    65    65
18   68    69    62    61    63    63    68
19   66    62    62    70    65    67    62
20   61    62    69    61    61    64    68
21   64    64    66    66    65    65    66
22   62    67    63    68    65    70    66
23   64    69    67    60    62    68    67
24   ;
25   run;
26
27   option linesize=min nonumber nodate;
28   proc print data=TemperatureFtoC4;
29    title 'TemperatureFtoC4 table';
30    title2 'Temperatures in Celsius';
31    format M T W TH F Sa Su best4.;
32   run;
```

The next program attempts to reference the array outside the DATA step but it doesn't work. An array exists only for the duration of the DATA step.

Program 16.4.3 *TemperatureFtoC5.sas*

```
1    dm log 'clear'; dm output 'clear';
2    data TemperatureFtoC5 (drop=i);
3    array Temperature[7] 8 M T W TH F Sa Su;
4    input Temperature[*];
5
6    week+1;
7    do i=1 to 7;
8      Temperature[i] = 5*(Temperature[i]-32)/9;
9    end;
10
11   datalines;
12   60    69    68    62    69    60    69
13   66    60    64    60    64    64    70
14   60    69    60    68    63    62    66
15   68    70    70    60    68    70    68
16   62    69    62    70    67    70    62
17   64    62    65    69    70    65    65
18   68    69    62    61    63    63    68
19   66    62    62    70    65    67    62
20   61    62    69    61    61    64    68
21   64    64    66    66    65    65    66
22   62    67    63    68    65    70    66
23   64    69    67    60    62    68    67
24   ;
25   run;
26
27   option linesize=min nonumber nodate;
28   proc print data=TemperatureFtoC5;
29    title 'TemperatureFtoC5 table';
30    title2 'Temperatures in Celsius';
31    format
32      Temperature[1]
33      Temperature[2]
```

```
34      Temperature[3]
35      Temperature[4]
36      Temperature[5]
37      Temperature[6]
38      Temperature[7]
39      best4.
40    ;
41  run;
```

Can you figure out why the next program doesn't work?

Program 16.4.4 *TemperatureFtoC6.sas*

```
1   dm log 'clear'; dm output 'clear';
2   data TemperatureFtoC6 (drop=i);
3   input M$ T W TH F Sa Su;
4
5   week+1;
6   array Temperature[7] 8 M T W TH F Sa Su;
7
8   do i=1 to 7;
9     Temperature[i] = 5*(Temperature[i]-32)/9;
10  end;
11
12  datalines;
13  60    69    68    62    69    60    69
14  66    60    64    60    64    64    70
15  60    69    60    68    63    62    66
16  68    70    70    60    68    70    68
17  62    69    62    70    67    70    62
18  64    62    65    69    70    65    65
19  68    69    62    61    63    63    68
20  66    62    62    70    65    67    62
21  61    62    69    61    61    64    68
22  64    64    66    66    65    65    66
23  62    67    63    68    65    70    66
24  64    69    67    60    62    68    67
25  ;
26  run;
```

M is a character variable in the INPUT statement, but it is declared to be numeric in the ARRAY statement. SAS writes the following to the log:

```
ERROR: All variables in array list must be the same type, i.e., all numeric or character.
```

The next program generates the correct output, but the code isn't clean. Can you figure out why?

Program 16.4.5 *TemperatureFtoC7.sas*

```
1   dm log 'clear'; dm output 'clear';
2   data TemperatureFtoC7 (drop=i);
3   array var[7] M T W TH F Sa Su;
```

```
4    input var[*];
5
6    week+1;
7    do i=1 to 7;
8      var[i] = 5*(var[i]-32)/9;
9    end;
10
11   datalines;
12   60    69    68    62    69    60    69
13   66    60    64    60    64    64    70
14   60    69    60    68    63    62    66
15   68    70    70    60    68    70    68
16   62    69    62    70    67    70    62
17   64    62    65    69    70    65    65
18   68    69    62    61    63    63    68
19   66    62    62    70    65    67    62
20   61    62    69    61    61    64    68
21   64    64    66    66    65    65    66
22   62    67    63    68    65    70    66
23   64    69    67    60    62    68    67
24   ;
25   run;
```

This is part of the log:

```
WARNING: An array is being defined with the same name as a
         SAS-supplied or user-defined function. Parenthesized
         references involving this name will be treated as
         array references and not function references.
```

The name of the array is `var`. However, it just so happens that `var()` is also a SAS function; `var()` returns the variance of the nonmissing arguments, hence SAS issues a warning in the log.

16.5 Declare an Array

You can reduce your ARRAY statement code by letting SAS do some work for you. The following statements are equivalent:

```
1    array Temperature[7] 8 M T W TH F Sa Su;
2    array Temperature[7]   M T W TH F Sa Su;
3    array Temperature[*]   M T W TH F Sa Su;
4    array Temperature      M T W TH F Sa Su;
```

Lines 2–4. If no length is specified for each variable in the variable list, each variable gets the default 8 bytes.

Lines 3–4. Since SAS can count the number of the variables in the variable list, the number of elements (called dimension) in the array doesn't need to be specified.

By the way, the asterisk in Line 3 cannot be changed into another symbol.

The following ARRAY statements are equivalent:

```
1  array x[5] x1 x2 x3 x4 x5;
2  array x[5] x1-x5;
3  array x[*] x1-x5;
4  array x x1-x5;
5  array x[5];
```

In Line 5, SAS automatically creates variable names by concatenating the array name with the numbers 1, 2, 3, and so on. If a variable name in the series already exists, SAS uses that variable instead of creating a new one.

16.6 Dynamically Set an Array Size

One common error is to dynamically set the size of an array by passing a variable as the dimension of an ARRAY. Here's an example.

```
n=7;
array Temperature[n];
```

The above ARRAY statement generates the following log:

```
ERROR: Too many variables defined for the dimension(s) specified for the array Temperature.
ERROR 22-322: Syntax error, expecting one of the following: an integer constant, *.
```

An array in SAS is syntax sugar for creating or identifying a group of DATA step variables via a common name. To create or identify multiple variables, SAS needs to know, at the DATA step compilation time, the name, the data type, and the length of each variable to be created or identified by the ARRAY statement.

At the compilation time, the assignment statement **n=7** causes **n** to get the same data type and length as the expression 7 on the right side of the assignment. As a result, **n** is an 8-byte numeric variable. Only at the DATA step execution time is n assigned the value 7.

To overcome the limitation that it's too late to pass, at the DATA step execution time, the value of the dimension to an ARRAY statement, you can store the dimension value in a macro variable and pass the value of the macro variable to an ARRAY statement.

```
%let n=7;
array Temperature[&n];
```

The macro processor will convert the above code into the following source code:

```
array Temperature[7];
```

The generated source code will create 7 numeric variables, **Temperature1** through **Temperature7**, each with length of 8 bytes. If any of these variables already exist in the DATA step, SAS will use that variable instead of creating a new one.

For another array example, see Program 19.1.1.

16.7 Further Reading

Using Arrays in SAS Programming

http://support.sas.com/resources/papers/97529_Using_Arrays_in_SAS_Programming.pdf

Arrays Data Step Efficiency

http://analytics.ncsu.edu/sesug/2011/CC17.Droogendyk.pdf

THE MANY WAYS TO EFFECTIVELY UTILIZE ARRAY PROCESSING

http://www.pharmasug.org/proceedings/2011/TU/PharmaSUG-2011-TU06.pdf

Chapter 17

Mass Convert Great Widget Co.'s Text Files to CSV Files

You wrote Program 8.1.2 to convert the Great Widget Co.'s February 2014 production text file `widgetFeb2014.txt` into two CSV files, `widgetFinal.csv` and `widgetFinalSum.csv`. In this chapter, you'll go one step further and convert all the production text files in the `C:\LearnSAS` folder or the `/home/userid/myProgram` folder into similar CSV files.

17.1 Objective

To understand what you need to accomplish, create 2 more production text files in the `C:\LearnSAS` folder. Find the `widgetFeb2014.txt` file created for Program 8.1.2. Make two copies of it. Rename one copy `widgetFeb2012.txt` and the other `widgetFeb2013.txt`. Now the `C:\LearnSAS` folder should have 3 production text files:

- `widgetFeb2012.txt`

- `widgetFeb2013.txt`

- `widgetFeb2014.txt`

If you use SAS in the cloud, you'll need to upload these 3 text files to the `/home/userid/myProgram` folder and replace `userid` with your user ID for SAS in the cloud.

You'll use the 3 text files to create 6 CSV files:

- `widgetFeb2012Final.csv` and `widgetFeb2012FinalSum.csv`

- `widgetFeb2013Final.csv` and `widgetFeb2013FinalSum.csv`

- `widgetFeb2014Final.csv` and `widgetFeb2014FinalSum.csv`

These 6 CSV files will be created in `C:\LearnSAS` if you use PC SAS or `/home/userid/myProgram` if you use SAS in the cloud.

The 3 input files are for explaining what you need to do and for testing your code. Your program should be able to convert a large number of raw text files into CSV files.

Assume all the production text files are named `widgetmmmyyyy.txt`, where `mmm` is the first three letters of a month and `yyyy` is the 4-digit year. Your program will convert each `widgetmmmyyyy.txt` file into two CSV files, `mmmyyyyFinal.csv` and `mmmyyyyFinalSum.csv`.

You may have noticed that one limitation of Program 8.1.2 is that it can only parse the January or February production text files. To see why, read Lines 11–12 of Program 8.1.2. For simplicity, the new program to be built in this chapter will still have this limitation and can only mass convert `widgetJanyyyy.txt` and `widgetFebyyyy.txt` text files. However, you can easily remove this limitation by modifying the program logic.

17.2 Skeleton Program

This is the pseudocode of the program to be built:

```
1. In C:\LearnSAS or /home/userid/myProgram, find all the widgetmmmyyyy.txt files.
2. Store all the widget text file names in a macro variable list.
3. Loop through the macro variable list; run the widgetFinalGeneric.sas program against
   each file name in the macro variable list to produce two CSV files.
```

The `widgetFinalGeneric.sas` program to be built will extend Program 8.1.2 `widgetFinal.sas` and process a generic input file `widgetmmmyyyy.txt`.

Now let's set up a skeleton program to implement the pseudocode:

Program 17.2.1 *widgetMassConvertMain.sas*

```
1    dm log 'clear'; dm output 'clear';
2    %let myfolder=C:\learnSAS; /*PC SAS*/
3
4    /*SAS in the cloud: (replace userid with your ID)*/
5    /*%let myfolder=/home/userid/myProgram;*/
6
7    /* find all the widget text files */
8    %include "&myfolder/getWidgetTextFiles.sas";
9
10   /*save the widget text file names into a macro var list*/
11   %include "&myfolder/procSqlCreateMacroVarList.sas";
12
13   /* loop through the macro variable list; geneate 2 csv files for each widget text file*/
14   %include "&myfolder/widgetLoopThruMacroVarList.sas";
```

If you use SAS in the cloud, delete Line 2 and uncomment Line 5. In addition, in Line 5, replace `userid` with your user ID for SAS in the cloud.

In Program 17.2.1, each `%include` statement calls a subprogram.

17.2.1   Call a Subprogram from a Main Program

You use a %include statement to call a subprogram. Suppose this is your original SAS program:

Program 17.2.2 *demo.sas*

```
1   dm log 'clear'; dm output 'clear';
2
3   /*Step 1 - create work.demo table*/
4   data demo;
5   do i=1 to 10;
6     output;
7   end;
8   run;
9
10  /*Step 2 - sum up i's*/
11  proc sql;
12  create table demoSum as
13  select sum(i) as total
14  from demo;
15  quit;
16
17  /*Step 3 - print demoSum*/
18  proc print data=demoSum;
19    title 'From demoSum table';
20  run;
```

This is the output:

```
From demoSum table

   Obs    total

    1      55
```

Instead of having a program with 3 steps, you can partition the 3 steps into 3 separate SAS programs: demoStep1.sas, demoStep2.sas, and demoStep3.sas. Then you can create a main program, demoMain.sas, to call the 3 subprograms. The main program and any subprogram can reside in different folders as long as the %include statement in the main program correctly specifies the full path of the subprogram so your operating system can find the subprogram.

For now we'll put the main program and the 3 subprograms in the same folder, which is C:\learnSAS if you use PC SAS or /home/userid/myProgram if you use SAS in the cloud.

Here are the 3 subprograms and the main program:

Program 17.2.3 demoStep1.sas

```
1   /*Step 1 - create work.demo table*/
2   data demo;
3   do i=1 to 10;
4     output;
5   end;
6   run;
```

Program 17.2.4 `demoStep2.sas`

```
1   /*Step 2 - sum up i's*/
2   proc sql;
3   create table demoSum as
4   select sum(i) as total
5   from demo;
6   quit;
```

Program 17.2.5 `demoStep3.sas`

```
1   /*Step 3 - print demoSum*/
2   proc print data=demoSum;
3     title 'From demoSum table';
4   run;
```

Program 17.2.6 `demoMain.sas`

```
1   dm log 'clear'; dm output 'clear';
2   options source2;
3   %let myfolder=C:/learnSAS; /*PC SAS*/
4   /*SAS in the cloud:(replace userid with your ID)*/
5   /*%let myfolder=/home/userid/myProgram;*/
6
7   %include "&myfolder/demoStep1.sas";
8   %include "&myfolder/demoStep2.sas";
9   %include "&myfolder/demoStep3.sas";
```

Each %include statement in Program 17.2.6 specifies the full path of the subprogram being called. The %include statement brings statements, data lines, or both, into a current SAS program. Submit Program 17.2.6 and you'll get the same output as Program 17.2.2.

In Program 17.2.6 Line 2, the source2 system option instructs SAS to write to the log the source code from the included files. This is the log generated by Program 17.2.6:

```
1    dm log 'clear'; dm output 'clear';
2    options source2;
3    %let myfolder=C:/learnSAS; /*PC SAS*/
4    /*SAS in the cloud:(replace userid with your ID)*/
5    /*%let myfolder=/home/userid/myProgram;*/
6
7    %include "&myfolder/demoStep1.sas";
NOTE: %INCLUDE (level 1) file C:/learnSAS/demoStep1.sas is file C:\learnSAS\demoStep1.sas.
8    +/*Step 1 - create work.demo table*/
9    +data demo;
10   +do i=1 to 10;
11   + output;
12   +end;
13   +run;

NOTE: The data set WORK.DEMO has 10 observations and 1 variables.
NOTE: DATA statement used:
```

```
        real time          0.00 seconds
        cpu time           0.00 seconds


NOTE: %INCLUDE (level 1) ending.
14   %include "&myfolder/demoStep2.sas";
NOTE: %INCLUDE (level 1) file C:/learnSAS/demoStep2.sas is file C:\learnSAS\demoStep2.sas.
15   +/*Step 2 - sum up i's*/
16   +proc sql;
17   +create table demoSum as
18   +select sum(i) as total
19   +from demo;
NOTE: Table WORK.DEMOSUM created, with 1 rows and 1 columns.


20   +quit;
NOTE: PROCEDURE SQL used:
        real time          0.01 seconds
        cpu time           0.00 seconds


NOTE: %INCLUDE (level 1) ending.
21   %include "&myfolder/demoStep3.sas";
NOTE: %INCLUDE (level 1) file C:/learnSAS/demoStep3.sas is file C:\learnSAS\demoStep3.sas.
22   +/*Step 3 - print demoSum*/
23   +proc print data=demoSum;
24   +  title 'From demoSum table';
25   +run;

NOTE: There were 1 observations read from the dataset WORK.DEMOSUM.
NOTE: PROCEDURE PRINT used:
        real time          0.01 seconds
        cpu time           0.01 seconds


NOTE: %INCLUDE (level 1) ending.
```

The default system option is **nosource2**, which instructs SAS not to write secondary source statements to the log. This is the log generated by Program 17.2.6 if Line 2 is deleted or if the statement in Line 2 is changed into **options nosource2**.

```
1    dm log 'clear'; dm output 'clear';
2    %let myfolder=C:/learnSAS; /*PC SAS*/
3
4    /*SAS in the cloud:(replace userid with your ID)*/
5    /*%let myfolder=/home/userid/myProgram;*/
6
7    %include "&myfolder/demoStep1.sas";

NOTE: The data set WORK.DEMO has 10 observations and 1 variables.
NOTE: DATA statement used:
        real time          0.00 seconds
        cpu time           0.00 seconds


14   %include "&myfolder/demoStep2.sas";
NOTE: Table WORK.DEMOSUM created, with 1 rows and 1 columns.
```

```
NOTE: PROCEDURE SQL used:
      real time             0.01 seconds
      cpu time              0.01 seconds


21    %include "&myfolder/demoStep3.sas";

NOTE: There were 1 observations read from the dataset WORK.DEMOSUM.
NOTE: PROCEDURE PRINT used:
      real time             0.01 seconds
      cpu time              0.01 seconds
```

Here's how a %include statement works using the PC SAS program as the example. After you submit Program 17.2.6, the &myfolder is replaced by the text C:\learnSAS and the first %include statement becomes:

```
%include "C:/learnSAS/demoStep1.sas";
```

In Windows, you can use either a forward slash or a backslash to specify a folder.

When the first %include statement is executed, SAS will search for the C:/learnSAS/demoStep1.sas file. Upon finding the file, SAS will open the file and copy and paste the contents of the file into Program 17.2.6. If the file C:/learnSAS/demoStep1.sas doesn't exist, SAS will stop processing and write the following messages to the log:

```
WARNING: Physical file does not exist, C:/learnSAS/demoStep1.sas.
ERROR: Cannot open %INCLUDE file C:/learnSAS/demoStep11.sas.

ERROR: File WORK.DEMO.DATA does not exist.
NOTE: The SAS System stopped processing this step because of errors.
```

Similarly, the second %include statement is replaced by the code in the C:/learnSAS/demoStep2.sas file and the third by the code in the C:/learnSAS/demoStep3.sas file. As a result, Program 17.2.6 and Program 17.2.2 are equivalent.

By the way, a %include statement is not part of the macro facility, even though it begins with the percent symbol.

Here's another example. Suppose this is your original program:

Program 17.2.7 *demo2.sas*

```
1   dm log 'clear'; dm output 'clear';
2   %let myfolder=C:\learnSAS; /*PC SAS*/
3
4   /*SAS in the cloud: (replace userid with your ID)*/
5   /*%let myfolder=/home/userid/myProgram;*/
6
7   /*Step 1 create work.demo table*/
8   data demo;
9   do i=1 to 10;
```

```
10    output;
11    end;
12    run;
13
14    /*Step 2 save all the i's into macro var list i*/
15    proc sql noprint;
16    select i into :i separated by ' '
17    from demo;
18    quit;
19
20    /*Step 3 loop through macro var i;
21    print each value in the log*/
22    %macro loopThruMacroVarList(text,delimiter=%str( ));
23    %local count;
24    %let count=0;
25
26    %do %while(%scan(&text,&count+1,&delimiter) ne);
27      %let count=%eval(&count+1);
28      %let word=%scan(&text,&count,&delimiter);
29
30      %put &word;
31
32    %end;
33    %mend;
34
35    %loopThruMacroVarList(&i)
```

In this program, the macro variable i created in Step 2 contains the following text:

```
1 2 3 4 5 6 7 8 9 10
```

The macro `loopThruMacroVarList` steps through each value in the macro variable list i and writes the value to the log via the macro PUT statement. Submit the program. This is the log:

```
    %loopThruMacroVarList(&i)
1
2
3
4
5
6
7
8
9
10
```

We can convert Program 17.2.7 into one main program and three subprograms:

Program 17.2.8 demo2Main.sas

```
1    dm log 'clear'; dm output 'clear';
2    %let myfolder=C:\learnSAS; /*PC SAS*/
3
```

```
4   /*SAS in the cloud:(replace userid with your ID)*/
5   /*%let myfolder=/home/userid/myProgram;*/
6
7   %include "&myfolder/demo2Step1.sas";
8   %include "&myfolder/demo2Step2.sas";
9   %include "&myfolder/demo2Step3.sas";
```

Program 17.2.9 demo2Step1.sas

```
1   /*Step 1 create work.demo table*/
2   data demo;
3   do i=1 to 10;
4    output;
5   end;
6   run;
```

Program 17.2.10 demo2Step2.sas

```
1   /*Step 2 save all the i's into macro var list i*/
2   proc sql noprint;
3   select i into :i separated by ' '
4   from demo;
5   quit;
```

Program 17.2.11 demo2Step3.sas

```
1    /*Step 3 loop through macro var i; print each value in the log*/
2    %macro loopThruMacroVarList(text,delimiter=%str( ));
3    %local count;
4    %let count=0;
5
6    %do %while(%scan(&text,&count+1,&delimiter) ne);
7      %let count=%eval(&count+1);
8      %let word=%scan(&text,&count,&delimiter);
9
10     %put &word;
11
12   %end;
13   %mend;
14
15   %loopThruMacroVarList(&i)
```

17.2.2 Call Many Subprograms in the Same Folder

If you have many subprograms to include in a main program, you can create a subfolder to contain all the subprograms. Let's experiment. Create a subfolder mysubs in C:\LearnSAS for PC SAS or /home/userid/myProgram for SAS in the cloud. Copy and paste the 3 subprograms demoStep1.sas, demoStep2.sas, and demoStep3.sas used for Program 17.2.6 to the mysubs folder. Submit the next program using any of the 8 methods. You should get the same output as in Program 17.2.2.

Program 17.2.12 *subsInSeparateFolderMain.sas*

```
1   dm log 'clear'; dm output 'clear';
2   %let subfolder=C:\LearnSAS\mysubs; /*PC SAS*/
3   /*SAS in the cloud*/
4   /*%let subfolder=/home/userid/myProgram/mysubs;*/
5
6   /*Method 1*/
7   %include "&subfolder/demoStep1.sas";
8   %include "&subfolder/demoStep2.sas";
9   %include "&subfolder/demoStep3.sas";
10
11  /*before using Methods 2 to 8, create a libname pointing to the subfolder*/
12  filename subDir "&subfolder";
13
14  /*method 2*/
15  %include subDir('demoStep1.sas', 'demoStep2.sas', 'demoStep3.sas');
16
17  /*method 3*/
18  %include subDir(demoStep1, demoStep2, demoStep3);
19
20  /*method 4*/
21  %include subDir('demoStep1.sas');
22  %include subDir('demoStep2.sas');
23  %include subDir('demoStep3.sas');
24
25  /*method 5*/
26  %include subDir(demoStep1);
27  %include subDir(demoStep2);
28  %include subDir(demoStep3);
29
30  /*method 6*/
31  %include subDir('demoStep*.sas');
32
33  /*method 7*/
34  %include subDir(demoStep*);
35
36  /*method 8*/
37  %include subDir('*.sas');
```

Methods 3, 5, and 7 omit the .sas file extension for each included file. If the file extension is omitted, SAS assumes that the file extension is .sas.

Methods 6 and 7 include all the .sas files whose names in the mysubs folder begin with demoStep. The files are included in ascending order of the file names. Methods 6 and 7 will include demoStep1.sas first, demoStep2.sas next, and demoStep3.sas last.

Method 8 includes all the SAS programs in the mysubs folder. The files are included in ascending order of the file names.

Be careful when using Methods 6, 7, and 8 if files need to be included in a specific order. For example, if the mysubs folder contains the fourth file demoStep11.sas, then Methods 6, 7, and 8 will include demoStep1.sas first, demoStep11.sas second, demoStep2.sas next, and demoStep3.sas last. This is because in ascending order the string demoStep11 appears after the string demoStep1 but before the string demoStep2. If your intention is to call demoStep11.sas last in the main program, then Methods 6, 7, and 8 will either not work or produce wrong results.

17.3   Subprogram 1 - Find the Widget Text Files

Now that you understand the main Program 17.2.1, let's build the three subprograms. For simplicity, the main program and the three subprograms are all in the sam folder, which is C:\learnSAS for PC SAS or /home/userid/myProgram for SAS in the cloud.

Program 17.3.1 *getWidgetTextFiles.sas*

```
1    filename mydir "&myfolder";
2    data myfiles;
3    length file_name $30;
4    drop rc did i;
5
6    did=dopen("mydir");
7    if did=0 then put 'Could not open folder';
8    else do;
9      do i=1 to dnum(did);
10        file_name=dread(did,i);
11        output;
12      end;
13
14      rc=dclose(did);
15    end;
16    run;
17
18    data widgetFiles;
19    set myfiles
20    (where=
21      (
22          substr(file_name,1,6)='widget'
23        and scan(file_name,-1,'.')='txt'
24        and length(file_name)=%length(widgetFeb2014.txt)
25      )
26    );
27    run;
```

Program 17.3.1 will be explained shortly. First, let's submit it and see the output.

17.3.1   How to Submit an Included Program

Submitting an included program is tricky if the included program uses any macro variables or systems options contained in the main program. If you directly submit Program 17.3.1, you'll get an error in the log:

```
WARNING: Apparent symbolic reference MYFOLDER not resolved.
```

The macro variable `myfolder` is defined not in any of the included files, but in the main program 17.2.1. To make the macro variable `myfolder` available to the files included in the main program, you need to submit the main program first.

There are two ways to submit the subprogram 17.3.1.

PC SAS Here's the first method. In the main program 17.2.1, highlight and submit the first 6 lines of code:

```
dm log 'clear'; dm output 'clear';
%let myfolder=C:\learnSAS; /*PC SAS*/

/*SAS in the cloud: (replace userid with your ID)*/
/*%let myfolder=/home/userid/myProgram;*/

/* find all the widget text files */
%include "&myfolder/getWidgetTextFiles.sas";
```

Now the main program will call the `getWidgetTextFiles.sas` program. You should get the following success log:

```
NOTE: The data set WORK.MYFILES has xxx observations and 1 variables.
```

```
NOTE: There were 3 observations read from the dataset WORK.MYFILES.
```

```
NOTE: The data set WORK.WIDGETFILES has 3 observations and 1 variables.
```

Here's the second method. First, highlight and submit the first 4 lines of code in the main program 17.2.1:

```
dm log 'clear'; dm output 'clear';
%let myfolder=C:\learnSAS; /*PC SAS*/

/*SAS in the cloud: (replace userid with your ID)*/
/*%let myfolder=/home/userid/myProgram;*/
```

This creates the macro variable `myfolder`, which can be referenced by another program in the same SAS session as long as the referencing program is submitted after the macro variable `myfolder` is created. Next, open the subprogram 17.3.1 under the same running instance of the SAS and submit it. You'll get the same success log.

SAS in the Cloud If you use SAS in the cloud, to use the first method to submit Subprogram 17.3.1, either the interactive mode or the non-interactive will work. However, to use the second method, you'll need to use the default non-interactive mode to submit the main program and the subprogram.

In SAS in the cloud under the interactive mode, macro variables will not persist from one program to another. After you submit the first 4 lines of code in the main program 17.2.1 in either the interactive mode or the non-interactive mode, when you submit the subprogram 17.3.1 using the interactive mode, the `myfolder` macro variable created in the main program is not accessible in the subprogram 17.3.1. SAS writes this message to the log:

```
WARNING: Apparent symbolic reference MYFOLDER not resolved.
```

If you use the second method to submit a subprogram in SAS in the cloud, you'll need to use the non-interactive mode to submit any code from different programs to allow the macro variables to persist from a program submitted earlier to another program submitted later.

17.3.2 Filename statement

In Subprogram 17.3.1, the `filename` statement creates a directory nickname or file nickname `mydir` pointing to the physical directory or folder "&myfolder", which resolves to "C:\LearnSAS" or "/home/userid/myProgram". We need to create a directory nickname because later we'll call the `dopen` function to open the `mydir`. The argument of the `dopen` function must be a directory nickname.

17.3.3 First DATA Step

In Subprogram 17.3.1, the variable `file_name` is specified as a 30-width string. When a variable without a specified length is assigned the return value of the `dread` function, that variable will get the default length 200. Setting `file_name` to be 200 column wide works but the `file_name` will contain many blanks.

The DROP statement tells SAS not to write `rc` (the return code), `did` (the directory identifier), or `i` to the output table `myfiles`. These three variables are still created in the PDV, but the DROP statement stops them from being written to the output table.

Instead of using the DROP statement, you can use the DROP= option. The DATA step in Program 17.3.1 can be rewritten as follows:

```
data myfiles (drop=rc did i);
length file_name $30;
did=dopen("mydir");

if did=0 then put 'Could not open folder';
else do;
  do i=1 to dnum(did);
     file_name=dread(did,i);
     output;
  end;

  rc=dclose(did);
end;
run;
```

The DOPEN function opens a directory and returns a directory identifier value (a number greater than 0) that is used to identify the open directory in other SAS external file access functions. If the directory could not be opened, DOPEN returns 0. The directory to be opened must be identified by a `fileref`.

The DCLOSE(`directory-id`) function closes a directory that was opened by the DOPEN function. DCLOSE returns 0 if the operation was successful.

The DNUM(`directory-id`) function returns the number of members in a directory.

The DREAD(`directory-id,nval`) function returns the name of a directory member. The parameter `directory-id` is a numeric value that specifies the identifier that was assigned when the directory was opened by the DOPEN function. The `nval` parameter is a numeric constant, variable, or expression that specifies the sequence number of the member within the directory.

DREAD returns a blank if an error occurs (such as when the second parameter `nval` is out-of-range). Use DNUM to determine the highest possible member number that can be passed to DREAD.

17.3.4 Second DATA Step

In Subprogram 17.3.1, Lines 20–25 use the WHERE= dataset option to restrict which incoming rows from the `myfiles` table will participate in the DATA step to create the output table `widgetFiles`. Here's an example of the WHERE= dataset option.

```
data widgetFiles;
set myfiles (where=(substr(file_name,1,6)='widget'));
/* additional processing logic; */
run;
```

From the input table `myfiles`, only the rows where the first 6 letters of the `file_name` column is the literal string `widget` are read into the PDV for DATA step processing; the rows that don't meet this condition are never brought into the PDV.

What does this program do?

```
data widgetFiles;
set myfiles (where=(1));
/* additional processing logic; */
run;
```

Since 1 evaluates to true, all the rows from the input table `myfiles` will be read into the PDV for DATA step processing. Submit the program and you'll get this log:

```
NOTE: There were x observations read from the dataset WORK.MYFILES.
      WHERE 1 /* an obviously TRUE where clause */ ;
NOTE: The data set WORK.WIDGETFILES has x observations and 1 variables.
```

The input table `myfiles` and the output table `widgetFiles` should have an equal number of rows.

The above block is equivalent to:

```
data widgetFiles;
set myfiles;
/* additional processing logic; */
run;
```

What does this program do?

```
data widgetFiles;
set myfiles (where=(0));
/* additional processing logic; */
run;
```

Since 0 evaluates to false, not a single row from the input table `myfiles` will be read into the PDV for DATA step processing. Submit the program and you'll get this log:

```
NOTE: There were 0 observations read from the dataset WORK.MYFILES.
      WHERE 0 /* an obviously FALSE where clause */ ;
NOTE: The data set WORK.WIDGETFILES has 0 observations and 1 variables.
```

Now back to the second DATA step in Program 17.3.1. This is the meaning of the WHERE conditions:

- the first 6 characters of `file_name` is `widget`

- the last 3 characters of `file_name` is `txt`

- `file_name` needs to be 17 character long

The condition `substr(file_name,length(file_name)-3,4)='.txt'` can be rewritten as:

```
scan(file_name,-1,'.')='txt'
```

In the `scan(string,count,charlist)` function, if the `count` is negative, `scan` counts the words from right to left. The `scan(file_name,-1,'.')` function returns the rightmost word delimited by a period.

In Program 17.3.1 Line 24, the macro `%length(widgetFeb2014.txt)` returns the string 17. Line 24 can be rewritten as:

```
and length(file_name)=17
```

You can always fine-tune the WHERE= option by adding new conditions. For example, adding the next condition will filter out only the first quarter Widget text files such as `widgetJanyyyy.txt`:

```
substr(file_name,7,3) in ('Jan','Feb','Mar')
```

By the way, the WHERE= option in a DATA step can be replaced with a WHERE statement. The second DATA step in Program 17.3.1 can be rewritten as follows without sacrificing any efficiency:

Program 17.3.2 *getWidgetFileWHERE.sas*

```
1   data widgetFiles;
2   set myfiles;
3
4   where
5         substr(file_name,1,6)='widget'
6     and scan(file_name,-1,'.')='txt'
7     and length(file_name)=%length(widgetFeb2014.txt)
8   ;
9   run;
```

IF versus WHERE   The second DATA step in Program 17.3.1 can be rewritten to a less efficient program as follows:

Program 17.3.3 *getWidgetFileIF.sas*

```
1   data widgetFiles;
2   set myfiles;
3
4   if    substr(file_name,1,6)='widget'
5     and substr(file_name,length(file_name)-3,4)='.txt'
6     and length(file_name)=%length(widgetFeb2014.txt)
7   ;
8
9   run;
```

In Program 17.3.3, during each iteration of the DATA step, the **set** statement reads the next row from the input table **myfiles** into the PDV. If any of the three conditions is not met, the current iteration immediately ends; the implicit **output** statement will not be executed; and the next iteration starts. If all three conditions are met, the implicit **output** statement will be executed, inserting one row into the output table.

Though Program 17.3.2 and 17.3.3 generate the same output table **widgetFiles**, Program 17.3.3 is less efficient. It reads each row from the input table **myfiles** into the PDV, whereas Program 17.3.2 reads into the PDV only the rows that meet the three conditions. This difference is reflected in the log.

This is the log generated by Program 17.3.3:

```
NOTE: There were x observations read from the dataset WORK.MYFILES.
NOTE: The data set WORK.WIDGETFILES has 3 observations and 1 variables.
```

The x in the log should be equal to the number of rows in the **myfiles** table. All the rows from the **myfiles** table are read into the PDV.

On the other hand, Program 17.3.2, which is the second DATA step in Program 17.3.1, generates the following log:

```
NOTE: There were 3 observations read from the dataset WORK.MYFILES.
NOTE: The data set WORK.WIDGETFILES has 3 observations and 1 variables.
```

The second DATA step in Program 17.3.1 reads in only 3 rows from the input table.

However, the WHERE statement or the WHERE= option can only subset an existing SAS table read into SAS via the **set** statement. When a DATA step reads in a raw input file via the **input** statement, only the subsetting IF statement can be used to restrict whether an observation will be further processed by a DATA step.

17.4 Subprogram 2 - Save the File Names into a Macro Variable List

We need to iterate through all the input Widget text files and generate two CSV files for each text file. First, let's save all the `widgetmmmyyyy.txt` file names into a macro variable.

Program 17.4.1 *procSqlCreateMacroVarList.sas*

```
1   proc sql noprint;
2   select file_name
3   into: file_name separated by ' '
4   from widgetFiles;
5   quit;
```

In Line 2, `file_name` is the name of the only column of the `widgetFiles` table. However, in Line 3, `file_name` is the name of a macro variable that will hold all the `file_name` column values to be delimited by one blank. SAS can tell which `file_name` is which. If it sees `&file_name` or `%let file_name=...`, SAS knows that `file_name` is a macro variable; otherwise, SAS knows that `file_name` refers to a column name. However, you can choose a different macro variable name such as `file_name_list` to avoid confusion.

There are also two ways to submit the second subprogram 17.4.1, as there are two ways to submit the first subprogram 17.3.1. Either way, submit the second subprogram. To verify that the second subprogram runs successfully and that the macro variable `file_name` is created, open a new enhanced editor window and submit the following code:

```
%put &file_name;
```

If you see the following log, your second subprogram has run successfully:

```
    %put &file_name;
widgetFeb2012.txt widgetFeb2013.txt widgetFeb2014.txt
```

17.5 Subprogram 3 - Iterate Through a Macro Variable List

To create Subprogram 3, we'll modify Program 14.7.1 as follows:

Program 17.5.1 *widgetLoopThruMacroVarList.sas*

```
1    %macro widgetLoopThruMacroVarList(text,delimiter=%str( ));
2    %local count;
3    %let count=0;
4
5    %do %while(%scan(&text,&count+1,&delimiter) ne);
6       %let count=%eval(&count+1);
7       %let word=%scan(&text,&count,&delimiter);
8
9       /* name of the text file without .txt extension */
10      %let name=%substr(&word,1, %length(&word)-4);
```

```
11
12     /* Define action */
13     %include "&myfolder/widgetFinalGeneric.sas";
14   %end;
15   %mend;
16
17   %widgetLoopThruMacroVarList(&file_name)
```

The major task is to write the `widgetFinalGeneric.sas` program, which is called by Line 13 during each iteration of the loop. The `widgetFinalGeneric.sas` program will read each widget text file into SAS and generate two CSV files.

17.5.1   Define a Generic Action

To create `widgetFinalGeneric.sas`, we just need to modify Program 8.1.2 `widgetFinal.sas`.

Program 17.5.2 *widgetFinalGeneric.sas*

```
1
2    filename InFile "&myfolder/&word";
3
4    data &name;
5    retain Branch Month Factory;
6    infile InFile truncover;
7    input @1 content $char100. @;
8    /*charw. informat doesn't trim leading or trailing blanks*/
9    /* @ = hold the pointer */
10
11   if index(content,'MONTH OF Jan')>0 then Month='Jan';
12   else if index(content,'MONTH OF Feb')>0 then Month='Feb';
13
14   if index(content,'Branch Office: North')>0 then Branch='North';
15   else if index(content,'Branch Office: South')>0 then Branch='South';
16
17   if index(content,'Factory')>0 then input @10 factory $1. @;
18
19   if index(content,'%')>0 and index(content,'total')=0 then do;
20   input
21      @20 WidgetCount comma9.
22      @51 SuccessRate percent7.
23      ;
24   end;
25   Line +1;
26   run;
27
28   data &name.Final (drop=content line);
29   set &name;
30   where WidgetCount NE .;
31   run;
32
33   proc sql;
34   create table &name.FinalSum as
35   select
36      Month
37      ,Branch
```

```
38      ,Factory
39      ,sum(widgetCount) as totalWidgetCount
40      ,ceil(sum(widgetCount * SuccessRate)) as goodWidgetCount
41
42    from &name.Final
43
44    group by
45      Month
46      ,Branch
47      ,Factory
48    ;
49    quit;
50
51    proc export
52        data=&name.Final
53        outfile="&myfolder/&name.Final.csv"
54        dbms=csv
55        replace;
56    run;
57
58    proc export
59        data=&name.FinalSum
60        outfile="&myfolder/&name.FinalSum.csv"
61        dbms=csv
62        replace;
63    run;
```

Compare `widgetFinal.sas` and `widgetFinalGeneric.sas`. They should pretty much match line by line except that some hard coding in the first program is replaced by dynamic values in the second program. For example, this is the `filename` statement in `widgetFinal.sas`

```
filename InFile C:\LearnSAS\widgetFeb2014.txt;
```

It is changed into:

```
filename InFile "&myfolder/&word";
```

`&word` is from Program 17.5.1 and represents the generic input text file name.

Notice we change the backslash to a forward slash. The forward slash path separator works for PC SAS and SAS in the cloud.

The two `dm` statements are not carried over to `widgetFinalGeneric.sas` because the main program 17.2.1 already has the two `dm` statements.

Now the three subprograms in Program 17.2.1 are created. If you run Program 17.2.1, it will read in the 3 production text files and create 6 CSV files as specified in Section 17.1.

17.6   Further Reading

A Recursive SAS Macro to Automate Importing Multiple Excel Worksheets into SAS Data Sets
```
http://www.pharmasug.org/proceedings/2011/CC/PharmaSUG-2011-CC10.pdf
```

Obtaining A List of Files In A Directory Using SAS Functions

```
http://www.wuss.org/proceedings12/55.pdf
```

Sample 24820: Creating a Directory Listing Using SAS for Windows

http://support.sas.com/kb/24/820.html

The Power of "The FILENAME"

www.lexjansen.com/wuss/2012/63.pdf

How do I read multiple raw data files with the same structure in one data step?

http://www.ats.ucla.edu/stat/sas/faq/multi_file_read.htm

Sample 24707: Reading multiple files with PROC IMPORT

http://support.sas.com/kb/24/707.html

Chapter 18

Mass Read High School Grade Files

18.1 Objective

In this fictitious case study, over 20,000 schools across the country each sent you their grade text file. Each grade file contains the student IDs, the first names, the last names, and the grades of various courses associated with a school. Your job is to combine the grade text files from all the schools into one SAS table and hand the table over to a statistician for further analysis.

The good news is that all the grade text files use common course abbreviations. For example, `bio` stands for biology and `alge` stands for algebra.

The bad news is that different schools offer different courses. You don't know which school offers which courses without examining each school's grade file. And it's impractical for you to examine over 20,000 files to compile an exhaustive list of all the courses offered by all the schools. Finally, the column names in a grade text file may appear in any random order.

To understand what you need to do, create three text files in C:\LearnSAS:

C:\LearnSAS\school1.txt:

```
School #1
ID fname lname  bio  chem  alge
1  Scott Fishers 75   82    80
2  May   Jones   65   70    92
```

C:\LearnSAS\school2.txt:

```
School #2
ID alge  chem  sci  hist  fname    lname
1  60    80    95   90    Peter    Wilson
2  50    85    70   80    Jennifer Brown
```

C:\LearnSAS\school3.txt:

```
School #3
ID  lname    fname  bio  alge  writing  hist  geo
1   Smith    Adam   61   89    90       95    90
2   Simpson  Mark   52   91    85       86    95
```

In each text file, the first line specifies the school ID. The second line specifies the column names. From the third line to the end of the file are the column values.

This is the table you need to create for the statistician:

```
                    All schools combined


  school ID fname     lname    bio chem alge sci hist writing geo

       1    1 Scott    Fishers  75  82   80    .   .      .     .
       1    2 May      Jones    65  70   92    .   .      .     .
       2    1 Peter    Wilson    .  80   60   95  90      .     .
       2    2 Jennifer Brown     .  85   50   70  80      .     .
       3    1 Adam     Smith    61   .   89    .  95     90    90
       3    2 Mark     Simpson  52   .   91    .  86     85    95
```

If you use SAS in the cloud, you'll need to upload the three text files to /home/userid/myProgram.

18.2   Parse One Text File

Before worrying about how to read 20,000+ grade text files into one SAS table, let's write a program to read in just one grade file, school3.txt.

Program 18.2.1 *parseOneSchoolFile.sas*

```
1   dm log 'clear'; dm output 'clear';
2   filename myfile 'C:\LearnSAS/school3.txt';
3   /*SAS in the cloud:(replace userid with your ID)*/
4   /*filename myfile '/home/userid/myProgram/school3.txt';*/
5
6   data grades (drop=content);
7   infile myfile firstobs=3 truncover;
8   input content   $char100.;
9
10  length id 3 fname lname $10 bio alge writing hist geo 3;
11  ID     =scan(content, 1, ' ');
12  fname  =scan(content, 2, ' ');
13  lname  =scan(content, 3, ' ');
14  bio    =scan(content, 4, ' ');
15  alge   =scan(content, 5, ' ');
16  writing=scan(content, 6, ' ');
17  hist   =scan(content, 7, ' ');
18  geo    =scan(content, 8, ' ');
19  ;
20  run;
21
22  options linesize=min nonumber nodate;
23  proc print noobs;
24   title 'Student grades from School #3';
25  run;
```

This is the output:

Student grades from School #3

ID	fname	lname	bio	alge	writing	hist	geo
1	Smith	Adam	61	89	90	95	90
2	Simpson	Mark	52	91	85	86	95

Similar to Program 8.1.1, this program first reads a whole line of the raw input file into the variable content. The firstobs=3 option in the infile statement instructs SAS to start reading the raw input file from Line 3.

To see the effect of the truncover option, remove truncover from the infile statement so the infile statement becomes:

```
infile myfile firstobs=3;
```

Re-submit Program 18.2.1 and you'll get this output:

Student grades from School #3

id	fname	lname	bio	alge	writing	hist	geo
2	Simpson	Mark	52	91	85	86	95

This is part of the log:

```
NOTE: 2 records were read from the infile MYFILE.
      The minimum record length was 52.
      The maximum record length was 52.
NOTE: SAS went to a new line when INPUT statement reached past the end of a line.
NOTE: The data set WORK.GRADES has 1 observations and 8 variables.
```

This is why the truncover option is needed in the infile statement. The width of the input file school3.txt is about 60 columns, less than the 100 width specified by the informat $char100. for the variable content. If the truncover option is omitted, the DATA step will use the default flowover option. The flowover option causes an INPUT statement to continue to read the next input data record if it does not find values in the current input line for all the variables in the statement. In contrast, the truncover option causes the DATA step to assign the raw data value to the variable content even if the value is shorter than expected by the INPUT statement.

You might wonder why we don't use an informat with a narrower width such as $char60. The reason is that our program needs to read in all the grade files with different widths. The solution is to specify a width large enough to accommodate all the input files. To read in the school3.txt file, the informat $char100. is sufficient. Later we'll use the informat $char300. to read all the grade text files on the assumption that 300 is the maximum width of all the grade text files.

In Program 18.2.1, if the length statement is removed, the 8 DATA step variables from ID to geo will all become character variables each with length 200. By default, the SCAN function returns a character value with length 200. To alter this default behavior, declare the data type and the length of a variable before setting this variable to the return value of the SCAN function. Due to the `length` statement, `fname` and `lname` are 10-column wide character variables and ID, `bio`, `alge`, `writing`, `hist`, and `geo` are 3-byte numeric variables.

18.3   Parse One Text File Without Hard Coding Variable Names

The next program reads in `school3.txt` without you specifying the column names or the column order.

Program 18.3.1 *parseOneSchoolFile2.sas*

```
1   dm log 'clear'; dm output 'clear';
2   filename myfile 'C:\LearnSAS\school3.txt'; /*PC SAS*/
3   /*SAS in the cloud:(replace userid with your ID)*/
4   /*filename myfile '/home/userid/myProgram/school3.txt';*/
5   options symbolgen mlogic mprint;
6
7   /***********************************************/
8   /* Step1 store # of vars into macro var numVars */
9   /***********************************************/
10  data countVars;
11  infile myfile firstobs=2 obs=2 truncover;
12  input content $char300.;
13
14  /*countw function requires SAS 9.2+*/
15  /*numVars=countw(content,' ');*/
16
17  /* This method works in all SAS versions */
18  numVars=0;
19  do while(scan(content,numVars+1,' ') ne ' ');
20    numVars = numVars +1;
21  end;
22
23  call symput('numVars',numVars);
24  run;
25
26  options linesize=min nonumber nodate;
27  proc print data=countVars;
28    title 'Result of Step 1';
29    title2 "This grade file has %left(&numVars) columns";
30  run;
31
32  /********************************************************/
33  /*Step2 store column names into macro variables v1, v2, ...*/
34  /********************************************************/
35  data _null_;
36  infile myfile firstobs=2 obs=2 truncover;
37  input content $char300.;
38
39  do i=1 to &numVars;
40    call symput('v'||trim(left(i)),scan(content, i, ' '));
41  end;
42  run;
43
```

```
44   /************************************************/
45   /* Step3 read in column names and values        */
46   /************************************************/
47   %macro getVarNameValue(N);
48    %do i=1 %to &N;
49       length
50              %if &&v&i=%str(fname) %then fname $10;
51       %else %if &&v&i=%str(lname) %then lname $10;
52       %else &&v&i 3;
53       ;
54
55       &&v&i=scan(content, &i, ' ');
56    %end;
57   %mend;
58
59   data school3(drop=content);
60   school=3;
61
62   infile myfile firstobs=3 truncover;
63   input @1 content $char300.;
64   %getVarNameValue(&numVars)
65   run;
66
67   proc print data=school3;
68     title 'Result of Step 3';
69     title2 "Values of the %left(&numVars) columns";
70   run;
```

This is the output:

```
                        Result of Step 1
                  This grade file has 8 columns


                                                      num
                                                      Vars
  Obs                            content

   1   ID   lname     fname   bio  alge  writing   hist   geo    8
                            Result of Step 3
                        Values of the 8 columns


  Obs   school   ID    lname    fname    bio  alge   writing  hist  geo

   1      3       1   Smith    Adam      61    89       90      95    90
   2      3       2   Simpson  Mark      52    91       85      86    95
```

In Line 11, the `firstobs=2 obs=2` options instruct SAS to read only the second record from the raw input file. These two options are explained in Program 2.4.5.

Lines 14–21 find `numVars`, the number of variables in the second record of the raw input file. If you have SAS 9.2+, you can use the `countw` function to find `numVars`. To use the `countw` function, uncomment Line 15 and comment out Line 18–21.

Line 23 stores the value of the DATA step variable `numVars` in a macro variable `numVars`. Though the DATA step variable and the macro variable have the same name `numVars`, SAS knows which is which.

If you have trouble understanding Lines 10–24, refer to Program 14.6.1 and Program 13.2.2.

Lines 26–30 print out the value of the macro variable `numVars` for debugging your code.

Lines 35–42 read the second record from the raw input file. This time, however, the purpose is to store the 8 variable names, ID, `lname`, `fname`, `bio`, `alge`, `writing`, `hist`, and `geo`, in 8 macro variables, v1, v2, ..., v8.

Lines 47–57 define a macro variable `getVarNameValue(N)`, which is called in Line 64 to create part of the source code of the final DATA step (Lines 59–65) in Program 18.3.1. This is the source code of the final DATA step:

Program 18.3.2 *parseOneSchoolFile2step3source.sas*

```
1   data school3(drop=content);
2   infile myfile firstobs=3 truncover;
3   school=3;
4
5   input @1 content $char300.;
6   length ID 3;
7   ID=scan(content, 1, ' ');
8
9   length lname $ 10;
10  lname=scan(content, 2, ' ');
11
12  length fname $ 10;
13  fname=scan(content, 3, ' ');
14
15  length bio 3;
16  bio=scan(content, 4, ' ');
17
18  length alge 3;
19  alge=scan(content, 5, ' ');
20
21  length writing 3;
22  writing=scan(content, 6, ' ');
23
24  length hist 3;
25  hist=scan(content, 7, ' ');
26
27  length geo 3;
28  geo=scan(content, 8, ' ');
29  run;
```

Program 18.3.1 Line 64 generates the source code Lines 6–28 in Program 18.3.2.

Let's analyze the source code generated by the first iteration of the macro `%getVarNameValue(8)` execution where $i = 1$. This is the macro code:

```
length
    %if &&v&i=%str(fname) %then fname $10;
%else %if &&v&i=%str(lname) %then lname $10;
%else &&v&i 3;
;

&&v&i=scan(content, &i, ' ');
```

It takes the macro processor two passes to convert &&v&i to the text ID. During the first pass, the macro processor converts a double ampersand && to a single ampersand & and converts &i to the text 1. At the end of the first pass, &&v&i becomes &v1. Since the macro variable v1 holds the text ID (see Step 2 of Program 18.3.1), during the second pass, the macro processor converts &v1 to the text ID.

The macro function %str(fname) returns a literal string fname. Similarly, %str(lname) returns a literal string lname. Since the literal string ID is not equal to the literal string fname or lname, the macro %else ID 3 statement will be executed, generating the text ID 3.

This is the source code generated by the first iteration of the macro %getVarNameValue(8) execution:

```
length ID 3;
ID=scan(content, 1, ' ');
```

In Program 18.3.1, if you omit Line 53, this will be the source code generated by the first iteration of the macro %getVarNameValue(8) execution:

```
length ID 3
ID=scan(content, 1, ' ');
```

The first line of the generated source code is wrong because it doesn't end with a semicolon.

Similarly, this is the source code generated by the second iteration of the macro execution:

```
length lname $10;
ID=scan(content, 2, ' ');
```

During the second iteration, the condition ID=%str(lname) evaluates to true because the macro variable v2 holds the text lname.

The macro IF condition %if &&v&i=%str(fname) ... can be rewritten as:

```
%if  "&&v&i"="fname" ...
```

The macro %getVarNameValue(N) can be rewritten as:

```
%macro getVarNameValue(N);
  %do i=1 %to &N;
    length
        %if "&&v&i"="fname" %then fname $10;
      %else %if "&&v&i"="lname" %then lname $10;
      %else &&v&i 3;
      ;

      &&v&i=scan(content, &i, ' ');
  %end;
%mend;
```

18.4 Read in the Grade Files from All the Schools

If we can read in school3.txt without hard coding the variable names, we can read in all the grade text files. Next, we set up a main program and a subprogram to read in all the grade files. For simplicity, we assume that any grade text file is named schoolj.txt, where j is the school ID. This is the main program.

Program 18.4.1 *parseAllSchoolFilesMain.sas*

```
1    dm log 'clear'; dm output 'clear';
2    %let myfolder=C:\LearnSAS; /*PC SAS*/
3    /*SAS in the cloud: (replace userid with your ID)*/
4    /*%let myfolder=/home/userid/myProgram;*/
5    options symbolgen mprint mlogic;
6
7    %macro parseAllSchoolFiles;
8    %do j= 1 %to 3;
9      %include "&myfolder/parseOneSchoolFileGeneric.sas";
10   %end;
11   %mend;
12   %parseAllSchoolFiles
```

The main program calls Subprogram 18.4.2. The subprogram reads in the raw input file from the j-th school.

Program 18.4.2 *parseOneSchoolFileGeneric.sas*

```
1    dm log 'clear'; dm output 'clear';
2    filename myfile "C:\LearnSAS/school&j..txt";
3    /*SAS in the cloud:(replace userid with your ID)*/
4    /*filename myfile "/home/userid/myProgram/school&j..txt";*/
5    options symbolgen mlogic mprint;
6
7    /***********************************************/
8    /* Step1 store # of vars into macro var numVars */
9    /***********************************************/
10   data countVars;
11   infile myfile firstobs=2 obs=2 truncover;
12   input content $char300.;
13
14   /*countw function requires SAS 9.1+*/
15   /*numVars=countw(content,' ');*/
16
17   /* This method works in all SAS versions */
18   numVars=0;
19   do while(scan(content,numVars+1,' ') ne ' ');
20     numVars = numVars +1;
21   end;
22
23   call symput('numVars',numVars);
24   run;
25
26   options linesize=min nonumber nodate;
```

```
27   proc print data=countVars;
28      title 'Result of Step 1';
29      title2 "This grade file has %left(&numVars) columns";
30   run;
31
32   /**********************************************************/
33   /*Step2 store column names into macro variables v1, v2, ...*/
34   /**********************************************************/
35   data _null_;
36   infile myfile firstobs=2 obs=2 truncover;
37   input content $char300.;
38
39   do i=1 to &numVars;
40     call symput('v'||trim(left(i)),scan(content, i, ' '));
41   end;
42   run;
43
44   /*************************************************/
45   /* Step3 read in column names and values         */
46   /*************************************************/
47   %macro getVarNameValue(N);
48    %do i=1 %to &N;
49      length
50            %if &&v&i=%str(fname) %then fname $10;
51      %else %if &&v&i=%str(lname) %then lname $10;
52      %else &&v&i 3;
53         ;
54
55      &&v&i=scan(content, &i, ' ');
56    %end;
57   %mend;
58
59   data school&j(drop=content);
60    school=&j;
61
62   infile myfile firstobs=3 truncover;
63   input @1 content $char300.;
64   %getVarNameValue(&numVars)
65   run;
66
67   proc print data=school&j;
68      title 'Result of Step 3';
69      title2 "Values of the %left(&numVars) columns";
70   run;
```

To create the subprogram 18.4.2, we just need to generalize Program 18.3.1. Let's identify all the statements in Program 18.3.1 that are specific only to the school3.txt input file:

```
filename myfile 'C:\LearnSAS\school3.txt';
data school3(drop=content);
school=3;
proc print data=school3;
```

We'll modify these four lines to reference the j-th school:

```
filename myfile "C:\LearnSAS\school&j..txt";
data school&j(drop=content);
school=&j;
proc print data=school&j;
```

Before writing your macro program, you'll typically want to first write a non-macro program and then generalize your non-macro program.

Finally, let's clean up the subprogram and the main program. Here's the new subprogram:

Program 18.4.3 *parseOneSchoolFileGeneric2.sas*

```
1   filename myfile "C:\LearnSAS/school&j..txt";
2   /*SAS in the cloud:(replace userid with your ID)*/
3   /*filename myfile "/home/userid/myProgram/school&j..txt";*/
4
5   /**********************************************/
6   /* Step1 store # of vars into macro var numVars */
7   /**********************************************/
8   data _null_;
9   infile myfile firstobs=2 obs=2 truncover;
10  input content $char300.;
11
12  /*countw function requires SAS 9.1+*/
13  /*numVars=countw(content,' ');*/
14
15  /* This method works in all SAS versions */
16  numVars=0;
17  do while(scan(content,numVars+1,' ') ne ' ');
18    numVars = numVars +1;
19  end;
20
21  call symput('numVars',numVars);
22  run;
23
24  /***************************************************/
25  /*Step2 store column names into macro variables v1, v2, ...*/
26  /***************************************************/
27  data _null_;
28  infile myfile firstobs=2 obs=2 truncover;
29  input content $char300.;
30
31  do i=1 to &numVars;
32    call symput('v'||trim(left(i)),scan(content, i, ' '));
33  end;
34  run;
35
36  /**********************************************/
37  /* Step3 read in column names and values      */
38  /**********************************************/
39  %macro getVarNameValue(N);
40  %do i=1 %to &N;
41    length
42        %if &&v&i=%str(fname) %then fname $10;
43    %else %if &&v&i=%str(lname) %then lname $10;
44    %else &&v&i 3;
```

```
45      ;
46
47      &&v&i=scan(content, &i, ' ');
48    %end;
49  %mend;
50
51  data school&j(drop=content);
52  school=&j;
53
54  infile myfile firstobs=3 truncover;
55  input @1 content $char300.;
56  %getVarNameValue(&numVars)
57  run;
```

Two changes are made to the subprogram. In the first DATA step, the output table `countVars` is replaced by `_null_`. The goal of the first DATA step is to store the number of variables into a macro variable `numVar`. This can be achieved without creating any output data set.

The second change is removing the two PROC PRINT jobs from the subprogram. These two PROC PRINT jobs were for debugging our code.

The main program is also updated:

Program 18.4.4 *parseAllSchoolFilesMain2.sas*

```
1   dm log 'clear'; dm output 'clear';
2   %let myfolder=C:\LearnSAS;
3   /*SAS in the cloud: (replace userid with your ID)*/
4   /*%let myfolder=/home/userid/myProgram;*/
5   options symbolgen mprint mlogic;
6
7   %macro parseAllSchoolFiles;
8   %do j= 1 %to 3;
9     %include "&myfolder/parseOneSchoolFileGeneric2.sas";
10    %end;
11  %mend;
12  %parseAllSchoolFiles
13
14  data schoolAll;
15  set school1 school2 school3;
16  run;
17
18  options linesize=min nonumber nodate;
19  proc print data=schoolAll(obs=9) noobs;
20    title 'All schools combined';
21  run;
```

Two things are new in Program 18.4.4. First, we added a DATA step, Lines 14–16. This step concatenates three tables, `school1`, `school2`, and `school3`, to build a bigger table `schoolAll` using a SET list. However, it's impractical to manually list over 20,000 tables in a SET list. You can use Program 10.5.1 to concatenate a large number of participating tables.

In addition, in Line 19, we added the `obs=9` option so only the first 9 records from the `schoolAll` table will be printed in the output window. When you actually read in 20,000+ files, your `schoolAll` table may have several hundred million rows and you don't want to print all the rows in the output window.

Run the main program 18.4.4 and you'll get a table that lists all the grades from all the schools.

18.5   Further Reading

A Macro for Reading Multiple Text Files

http://www2.sas.com/proceedings/sugi29/057-29.pdf

Chapter 19

Parse Emails and Verify Social Security Numbers

19.1 Parse Emails

You are given a list of emails. Each email has a mandatory last name followed by a mandatory 4-character ID. It may have two optional fields: a first name and a middle name. Your job is to extract the first name, the middle name, the last name, and ID from each email as follows:

```
            email                   fname mname lname   ID
-----------------------------------------------------------
<clark.9mu2@xyz.com>                            clark  9mu2
<jones.be32@xyz.com>                            jones  be32
<betty.davis.d8km@xyz.com>        betty         davis  d8km
<dawn.jones.mn49@xyz.com>         dawn          jones  mn49
<jane.m.white.q5bc@xyz.com>       jane    m     white  q5bc
<mark.v.miller.d2my@xyz.com>      mark    v     miller d2my
```

Your first instinct is probably to use IF-THEN-ELSE statements and string functions to parse each email. But wait! Regular expressions are perfect for reading messy strings when no existing informat fits your need.

Program 19.1.1 *extractEmail.sas*

```
1   dm log 'clear'; dm output 'clear';
2   data extractEmail(drop=j);
3   infile datalines truncover;
4   input email $char50.;
5   if _n_=1 then re=prxparse('/<([a-z]+\.)?([a-z]+\.)?([a-z]+\.)([a-z0-9]{4}\@)/');
6   retain re;
7
8   array info[*] $10 fname mname lname ID;
9
10  if prxmatch(re, email) then do;
11    do j=1 to 4;
12      info[j]=prxposn(re,j,email);
```

```
13      if info[j] NE '' then info[j]=substr(info[j],1,length(info[j])-1);
14    end;
15  end;
16
17  datalines;
18  <clark.9mu2@xyz.com>
19  <jones.be32@xyz.com>
20  <betty.davis.d8km@xyz.com>
21  <dawn.jones.mn49@xyz.com>
22  <jane.m.white.q5bc@xyz.com>
23  <mark.v.miller.d2my@xyz.com>
24  ;
25  run;
26
27  option linesize=min nonumber nodate;
28  proc print data=extractEmail;
29    title 'extractEmail';
30  run;
```

Regular expressions were introduced in SAS version 9.0. If you have SAS version 9.0+ or if you use SAS in the cloud, submit the program and you'll get this output:

```
                   extractEmail

Obs           email            re fname mname lname   ID

  1  <clark.9mu2@xyz.com>       1                clark  9mu2
  2  <jones.be32@xyz.com>       1                jones  be32
  3  <betty.davis.d8km@xyz.com> 1 betty          davis  d8km
  4  <dawn.jones.mn49@xyz.com>  1 dawn           jones  mn49
  5  <jane.m.white.q5bc@xyz.com> 1 jane     m    white  q5bc
  6  <mark.v.miller.d2my@xyz.com> 1 mark    v    miller d2my
```

The re column in the extractEmail table is for you to see the return value of the prxparse function in Line 5. To remove the re column, change Line 2 from data extractEmail(drop=j) into data extractEmail(drop=j re).

Program 19.1.1 is succinct because it uses an array and a regular expression. Let's remove the array so we can focus on the regular expression. Rewrite Program 19.1.1 as follows:

Program 19.1.2 *extractEmail2.sas*

```
1   dm log 'clear'; dm output 'clear';
2   data extractEmail;
3   infile datalines truncover;
4   input email $char50.;
5   if _n_=1 then re=prxparse('/<([a-z]+\.)?([a-z]+\.)?([a-z]+\.)([a-z0-9]{4}\@)/');
6   retain re;
7
8   length fname mname lname ID $ 10;
9
10  if prxmatch(re, email) then do;
11    fname=prxposn(re,1,email);
12    mname=prxposn(re,2,email);
```

```
13    lname=prxposn(re,3,email);
14    ID=prxposn(re,4,email);
15
16    if fname NE '' then fname=substr(fname,1,length(fname)-1);
17    if mname NE '' then mname=substr(mname,1,length(mname)-1);
18    if lname NE '' then lname=substr(lname,1,length(lname)-1);
19    if ID    NE '' then ID=substr(ID,1,length(ID)-1);
20  end;
21
22  datalines;
23  <clark.9mu2@xyz.com>
24  <jones.be32@xyz.com>
25  <betty.davis.d8km@xyz.com>
26  <dawn.jones.mn49@xyz.com>
27  <jane.m.white.q5bc@xyz.com>
28  <mark.v.miller.d2my@xyz.com>
29  ;
30  run;
31
32  option linesize=min nonumber nodate;
33  proc print data=extractEmail;
34    title 'extractEmail';
35  run;
```

Submit Program 19.1.2. It generates the same output as Program 19.1.1.

To understand Program 19.1.2, let's use a regular expression to extract only the ID field.

Program 19.1.3 *extractID.sas*

```
1   dm log 'clear'; dm output 'clear';
2   data extractID;
3   infile datalines truncover;
4   input email $char50.;
5   if _n_=1 then re=prxparse('/<?([a-z0-9]{4})\@/');
6   retain re;
7
8   if prxmatch(re,email) then ID=prxposn(re,1,email);
9
10  datalines;
11  <clark.9mu2@xyz.com>
12  <jones.be32@xyz.com>
13  <betty.davis.d8km@xyz.com>
14  <dawn.jones.mn49@xyz.com>
15  <jane.m.white.q5bc@xyz.com>
16  <mark.v.miller.d2my@xyz.com>
17  ;
18  run;
19
20  option linesize=min nonumber nodate;
21  proc print data=extractID;
22    title 'extractID';
23  run;
```

This is the output:

```
                        extractID

    Obs            email            re     ID

     1     <clark.9mu2@xyz.com>      1    9mu2
     2     <jones.be32@xyz.com>      1    be32
     3     <betty.davis.d8km@xyz.com>  1   d8km
     4     <dawn.jones.mn49@xyz.com>   1   mn49
     5     <jane.m.white.q5bc@xyz.com>  1  q5bc
     6     <mark.v.miller.d2my@xyz.com>  1 d2my
```

In Program 19.1.3 Line 5, `<?([a-z0-9]{4})\@` is a regular expression or regex for short. A regular expression specifies a pattern to be matched in a string. The two forward slashes in Line 5 specify the beginning and the end of a pattern to be matched.

- `<?` will match 0 or 1 occurrence of a less-than sign. The question mark means occurring 0 or 1 time. `?` can be rewritten as `{0,1}` and `<?` is the same as `<{0,1}`. The expression `{m,n}` means occurring at least m times but no more than n times. `{m,m}` can be shortened to `{m}`; both mean occurring exactly m times. `{m,}` means occurring at least m times.

- `[a-z0-9]` will match one symbol that is a lowercase letter from a to z or a number from 0 to 9. The `-` symbol means a range. `[a-z0-9]{4}` will match 4 symbols of a lowercase letter from a to z or a number from 0 to 9.

- `\@` is a literal at-sign. The backslash escapes the at-sign. An at-sign, if not escaped, means an array in Perl.

What do parentheses do in the regular expression `<?([a-z0-9]{4})\@` in Line 5? Parentheses group parts of a regular expression together. They capture the text matched by a regular expression within into a numbered group that can be reused with a numbered backreference.

`<?([a-z0-9]{4})\@` means the following. If a less-than sign followed by 4 characters of a to z or 0 to 9 and followed by an at-sign is found, the 4 characters of a to z or 0 to 9 can later be referenced by the number 1. The number 1 is the reference number because the pattern `[a-z0-9]{4}` is in the first pair of parentheses inside a regular expression.

In Line 5, the **prxparse** function returns a pattern identifier number that is used by other Perl functions and CALL routines to match patterns. If an error occurs in parsing the regular expression, SAS returns a missing value.

In Line 8, the **prxmatch(re,email)** function searches **email** for a pattern specified by **re** in Line 5 and returns the position at which the pattern is found. The **prxposn(re,1,email)** function uses the result of the function **prxmatch(re,email)**, searches **email**, and returns the pattern enclosed in the first pair of parentheses in the regular expression identified by **re**. By the way, a match must be found by the **prxmatch**, **prxsubstr**, **prxchange**, or **prxnext** function before the **prxposn** function can be used.

In Line 5, even if you omit `if _n_=1 then`, the **prxparse** function will still be compiled only once. In a DATA step, if a Perl regular expression is a constant as in Program 19.1.3 or if it uses the `/o` option, it is compiled only once. Successive calls to the **prxparse** function will not cause a recompile, but will return the regular expression ID for the regular expression that was already compiled. However, the condition if _n_=1 explicitly requests the compile-once behavior and makes your code easier to understand.

The compile-once behavior occurs when you use **prxparse** in a DATA step. For all other uses, the Perl regular expression is recompiled for each call to **prxparse**.

The next program extracts the last name and ID from each email.

Program 19.1.4 *extractLnameID.sas*

```
1   dm log 'clear'; dm output 'clear';
2
3   data ExtractLnameID;
4   infile datalines truncover;
5   input email $char50.;
6   if _n_=1 then do;
7    reID=prxparse('/<?([a-z0-9]{4})\@/');
8    reLname=prxparse('/\.?([a-z]+)\.[a-z0-9]{4}\@/');
9   end;
10
11  retain reID reLname;
12
13  if prxmatch(reID,email) then ID=prxposn(reID,1,email);
14  if prxmatch(reLname,email) then lname=prxposn(reLname,1,email);
15
16  datalines;
17  <clark.9mu2@xyz.com>
18  <jones.be32@xyz.com>
19  <betty.davis.d8km@xyz.com>
20  <dawn.jones.mn49@xyz.com>
21  <jane.m.white.q5bc@xyz.com>
22  <mark.v.miller.d2my@xyz.com>
23  ;
24  run;
25
26  option linesize=min nonumber nodate;
27  proc print data=ExtractLnameID;
28   title 'ExtractLnameID';
29  run;
```

This is the output:

ExtractLnameID

Obs	email	reID	re Lname	ID	lname
1	<clark.9mu2@xyz.com>	1	2	9mu2	clark
2	<jones.be32@xyz.com>	1	2	be32	jones
3	<betty.davis.d8km@xyz.com>	1	2	d8km	davis
4	<dawn.jones.mn49@xyz.com>	1	2	mn49	jones
5	<jane.m.white.q5bc@xyz.com>	1	2	q5bc	white
6	<mark.v.miller.d2my@xyz.com>	1	2	d2my	miller

In this program, `\.?([a-z]+)\.[a-z0-9]{4}\@` in Line 8 will match an optional period, followed by one or more lowercase letters, followed by a period, followed by 4 characters of a to z or 0 to 9, and ending with an at-sign. The expression `\.` matches a period. The backslash escapes the period. If not escaped, a period means any character. The plus sign means occurring 1 or more times and is the same as `{1,}`. The expression `[a-z]+` is the same as `[a-z]{1,}`.

Now let's figure out how Program 19.1.2 works. Comment out the four IF statements (Lines 16–19) in Program 19.1.2 and re-submit the program. This is the output:

```
                             extractEmail

Obs          record           re fname  mname  lname    ID

  1   <clark.9mu2@xyz.com>      1                clark.   9mu2@
  2   <jones.be32@xyz.com>      1                jones.   be32@
  3   <betty.davis.d8km@xyz.com>  1 betty.       davis.   d8km@
  4   <dawn.jones.mn49@xyz.com>   1 dawn.        jones.   mn49@
  5   <jane.m.white.q5bc@xyz.com> 1 jane.   m.   white.   q5bc@
  6   <mark.v.miller.d2my@xyz.com> 1 mark.  v.   miller.  d2my@
```

In Program 19.1.2 Line 5, `<([a-z]+\.)?([a-z]+\.)?([a-z]+\.)([a-z0-9]{4}\@)` contains 4 capturing groups representing the optional `fname` and a period, the optional `mname` and a period, the mandatory `lname` and a period, and the mandatory `ID` and an at-sign.

If you uncomment the four IF statements (Lines 16–19), the unwanted period or the unwanted at-sign from each capturing group will be removed.

In Line 8, the `length` statement defines `fname`, `mname`, `lname`, and `ID` as 10-byte strings. If a variable whose length is not specified is assigned the return value of the `prxposn` function, that variable will get the default length 200. Without the `length` statement, `fname`, `mname`, `lname`, and `ID` will all become 200 byte string columns.

19.2 Verify Social Security Numbers

You need to verify social security numbers against the following rule. An SSN is a nine-digit number in the form of `AAA-GG-SSSS`. The area number `AAA` cannot be 000, 666, or 900 through 999. The group number `GG` ranges from 01 to 99. Finally, the serial number `SSSS` ranges from 0001 to 9999.

Program 19.2.1 *verifySSN.sas*

```
1   dm log 'clear'; dm output 'clear';
2   data verifySSN;
3   infile datalines truncover;
4   retain re;
5   input ssn $20.;
6   if _n_=1 then re=prxparse('/\b(?!000|666|9\d{2})\d{3}-?(?!00)\d{2}-?(?!0000)\d{4}\b/');
7   if prxmatch(re, ssn) then good=1; else good=0;
8
9   datalines;
10  000-22-3333
```

```
11    111-00-3333
12    111-22-0000
13    111-22-4444
14    666-22-3333
15    900-11-2222
16    999-22-3333
17    11-22-3333
18    111-2-3333
19    111-22-3333
20    345-22-3333
21    3456-22-3333
22    x456-22-3333
23    345-22-3333y
24    x345-22-3333y
25    111223333
26    ;
27    run;
28
29    options linesize=min nodate nonumber;
30    proc print data=verifySSN;
31     title 'verifySSN';
32    run;
```

This is the output:

verifySSN

Obs	re	ssn	good
1	1	000-22-3333	0
2	1	111-00-3333	0
3	1	111-22-0000	0
4	1	111-22-4444	1
5	1	666-22-3333	0
6	1	900-11-2222	0
7	1	999-22-3333	0
8	1	11-22-3333	0
9	1	111-2-3333	0
10	1	111-22-3333	1
11	1	345-22-3333	1
12	1	3456-22-3333	0
13	1	x456-22-3333	0
14	1	345-22-3333y	0
15	1	x345-22-3333y	0
16	1	111223333	1

To understand the regular expression in Program 19.2.1 Line 6, let's simplify Line 6 to:

```
if _n_=1 then re=prxparse('/\b\d{3}-?\d{2}-?\d{4}\b/');
```

Re-submit Program 19.2.1. This is the output:

verifySSN

Obs	re	ssn	good
1	1	000-22-3333	1
2	1	111-00-3333	1
3	1	111-22-0000	1
4	1	111-22-4444	1
5	1	666-22-3333	1
6	1	900-11-2222	1
7	1	999-22-3333	1
8	1	11-22-3333	0
9	1	111-2-3333	0
10	1	111-22-3333	1
11	1	345-22-3333	1
12	1	3456-22-3333	0
13	1	x456-22-3333	0
14	1	345-22-3333y	0
15	1	x345-22-3333y	0
16	1	111223333	1

The regular expression \b\d{3}-?\d{2}-?\d{4}\b matches the beginning of a word (\b stands for a word boundary), followed by 3 digits (\d is the same as [0-9], meaning one digit), followed by an optional dash, followed by 2 digits, followed by an optional dash, followed by 4 digits, and ending with a word boundary.

If you enclose a pattern inside a pair of \b symbols, then that pattern must appear as a whole word. That's why x456-22-3333, 345-22-3333y, and x345-22-3333y are invalid SSNs.

Next, let's add more requirements. The area number can be any 3 digits except 000, 666, and 900 through 999. Any 3 digits is \d{3}. Any 3 digits except 000 is (?!000)\d{3}. Any 3 digits except 000 and 666 is (?!000|666)\d{3}. The vertical bar | means OR. Any 3 digits except 000, 666, and 900 through 999 is (?!000|666|9d{2})\d{3}.

The regular expression (?!regex) is a zero-width negative lookahead assertion. A zero-width negative lookahead works differently depending on whether it is placed before or after another regular expression. In regex1(?!regex2), a match is found if a string matches regex1 and the new string after the one that matches regex1 doesn't match regex2. Thus foo(?!bar) matches foo that isn't followed by bar.

However, in (?!regex1)regex2, a match is found if the same string that matches regex2 doesn't match regex1. Internally, the regular expression engine traverses a string to search for a no-match of regex1. If a no-match is found, the regular expression engine traverses back to the first position of the string and searches for a match of regex2.

Hence (?!foo)bar doesn't mean bar that is not preceded by foo. It means bar except when bar is foo. Since bar is never foo, (?!foo)bar is equivalent to bar and matches any bar such as bar in foobar.

Similarly, (?!0)\d{1} matches any one digit except 0 and is equivalent to [1-9]. And (?!u)[a-zA-Z] matches any letter except the lowercase u and is equivalent to [a-tv-zA-Z]. And (?!u)[a-zA-Z]+ matches any letter or letters that don't begin with the lowercase u.

A zero-width negative lookahead assertion is called zero-width because it doesn't consume any characters. If a no-match is found, the pointer moves back to the first position of the string.

Let's add more validation rules. The group number GG can be any 2 digits except 00. This is (?!00)\d{2}. And the serial number SSSS is 4 digits except 0000. This is (?!0000)\d{4}.

By the way, Program 19.2.1 Line 6 can be rewritten as:

```
if _n_=1 then re=prxparse
    ('/\b(?!000|666)[0-8][0-9]{2}-?(?!00)[0-9]{2}-?(?!0000)[0-9]{4}\b/');
```

Convince yourself that this rewrite is correct.

The next program uses the uniform distribution to generate 100,000 random SSNs for testing. It creates two CSV files, goodSSN.csv and badSSN.csv. You can use these CSV files to verify that Program 19.2.2 works.

Program 19.2.2 *testVerifySSN.sas*

```
1   dm log 'clear'; dm output 'clear';
2   %let myfolder=C:\learnSAS; /*PC SAS*/
3   /*SAS in the cloud:(replace userid with your ID)*/
4   /*%let myfolder=/home/userid/myProgram;*/
5
6   data goodSSN badSSN;
7   call streaminit(123);  /*set random number seed*/
8
9   if _n_=1 then re=prxparse('/\b(?!000|666|9\d{2})\d{3}-?(?!00)\d{2}-?(?!0000)\d{4}\b/');
10  retain re;
11
12  do i = 1 to 1e5;        /*1e5=100,000*/
13    u = rand("Uniform"); /* u is U[0,1] */
14    ssnRaw = floor(5e8*u);
15    ssn=put(ssnRaw,ssn11.);
16
17    if prxmatch(re, ssn) then do; good=1; output goodSSN; end;
18    else do; good=0; output badSSN; end;
19  end;
20  run;
21
22  %macro table2csv(table);
23  proc export
24  data=&table
25  outfile="&myfolder/&table..csv"
26  dbms=csv
27  replace;
28  run;
29  %mend;
30
31  %table2csv(goodSSN)
32  %table2csv(badSSN)
```

19.3   Double Swap

Program 19.3.1 *doubleSwap.sas*

```
1    dm log 'clear'; dm output 'clear';
2
3    data phrases;
4    infile datalines truncover;
5    input phrase $30.;
6    length phrase2 $40;
7    phrase2=prxchange('s/(\w+)\s+(\w+)/I like $2$2 $1$1/',-1,phrase);
8
9    datalines;
10   Hello World
11   United States
12   day night
13   ;
14
15   run;
16
17   proc sql;
18   create table newphrases as
19   select
20     phrase
21     ,prxchange('s/(\w+)\s+(\w+)/$2 $1, not $1 $2/',-1,phrase) as phrase2 length=40
22   from phrases;
23   quit;
24
25   options linesize=min nonumber nodate;
26   proc print data=phrases; title 'phrases'; run;
27   proc print data=newphrases; title 'newphrases'; run;
```

This is the output:

```
                           phrases

       Obs      phrase                  phrase2

        1    Hello World     I like WorldWorld HelloHello
        2    United States   I like StatesStates UnitedUnited
        3    day night       I like nightnight dayday
                           newphrases

       Obs      phrase                  phrase2

        1    Hello World     World Hello, not Hello World
        2    United States   States United, not United States
        3    day night       night day, not day night
```

In Line 7 and 21, the **prxchange** function performs a pattern-matching replacement. Inside the **prxchange** function, the beginning letter s means replacement and the negative 1 parameter means that all matches will be replaced.

The regular expression \s matches any whitespace character (a space, tab, newline, or carriage return). The expression \s+ matches 1 or more white space characters. The expression \w is the same as [a-zA-Z0-9_] and will match any letter (lowercase or uppercase), a number, or an underscore.

19.4   Further Reading

An Introduction to Perl Regular Expressions in SAS 9

http://www2.sas.com/proceedings/sugi29/265-29.pdf

SAS 9 Perl Regular Expressions Tip Sheet

http://support.sas.com/rnd/base/datastep/perl_regexp/regexp-tip-sheet.pdf

SSN Validation - Virtually at no cost

http://analytics.ncsu.edu/sesug/2007/P023.pdf

Identifying Invalid Social Security Numbers

http://www.lexjansen.com/nesug/nesug07/ap/ap19.pdf

Using the New Features in PROC FORMAT

https://support.sas.com/resources/papers/proceedings12/245-2012.pdf

Perl Regular Expressions in SAS 9.1+ - Practical Applications

http://www.pharmasug.org/proceedings/2012/TA/PharmaSUG-2012-TA08.pdf

How to generate random numbers in SAS

http://blogs.sas.com/content/iml/2011/08/24/how-to-generate-random-numbers-in-sas/

Chapter 20

Where to Go from Here

Miss one day of practice, I notice; miss two, the critics notice; miss three, the audience notices.

— The Hungarian composer and pianist Franz Liszt (1811-1886)

If you mastered all the programs in this book and understood some, if not all, of the additional reading assignments, you have learned the fundamentals of SAS programming and are well on your way to becoming an advanced SAS programmer. With your newfound knowledge of SAS plus some Googling, you are ready to tackle challenging real-world problems.

The best way to improve your SAS programming skills is to write code to solve problems. If you are already a professional SAS programmer or if you are a business user regularly programming in SAS, you can use SAS to solve more business problems. The more problems you solve using SAS, the better you will be at SAS programming.

If you are a college student or an independent learner, you can create your own projects using Sashelp data sets. SAS provides over 200 data sets in the Sashelp library. You can access Sashelp data sets in PC SAS or SAS in the cloud. Here are some papers on Sashelp data sets to get you started:

SASHELP: A Backstage Pass

http://www.lexjansen.com/nesug/nesug00/cc/cc4008.pdf

Application of DICTIONARY Tables and SASHELP Views

http://www.wuss.org/proceedings10/databases/2908_4_DDI-Lafler.pdf

Besides solving your own data problems using SAS, you can learn how other SAS programmers solve their real-world problems. Refer to http://lexjansen.com/.

General Index

Index of 263 SAS Programs

Index of Major Text Files

Made in the USA
Coppell, TX
08 August 2020

32645683R00214